ScottForesman

SPELLING

Authors

James Beers

Ronald L. Cramer

W. Dorsey Hammond

 ScottForesman

A Division of HarperCollins*Publishers*

Editorial Offices: Glenview, Illinois
Regional Offices: Sunnyvale, California • Tucker, Georgia
Glenview, Illinois • Oakland, New Jersey • Dallas, Texas

■ ACKNOWLEDGMENTS

ILLUSTRATIONS

pp. 12, 13, 15, 19, 23, 27, 31: Roger Chandler; pp. 12Center, 20, 38C, 39, 76, 90, 146: Randy Verougstraete; pp. 14, 26, 40, 66, 92, 118, 142, 143, 144, 145, 149, 153, 157, 161: Thomas Kovacs; pp. 16, 36Bottom, 89, 113, 166B: Paul G. Somers; pp. 17, 47, 54, 58, 72, 90, 91, 93, 97, 101, 105, 109, 110, 139, 154, 162: Corasue Nicholas; pp. 18, 44, 64, 65, 67, 70, 71, 75, 79, 83, 96, 122, 148: David Wink; p. 21: Gwen Connelly; pp. 22, 24, 48, 50, 74, 100, 126, 152: C.K. Poedtke; pp. 28, 158Top, 158C: Richard Syska; pp. 29, 51Bottom Left, 51BC: Mary Frances Gregory; pp. 30, 56, 82, 85Left, 85C, 85Right, 108, 134, 160: Donna Ingemanson; p. 32: Gil Ashby; pp. 33, 163L, 163C, 163R: Randy Chewning; pp. 34, 60Top Left, 86TL, 112, 138, 164: Maria Stroster; pp. 35C, 36C, 60B: Marianne D. Wallace; pp. 35B, 87, 107, 150: Joe Rogers; pp. 38T, 41, 45, 49, 53, 57: Kelly Hume; p. 42: Melinda Levine; pp. 43L, 43C, 43R, 86Bottom Right, 88, 102, 120, 124, 141, 147L, 147C, 147R: Yoshi Miyake; p. 46: Craig Rex Perry; pp. 52, 59T, 78, 104, 130, 137L, 137C, 156, 166T: Teresa R. Jonik-Heine; p. 68: Jack Wallen; p. 80: Terry J. Sirrell; pp. 94TL, 94Center Left: Susan J. Shipley; p. 98: Laura Derichs; pp. 99, 116, 117, 119, 123, 127, 131, 135: Rebecca Brown; p. 103: Darryl Goudreau; pp. 114, 136: Kees de Kiefte; pp. 115, 132: Paul Sharp; pp. 125L, 125C, 125R: Barbara Samanich; p. 140: Ann Rebidas; p. 167: Mary Jones; pp. 196, 197: Mark Sobey; pp. 198, 199, 218, 219, 225: Kelly Booth; pp. 200, 201, 216, 217: Larry Frederick; pp. 202, 203: Charles Thomas; p. 204: Susanne Beringer; pp. 205, 208, 209: Damien Reynolds; pp. 206, 207: Connie M. Eichberger; pp. 221, 222: Randy Minor

PHOTOGRAPHS

pp. 170Left, 171, 178Right, 179Center, 264, 278: Library of Congress; p. 170R: Museum of the City of New York; p. 171Bottom Right: Anne S. K. Brown Military Collection, Brown University Library; p. 171BR: Yale University Art Gallery; p. 172: Independence Historical Park Collection, Easter National Park & Monument Association; p. 173Top: Montana Historical Society; p. 173Top Right, BR: Missouri Historical Society; p. 173C: The American Philosophical Society; p. 177: New York Public Library, Astor, Lenox & Tilden Foundation, Picture Collection; p. 178L: The Huffman Pictures, Miles City, MT; p. 179Top Left, Bottom: Panhandle-Plains Historical Museum; p. 179TR: Jim Strawser/Grant Heilman Photography, Inc.; p. 182L: The National Police Gazette, New York Public Library; p. 182BR: New York Historical Society; p. 183: Hogan Jazz Archives, Tulane University; p. 183: Norman Owen Tomalin/Bruce Coleman, Inc.; p. 184L: American Legion; p. 184R: George Rodgers/Life Magazine, Time Warner, Inc.; p. 185TR, L: U.S. Army Photograph; p. 185B: Jean-Loup Charmet; pp. 186, 187: Robert Kelley/Life Magazine; pp. 188, 189TL: Carolyn George d'Amboise; p. 189TR: © 1993 Martha Swope Photography; pp. 190L, 200, 201: Runk/Schoenberger/Grant Heilman Photography, Inc.; p. 190R: Photo Researchers; p. 191: Drawing by Lowell Hess from *Marvels & Mysteries of Our Animals World,* © 1964, The Reader's Digest Association; p. 193: George Disario/The Stock Market; p. 194: Custom Medical Stock; p. 195TR: A. Allerano/Custom Medical Stock; p. 199: The Granger Collection; p. 204: The Science Museum, London; p. 205: Mount Wilson & Palomar Observatories; p. 205: Lee Milne/The Stock Broker; p. 208: Ken Ross/Viesti Associates, Inc.; p. 209: Photogroup/FPG International; p. 209: Don & Pat Valenti; p. 210: California Institute of Technology; pp. 210, 211: Courtesy NASA; p. 211: Harvard/Smithsonian Center for Astrophysics; p. 214: The Kobal Collection; p. 215: Don Ornitz/Globe Photos; pp. 254, 255, 256T, 259T, 260T, 269B, 270T, 272, 274T, 274B, 277B, 279T, 279B, 287, 288T, 290, 291, 298T, 305, 308: Cynthia Clampitt; pp. 257, 261, 300, 302: E.G. Stout; p. 260B: Don Dixon; p. 262B: Naval Photographic Center, Naval Station; p. 267B: Smithsonian Institute; p. 275: NSSL/NOAA; p. 280: National Park Service; p. 295: The White House; p. 301: Naval Photographic Center, Naval Station; p. 310: Reprinted with permission of UNICEF; p. 312B: P. & A. Photo

All photographs not specifically credited are ScottForesman photographs.

■ CONTENTS

UNIT 6

Cross-Curricular Lessons

CONTENTS

Commonly Misspelled Words

Do you know what this symbol ♻ means? It means that something is used over and over again—it is recycled. Most students your age use the same words over and over when they write, and they often misspell some of those words.

Look through your spelling book. On the next two pages and in many of the lessons are words marked with the recycled symbol. These are the words you need to give special attention. They are the words most frequently misspelled by students your age.*

a lot	really	no one
too	allowed	our
it's	didn't	than
you're	off	especially
their	TV	let's
that's	until	then
there	something	weird
they're	going to	favorite
because	through	friends
probably	they	know
don't	to	outside
we're	which	always
finally	different	beginning
there's	everything	college
where	believe	maybe
can't	Christmas	now
usually	clothes	wear
doesn't	I'm	

*__Research in Action__ is a research project conducted in 1990-1993. The misspelled word list is one result of an analysis of 18,599 unedited compositions. Words are listed in the order of their frequency of misspelling.

strategy Workshop

Developing Spelling Consciousness

DISCOVER THE STRATEGY Everyone misspells words like these—words we know how to spell, or ought to.

know	now	I'm	outside
our	which	their	Christmas
we're	don't	let's	friends
where	they	to	there
you're	than	they're	off
always	too	then	TV
can't	until	there's	it's
didn't	wear	that's	

They're called **recycled words** in this book. Students your age misspell them again and again when they write.

> Which three of these words did the writer misspell in the LOST notice above? Find them and write them correctly.

These mistakes are mostly with easy words we know how to spell, such as leaving the apostrophe out of a contraction, so misspelling these words makes us look bad. If we could learn too notice these mistakes, we'd catch them. (Did you catch the misspelling in that last sentence?)

We need to make ourselves aware of these words. We need to develop our **spelling consciousness.**

† TRY IT OUT   Find the nine misspelled words in these notices and write them correctly. *Hint:* A word that looks right may actually be the wrong word, so proofread carefully for meaning.

FREE KITTENS!
   You may choose from six cute kittens. Thay all need a good home. Dont wait untill all six are gone. Hurry! Call me right away at . . .

FOR SALE
   See the stars through a telescope in almost perfect condition. It would make a great Chrismas gift or buy it for yourself. It will provide hours of entertainment and has educational value to. Call no for the best deal.

FOR RENT
   If you cant afford to buy a boat, rent one. I'm the proud owner of a 20-foot luxury cruiser. Fish of the bow or sunbathe on the deck. Sleep in a cabin or out side under the stars. Call me at . . .

† LOOK AHEAD   More recycled words appear in the spelling lessons that follow. Each one is marked by the recycle symbol you see in this lesson. You'll also find them in proofreading exercises. Look through the lists for the next five lessons and write down any recycled words that are spelling problems for you.

Getting Letters in Correct Order

1

■ **FOCUS** Look at each word, paying special attention to the underlined letters. Then read the meaning phrases.

preliminary	a **preliminary** match before the contest
preferable	**preferable** to the other choices
tremendous	an old tree of **tremendous** size
mediocre	won't choose **mediocre** players first
perspective	put the loss in proper **perspective**
perception	a clear **perception** of the problem
believe	can **believe** what he says
retrieve	can **retrieve** my ring from the trash
deceitful	**deceitful** about the missing book
weird	played **weird** music on Halloween
perceive	can **perceive** her friends' feelings
glimpse	a brief **glimpse** of the President
collapse	sudden **collapse** of the bridge
through	walking **through** the doorway
thoroughly	**thoroughly** cleaned up the mess
naïve	**naïve** about city subway travel
because	can't **because** I said so
neutral	be **neutral** rather than take sides
doesn't	**doesn't** want to go skating
irrelevant	important to him but **irrelevant** to me

■ **DISCOVER** It's easy to write the underlined letters in the wrong order, so concentrate on them. For example, in **perspective**, the **e** comes before the **r**. What letters should you concentrate on in **believe** and **doesn't?**

■ **WRITE** Look over the list words carefully. First write the words that you think are most difficult for you to spell. Then write the rest of the words. If there are letters that you sometimes confuse in any of the words, underline them.

CHALLENGE!

kaleidoscope
preposterous
surveillance
inconceivable
interpretation

SYNONYMS   Write the list word that means the same as each pair below.

1. completely, totally
2. unimportant, trivial
3. fall, plummet
4. recover, regain
5. sense, detect
6. trust, be certain
7. neither side, objective
8. beforehand, prior
9. since, whereas
10. simple-minded, trusting
11. misleading, false
12. better, favored

RHYMES   Write a list word that rhymes with each underlined word or phrase and makes sense in the sentence. Underline each list word in which the rhyming part is spelled differently from the word it rhymes with.

13. Just as I had <u>feared</u>, my new hairdo is ____.
14. We caught a ____ of the performing <u>chimps</u>.
15. Is it your ___ that the game was won through <u>deception</u>?
16. The wait in line was <u>horrendous</u>, but the roller coaster ride was ____.
17. Please don't sit and <u>stew</u>. I'll take you there when I'm ____.
18. It took a new <u>detective</u> to give the case a fresh ____.
19. If you want to <u>provoke her</u>, say the show was ____.
20. It should make sense, but it____. He was here when he said he <u>wasn't</u>.

Developing Spelling Consciousness

We sometimes misspell familiar words that we shouldn't miss. Proofread this passage. Write the four misspelled words correctly.

21–24. You can't beleive everything you hear. Just becuase a word is short dosen't mean it's easy to spell! In fact, really easy words are the ones we're most likely to spell wrong. When you're threw writing something, make sure you proofread for easy words too!

RECYCLED WORDS

Believe is a recycled word because students often misspell it. Maybe this will help: Don't bel<u>ie</u>ve a l<u>ie</u>.

≡	Make a capital.
/	Make a small letter.
∧	Add something.
ℯ	Take out something.
⊙	Add a period.
⌗	New paragraph

PROOFREAD FOR PUNCTUATION

When you write a contraction, remember to include an apostrophe. For example:

I dont like baby-sitting anymore because the kids just wont listen to me.

Check Contractions Read each sentence. Add apostrophes to contractions that need them. If they are correct, write "Correct."

1. Its a tremendous responsibility to be a baby-sitter.
2. You cant be too naive around little kids.
3. I have found that theyll try to get away with a lot.
4. I believe, however, that kids aren't ever really too bad.
5. Ive found it to be the best way to earn extra money.

PROOFREAD A JOURNAL ENTRY   Find the eight misspelled

words in Mariko's journal entry. Write them correctly. Some may be words you learned before. Three are contraction errors.

> I cant believe the kid I baby sat for. She was decietful, dishonest, and disrespectful. It was wierd. She didnt want to watch teevee, so I had to play with her all night. When I got home, I was throughly exhausted and ready to collaspe. I don't think Ill ever stay with her again.

WRITE A JOURNAL ENTRY   Write a journal entry about

your most recent baby-sitting experience or about a time you've spent with young children. Use three spelling words and a personal word.

Word List

preliminary	perception	perceive	naive
preferable	believe	glimpse	because
tremendous	retrieve	collapse	neutral
mediocre	deceitful	through	doesn't
perspective	weird	thoroughly	irrelevant

Personal Words 1.___ 2.___

CONNOTATIONS Words have **connotations**—what is suggested in addition to their exact meaning. Often these connotations are either positive or negative. Write *innocent* and *naive* to complete the chart and the sentence that follows.

Word	Exact Meaning	Connotations
1. ____	trusting	blameless, free from evil or guilt, childlike
2. ____	trusting	unsophisticated, simple-minded, foolish

The word __(3)__ has mostly negative connotations, while __(4)__ has mostly positive connotations.

Look over these pairs: *unusual* and *weird, mediocre* and *normal, painstakingly* and *thoroughly.* Sort them by the type of connotation each has.

Positive

5.____
6.____
7.____

Negative

8.____
9.____
10.____

ENRICHMENT Pick one.

A Job Is a Job

Jobs and *chores* have similar meanings, but you probably picture them differently. Label a column **jobs** and another column **chores.** List at least ten tasks that you think go under each label.

My Home Is My Castle

With a partner, brainstorm lists of words that mean "thin," "house," and "talk."
Then, working separately, arrange the words in order, starting with the most positive connotation to the most negative. Compare lists with your partner.

CHALLENGE!

Use art and word pictures to illustrate the differences between these words with similar meanings: *short-order cook* and *chef; antique* and *secondhand; shack* and *mansion.* Use a dictionary if you need help. Create a poster to show the different connotations.

One Consonant or Two?

■ **FOCUS** Read each word, paying special attention to sets of double consonants. Then read each meaning phrase.

dilemma	a **dilemma** about which twin to choose
compassionate	a **compassionate** hug to comfort him
commemorate	will **commemorate** their bravery
aggressive	an **aggressive** move on the playing field
cancellation	a **cancellation** because of rain
moccasin	a fringed and beaded **moccasin**
unnecessary	avoided **unnecessary** work
accompany	can **accompany** us on the trip
exaggerate	stories that **exaggerate** his talent
embarrassment	red-faced with **embarrassment**
challenge	will **challenge** them to a game
possessive	**possessive** of her new bike
trespass	shouldn't **trespass** in his yard
dismissed	**dismissed** the class early
forbidden	**forbidden** to go there
accumulate	**accumulate** a collection of pens
occasionally	**occasionally** gives us candy
immediately	**immediately** called the police
appropriate	an **appropriate** coat for the cold weather
accessory	a scarf as an **accessory** for the dress

■ **DISCOVER** The double letters in **embarrassment** and **dilemma** spell only one sound, but you have to use two letters to spell it correctly. What letters are double in **dismissed, possessive,** and **forbidden?**

■ **WRITE** Sort the list words by writing
- six words with two sets of double consonants
- five other words with double **s** or **l**
- six other words with double **c** or **m**
- three words with double **g, p,** or **d**

CHALLENGE!

preoccupation
saccharin
insufficient
constellation
commiserate

ANTONYMS   Write a list word that means the opposite of the underlined word in each sentence.

1. We stocked our first-aid kit with <u>essential</u> supplies.
2. Of course you'll be <u>permitted</u> to attend the carnival.
3. That lifeguard is not as <u>unfeeling</u> as he seems to be.
4. Our new kitten has a <u>passive</u> personality.
5. It is considered <u>improper</u> behavior to interrupt the speaker.
6. Will you get me that new software <u>sometime</u>?
7. I <u>generally</u> lock the front door when I leave the house.
8. I hope you didn't <u>lose</u> all your money playing video games.
9. The <u>solution</u> is simple; invite both of your friends over.
10. The hero was modest and tended to <u>understate</u> his actions.

CONTEXT   Write the list word that completes each sentence.

11. No, I didn't lose a gray sandal; it was a gray ____.
12. We are ____ from class for lunch at 11:45 every day.
13. Pouring rain forced the ____ of our picnic.
14. I fell in front of the audience. What an ____!
15. My sister gets ____ and won't let me borrow her clothes.
16. Some people consider a watch an ____, but I think it's a necessity.
17. I hope you didn't ____ on our neighbor's land.
18. Would you like me to ____ you to your appointment?
19. I'd like to see a new stamp to ____ the end of the war in Vietnam.
20. I ____ you to a game of chess.

Using the Problem Parts Strategy

21–24. Double letters are often the problem parts of words. Write *embarrassment, commemorate, occasionally,* and *aggressive.* Mark the double letters in each word to help you remember them.

> **Did You Know?**
> **Compassionate** comes from a Latin prefix that means "with" and a root that means "suffer"; so the literal meaning of compassionate is "to suffer with your friend."

≡	Make a capital.
/	Make a small letter.
∧	Add something.
ℯ	Take out something.
⊙	Add a period.
⌐	New paragraph

PROOFREAD FOR USAGE To fix a run-on sentence, end the first one with a period and start the second one with a capital letter.

I had to make a police report, those kids were in the wrong place.

Check for Run-on Sentences Read this paragraph. If a sentence is a run-on, write "RO." If it is correct, write "Correct."

(1) Kids trespassed on my neighbor's land, I saw them and called the police. (2) The police challenged the kids' story and called their parents. (3) They called my neighbor too, he had the charges dismissed. (4) He's really very nice.

PROOFREAD A POLICE REPORT Find six misspelled words in this shoplifting report and write them correctly. Some may be words you learned before. Fix two run-on sentences.

> I hate to cause any embarassment, but I'm sure I saw that man shoplift. I was in the accessory area. I caught a glimspe of him taking a mocassin from a display, I saw him take earrings from the jewelry counter. I imediately reported it to the manager, he tried not to bring any uneccessary attention to him.

WRITE A POLICE REPORT Describe an incident you witnessed. Use three list words and a personal word.

Word List

dilemma	moccasin	challenge	accumulate
compassionate	unnecessary	possessive	occasionally
commemorate	accompany	trespass	immediately
aggressive	exaggerate	dismissed	appropriate
cancellation	embarrassment	forbidden	accessory

Personal Words 1.___ 2.___

MULTICULTURAL CONNECTION: LANGUAGES The Europeans who came to America in the 1500s and 1600s owed a great deal to the **North American Indians.** The Europeans encountered many plants, animals, and tools for daily living that were new to them, but certainly not new to the Indians. The Europeans had no words for these new things. That's how these words came to English from Native American languages.

moccasin	woodchuck	muskrat	hickory
hogan	caucus	hominy	pecan

Write the word from the list above that each sentence describes. Use your Spelling Dictionary if you need help.

1. The fur of this water rodent was valuable for Indians in their early trade with the Europeans.
2. This nut is the most valuable edible nut in North America.
3. This soft leather shoe with no seams protected the Indians' feet from dampness.
4. This tree with edible nuts has tough, hard wood.
5. This is a Navajo house that is made of logs covered with earth.
6. This groundhog digs holes in fields.
7. This is a meeting for political leaders that comes from an Algonquin word for elders or advisers.
8. This ground or hulled corn, usually eaten boiled, comes from an Algonquin word meaning "parched corn."

ENRICHMENT Pick one.

CHALLENGE!

Pemmican Snacks?
Here are some more North American Indian words: *anorak, pemmican, mugwump, tupelo, pipsissewa.* Look up any words you don't know in your Spelling Dictionary. Use each word in a sentence or story that shows what it means.

Tell Me a Story
Folk tales are an important part of American Indian culture. With a partner, choose a Native American folk tale and prepare a dramatic reading of it for your class.

The names of many states came from Indian languages. Look up information and prepare a map of the United States, marking each state that has a Native American name. Include a chart explaining what each name means and where it came from.

Words with Digraphs

■ **FOCUS** Read each word and look for the **ci, ss, ti,** or **tu.** Then read each meaning phrase.

adventurous	a cave hike for **adventurous** people
impression	first **impression** when you meet
emotional	cried at hearing an **emotional** story
unnatural	**unnatural** shape of the melted candle
beneficial	**beneficial** rains to end the drought
posture	good **posture** and good health
sufficient	**sufficient** gas for the drive home
reassure	can **reassure** us that we're safe
intermission	short **intermission** after the first act
ancient	**ancient** ruins overgrown with brush
expression	puzzled **expression** on her face
negotiate	will **negotiate** a new contract
efficient	well packed by **efficient** workers
spacious	**spacious** rooms in the large house
questionable	story of **questionable** truth
capture	will **capture** the bank robbers
congestion	city streets clogged by **congestion**
punctual	being **punctual** for every class
cultural	**cultural** differences between two countries
initiation	**initiation** into an honorary club

■ **DISCOVER** One sound can be spelled several different ways. Both of these underlined digraphs stand for the sound /ch/ in **chat: punctual, congestion.** All three of these underlined digraphs make the sound /sh/ in **shall: intermission, negotiate, ancient.** Which sound, /ch/ or /sh/, is made by the digraph **ti** in **questionable?**

■ **WRITE** ▪ five words with **ci**
▪ four words with **ss**
▪ five words with **ti**
▪ six words with **tu**

CHALLENGE!
picturesque
auspicious
repercussion
minutia
caricature

WORD FORMS   Write the list word that contains each base word below.

1. assure
2. emotion
3. express
4. adventure
5. nature

6. congest
7. initiate
8. culture
9. question
10. impress

RELATIONSHIPS   Write the list word that completes each analogy.

11. Modern is to new as ____ is to old.
12. Half time is to a football game as ____ is to a play.
13. Small is to crowded as large is to ____ .
14. Terrible is to awful as ____ is to good.
15. Satisfactory is to adequate as enough is to ____ .
16. Release is to free as ____ is to grab.
17. Slouching is to curved back as good ____ is to straight back.
18. Delayed is to late as ____ is to on time.
19. Compromise is to meet halfway as ____ is to talk over.
20. Incompetent is to unable as ____ is to capable.

Seeing Meaning Connections

nature
natural
naturalist
unnatural

The words in the box, including the list word **unnatural,** are related in spelling and meaning. Complete the sentences with these words.

My friends and I went on a _(21)_ walk in a nearby forest preserve. We were guided by a _(22)_ who works there. Our guide was able to point out plants, animals, and birds that are native to our region. It's great to see them in their _(23)_ habitat. What wasn't great, though, was seeing the litter that people had left. It looked so _(24)_ .

Did You Know?
Ancient, which means "very old," actually comes from a Latin word meaning "before"; so something that is **ancient** certainly came before now.

☰	Make a capital.
/	Make a small letter.
∧	Add something.
ℒ	Take out something.
⊙	Add a period.
¶	New paragraph

PROOFREAD FOR CAPITALIZATION

Capitalize the names of countries, cities, states, and nationalities. For example:

How many people left mexico with you?

Check Capitalization Read each interview question. Correct any capitalization errors. If it's correct, write "Correct."

1. What do you like most about chicago?
2. What has been most exciting for you since coming to Illinois?
3. Is there more traffic congestion in guadalajara than here?
4. What are the ancient Mayan ruins in your country like?
5. Do we use english expressions that you don't understand?

PROOFREAD INTERVIEW QUESTIONS Find the five

misspelled words in Marcia's questions. Write them correctly. They may be list words or words you have learned before. Fix three capitalization errors too.

1. What was your first impreshin of fairfield?

2. What advencherous things have you done since coming to the United states?

3. What cultoral differences have you seen?

4. Were you emoshinal when you arrived?

5. Wich american TV shows do you like?

WRITE INTERVIEW QUESTIONS Write a list of questions

that you would like to ask someone who just moved to this country. Try to use three list words and a personal word.

Word List

adventurous	posture	expression	capture
impression	sufficient	negotiate	congestion
emotional	reassure	efficient	punctual
unnatural	intermission	spacious	cultural
beneficial	ancient	questionable	initiation

Personal Words 1.___ 2.___

GREEK AND LATIN ROOTS: *bene* The list word **beneficial** comes from the Latin root *bene,* and so do the rest of the words in the box.

beneficial
benign
beneficiary
benefit
benevolent

Each of these words has a different meaning, but they are all related to something good. That's because *bene* means "good or well." Complete the word web below with these *bene* words. Use your Spelling Dictionary if you need help.

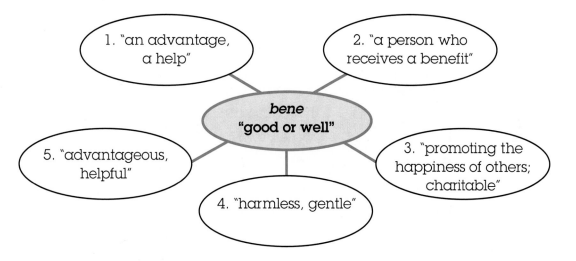

1. "an advantage, a help"
2. "a person who receives a benefit"

bene "good or well"

5. "advantageous, helpful"
3. "promoting the happiness of others; charitable"
4. "harmless, gentle"

Now that you know their meanings, use one of the *bene* words to complete each sentence.

6. Exercising is ____ to your health.
7. His ____ actions brought much joy to those in need.
8. Eating the extra doughnuts is a ____ of this bakery job.
9. Who is the ____ on your insurance policy?
10. We were thankful that the tumor was ____.

ENRICHMENT Pick one.

Prime Benefits
A *benefit* of exercising is being physically fit. A *benefit* of having a savings account is earning interest on your money. Write five sentences about things you can benefit from. Explain why each one is good for you.

Acts of Kindness
If you took turns sweeping the hall every day for a week, you could be called *benevolent.* With a small group, think of a project that will benefit your school. You could scrub lockers or wash desks. Carry out your project.

CHALLENGE!
A will is a legal document that says what happens to your property after you die. A *beneficiary* is the person who gets the property. Write a will for yourself. Who will be the beneficiaries of your most prized possessions?

4

Greek Word Parts

■ **FOCUS** Read each word and meaning phrase. Notice that some words have similar parts.

hydrant	**hydrant** with a fire hose attached
hydrophobia	avoids the beach because of **hydrophobia**
chronicle	a **chronicle** of the Gold Rush days
diameter	**diameter** of a softball
thermostat	adjusted the **thermostat** for winter
speedometer	55 mph on the **speedometer**
thermos	hot chocolate in a **thermos**
hydrogen	water from **hydrogen** and oxygen
synchronize	**synchronize** our watches so they match
barometer	rain indicated by the **barometer**
hydroelectric	**hydroelectric** plant at the dam
chronic	a constant, **chronic** cough
thermometer	the red line in the **thermometer**
geometry	angles and lines in **geometry**
hydraulic	a car up on the **hydraulic** lift
symmetry	**symmetry** of one half with the other
dehydrated	dried, **dehydrated** vegetables
thermal	**thermal** underwear for cold days
centimeter	a **centimeter** compared to an inch
chronological	story told in **chronological** order

■ **DISCOVER** The Greek word part **hydro** means "water." What is the meaning of **hydrant? Chronos** means "time." What does **synchronize** mean? **Thermo** means "heat" and **meter** means "a device for measuring." What does **thermometer** mean?

■ **WRITE**
- four words with **chronos**
- six words with **hydro**
- a word with both **thermo** and **meter**
- three more words with **thermo**
- six more words with **meter**

CHALLENGE!

metronome
thermodynamic
asymmetrical
chronograph
thermonuclear

MAKING CONNECTIONS Write the list word that matches each clue.

1. This is where you would get water to put out a fire.
2. This electricity is generated using water power.
3. It's a gas that combines with oxygen to form water.
4. This describes a machine that is powered by water pressure.
5. This is the fear of water.
6. The water has been taken out.
7. This is another word for time order.
8. When something lasts a long time, it is this.
9. This is to arrange for two things to happen at the same time.
10. This is a history of events based on their time order.

DEFINITIONS Write the list word that matches each clue.

11. I'm a line segment that goes from one side to the other through the center of a circle.
12. Use me when you want to know how fast a car is going.
13. I'll keep your soup hot and your lemonade cold.
14. You use me to find out if you have a fever.
15. When something is the same on both sides, it has this.
16. When you want to see if the weather will change, I'm there.
17. Wool-lined gloves like me can be described as this.
18. I am one-hundredth of a meter.
19. When it gets too cold, I tell the furnace to get to work.
20. In math, I'm the study of circles, squares, and other shapes.

Seeing Meaning Connections

These words come from **phobia,** meaning "fear." Write the word that fits each definition. One is from your word list. *Hint:* **pyro** means "fire" and **arachnē** means "spider."

| hydrophobia |
| arachnophobia |
| pyrophobia |

21. fear of water
22. fear of fire
23. fear of spiders

Did You Know?
When the Thermos bottle was patented in 1904, **Thermos** was a trademark. Since then it's been used so much it's no longer considered a trademark and is not capitalized.

≡	Make a capital.
/	Make a small letter.
∧	Add something.
ℓ	Take out something.
⊙	Add a period.
¶	New paragraph

PROOFREAD FOR CARELESS ERRORS

Adding and dropping letters are usually careless errors. For example:

You have to find ever~~ey~~ item on th∧list.

Check for Careless Errors Read each sentence. Correct any words with added or dropped letters.

1. Pleas remain in our immediate neighborhood.
2. Try to find all of you items in your assigned area.
3. Do note go beyond the fire hydrant on South Street.
4. Smile for they photographer from *The Daily Chronicle.*
5. Hurry, because there is and time limit.

PROOFREAD DIRECTIONS

Find the eight misspelled words in the rest of the directions and write them correctly. Three are careless errors. Some may be words you learned before.

You have exactly thirty minutes to find everything. Let's synkronize our watches and go! You need too find the following: a thermometer, a measuring cup, a pair off thermle underwear, a mocassin, a ruler with centameter marks, a thimble, tree safety pins, a wooden coat hanger, a thermus jug, and a compass.

WRITE DIRECTIONS

Plan your own scavenger hunt. Write directions and brainstorm a list of items that you want your friends to find. Try to use three list words and a personal word.

Word List

hydrant	speedometer	hydroelectric	symmetry
hydrophobia	thermos	chronic	dehydrated
chronicle	hydrogen	thermometer	thermal
diameter	synchronize	geometry	centimeter
thermostat	barometer	hydraulic	chronological

Personal Words 1.___ 2.___

DICTIONARY: PARTS OF AN ENTRY A dictionary gives
you all sorts of interesting information about a word. Look at this
dictionary entry for *synchronize*.

pronunciation — inflected forms — part-of-speech label

entry word —— **syn chro nize** (sing′krə nīz), *v.,* **-nized, -nizing.**—*v.i.* **1** occur at the same —— definition
time; agree in time. **2** move or take place at the same rate and exactly
together. —*v.t.* **1** make agree in time: *synchronize all the clocks in a building.*
2 assign to the same time or period. [< Greek *synchronizein* < *synchronos* <
etymology —— *syn-* together + *chronos* time] **—syn′chro ni za′tion,** *n.* **—syn′chro niz′er,** *n.*

run-on entry ——

illustrative sentence
or phrase

Answer these questions using the entry for *synchronize*.

1. How many syllables are there in *synchronize*?
2. What part of speech is *synchronize*?
3. How do you spell the past tense?
4. How many definitions are given?
5. From what language did we get *synchronize*?

Use your Spelling Dictionary to answer these questions about the
dictionary entries for some of your list words.

6. How many definitions are given for *chronic*?
7. What part of speech is *thermal*?
8. What word is given in the run-on entry of *chronic*?
9. What did *thermos* used to be? *Hint:* See the etymology.
10. Which definition for *barometer* has an illustrative sentence?

ENRICHMENT Pick one.

Multiple Meanings
Look up *posture* in your
Spelling Dictionary. It
has three illustrative
sentences. Write new
illustrative sentences for
the three definitions. For
an extra challenge, try
to write sentences for the
other two definitions too.

kan yü rēd ᴛʜis?
If you can read that title,
you are able to read
pronunciations. Write
five sentences like this
using the pronunciations
in your dictionary.
Exchange them with a
partner and rewrite each
other's sentences.

CHALLENGE!
Use a dictionary to look
up the etymologies of
*flamboyant,
delicatessen, helicopter,*
and *launch.* What
languages do they come
from? Write a short story
that uses these words.

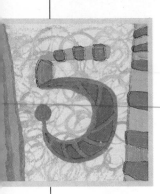

Irregular Plurals

■ **FOCUS** Look at the words in each column. Does the base word change spelling when it's made plural?

wharf	**wharves**
wife	**wives**
giraffe	**giraffes**
tariff	**tariffs**
pistachio	**pistachios**
ghetto	**ghettos**
memento	**mementos**
veto	**vetoes**
mosquito	**mosquitoes**
embargo	**embargoes**
sister-in-law	**sisters-in-law**
great-aunt	**great-aunts**
criterion	**criteria**
stimulus	**stimuli**
phenomenon	**phenomena**
crisis	**crises**
diagnosis	**diagnoses**
analysis	**analyses**
Sioux	**Sioux**
species	**species**

■ **DISCOVER** Add **-s** or **-es** to most words, but
- sometimes **f** or **fe** changes to **v** before **-es** is added: **wives**
- some plurals are in a new form: **crises**
- some plurals are the same as the singular: **species**

■ **WRITE**
- two plurals identical to their singular form
- three plurals in which **is** becomes **es**
- three plurals that aren't formed with **-s** or **-es**
- five plurals to which **-es** was added
- seven plurals to which **-s** was added

CHALLENGE!

armadillos
supercargoes
memoranda
radii
commandos

WORD FORMS   Write the plural forms of the words in parentheses.

1. We had (analysis) of the problem done by three scientists.
2. I bought (memento) of our trip to the Smoky Mountains for my traveling companions.
3. The (tariff) on some imports are high.
4. A set of (criterion) had to be met before it was accepted.
5. The (stimulus) for achievement are punishment and reward.
6. A series of (crisis) cause a lot of stress in our lives.
7. The President's (veto) kept several bills from becoming laws.
8. The (diagnosis) of the two diseases were quite similar.
9. Will their government lift the (embargo) on our ships?

CLASSIFYING   Write the list word that belongs in each group.

10. macadamias, pecans, cashews
11. happenings, events, occurrences
12. Navajo, Iroquois, Cheyenne
13. mothers-in-law, fathers-in-law, brothers-in-law
14. neighborhoods, areas, districts
15. great-uncles, great-grandmothers, great-grandfathers
16. grasshoppers, bees, flies
17. piers, docks, platforms
18. sisters, brothers, husbands
19. kingdoms, phylums, genuses
20. elephants, aardvarks, lions

Strategic Spelling

Building New Words

Form the plurals of these words: *portfolio, volcano, motto, handcuff.* Use your Spelling Dictionary if you need to.

Plurals with -s
21.____
22.____

Plurals with -es
23.____
24.____

Take a Hint
Need help spelling **mementos**? Remember that <u>mem</u>entos are to preserve <u>mem</u>ories.

☰	Make a capital.
/	Make a small letter.
∧	Add something.
℮	Take out something.
⊙	Add a period.
⌐f	New paragraph

PROOFREAD FOR USAGE Having verb tenses consistent keeps your writing from being confusing. For example:

We went to South Dakota first. Then we traveled ~~travel~~∧ to Montana.

Check Verb Tense Read each sentence. If the underlined verb is correct, write "Correct." If not, write it correctly.

1. First we were in Iowa, and then we <u>go</u> to South Dakota.
2. The Badlands were beautiful. We <u>explore</u> them.
3. We found a campground that <u>had</u> a fantastic view.
4. I was amazed at how cold it got. I <u>needed</u> a heavy sweater.
5. We left early the next morning and <u>drive</u> to the Black Hills.

PROOFREAD A TRAVEL DIARY Find five misspelled words in this travel diary. Write them correctly. Some may be words you have learned before. Fix three errors with verb tense too.

> We spent the morning at Mt. Rushmore. I buy mementos their. I bought gifts for my great-aunts and sister-in-laws too. We left for Montana at noon. We didn't stop for lunch but munch on pistachioes in the car and tried to find as many animal speces as we could. We also go to where the Soux defeated Custer.

WRITE A TRAVEL DIARY Write a travel diary about a trip that you enjoyed. Use three list words and a personal word.

Word List

wharves	ghettos	sisters-in-law	crises
wives	mementos	great-aunts	diagnoses
giraffes	vetoes	criteria	analyses
tariffs	mosquitoes	stimuli	Sioux
pistachios	embargoes	phenomena	species

Personal Words 1.____ 2.____

EXPLORING LANGUAGE: ANALOGIES An **analogy**
shows how two pairs of words are related. In the analogy
mammal : giraffes :: insect : mosquitoes, the first word is a *class*
and the second is a *member* of the class. The analogy is read
"mammal is to giraffes as insect is to mosquitoes." Some other
types of analogies, besides class and member, are *Worker and
Tool*—**painter : brush :: golfer : club** and *Part to Whole*—**finger :
hand :: letter : alphabet.**

Label each analogy as *Class and Member, Worker and Tool,* or
Part to Whole.

1. furniture : sofa :: tree : maple
2. doctor : stethoscope :: carpenter : hammer
3. leaf : tree :: petal : flower
4. poem : limerick :: song : ballad
5. pilot : airplane :: artist : easel

Now that you know some types of analogies, use these words to
complete the analogies: *whale, pistachio, tractor, stove, team.*

6. vegetable : carrot :: nut : ____
7. page : book :: player : ____
8. judge : gavel :: farmer : ____
9. fish : trout :: mammal : ____
10. conductor : baton :: chef : ____

ENRICHMENT Pick one.

Working for a Living
Think of a tool that each
one of these workers
would use: *teacher,
banker, architect, nurse,
postal worker,
accountant.* Then write
three analogies using
the workers and tools.
Need an extra
challenge? Think
of some more worker
and tool relationships
on your own.

Just Alike
Try your hand at writing
antonym analogies to
stump your partner.
Think of ten sets of
antonyms, such as *hot—
cold* and *up—down.*
Then pair them to create
five analogies. Leave
one word out of each:
cold : hot :: up : ____.
Have your partner
complete your
analogies.

CHALLENGE!
Sometimes the
relationships can be
hard to see. Think about:
department store : zoo.
Explore the relationship,
making a list of ways
they're alike. Come up
with another pair that
shares the same
relationship. Write an
explanation of the
relationship they share.

Review

Look back at the word lists in Lessons 1–5 and think about how you are doing in spelling.

1. The hardest words for me to spell were ____.

2. I sometimes misspell familiar words, but I catch these mistakes when I proofread. **Yes   No   Sometimes**

3. If someone asked me how to tell whether the plural of **mosquito** is formed by adding **-s** or **-es,** I would tell them ____.

4. I remember that the plural of most nouns ending in **-is** is formed by changing **-is** to **-es (crisis—crises). Yes   No   Sometimes**

5. The most interesting word that I have learned to spell is ____.

■ PROOFREADING

Find the spelling errors in each passage and write the words correctly. All passages have seven errors except the last one, which has eight.

PROOFREAD A MOVIE REVIEW

The Gnat

The movie *The Gnat* is an embarassment by any ordinary criteria for judging films. When a niave scientist accidentally injects a pair of gnats with a chemical, they grow to the size of girraffes and immediatly start eating Washington, D.C. The mutant specis manages to cause conjestion on Constitution Avenue and panic in the Pentagon. You can fly away from this one.

PROOFREAD A REPORT

Origins of State Names

Many states take their names from Native American or Spanish words. Others comemorate a person or place. Kansas is a Suoix word meaning "south wind people." The origin of Mississippi is questionible. It may come from a Chippewa or an Algonquin word. New Hampshire was named by Capt. John Mason becuse his home was originally in the county of Hampshire in England. Louisiana was named by the adventurus explorer Sieur de La Salle for Louis XIV, a French king. Nevada is a Spanish word meaning "covered with snow," certainly approppriate for northern Nevada. Washington State was originally the Territory of Columbia, but Congress thought Washington perferable because of the already-named District of Columbia.

PROOFREAD A CHARACTER SKETCH

My Granddad

My granddad is an amateur weatherman. Not only does he have a thermometre, but he also has a barmeter, a rain gauge, and a device for measuring wind speed. He records all the data measured by his instruments three times a day. He also studies the clouds. From his analises of all this information, he can forecast local weather. He has predicted all kinds of fenomena, including a ten-inch snowfall when school was dismised. He says his methods are based on a close preception of nature and a tremedous intellect.

PROOFREAD A FRIENDLY LETTER

November 19, 19--

Dear Karen,

In looking though a box of momentoes and photographs, I foiund the enclosed picture of three of our great-ants taken when they were young women. They are all wearing rather wierd clothes, and Emily seems to be holding up a mocassin! The house in the background looks very spacouis. There is a mystery, however. Who is the fourth woman in the photo with the amused exspression? Is she one of your sister-in-laws?

Love from your cousin,

Felicia

PROOFREAD A SCIENCE REPORT

The Planet Mercury

Mercury is the nearest planet to the sun. With a diamter of 3100 miles, it is the second smallest of the planets. Scientists now belive that Mercury has an atmosphere, probably made up of hydragen and helium. In Roman mythology, Mercury was a messenger to the gods. Like the anchant Roman god for whom it is named, the planet Mercury moves quickly. It completes its journey around the sun in 88 days. It dosen't have a great climate, however. The temperature probably reaches 800 degrees Fahrenheit. We can often glipse the planet during early morning or early evening hours, but we cannot percieve it from Earth against a night sky, for it is too much in line with the sun.

PROOFREAD AN INSTRUCTION SHEET

Instructions for Minnesota Expedition

Please read these instructions. They tell you about the Minnesota Expedition in October.

In addition to your usual hiking gear, please remember to bring these items:

thermel jacket
sleeping bag
something to repel mosquitos

flashlight
thermus or canteen

We will supply these items:

dehidrated food

cooking equipment

The bus leaves October 1 at 6:00 A.M. from Sharp School. Please be punchual! Do not bring uneccessary items. Hikers are not to tresspass on private property.

PROOFREAD A SPORTS STORY

Cougars Win

The Cougars throughly trounced the Tigers last Friday in a 43-38 victory in the first home game of the season. After a medioakre first quarter, the Cougars caught fire when Charles Green scored six baskets, and they led 25-17 at the half. The Tigers mounted an agressive challange in the third quarter but couldn't acumulate sufficent points to win. With three lay-up shots by the Tiger's Joseph Porter and Jose Rico's spirited attempts to capshure the ball in the fourth quarter, the Tigers occaisonally showed some of last year's spunk, but missed free throws finally told the story.

Pronouncing for Spelling

DISCOVER THE STRATEGY 1   Annie misspells the middle part of *probably* because she mispronounces it. She needs to try this correct pronunciation strategy:

1. Read the word aloud carefully and correctly. Listen to the sound of each letter.
2. Pronounce the word again as you write it.

✝ **TRY IT OUT**   Now practice this strategy. Pronounce the words in dark type slowly and correctly. As you do, listen carefully to the sounds of the underlined letters. Pronounce each word again as you write it.

    1. **fin<u>a</u>lly** (not "fin▪ly")
    2. **med<u>i</u>cine** (not "med▪cine")
    3. **cand<u>i</u>date** (not "can▪i▪date")
    4. **accident<u>a</u>lly** (not "ac▪ci▪dent▪ly")
    5. **mem<u>o</u>ry** (not "mem▪ry")

"PROB-AB-LY" THAT'S BETTER. BUT WHAT ABOUT VEHICLE? I MISS THAT H BECAUSE IT'S SILENT. SO HOW WOULD PRONOUNCING THE WORD CORRECTLY HELP ME?

DISCOVER THE STRATEGY 2 It wouldn't—but making up a secret pronunciation might help.

- Pronounce the silent letters in the word as you write it. For example, say the sound of the **h** in *vehicle*: "ve-**hi**-cle."
- Or change the way you say a tricky sound in the word. For example, to remember the **o** at the end of *conductor*, say it to yourself like the word *or:* "con-duct-**or**." To remember the **i** in *gratitude*, say it like the letter **i**: grat-**i**-tude.

✝ **TRY IT OUT** Practice this secret pronunciation strategy on words that aren't spelled the way they're spoken. Make up secret pronunciations for these words. Concentrate on the underlined letters. Write each word as you say its secret pronunciation.

6. shep<u>h</u>erd
7. uniq<u>ue</u>
8. ca<u>l</u>ves
9. as<u>th</u>ma
10. vic<u>ti</u>m

✝ **LOOK AHEAD** Look ahead at the next five lessons. Write three list words that you could use the strategy with. Mark the part of each word that you'll pay special attention to when you pronounce it.

Words with No Sound Clues

■ **FOCUS** Read each list word, paying special attention to how you say each one. Then read each meaning phrase.

identify	will **identify** your lost billfold
government	the legislative branch of our **government**
everything ♻	must put **everything** in the desk
environment	polluting the **environment**
automatically	opens the garage door **automatically**
mortgage	**mortgage** on the house
temperamental	bought a **temperamental** old car
probably ♻	**probably** can go with you
consequences	the **consequences** of telling a lie
trampoline	jumped on the **trampoline**
really ♻	pitches **really** well
therapy	**therapy** to regain use of her arm
semester	first **semester** of eighth grade
catastrophe	survived the **catastrophe**
luckily	**luckily** found me in the crowd
distribute	will **distribute** the tests
favorite ♻	sang my **favorite** song
delicate	**delicate** glass vase
criticism	unfair **criticism** of whatever I do
hideous	**hideous** face of the monster

■ **DISCOVER** Some words are misspelled because they're spelled and pronounced differently. When you say **mortgage** correctly, you don't hear the **t.** What don't you hear in **everything?** In other words, the same exact sound can be spelled by different letters: **luckily, favorite, catastrophe.**

■ **WRITE** Look over the list words carefully. First write the words that are most difficult for you to spell. Then write the rest of the words. Underline any letters that cause you a particular problem.

CHALLENGE!

mannequin
annihilate
aesthetic
apropos
aerobics

SEEING RELATIONSHIPS   Write the list word that completes each sentence.

1. I'm absolutely, positively certain. I'm ____ certain.
2. Physical and occupational are two kinds of me. I'm ____.
3. Two of me together make a school year. I'm a ____.
4. I'm made up of the executive, judicial, and legislative branches. I'm your ____.
5. You lost a ring and want to claim it. You must ____ it first.
6. I include everything around you. I'm your ____.
7. A volcano, hurricane, or tornado is an example of me. I'm a natural ____.
8. Acrobatically speaking, I'm "hopping" fun. I'm a ____.
9. Follow directions exactly or you will suffer me. I'm the ____.
10. You want everyone to have the same amount. You need to ____ the money evenly.
11. You borrow money to buy a house, but the bank gets the house if you can't pay. That's a ____.

ANTONYMS   Write the list word that completes each phrase.

12. not nothing, but ____
13. not manually, but ____
14. not easy to get along with, but ____
15. not beautiful, but ____
16. not unfortunately, but ____
17. not approval, but ____
18. not strong, but ____
19. not the least-liked, but the ____
20. not unlikely, but ____

> **Did You Know?**
> **Trampoline** comes from a German word that means "to trample." When you bounce on a trampoline, are you trampling, or "walking heavily," on it?

STRATEGIC SPELLING
The Pronouncing for Spelling Strategy

21.–24. We sometimes spell words wrong because we say them wrong. Write *identify, government, temperamental,* and *automatically*. Now say each word carefully. Be sure to pronounce the sounds of the underlined letters.

≡	Make a capital.
/	Make a small letter.
∧	Add something.
ℯ	Take out something.
⊙	Add a period.
¶	New paragraph

PROOFREAD FOR CARELESS ERRORS

Proofread carefully so you don't carelessly leave out words when you write. For example:

We need ∧to⁣ start a recycling program at Hillside Middle School.

Check for Careless Errors Read more of this editorial. Write any words that were left out. Write "Correct" if the sentence is correct.

1. It going to be up to us to save our environment.
2. If we don't, we'll have face future consequences.
3. Luckily for us, it's not too late.
4. There are lot of things we can do around our school.
5. To start, we will distribute recycling bins around the school.

PROOFREAD AN EDITORIAL

Find the six misspelled words in the rest of this editorial and write them correctly. Some may be words you learned before. Write three missing words too.

> We'll idenify the bins by color. Orange is for cans and green is for paper. Are world doesn't seem delacate, but it. It probably take awhile get used to recycling. We hope that by next smester, recycling will come automaticly to you. We're trying realy hard to make a difference.

WRITE AN EDITORIAL

Identify a situation in your school that you think needs to change. Write an editorial calling for action. Try to use three list words and a personal word.

Word List

identify	mortgage	really	distribute
government	temperamental	therapy	favorite
everything	probably	semester	delicate
environment	consequences	catastrophe	criticism
automatically	trampoline	luckily	hideous

Personal Words 1.___ 2.___

MULTICULTURAL CONNECTION: LANGUAGES For years we called the natural catastrophe that can follow an underwater earthquake a tidal wave. Now this ocean wave is more accurately called by the Japanese word *tsunami* because it really has nothing to do with tides. In the box are other words from **Asian languages** that have become part of our language.

tsunami
bamboo
kumquat
sukiyaki
tycoon
tatami
orangutan
chop suey

Write the word from the box that best fits each clue. Use your Spelling Dictionary if you need help.

1. From the Chinese *tai kiun,* it now means "a businessperson with wealth and power."
2. From the Chinese word *kamkwat,* it is a yellow fruit, somewhat like a small orange.
3. From a Malay word, it is a treelike, woody grass.
4. This combines the Japanese words meaning "harbor" and "wave."
5. This word from Malay for a large ape literally translates "man of the woods."
6. This dish of meats and vegetables comes from the Chinese word *tsap sui,* meaning "odds and ends."
7. This is a Japanese dish of strips of meat with vegetables.
8. This is a straw floor mat used in Japanese homes.

ENRICHMENT Pick one.

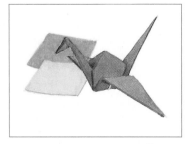

Let's Take a Ride
Here are more words that come from Asian languages: *sampan, jinrikisha, palanquin.* Look up these words in your Spelling Dictionary. Write a short explanation of what these three things have in common and how they're used in their country of origin.

Children's Day
The Chinese celebrate Children's Day on April 4. They honor children who have done well in school, citizenship, and other activities. With a small group, plan a Children's Day celebration. Be sure to honor each of your classmates with an award.

CHALLENGE!
Origami is a well-known Japanese art form of paper folding. Find some illustrated instructions for origami and try your hand at it. After you have perfected a pattern, teach a classmate how to create it.

Related Words 1

FOCUS Say each pair of related words. Notice that the spellings are similar. Then read each meaning phrase.

stable	a **stable** table that won't wobble
stability	doubtful **stability** of the tent
congratulate	will **congratulate** the winners
congratulations	smilingly accepted **congratulations**
graduate	will **graduate** from eighth grade this year
graduation	a crowded gym for **graduation**
narrate	will **narrate** the suspenseful story
narrative	a **narrative** about the pioneers
strategy	a winning **strategy** for the game
strategic	**strategic** base for defense
define	can't **define** this strange word
definition	will find the **definition** in the dictionary
inspect	will **inspect** our lockers on June 1
inspection	an **inspection** by the fire chief
victory	a trophy for their **victory**
victorious	honored the **victorious** team
politics	democratic and republican **politics**
political	the two **political** parties
protect	will **protect** you from mosquitoes
protection	**protection** from the wind and rain

DISCOVER These words are related in spelling and meaning. When a suffix is added, the sound of a letter may change, but the spelling usually stays the same: **inspect—inspection**. What happens to the sound of **a** in **stable—stability**?

WRITE Sort the list words by writing
- five pairs of words in which the suffix **-ion** or **-ition** is added
- two pairs of words in which the suffix **-ity** or **-ive** is added
- two pairs of words in which the suffix **-al** or **-ous** is added
- one pair of words in which the suffix **-ic** is added

CHALLENGE!

immune
immunize
tranquil
tranquility
intuitive
intuition

WORD RELATIONSHIPS Write the list word that matches each clue. Then write the list word that is related to it.

1.–2.   to tell a story about
3.–4.   to give the meaning of
5.–6.   not likely to fall
7.–8.   to shield from harm
9.–10. to look closely at

DRAWING CONCLUSIONS Write the list word that answers each question.

11. If your dog finishes its training class, it will what?
12. What do you call a win?
13. What would you say to someone who just won an award?
14. What is another name for a plan of attack?
15. What word would you use to describe the winning team?
16. What do you call the science and art of government?
17. What is the ceremony for when you finish high school?
18. What would you call the methods of a politician?
19. If you set yourself up in exactly the right spot, what word would you use to describe your location?
20. If you were really happy for the bride and groom, what would you do to them?

STRATEGIC SPELLING
Building New Words

Add the suffix **-ic** to make new words. Circle the words that have spelling changes. Use your Spelling Dictionary if you need help.

21. strategy
22. telescope
23. hero
24. scene
25. economy

Take a Hint
Exaggerating the pronunciation of
congratulations can help you spell it
correctly. Try to emphasize the first **t.**

≡	Make a capital.
/	Make a small letter.
∧	Add something.
ℰ	Take out something.
⊙	Add a period.
⨍	New paragraph

PROOFREAD FOR PUNCTUATION

Most abbreviations that are the initials of words need periods. For example:

When: Saturday, August 4, at 10:00 AM
                                      ⊙⊙

Check Abbreviations Write these abbreviations from party invitations correctly. If they are correct, write "Correct."

1. DJ Johnson has just completed college.
2. Let's congratulation D.J. on completing his BA in business.
3. Where: at the Lincoln Memorial, Washington, DC
4. Please send all replies to PO Box 348.
5. When: 4:00 P.M. on Sunday

PROOFREAD AN INVITATION

Find the five misspelled words in this party invitation and write them correctly. Some may be words you learned before. Find two abbreviation errors too.

Its a surprise graduation party!

Help us congradulate Shawn.

When: Sunday, June 6

2:00 PM (Please be prompt.)

Where: 1453 Madison Ave.

Please write a short narritive about the graduite to share. Anything that will cause embarasment is preferred! RSVP by June 4.

WRITE AN INVITATION

Write an invitation to a party you might like to give. Be sure to write the dates and addresses correctly. Use three list words and a personal word.

Word List

stable	graduation	define	victorious
stability	narrate	definition	politics
congratulate	narrative	inspect	political
congratulations	strategy	inspection	protect
graduate	strategic	victory	protection

Personal Words 1.___ 2.___

LATIN ROOTS: MILITARY WORDS The words *victory*, *convict*, *convince*, and *invincible* come from the Latin root *vict*, meaning "to conquer." Answer the questions below with one of these military words. Use your Spelling Dictionary if you need help.

1. What are you if you can't be conquered?
2. What do you call a person who is serving a prison sentence?
3. What can you claim when you conquer an opponent?
4. What do you do when you persuade a person to change his or her mind?

The words *command*, *demanding*, *mandates*, and *commander* come from another Latin root, *mand*, which means "to order." Complete each of these sentences with one of these military words. Use your Spelling Dictionary if you need help.

5. The ___ ordered the troops to march.
6. George Washington was in ___ during the Revolutionary War.
7. The military is ___ that we follow all of the rules and regulations.
8. The Pentagon passed down new ___ about training and educational levels for recruits.

ENRICHMENT Pick one.

Rebel with a Cause
Another military Latin root is *bellum,* meaning "war." Look up *rebel*, *belligerent, bellicose,* and *antebellum* in your Spelling Dictionary. Think of a person you consider to be a rebel. Write a short description of that person. Try to use other *bellum* words in your description.

A Plan of Attack
Many games involve military strategy, or a plan of attack for winning. With a partner or small group, think of games you know that involve plans of attack. Choose one and read the directions carefully. Decide what strategy will help you win the game; then give it a try.

CHALLENGE!
Mars was the Roman god of war. The word *martial*, which means " of war," comes from his name. Research these mythological characters: *Ceres, Terra, the Muses,* and *Helios.* What were they the gods or goddesses of? Then find some English words that come from their names.

Latin Roots 1

■ **FOCUS** Read each word and meaning phrase. Notice that some words have similar parts.

sensational	a **sensational** movie stunt
construction	road **construction** ahead
preferred	**preferred** reading to watching TV
sensibility	a **sensibility** for people's feelings
different ♻	socks of many **different** colors
consensus	reached **consensus** on a solution
destructive	a **destructive** forest fire
fertilize	must **fertilize** the garden
instructor	swimming **instructor**
sensitize	**sensitize** your eyes to the light
referral	a **referral** to another dentist
obstruction	drove around the **obstruction**
transfer	will **transfer** to another school
resentment	felt **resentment** at being called lazy
structural	**structural** differences in the buildings
inference	an **inference** from the clues
sensitivity	**sensitivity** to sunlight
conference	a **conference** with your teacher
consent	need **consent** to paint my room black
reconstruct	will **reconstruct** the collapsed bridge

■ **DISCOVER** The root *ferre,* written in English as **fer,** means "to carry," so **transfer** means "to carry across." The root *struere,* or **struct,** means "to build." What does **reconstruct** mean? The root *sentire,* written as **sens** or **sent,** means "to feel." What does **sensitive** mean?

■ **WRITE** Sort the list words by writing
- seven words with **fer**
- six words with **struct**
- seven words with **sens** or **sent**

CHALLENGE!

sentimental
preferential
differentiate
indestructible
insensitive

WORD ENDINGS   Write the list words that end with each of these suffixes.

1.–2.   -ion
3.–4.   -ence
5.–6.   -ize
7.–8.   -ity

CONTEXT   Write the list word that completes each sentence.

9. We faced a new challenge every week because we played a ____ team.
10. We were amazed at how ____ a tornado can be.
11. The swimming ____ had to cancel class this week.
12. When you think you are being treated unfairly, you build up a lot of ____.
13. My mom found a piano teacher on a ____ from your mom.
14. We were unable to reach a ____, so no decision was made.
15. The fire caused smoke damage, but fortunately there was no ____ damage to the house.
16. My parents gave their ____ for me to go on the field trip.
17. My toothpick model of the bridge collapsed on the way to school, so I had to ____ it when I got there.
18. I would have ____ to see the other movie.
19. Because we moved, I have to ____ to a new school.
20. The outfielder made a ____ catch and threw the runner out at home plate.

Add the suffix **-al** to make new words. Use your Spelling Dictionary if you need help.

21. transfer
22. instruction
23. environment
24. exception

RECYCLED WORDS

When you say **different,** make sure to say three syllables: dif•fer•ent. This will help you include all the letters when you write it.

⚌	Make a capital.
/	Make a small letter.
∧	Add something.
℘	Take out something.
⊙	Add a period.
¶	New paragraph

PROOFREAD FOR CAPITALIZATION

Capitalize proper names, the first word of a sentence, and the pronoun *I*. For example:

My parents think gary is a bad influence.

Check Capitalization Correct capitalization errors in these sentences from a letter. If there are no errors, write "Correct."

1. If Mom sees me with Gary, she thinks we're causing trouble.
2. We really aren't doing anything wrong. we're just laughing.
3. One time we took some flowers out of Mrs. steen's garden.
4. He and i have been in trouble because of that ever since.

PROOFREAD A LETTER
Find five misspelled words in this letter to an advice columnist and write them correctly. Some may be words you learned before. Fix three capitalization errors.

November 1, 19--

Dear Mr. Fix-it,

My parents had a confrence with Mr. strong, my language arts instructer. He wanted me to move to a diffrent class because i'm a good writer. I asked my parents not to make me transfer until next smester, but there making me go now. I don't want to. what should I do?

LeRoy

WRITE A RESPONSE
Write a response, giving LeRoy your best advice. Use three list words and a personal word.

Word List

sensational	consensus	referral	inference
construction	destructive	obstruction	sensitivity
preferred	fertilize	transfer	conference
sensibility	instructor	resentment	consent
different	sensitize	structural	reconstruct

Personal Words 1.____ 2.____

50

IDIOMS   An **idiom** is an expression whose meaning can't be understood from the ordinary meanings of the words in it. For example, the idiom *sing a different tune* doesn't mean you're singing "Happy Birthday" while everyone else is singing "America the Beautiful." It means that you have changed your mind about something.

> off the record
> hit the roof
> chew the fat
> take the cake
> out of line

Write the idiom from the box that matches each definition. Use your Spelling Dictionary if you need help. Look up idioms under the most important word in the phrase. For example, look up *off the record* under the entry for *record.*

1. win the first prize
2. become angry or excited
3. uncalled-for, improper
4. friendly talk or chatting
5. not to be quoted

Now that you know what these idioms mean, write the idiom that best completes each sentence.

6. My mom ____ when I broke her antique vase.
7. The informant would only talk to the reporter ____.
8. Why don't you ____ with Chris while I finish reading this chapter.
9. Our class's behavior in the assembly was ____.
10. The Cougars ____ at runs-batted-in, but are not very good at hitting home runs.

ENRICHMENT   Pick one.

Batter Up
Many idioms are sports-related. Look up these idioms in your Spelling Dictionary: *neck and neck, throw in the towel, jump the gun, out in left field.* Create a conversation that is unrelated to sports. Have the speakers use these idioms.

Take the Cake
Picture a thief sneaking a cake off a table. He is truly *taking the cake.* With a partner, make a poster picturing the exact meanings of *walk on eggs, bring home the bacon, cry over spilled milk,* and *a finger in the pie.*

CHALLENGE!
Our language probably has so many idioms because we need new expressions to express new ideas. Try to invent four idioms of your own. Topics that you might try are *time, traveling,* or *making noise.* Write a story using your new idioms in context.

Suffixes -age, -ism, -ure

10

■ **FOCUS** Read each word. Notice how the suffixes affect the spelling and meaning of the base words.

mile + age =	**mileage**
store + age =	**storage**
post + age =	**postage**
bag + age =	**baggage**
wreck + age =	**wreckage**
pass + age =	**passage**
journal + ism =	**journalism**
real + ism =	**realism**
manner + ism =	**mannerism**
hero + ism =	**heroism**
vandal + ism =	**vandalism**
capital + ism =	**capitalism**
optimist + ism =	**optimism**
please + ure =	**pleasure**
compose + ure =	**composure**
legislate + ure =	**legislature**
sculpt + ure =	**sculpture**
moist + ure =	**moisture**
fail + ure =	**failure**
press + ure =	**pressure**

■ **DISCOVER** The suffixes **-age**, **-ism**, and **-ure** form nouns when they are added to words. When **-ure** is added to the verb **sculpt**, you get **sculpture**. What noun is formed when **-ism** is added to **hero?** Sometimes the spelling changes: **bag—baggage**. What spelling change occurs in **please—pleasure?**

CHALLENGE!

architecture
enclosure
acreage
metabolism
materialism

■ **WRITE**
- Alphabetize the seven words with **-ure**.
- Alphabetize the six words with **-age**.
- Alphabetize the seven words with **-ism**.

DEFINITIONS   Write the list word that fits the definition.

1. tendency to look on the bright side of things
2. amount paid on anything sent by mail
3. the work of writing for a newspaper or magazine
4. put a lot of stress or strain in one spot
5. an economic system in which individual people own businesses and compete with others for profit
6. calmness; quietness; self-control
7. an odd habit or behavior
8. a way through or between parts of a building
9. a feeling of enjoyment or delight
10. a place for storing goods

WORD FORMS   Write the list word that has each meaning and ending indicated below.

11. the art of making figures + ure
12. actual + ism
13. a sack + age
14. to make or enact laws + ure
15. to not succeed + ure
16. a person admired for bravery + ism
17. slightly wet + ure
18. the partial or total destruction of a vehicle + age
19. a person who destroys or damages valuable things + ism
20. five thousand two hundred and eighty feet + age

STRATEGIC SPELLING
Seeing Meaning Connections

Write the words from the box that fit the definitions. One is a list word.

Words with *real*

realism
realize
unreal
real estate

21. picturing life as it is
22. imaginary
23. to understand clearly
24. land you can own

Did You Know?
The Vandals were early Europeans who earned a destructive reputation as they invaded parts of Spain and North Africa. Do you see the connection with the current meaning of **vandalism?**

☰	Make a capital.
/	Make a small letter.
∧	Add something.
ℯ	Take out something.
⊙	Add a period.
⁋	New paragraph

PROOFREAD FOR PUNCTUATION

Be sure to use commas and capital letters correctly in the heading, greeting, and closing of a personal letter. For example:

October 20 19--

dear Hong

Check Commas and Capitals Fix comma and capitalization errors in these headings, greetings, and closings from letters.

1. march 11, 19--
2. Dear Felicia
3. June 23 19--
4. Dear Mrs. Lopez
5. Yours truly
6. sincerely,

PROOFREAD AN APOLOGY LETTER Find five misspelled

words in the letter and write them correctly. Fix three errors with commas and capital letters too.

August 25 19--

Dear Sophie

I'm sorry for my faliure to put postige on your birthday gift. I didint mean for you to pay. The preshure of getting it to you on time got to me. I hope you enjoy the sculpsure. To apologize, may I treat you to dinner?

sincerely,

Melissa

WRITE AN APOLOGY LETTER Write a letter of apology to a

friend. Use three list words and a personal word.

Word List

mileage	passage	vandalism	legislature
storage	journalism	capitalism	sculpture
postage	realism	optimism	moisture
baggage	mannerism	pleasure	failure
wreckage	heroism	composure	pressure

Personal Words 1.___ 2.___

CONTEXT: EXAMPLES   Often you can guess the meaning of an unfamiliar word by its **context**—the words around it. Sometimes this context comes in the form of an example. Read this sentence: "Her soothing words helped us keep our *composure* during the tornado." The word *composure* may be unfamiliar to you, but the example, "her soothing words," gives you a clue that *composure* means "calmness."

Write an example that gives you a clue to the meaning of each underlined word.

1. <u>Sportsmanship</u> is often demonstrated by opponents shaking hands after a match.
2. Frogs are among the <u>amphibians</u> that inhabit our pond.
3. In my <u>floriculture</u> class this week, we made arrangements with carnations.
4. <u>Theropods</u>, such as the tyrannosaurus, walked on two legs and came in a variety of sizes.

Now, write the word or words in each sentence that the underlined examples give you clues about.

5. <u>Kangaroos and koalas</u> live in Australia, but the only marsupial in North America is the <u>opossum</u>.
6. Some archipelagos, such as the <u>Hawaiian Islands</u>, have become heavily populated.
7. Woodwind instruments, like the <u>clarinet and flute</u>, are an important part of an orchestra.
8. <u>Mark Twain</u> was the nom de plume of Samuel Clemens.

ENRICHMENT   Pick one.

Set an Example
You can practice writing context clues. Choose five list words, such as *legislature, vandalism, capitalism, heroism,* and *optimism.* Write a sentence for each one that contains an example so that others could figure out the meaning from the context.

Context Contest
Grab a dictionary and find at least five big words that you don't know. Nouns will work best. Write a sentence for each one, giving at least one example. Exchange sentences with a partner and try to figure out what the unfamiliar words mean from the context.

CHALLENGE!
Make up five or six new words. Then use your new words in a story. Make sure that you use plenty of examples of your created words in your story so that your classmates can figure out what they mean.

Compound Words

■ **FOCUS**   Read each compound. Notice the words that form it and how they are joined. Then read each meaning phrase.

thunderstorm	lightning during a **thunderstorm**
granddaughter	tickled his baby **granddaughter**
remote control	a **remote control** toy car
no one ♻	has told **no one** the secret
bookkeeper	**bookkeeper** for the music store
vice-president	**vice-president** of the student council
wheelchair	will need a motorized **wheelchair**
great-grandmother	a picture of my **great-grandmother**
shopping center	a day at the **shopping center**
seventy-two	**seventy-two** years ago
halfway	**halfway** around the world
outside ♻	stood **outside** the door
underground	an **underground** stream
life jacket	a **life jacket** for each person in the boat
self-esteem	the importance of **self-esteem**
throughout	chocolate chips **throughout** the ice cream
well-known	a **well-known** singing group
role model	admires her **role model**
underrated	**underrated** by the movie reviewers
daydream	seems to **daydream** in class

■ **DISCOVER**   In an open compound a space remains between the two words: **no one.** In a hyphenated compound the two words are joined by a hyphen: **seventy-two.** How are the words in a closed compound such as **bookkeeper** joined? Notice that no letters are left out when joining the words in a compound.

■ **WRITE**   Sort the list words by writing
- five open compound words
- five hyphenated compound words
- ten closed compound words

CHALLENGE!

straight-faced
daylight-saving
    time
stage fright
report card
straightforward

JOINING WORDS Find two words in each sentence that make up a compound word from the list and write the word.

1. Did you go shopping at the center near your home?
2. I won't be through until I'm out of time.
3. It's great that your grandmother could come for a visit.
4. We split the sandwich in half and ate it on our way to school.
5. The thunder told us that there was a storm approaching.
6. No, you may have only one cookie.
7. There were seventy pieces to the puzzle, but we lost two.
8. She has never in her life owned a jacket like that.
9. The possibility is remote, but can you control your dog?
10. Take that out and put it by the side of the house.

COMPOUND COMBINATIONS Write the list word that includes the underlined part of each of these compound words.

11. daughter-in-law
12. daybreak
13. overrated
14. role-play
15. playground

16. shopkeeper
17. president-elect
18. myself
19. wheelbarrow
20. well-meaning

STRATEGIC SPELLING

Seeing Meaning Connections

Words with *life*

life jacket
life expectancy
life insurance
lifeguard
life-size

Write the word from the box that fits each definition. One is a list word.

21. I keep a watchful vigil over the beach and water.
22. I'll help support your loved ones after you die.
23. I am equal to the size of the original.
24. I'll keep you afloat if you fall overboard.
25. I'm how long you will probably live.

RECYCLED WORDS

To remember that **no one** is two words, think about how you say it. Two **o's** written together are rarely pronounced separately as they are in **no one.**

≡	Make a capital.
/	Make a small letter.
∧	Add something.
℮	Take out something.
⊙	Add a period.
⁋	New paragraph

PROOFREAD FOR USAGE   The pronouns *me, him, her, us,* and *them* are used as the object of a preposition or the direct object.

Between you and ~~I~~, Great-grandmother [me]
allows ~~he~~ and ~~I~~ to get away with a lot. [him] [me] [∧]

Check Pronouns Read each sentence. Correct any pronoun errors. Write "Correct" if all the pronouns are correct.

1. Great-grandmother is a good role model for my mom and I.
2. She gives Mom and I a care package to take home with us.
3. I try to help her do things around the house when I can.
4. No one is as nice to Mom and me as Great-grandmother is.

PROOFREAD A DESCRIPTION   Find six misspelled words in this description and write them correctly. Some may be words you learned before. Fix three pronoun errors too.

My great-grandmother's house is neat. She is seventytwo and in a wheel chair, so she has ramps througout her house. She lets my freinds and I ride our bikes on the one outside. There's an under ground tunnel that connects the house to a cellar. My friend and I went down it but got scared because noone was with he and I.

WRITE A DESCRIPTION   Do any of your friends or relatives live in an interesting place? Write a description of a house you think is neat. Try to use three list words and a personal word.

Word List

thunderstorm	vice-president	halfway	throughout
granddaughter	wheelchair	outside	well-known
remote control	great-grandmother	underground	role model
no one	shopping center	life jacket	underrated
bookkeeper	seventy-two	self-esteem	daydream

Personal Words 1.____ 2.____

EXPLORING LANGUAGE: JARGON

A life jacket is a basic piece of equipment for sailing, and almost everyone knows what one is. However, sailing also has its own special language, or **jargon,** that is mostly known only by those who actually sail. Look at these parts of a sailboat:

Some of these words, such as *boom* and *painter,* have familiar meanings, but they have their own special meanings in sailing jargon. Write the sailing word that fits each definition. Use the illustration and your Spelling Dictionary if you need help.

mast

boom

sheet

painter

rudder

centerboard

1. the pole that holds up the sail
2. the pole that holds the bottom edge of the sail
3. board that keeps the boat from slipping sideways in the water
4. the piece at the rear of the boat used to steer it
5. line used for controlling the sail
6. rope for tying the boat to the pier

ENRICHMENT   Pick one.

Sail Away
Sailing has a lot more jargon than these six words. Look up this sailing jargon in your Spelling Dictionary: *luffing, keel, windward, leeward, port,* and *starboard.* Write a short description of a sailing trip, using these words.

Sail Safely
Safety gear in sailing also has its own jargon. With a partner, investigate the safety equipment, in addition to life jackets, that you should find on a sailboat. Make a list of the safety gear that is important to sailing.

CHALLENGE!
Tying knots is an important sailing skill. Some basic boating knots are the *clove hitch,* the *square knot,* the *bowline,* and the *figure eight.* Get some rope and information about knot-tying. Learn how to tie these knots.

Review

Look back at the word lists in Lessons 7–11 and think about how you are doing in spelling.

1. The hardest words for me to spell were ____ ____ ____

2. It's easy for me to remember how to spell compound words like **outside** or **life jacket.** **Yes**   **No**   **Sometimes**

3. If someone asked me how to tell which compound words are spelled with a hyphen and which are not, I would tell them ____.

4. You learned that careful pronunciation can help you spell some words. Have you used this strategy?   **Yes**   **No**   **Sometimes**

5. The most interesting word that I have learned to spell is ____.

■ PROOFREADING

Find the spelling errors in each passage and write the words correctly. All passages have seven errors except the last one, which has eight.

PROOFREAD A NOTICE

Several articles are in the lost-and-found boxes in the main office. If you have lost something, you may insect or idenify the articles from noon until 3:00 today. We will distribyute every thing not picked up to the children's home. Items in the boxes include a book of postige stamps, a remotcontrol car, four sweaters, a black notebook, a softball, a tape by a wellnown rock group, and two mismatched athletic socks.

PROOFREAD BABY-SITTER INSTRUCTIONS

Angela,

Please put the baby to bed. She has been fed, but she was rather tempramental today, so she may not go to sleep right away.

Dinner for you and the twins is in the oven, which will automaticly turn off at 6:30. Each of you may have a diffrent fruit for dessert. Tim's favorit is in the bowl out side the refrigerator. Luckly, I shopped today.

The twins are to be in bed by 8:00. They know the consiquences if they are not. I'll be home by 9:30.

Mrs. Fitzgerald

PROOFREAD A NEWS STORY

Vandals at Work

Several exhibits in the indoor sculpsure garden were damaged by vandalsm last week. Art instructer Tad Morelli said that students can reconstrut some of the work, but that the most delecate pieces are probly not replaceable. The exhibit was completed last smester by students from three middle schools, and several of the pieces won awards. One of the works damaged was a sea gull made from clay, which won a blue ribbon. It was sculpted by Blaine Newsome.

PROOFREAD A JOURNAL ENTRY

We had a hard time getting to grategrandmother Rosa's house today. In fact, Mom lost her composer. We were driving on the expressway when we saw the reckage from an accident. Then there was an abstruction on a bridge. After that we hit a sentsational storm with thunder and lightning. I was about to congradulate Mom on her driving when we had a flat tire. Mom says she would have prefered to have stayed home.

PROOFREAD A SOCIAL STUDIES REPORT

Benjamin Franklin

Benjamin Franklin (1706-1790) was active and influential in journlism, science, and politicks. He started his career as a printer's apprentice and went on to become owner of his own newspaper in Philadelphia. There he helped establish the first public library in the colonies and became postmaster of Philadelphia. In his famous kite experiment, he made a kite of silk, strips of cedar, and a wire and attached a key to the string. When he flew the kite in a thunderstrom, he drew down lightning. He developed important ideas about electricity and also invented the lightning rod. He was a signer of the Declaration of Independence and was sent by the goverment to France as a diplomat. He remained active in politickal affairs threwout his career. His famous autobiography is a narritive of his unusual life.

PROOFREAD A FRIENDLY LETTER

November 3, 19--

Dear Uncle Ignacio,

Congradulations on winning an award for
heroizm. We read about your rescue of the boy
in the river. It's a good thing that you were
wearing a lifejacket. That swimmer was
realy lucky that you were in a stategic spot
when he fell in. The newspaper reported that
he is in stabel condition. We hope you are too.

Will you be able to come to my graduate-
tion in June? It would be great to see you
again.

Your nephew,

Roberto

PROOFREAD A FEATURE STORY

Hurricanes: Costly and Cruel

Hurricanes usually start over tropical ocean waters and can do much strutural damage to buildings as well as damage to the enviroment. Often high waves are as distructive as the wind. Offshore islands, which extend from New England to Texas, have been seriously eroded over the years, and there has been critisim of the construcshin that has taken place on coastal areas. Mobile homes in particular offer little pertection from hurricane winds.

Hurricane winds rotate in a circle or oval that may be as big as 500 miles in diameter. In 1993, Hurricane Emily's winds reached 115 miles per hour. Since knowone can predict exactly which direction a hurricane will take, a catastrope can occur with very little warning.

STRATEGY WORKSHOP

Divide and Conquer

DISCOVER THE STRATEGY Here's a strategy for studying extra-long words that you keep having trouble with. Cut them down to size by cutting them up. Then study them piece by piece. How do you divide these words for study? That depends on the kind of word you're working with.

Compounds: divide between base words	Words with Affixes: divide between affix and base word	Other Words: divide between syllables
grand/daughter through/out under/ground	re/construct/ion fertil/ize compos/ure	tram/po/line ca/tas/tro/phe i/den/ti/fy

†† TRY IT OUT Now try this divide and conquer strategy.

Compounds Write these compounds:

thunderstorm bookkeeper underrated wheelchair daydream

1.–5. Draw a line between the two base words that make up each compound. *Note:* This will show you that two words have been put together with no letters lost.

Affixes Write these words:

| subdivision | structural | pleasure | failure | mileage |

6.–10. Draw lines between each base word and any prefixes or suffixes. *Note:* This will show you whether adding a suffix changes the spelling of the base word.

Now look back at the words you wrote. Three base words changed spelling when the suffix was added. Underline the base words that changed spelling.

Syllables Write these words:

| consequences | pistachios | temperamental |
| diagnoses | thermostat | |

11.–15. Say each word. Listen carefully for the syllables and draw lines between them. Check a dictionary for how to divide any words that you're not sure of.

✝ LOOK AHEAD Look ahead at the next five lessons. Write six list words that you could use these strategies with. Say each word to yourself and divide it into smaller pieces. Divide each word the way that works best for you.

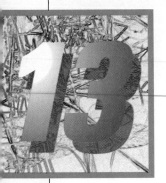

Directional Prefixes

■ **FOCUS**   Look at each word and read the meaning phrase. Notice what happens to the base words when the prefix is added.

submarine	a **submarine** exploring the sea bottom
transportation	**transportation** by bus, car, or plane
supernatural	imagining **supernatural** noises in the night
subheading	a chapter **subheading** in a book
transfusion	a blood **transfusion** after the accident
subtraction	addition, **subtraction,** multiplication
translate	**translate** a book from English to French
supermarket	went to the **supermarket** for groceries
subcommittee	a senate **subcommittee** studying taxes
subsection	a section and **subsection** of a contract
superficial	**superficial** scratches that aren't deep
transaction	a **transaction** on my credit card bill
superstition	a silly old **superstition** about black cats
transparent	looked through the **transparent** curtain
supersede	**supersede,** or overrule, the earlier rules
submerge	**submerge** my head underwater
supersonic	**supersonic** speed of the jet
transcript	the **transcript** of your school records
subdivision	a new **subdivision** near our neighborhood
transmit	tried to **transmit** a message to the ship

■ **DISCOVER**   The prefixes in these words all indicate direction. The prefix **sub-** means "below," so a **subheading** is "below the heading". The prefix **trans-** means "across." What does **transmit** mean? The prefix **super-** means "greater than." What does **supersonic** mean?

■ **WRITE**   Sort the list words by writing
- seven words with **sub-**
- six words with **super-**
- seven words with **trans-**

CHALLENGE!

subterranean
translucent
superimpose
subordinate
transoceanic

MAKING CONNECTIONS Write the list word that matches each clue.

1. I am a boat found below the surface of the water.
2. You can see through me.
3. I am not deep.
4. I am a part of a section.
5. I travel faster than the speed of sound.
6. I am the transfer of blood from one person to another.
7. I am above or beyond what is natural.
8. I mean "to put under water."
9. I am a piece of land divided into smaller parts.
10. I mean "to be greater than something that came earlier."

CONTEXT CLUES Write the list word that completes each sentence.

11. My grandmother had a ____ about walking under ladders.
12. A ____ of the chapter titled "Ecology" is "Saving Our Environment."
13. Some members of the dance committee formed a ____ to choose songs.
14. Could you ____ this Spanish song into English for me?
15. An airplane is usually the fastest mode of ____.
16. I find it easier to do ____ than multiplication.
17. The college will want a ____ of your high school grades before it will consider accepting you as a student.
18. I'm on my way to the ____ to buy some milk.
19. This ____ won't be on your bill until next month.
20. We ____ documents over the phone lines now.

The Divide and Conquer Strategy

21.–24. It often helps to study longer words piece by piece. Write *transportation, supernatural, subheading,* and *subtraction.* Draw lines to break them into smaller parts. Study the parts.

> **Did You Know?**
> **Supersede** is the only word in English that ends in *sede.*

≡	Make a capital.
/	Make a small letter.
∧	Add something.
ℓ	Take out something.
⊙	Add a period.
¶	New paragraph

PROOFREAD FOR USAGE Some indefinite pronouns, such as *each, either, everyone, neither, no one, somebody,* and *one,* are singular and need singular verbs.

Each one of the committee members looking into the bike rack situation ~~have~~ ∧has come up with a plan.

Check Subjects and Verbs Read each sentence. Correct the verbs that do not fit subjects. If a verb is correct, write "Correct."

1. Somebody on the committee objects to the investigation.
2. No one on the council really have an opinion.
3. Everyone at school uses bicycles as a form of transportation.
4. Each of the teachers have voiced an opinion on the subject.
5. Neither of the advisers feel this issue supersedes all others.

PROOFREAD MEETING MINUTES Find five misspelled words in the rest of the student council minutes and write them correctly. Some may be words you learned before. Correct three incorrect verbs following indefinite pronouns too.

> The subcommitee looking into the cost of new bike racks reported that every one of the existing racks are in terrible condition. Each have been partly submerjed in water and are rusting. Racks range in price, but the differences among them are superfishal. Were hoping to complete a transackton for four new racks soon.

WRITE MEETING MINUTES Write the minutes of a meeting concerning plans for a community clean-up project. Use three list words and a personal word.

Word List

submarine	subtraction	superficial	submerge
transportation	translate	transaction	supersonic
supernatural	supermarket	superstition	transcript
subheading	subcommittee	transparent	subdivision
transfusion	subsection	supersede	transmit

Personal Words 1.____ 2.____

GREEK AND LATIN ROOTS: *fundere*   *Transfusion* comes from the Latin root *fundere,* which means "melt or pour." The rest of the words in the box also have something to do with melting or pouring because they come from *fundere.* Write the word from the box that fits each definition in the word web. Use your Spelling Dictionary if you need help.

refund
fuse
funnel
transfusion
foundry

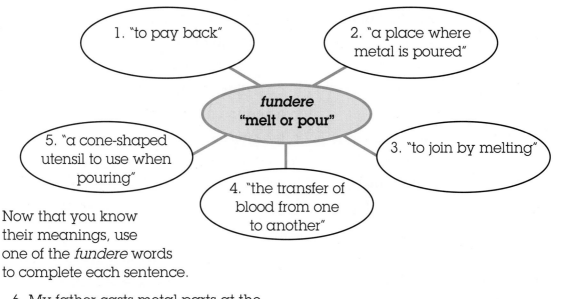

1. "to pay back"

2. "a place where metal is poured"

fundere "melt or pour"

3. "to join by melting"

4. "the transfer of blood from one to another"

5. "a cone-shaped utensil to use when pouring"

Now that you know their meanings, use one of the *fundere* words to complete each sentence.

6. My father casts metal parts at the ____.
7. When I return this sweater, the store will ____ my money.
8. The accident victim needed a ____.
9. To fix the crack in my ring, the jeweler had to ____ the metal.
10. To avoid spilling, I used a ____ to put oil in my car.

ENRICHMENT   Pick one.

Root Awareness
Look up the word histories of *transparent, translate, submerge, supersede,* and *superstition* in your Spelling Dictionary. Make a chart that shows for each word the prefix with its meaning, the Latin root with its meaning, and a context sentence.

Across the Country
The prefix *trans-* means "across," so a word like *transoceanic* means "across the ocean." With a partner, brainstorm other places you can go across, and coin some new words that start with *trans-.* Choose your favorite and make a poster illustrating the crossing.

CHALLENGE!
The prefixes *sub-,* meaning "under or below," and *super-,* meaning "over or above," can be opposites. How many opposite pairs, like *subscript* and *superscript,* can you think of? Use a dictionary if you need help.

Related Words 2

■ **FOCUS** Say each pair of related words. Notice how the spelling and pronunciation change. Read each meaning phrase.

exclaim	did **exclaim** that he didn't do it
exclamation	heard a fearful **exclamation**
commit	didn't **commit** the crime
commission	a ten percent **commission** on each sale
detain	should **detain** them for questioning
detention	a **detention** period after school
ferocious	a **ferocious** wild tiger
ferocity	feared the **ferocity** of the verbal attack
comprehend	can't **comprehend** the explanation
comprehension	a good **comprehension** of the process
pertain	comment didn't **pertain** to the question
pertinent	**pertinent** facts to help make the decision
intrude	**intrude** into a private conversation
intrusion	an **intrusion** into our campsite
recede	**recede** to the river's normal level
recession	factory closing because of the **recession**
sustain	must study hard to **sustain** good grades
sustenance	without **sustenance** and almost starving
invade	will **invade** a neighboring country
invasion	an **invasion** of ants in the cookie jar

■ **DISCOVER** The words **sustain** and **sustenance** are similar in spelling and meaning, but are pronounced differently. Say **commit** and **commission.** Which letter changes between the base word and the related word?

■ **WRITE** Sort the list words by writing
- four pairs of words in which **ai** changes to **a, e,** or **i**
- five pairs of words in which **d** or **t** changes to **s** or **ss**
- one pair of words in which **ous** disappears

CHALLENGE!

atrocious
atrocity
abstain
abstention
apprehend
apprehension

SYNONYMS Write the list word that means the same as the underlined word or phrase in each sentence.

1. How long can you <u>hold</u> that high note?
2. Let's limit ourselves to facts that <u>relate</u> to the problem.
3. Is our economy starting to recover from the latest <u>slump</u>?
4. Ann led the midnight <u>raid</u> of the kitchen.
5. Please pardon our <u>barging in</u> on your quiet time.
6. I know you're in a hurry, so I won't <u>delay</u> you any longer.
7. I heard him <u>yell</u> with pain when he hit his thumb with the hammer.
8. Did you <u>promise</u> your time to picking up litter this Saturday?
9. You shouldn't <u>meddle</u> in your friend's private affairs.
10. Do you receive a <u>portion of the profit</u> on each sale?
11. The prisoner was placed in a small <u>confinement</u> room before she was moved to her cell.
12. The Blue Team will attempt to <u>enter</u> the Orange Team's territory in the game of military strategy.

SYLLABLES Write the list word that matches the number of syllables shown. The last syllable has been given.

13. ____ ■ ____ ■ ____ ■ sion   17. ____ ■ ____ ■ ____ ■ tion
14. ____ ■ ____ ■ ____ ■ ty   18. ____ ■ ____ ■ cious
15. ____ ■ ____ ■ nent   19. ____ ■ ____ ■ hend
16. ____ ■ ____ ■ nance   20. ____ ■ cede

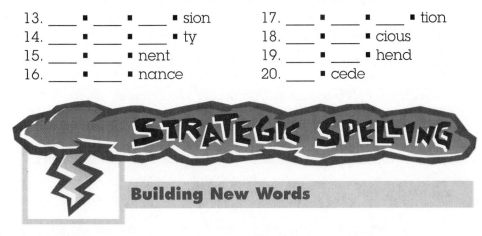

STRATEGIC SPELLING

Building New Words

Add the suffix **-ent** to make new words. Circle the words with spelling changes. One is a list word. Use your Spelling Dictionary if you need help.

21. pertain
22. depend
23. precede
24. excel
25. persist

Did You Know?
Not only can an army **invade** a country, but tourists can **invade** a city and ants can **invade** a picnic.

≡	Make a capital.
/	Make a small letter.
∧	Add something.
℮	Take out something.
⊙	Add a period.
⁋	New paragraph

PROOFREAD FOR USAGE Use only one negative word, such as *no, never, not* (or its contraction *n't*), *nothing, nobody,* or *neither,* when you mean "no." For example:

Serving time in detention isn't ~~no~~ $\overset{any}{\wedge}$ fun.

Check for Double Negatives Write the word from the parentheses that correctly completes each sentence.

1. I don't like (any, none) of the rules in detention.
2. You can do (anything, nothing) but schoolwork there.
3. I have had (any, no) pertinent schoolwork all week.
4. The detention teacher makes sure you're not doing (anything, nothing) that you're not supposed to do.
5. I can't take (any, no) more invasion of my privacy.

PROOFREAD A COMPLAINT Find five misspelled words in the rest of this complaint. Write them correctly. Some may be words you learned before. Fix two double negatives too.

> For one thing, you're supposed to work on pertnent schoolwork, but you can't do that if you don't have nothing that day. Also, if you comit a second offense while your in detension, you should get a diffrent punishment pertaining to the new violation. You shouldn't never have the same punishment for different crimes.

WRITE A COMPLAINT What rule around your school would you like to change? Write a complaint to your principal, making sure to give reasons. Use three list words and a personal word.

Word List

exclaim	detention	pertain	recession
exclamation	ferocious	pertinent	sustain
commit	ferocity	intrude	sustenance
commission	comprehend	intrusion	invade
detain	comprehension	recede	invasion

Personal Words 1.____ 2.____

DICTIONARY: MULTIPLE MEANINGS Some words have more than one meaning. To help choose the right one, use the part-of-speech label and the sample sentences or phrases. Look at all the different meanings in this dictionary entry for *commit*.

> **com mit** (kə mit′), *v.t.,* **-mit ted, -mit ting. 1** do or perform (usually something wrong): *commit a crime.* **2** hand over for safekeeping; deliver. **3** send to prison or an asylum. **4** give over; carry over; transfer: *commit a poem to memory.* **5** reveal (one's opinion). **6** involve; pledge: *I would not commit myself in any way.* [< Latin *committere* < *com-* with + *mittere* send, put] **—commitable,** *adj.*

Write the number of the definition of *commit* that fits each sentence. Some definitions are used more than once.

1. Did you commit your new locker combination to memory?
2. We are committed to working to save our environment.
3. A person who steals is committing a crime.
4. I commit my child to your care until I return.
5. When asked if he was a candidate for president, he refused to commit.
6. The convicted thief was committed to the state prison.
7. He received a five-year sentence for committing bribery.
8. I have committed to going and will not change my mind.

ENRICHMENT Pick one.

Sustained Sentences

Other list words have multiple meanings too. Read the entry for *sustain* in your Spelling Dictionary. Use the existing illustrative sentences as guides, and write new sentences illustrating each of the seven definitions.

Multiple Meanings Game

Get a partner. One of you look up the three meanings of *detain* in your Spelling Dictionary and write five sentences, using each definition at least one time. The other do the same for *invade.* Exchange papers and label each other's sentences with the correct definition.

CHALLENGE!

Often the easiest words have the most meanings. Look up *fit* or *run* in a dictionary. How many different meanings do you find? Choose an easy word with many meanings and use it in a short story. Use as many of its different meanings as you can.

Latin and Greek Word Parts 1

■ **FOCUS** Read each word and meaning phrase. Notice that some words have similar parts.

subscribe	will **subscribe** to the paper for a year
eloquent	an **eloquent** speech about teamwork
biography	a **biography** of Abraham Lincoln
revoke	**revoke** their privileges if they misbehave
graphic	made real by the **graphic** description
loquacious	a **loquacious** child talking endlessly
scribble	shouldn't **scribble** in the book
geography	the **geography** of the Middle East
vocation	thought his **vocation** was to be a lawyer
postscript	**postscript** at the end of the letter
advocate	an **advocate** promoting children's rights
colloquial	a formal speech with no **colloquial** words
manuscript	screenplay **manuscript** sent to a producer
paragraph	wrote a **paragraph** about Chinese cooking
describe	will **describe** your room in detail
invoke	**invoke,** or appeal for, police protection
soliloquy	on stage alone delivering a **soliloquy**
vocalize	should **vocalize** our ideas, not keep silent
photography	portrait done at a **photography** studio
inscription	will read the **inscription** on the plaque

■ **DISCOVER** These words from Greek and Latin are related to communicating. The Latin word *vocare* means "to call." What does **revoke** mean? The Latin word *scribere* and the Greek word *graphein* mean "write." What do **scribble** and **graphic** mean? The Latin word *loqui* means "speak." What does **eloquent** mean?

CHALLENGE!

circumlocution
irrevocable
choreograph
cartographer
circumscribe

■ **WRITE** Sort the list words by writing
- six words from *scribere,* written **scrib** or **script** in English
- five words from *graphein,* written **graph** in English
- five words from *vocare,* written **voc** or **vok** in English
- four words from *loqui,* written **loq** in English

WORD PARTS Write the list word that includes the underlined part of each word.

1. <u>bio</u>degradable
2. manu<u>fac</u>ture
3. sol<u>it</u>ary
4. <u>photo</u>copy
5. post<u>hum</u>ous
6. para<u>phrase</u>
7. re<u>peal</u>
8. <u>geo</u>metry

ROOTS AND MEANING Write the word that fits the Latin or Greek word and the definition. Use your Spelling Dictionary.

9. From *loqui,* this means "talkative."
10. From *scribere,* this means "to write carelessly."
11. From *graphein,* this means "shown with a picture."
12. From *scribere,* this is your promise that you'll pay for the daily newspaper that is delivered every morning.
13. From *vocare,* this is "an occupation or profession."
14. From *scribere,* this is "something engraved on a plaque."
15. From *vocare,* this means "to support or promote."
16. From *loqui,* this describes "everyday, informal conversation."
17. From *vocare,* this means "to use your voice."
18. From *loqui,* this is "speech that is expressive and graceful."
19. From *vocare,* this means "to appeal for help."
20. From *scribere,* this is "to tell about something in detail."

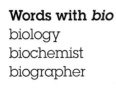

STRATEGIC SPELLING

Seeing Meaning Connections

Words with *bio*
biology
biochemist
biographer

The root **bio** means "life." Write the words from the box that fit the definitions. Use your Spelling Dictionary if you need help.

21. scientist who studies the chemical processes of life
22. the scientific study of life
23. one who writes about someone else's life

Did You Know?
Before printing was invented, all books were written by hand, a long and laborious task. Combine the Latin words for "hand" and "write" and you get **manuscript.**

☰	Make a capital.
/	Make a small letter.
∧	Add something.
ℓ	Take out something.
⊙	Add a period.
⁋	New paragraph

PROOFREAD FOR PUNCTUATION

Add an apostrophe and **s ('s)** to form the possessive of singular nouns. Add an apostrophe to form the possessive of most plural nouns. For example:

All classes' plays are about a time in America's history.

Check Apostrophes Add apostrophes to possessives that need them. If a possessive is correct, write "Correct."

1. Each class's play will be performed Saturday.
2. The seventh-graders performance will be first.
3. Their play is based on Helen Kellers autobiography.
4. Their teachers husband designed a set for them.
5. He used photography to show Helen's house in the background.

PROOFREAD A REVIEW
Find the five misspelled words in this review of a school play. Write them correctly. Some may be words you learned before. Fix three possessive errors too.

> The eighth-graders play, <u>Huckleberry Finn</u>, was about two friends on a river. It also told about the river's geagraphy. Hucks soliloqwey helped to discribe the scenery. Coloquial language added to the charm. The actors costumes were neat. They had to where them to school the day before the play for publicity.

WRITE A REVIEW
Choose a movie or play you've seen recently and write a review of it. Describe the sets, costumes, and acting. Try to use three list words and a personal word.

Word List

subscribe	loquacious	advocate	invoke
eloquent	scribble	colloquial	soliloquy
biography	geography	manuscript	vocalize
revoke	vocation	paragraph	photography
graphic	postscript	describe	inscription

Personal Words 1.____ 2.____

EXPLORING LANGUAGE: INITIALS AND ACRONYMS

Have you ever added **PS** to the bottom of a letter? These are the **initials** for *postscript.* When you address the envelope for that letter, you should write a Zip code. **Zip** is an **acronym** for *Zone Improvement Plan.* What's the difference between initials and acronyms? Each letter of an initial is pronounced, but acronyms are pronounced as a single word. The box lists other initials and acronyms.

Write the initials or acronyms from the box that stand for these phrases.

laser	VISTA
IQ	NATO
snafu	UNICEF
NASA	SWAT
D.J.	RV

1. situation normal—all fouled up
2. North Atlantic Treaty Organization
3. United Nations International Children's Emergency Fund
4. recreational vehicle
5. light amplification by stimulated emission of radiation
6. Special Weapons and Tactics
7. Volunteers in Service to America
8. National Aeronautics and Space Administration
9. disc jockey
10. intelligence quotient

ENRICHMENT   Pick one.

MIAP
This is More Initials and Acronyms Practice. (Look at the title again!) Look these up in your Spelling Dictionary: *R.S.V.P., scuba, BLT, radar.* Find out where each one comes from. Write sentences that show how each would be used in everyday communication.

Secret Acronyms
Working with a small group, make up some secret clubs or organizations to do good deeds around your school. Create acronyms for the names of your clubs. See if your classmates can break your acronym code!

CHALLENGE!
Your name (first and last) could be an acronym or initials. For example, if you are Ann Smith, your name could stand for: A Naturally Nice Safety-patroller and role-Model In The Hallway. Write a sentence to create an acronym for your name.

Easily Confused Words

■ **FOCUS** Read each word and meaning phrase. Notice how the pairs of words sound similar but have different meanings.

collage	framed her **collage** of photos and words
college	might study engineering in **college**
liable	**liable** to break if you drop it
libel	newspaper defending itself in a **libel** suit
emigrants	**emigrants** leaving Korea for America
immigrants	**immigrants** arriving in America from Korea
allude	didn't even **allude** to your secret
elude	**elude** the tacklers to score a touchdown
rational	not **rational** when angry
rationale	explained the **rationale** behind the decision
persecute	used to **persecute** and harass them
prosecute	will **prosecute** them in a court of law
hardy	**hardy** people living in the Arctic Circle
hearty	sides hurting from a **hearty** laugh
envelop	fog to **envelop** the entire city
envelope	a stamped, self-addressed **envelope**
imply	**imply,** or suggest, anger with clenched fists
infer	can **infer** facts from the hints given
magnet	held to the refrigerator with a **magnet**
magnate	railroad **magnate** who owns ten mansions

■ **DISCOVER** Some of these word pairs sound alike but have very different meanings: **magnet, magnate.** The spellings of other words on the list differ by only one or two letters: **persecute, prosecute.** Think about what these words mean to be sure you're using the right one.

effective
affective
eminent
imminent
perpetrate
perpetuate

■ **WRITE** Some of these word pairs are more confusing than others. Write the word pairs that you use correctly. Then write the pairs that you aren't sure of.

DEFINITIONS   Write the list word that matches each clue.

1. people who move into a country
2. people who move out of a country
3. to refer to or mention in passing
4. to cleverly avoid or escape
5. to draw conclusions from hints
6. to mean something without saying it directly
7. to cause to suffer
8. to bring before a court of law

CLASSIFYING   Write the list word that relates to each group.

9. durable, robust, lasting
10. stationery, stamp, address
11. attract, pull, polar
12. university, school, institution
13. warm, friendly, strong
14. explanation, justification, reason
15. mosaic, mural, montage
16. likely, possible, probable
17. businessperson, tycoon, entrepreneur
18. sensible, reasonable, logical
19. cover, enfold, conceal
20. falsehood, slander, lie

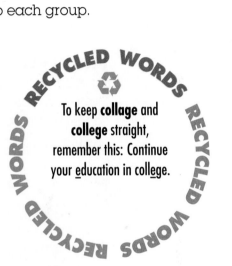

RECYCLED WORDS

To keep **collage** and **college** straight, remember this: Continue your <u>e</u>ducation in coll<u>e</u>ge.

STRATEGIC SPELLING

Seeing Meaning Connections

| immigrants |
| emigrated |
| immigrating |
| immigration |

Complete the sentences in this passage with words from the box. One is a list word.

Between 1892 and 1943, Ellis Island in Upper New York Bay was the main __(21)__ center in the United States. As many as one million __(22)__ were processed there in a year. People __(23)__ from their native countries for various reasons, such as fleeing persecution. They hoped to get a better life by __(24)__ to the U.S.

≡	Make a capital.
/	Make a small letter.
∧	Add something.
ℓ	Take out something.
⊙	Add a period.
¶	New paragraph

PROOFREAD FOR CARELESS ERRORS

Capitalize nouns only if they name a specific person, place, or thing. For example:

Fourteen-year-old Tex lives with his seventeen-year-old Brother, Mason.

Check for Capital Letters Write correctly the five incorrectly capitalized words in the rest of this blurb for *Tex,* by S.E. Hinton.

The two Brothers are often in conflict. No one has seen their Father for months. Mason has dreams of going to College, while Tex has a hard time just keeping out of Trouble. A terrifying Experience forces them together.

PROOFREAD A BLURB Find five spelling errors in this blurb for *I Am the Cheese,* by Robert Cormier. Write them correctly. Some may be words you learned before. Fix three words that shouldn't be capitalized too.

> The goverment and a Criminal organization envelope Adam's family in danger. His father gave testimony to help persecute the Organization, but Adam has blanked it out. The Family has been in witness protection, but the are no longer able to allude the organization. Adam is finally let in on the horrible secret.

WRITE A BLURB Choose a book or story that you have recently read and write a blurb for it. Try to use three list words and a personal word.

Word List

collage	immigrants	persecute	envelope
college	allude	prosecute	imply
liable	elude	hardy	infer
libel	rational	hearty	magnet
emigrants	rationale	envelop	magnate

Personal Words 1.___ 2.___

MULTICULTURAL CONNECTION: ART The collage is a relatively new art form, really only begun within the last hundred years. **Mosaic**—pictures made of pieces of stone, glass, or wood—has been around for thousands of years. Mosaics recovered in the Middle East were completed as long as five thousand years ago.

Look at these mosaics from various times and places. Use the information at the right to help you label each with its country of origin.

1. ____

3. ____

2. ____

4. ____

Israel Thousands of years ago, Middle Eastern people used mosaic in geometric patterns to decorate buildings.

Mexico In the 7th or 8th century, Aztecs often used mosaic to decorate ceremonial masks.

Italy The mosaics of Italy, dating from the 1st century to the present, often resemble paintings.

Spain In the 20th century, mosaic was revived to decorate the outside of modern buildings in Spain.

ENRICHMENT Pick one.

A Collage About You
Use words and pictures to make a collage that tells about you. Bring in magazines and newspapers for pictures and words, or write and draw them yourself. Some things you may want to tell about are your family, interests, hobbies, pets, and home.

Mosaic Mascot
Working with a partner, think about something that makes your school unique. Create a mosaic to represent your object by cutting up squares of colored construction paper and gluing them onto paper. Display your mosaic in your classroom or school.

CHALLENGE!
In addition to mosaic, Mexico also is known for its murals. Find out more about the art of Mexican mural painting, especially the subject matter. Perhaps organize a class mural that imitates the subject matter of Mexican murals.

Words from Many Cultures 1

■ **FOCUS** Say each word and read the meaning phrase that goes with it.

calligraphy	a letter handwritten in **calligraphy**
hammock	**hammock** swinging between two trees
toboggan	down the snowy hill on the **toboggan**
tambourine	**tambourine** shaken in time with the music
slalom	lose a ski on the **slalom** course
rodeo	the bucking horses at the **rodeo**
snorkel	breathed underwater with a **snorkel**
banjo	strumming a tune on the **banjo**
amateur	excellent violinist for an **amateur**
origami	an **origami** cat of folded rice paper
jukebox	play a favorite song on the **jukebox**
luggage	having too much **luggage** for a short trip
ukulele	played the **ukulele** I bought in Hawaii
batik	dye, cloth, and heated wax for **batik**
machete	chopped sugar cane with a **machete**
macramé	a **macramé** wall hanging of white rope
umbrella	bright red **umbrella** for a gray, misty day
safari	a photo **safari** looking for elephants
encore	clapped and cheered for an **encore**
karate	will study **karate** for self-defense

■ **DISCOVER** Words come into the English language in many different ways. We commonly borrow words from other languages and make them part of our language. The words in this list are all borrowed from other languages.

CHALLENGE!

mah-jongg
jai alai
boccie
croquet
canasta

■ **WRITE** Sort the list words by writing:
■ four words that have to do with arts and crafts
■ six words that have to do with sports or adventure
■ six words that have to do with music or performance
■ four words that name tools or things we use

RIDDLES   Write the list word that answers each riddle.

1. I am a hanging bed from the Spanish word *hamaca.*
2. From the German *schnorchel,* I am a tube you can breathe through while underwater.
3. From a Swahili word, I am an expedition in Africa.
4. I'm a Javanese word describing a method of dyeing fabric.
5. I am from a Greek word meaning "beautiful handwriting."
6. I am the Japanese art of paper folding.
7. I am the French word you shout when you have especially enjoyed a performance.
8. From a Norwegian word, I am a zigzag race downhill.
9. I am baggage, from a Swedish word for pull.
10. I am a small guitar of Hawaiian origin.

DEFINITIONS   Write the list word that fits each definition.

11. From the French word meaning "to love," this describes a person who does a sport for love, not money.
12. From Arabic, this instrument can be shaken and drummed.
13. An automatic record machine, part of its name is from Bantu.
14. This French word describes lace made from knotting patterns with thread or cord.
15. This tool to protect you from the rain is from an Italian word.
16. From Spanish, it is a contest in roping cattle and riding horses.
17. Of Algonquin origin, this is a sled without runners.
18. This is a Spanish word for a large knife used for cutting brush and sugar cane.
19. This stringed musical instrument is from the Bantu language.
20. This is a Japanese style of fighting without weapons.

STRATEGIC SPELLING

Building New Words

21.–24. Write the plural form of each of these list words: *rodeo, banjo, jukebox, safari.*

Did You Know?
Ukulele combines two Hawaiian words: **uku** and **lele.** Literally, ukulele means "the jumping flea," probably because of the quick way the player's fingers move over the strings.

≡	Make a capital.
/	Make a small letter.
∧	Add something.
ℯ	Take out something.
⊙	Add a period.
⁋	New paragraph

PROOFREAD FOR PUNCTUATION

Items in a series should be separated by commas. For example:

> The International Day program will
> include arts and crafts food, and a parade of world flags.
> ∧

Check Commas Read this passage. Write the four words that should have commas after them.

> Mrs. Osawa will make origami cranes fish, and flowers. Then Mr. Osawa will demonstrate karate. For lunch we will serve foods from Sweden China Turkey, and Brazil. In the afternoon we will explore holidays in Korea Mexico, and Poland. At the end of the day, we will see many flags from around the world.

PROOFREAD A PROGRAM

Find five spelling errors in this program for International Day and write them correctly. Some may be words you learned before. Fix three comma errors too.

8:00	The Arts: Chinese caligraphy macramé plant hangers, and photografhy
10:00	Music: uklele drum banjoe, and accordion
12:00	International Lunch
1:00	Presentation: Chrismas Around the World

WRITE A PROGRAM

Plan a program for a special day at your school. It could be an International Day or some other occasion. Write the program and decorate a cover for it. Try to use three list words and a personal word.

Word List

calligraphy	rodeo	jukebox	macramé
hammock	snorkel	luggage	umbrella
toboggan	banjo	ukulele	safari
tambourine	amateur	batik	encore
slalom	origami	machete	karate

Personal Words 1.____ 2.____

FIGURATIVE LANGUAGE: PERSONIFICATION
"The hammock groaned from the weight of the three sisters." Can a hammock really groan? Of course it can't, but the writer is using **personification**—giving human qualities (in this case, groaning) to nonhuman things (a hammock). Personification helps make the descriptions in your writing come alive. The writer could have said: "The hammock stretched under the weight of the three sisters." Doesn't the first sentence give you a clearer picture of the scene?

Read this passage and find four examples of personification. For each example, write both the thing being personified and the human quality given to it.

It was a lovely summer day. As a cool breeze whispered through the trees, the sun teased the flowers growing on the forest floor. A mature oak tree off in the distance wrapped its arms around a young maple. The maple sighed as it leaned into the oak. This was my favorite place to get away from my brother.

Now try your hand at personification. For each of the following things, write a phrase that gives it a human quality.

5. chair
6. doorbell
7. coffee pot
8. thunderstorm

ENRICHMENT Pick one.

Personify Some More
Practice personification by writing sentences giving human qualities to these things: *balloon, ocean, leaves, shoe, guitar.* After you've given them the human qualities, see if you can work your sentences into a short story.

The Desk Did It!
With a partner, choose five ordinary objects from your classroom. Think of phrases or sentences that give them human characteristics. For example: The desk devoured my books. Then draw silly pictures that show the personification.

CHALLENGE!
Look around your bedroom. What ordinary objects can you give human qualities to? Write a short story about your bedroom that makes it come alive. Then make your story into a picture book, showing the human qualities of the usually nonhuman things.

Review

18

HOW AM I DOING?

Look back at the word lists in Lessons 13–17 and think about how you are doing in spelling.

1. Which types of words are most difficult for you to spell?
   - ❏ words that have three or four syllables
   - ❏ words that have silent letters
   - ❏ words like **libel** and **liable** that sound and look alike

2. If someone asked me how to remember the difference between **emigrants** and **immigrants,** I would tell them ____.

3. I remember that it helps to carefully pronounce words that are hard to spell.   **Yes   No   Sometimes**

4. I try to use words I am learning to spell in my writing.
   Yes   No   Sometimes

5. The most interesting word that I have learned to spell is ____.

■ **PROOFREADING**

Find the spelling errors in each passage and write the words correctly. All passages have seven errors except the first one, which has eight.

PROOFREAD A NEWSLETTER

Main Street Messenger

Fall classes at the Main Street Center begin September 22. New offerings this year include classes in caligraphy, oragami, photogaphy, knitting, and macramay. Guitar, banjoe, and uklele classes will start October 5. Classes in krate have been postponed until January. You may transmitt your enrollment form by mail or fax.

PROOFREAD A SOCIAL STUDIES REPORT

At the start of the War for Independence, the American militia was poorly trained, poorly armed, and inexperienced, but these emigrants to America were hearty, and they fought with a feriocity and skill that amazed the British. The Americans attacked from behind barns and bushes at any time of the day or night, warfare the British could not at first comprahend. Americans had geagraphy on their side too and could quickly allude their enemies, who were often unfamiliar with the landscape. The winter at Valley Forge tested even the strongest, however. Hundreds of Americans died while the British were able to sustane themselves only a few miles away in Philadelphia.

PROOFREAD A DESCRIPTIVE PARAGRAPH

The Welles Mansion was built by Ashton Welles, a steel magnet. Visitors often exclaime when they see the beautiful curving staircase that rises from the entrance hall. Over the dining room fireplace is a Latin enscription that may refer to Welles. Left of the entrance hall is a parlor with several oil paintings, a small college over a mahogany desk, and a framed batick print over a sofa. There is a supersition about this house: Annabelle Welles considered herself an expert on the super-natural, and she believed the mansion was haunted.

PROOFREAD A LETTER TO THE EDITOR

Help us clean up our neighborhood

For a number of years a large vacant lot next to the Sheffield sub division has been a dumping ground. Now an eloqent advacate for a cleaner neighborhood, whose vacation is landscape design, wants to buy this lot and transform it into a park. Although she is ready to spend her own money, the owners are unwilling to sell, which is beyond my comprehenshon. I can only inferr the rational behind this refusal, but surely something should be done to clean up this lot.

PROOFREAD A BOOK REVIEW

The Jericho Scroll is part thriller, part detective story set in the Middle East. A valuable manusript is stolen from a library by a scholar given permission to tranlate the work. After gaining the confidence of a commision on antiquities, he rolls up the manuscript, places it in his umberella, walks out of the library, and vanishes. The chief librarian becomes an amature sleuth and sets out to track down the scholar. His only clues are a torn piece of paper with a mysterious scribbel and a biografy of the thief taken from a reference work.

PROOFREAD A REPORT

Over 3,000 miles of canals, in combination with roads and rivers, created a vast transportation network north of the Ohio River by 1840. Writer Charles Dickens told of his experiences on a canal boat in <u>American Notes</u>. Passengers' lugage was heaped in the middle of the deck and passengers had to lie down nearly flat when the helmsman shouted, "Low bridge!" Dickens also wrote of a loqwacious fellow passenger and remarked on the coloquial speech of Americans. The usual sustanance was plain but ample, and passengers slept in a sort of wooden hamock, which Dickens described in a grafic way as a "hanging bookshelf" with a "microscopic blanket."

PROOFREAD THE MINUTES OF A MEETING

Forty student council members were present at the October 21 meeting when several pertnent matters were discussed. Eugene Slater asked if the council could send a letter to the school board about locker searches, which he said seemed to immply distrust of students and were an envasion of privacy. Members also voted to comit volunteer time to helping at the Walkathon. A subcommitee was appointed to explore locations and cost of a tobbogan party in December. Tiffany Baker passed an envelop around for contributions for flowers for Mr. Adkins, who is in the hospital. The next meeting is in November.

STRATEGY WORKSHOP

Creating Memory Tricks

DISCOVER THE STRATEGY   We all have words that give us trouble. Outwit these tricky words with tricks of your own. Give this strategy a try.

First, mark the letters that give you problems.

~~mosquetoes~~   mos<u>qui</u>toes

Then think of memory helpers—words or phrases you already can spell—that have the same letters.

<u>qui</u>ck   <u>qui</u>te   (<u>qui</u>t)

Now you're ready to create your memory trick. Link your word with a memory helper that helps you remember it.

Tell these mos<u>qui</u>toes to <u>qui</u>t biting!

Tips: It helps to **visualize** the scene as you say the trick. Also, your trick doesn't have to be serious, nor does it have to make sense. It only has to help you remember how to spell the word.

†† TRY IT OUT Now try this memory tricks strategy with a partner.

crew	hideout	quacks	cute, cozy shoes

Write a helper from the box to complete each memory trick.
Underline the matching letters. *Note:* A helper could be one word
or more. A memory trick could be a phrase **(the eloquent queen)**
or a sentence **(Al always acts).**

1. a hideous ___
2. a mediocre ___
3. My moccasins are ___.
4. The loquacious duck ___ often.

†† Pick a helper from the box and create a memory trick for each
word below. Underline the matching letters in the word and
helper. Draw any tricks you can visualize.

rough	brain	comma	Mort

5. mortgage
6. dilemma
7. naive
8. thoroughly

† LOOK AHEAD Look ahead at the next five lessons for list
words that might give you problems. Create memory tricks for
two of them. Share your results with the class.

Unusual Letter Combinations

19

■ **FOCUS** Say each word and read the meaning phrase.

limousine	rode to the airport in a fancy **limousine**
guarantee	a money-back **guarantee** on my radio
counterfeit	fooled by the **counterfeit** signature
archaeology	studied ancient tools in **archaeology** class
camouflage	wore **camouflage** clothes to blend in
connoisseur	a **connoisseur** of fine foods
cantaloupe	juicy orange flesh of a **cantaloupe**
turquoise	a bluish **turquoise** stone in the bracelet
parliament	Canadian laws made by **parliament**
silhouette	**silhouette** of a skyscraper against the sky
porcelain	delicate **porcelain** cup and saucer
nuisance	that buzzing **nuisance** of a fly
ricochet	**ricochet** of a rock from wall to wall
sergeant	promoted from corporal to **sergeant**
matinee	the Saturday **matinee** starting at 2:00 P.M.
sleuth	a **sleuth** hunting for clues to the crime
liaison	a **liaison** between school and community
pageant	**pageant** reenacting the first Thanksgiving
aerial	an **aerial** photo shot from a helicopter
forfeit	**forfeit** the game for lack of players

■ **DISCOVER** These words have sounds made by letter combinations that are unusual in English, such as the long **a** sound spelled **et** in **ricochet.** What letters spell the long **a** sound in **matinee?** What letters spell the sound /ü/ in **sleuth?**

■ **WRITE**
- one word that has one syllable
- five words that have two syllables
- thirteen words that have three syllables
- one word that has five syllables

CHALLENGE!

hors d'oeuvre
bureaucrat
reveille
entrepreneur
reconnaissance

ANALOGIES   Write the list word that completes each analogy.

1. Orange is to citrus as ___ is to melon.
2. Congress is to United States as ___ is to England.
3. Pilot is to airplane as chauffeur is to ___.
4. Superman is to superhero as Sherlock Holmes is to ___.
5. Victory is to win as give up is to ___.
6. Corporal is to private as lieutenant is to ___.
7. Biology is to living things as ___ is to ancient life.
8. Evening is to late show as afternoon is to ___.
9. Real is to genuine as fake is to ___.
10. Silver is to metal as ___ is to stone.

WORD ASSOCIATIONS   Write the list word that is associated with each group.

11. disguise, conceal, hide
12. china, pottery
13. form, outline, shadow
14. money-back, warranty, promise
15. pesky, annoying
16. go-between, middleman, mediator
17. bounce, spring, boomerang
18. beauty contest, spectacle
19. aeronautic, aerospace
20. expert, professional

STRATEGIC SPELLING
Using the Memory Tricks Strategy

Use memory tricks to help you spell. Create memory tricks using the list words and helpers below. Underline the matching letters.

21. camouflage—amount
22. pageant—age

> **Did You Know?**
> The French word that **turquoise** comes from means "Turkish stone."

≡	Make a capital.
/	Make a small letter.
∧	Add something.
ℰ	Take out something.
⊙	Add a period.
⸮	New paragraph

PROOFREAD FOR USAGE Most nouns are made plural by adding **-s** or **-es.** Some words change spelling and others remain the same word. For example

Clarke's makes fine porcelain figures that
won't just sit on your ~~shelfs.~~ *shelves*

Check Plurals Correct the mistakes in this advertisement by writing the five misspelled plurals correctly.

Clarke's new line of dishs and utensils is a sight to behold. The knifes, forks, and spoons have lovely porcelain handles. The first two serieses of patterns are decorated with delicate, hand-painted summer daisies and winter berrys. A new pattern, available this October, will use autumn leafs.

PROOFREAD AN ADVERTISEMENT Find the eight misspelled words in this advertisement and write them correctly. Some may be words you learned before. Three of the misspellings are incorrect plurals.

Are you a connoseur of modern art? If so, you'll love our new turqiuose jewelry designes. Furthermore, you won't have to forfit other luxurys to afford them. We garenty you'll wear these unique creationes know and for years to come.

WRITE AN ADVERTISEMENT Plan and write an advertisement for a product you like. Try to use three list words and a personal word.

Word List

limousine	connoisseur	porcelain	sleuth
guarantee	cantaloupe	nuisance	liaison
counterfeit	turquoise	ricochet	pageant
archaeology	parliament	sergeant	aerial
camouflage	silhouette	matinee	forfeit

Personal Words 1.___ 2.___

WORDS FROM NAMES AND PLACES Did you know that the word **cantaloupe** comes from Cantalupo, an area near Rome where the melons were originally grown? Many English words come from the names of people and places. Write the words from the box that are from the names of the people and places described. Use your Spelling Dictionary if you need help.

> leotard
> zeppelin
> napoleon
> tangerine
> graham crackers
> teddy bear
> forsythia
> Ferris wheel

1. Sylvester Graham invented a healthful snack made with unsifted whole wheat flour.
2. Legend has it that a small, orange citrus fruit came to us by way of Tangier, Morocco.
3. William Forsyth, a Scottish horticulturist, was honored for his work by having a flowering shrub named for him.
4. Count Ferdinand von Zeppelin invented the dirigible, a kind of airship.
5. A stuffed toy was named for President Theodore Roosevelt, who refused to shoot a small animal that had been tied to a tree to ensure a successful hunting trip.
6. George Washington Ferris designed a huge revolving amusement park ride that was a big attraction at the 1893 Chicago World's Fair.
7. This custard-filled sweet is probably named for an emperor of France.
8. Jules Léotard, a nineteenth-century circus performer, designed his own stretchy, tight-fitting costume.

ENRICHMENT Pick one.

You Name It!
Many people's inventions are named for them. Invent a special concoction that you like to make and eat that no one else seems to know about. Write the recipe for it and name it after yourself.

My Kind of Town
With a partner, brainstorm foods, flowers, fashions, or inventions that are particular to your area. Are any of these items named for local people or places? If not, name a few items after local people. Write explanations for your choices.

CHALLENGE!
Design an article of clothing or a child's toy. Make a sketch of it and use your first or last name to name it.

Latin and Greek Word Parts 2

■ **FOCUS** Read each word and meaning phrase. Notice that some words have similar parts.

judicial	the **judicial** branch of government
democracy	a government such as a **democracy**
regular	on our **regular** schedule all week
justify	good reasons to **justify** the decision
policy	their **policy** on eligibility for athletics
cosmopolitan	a **cosmopolitan,** well-traveled person
jurisdiction	under the **jurisdiction** of the police
demographic	**demographic** study of our neighborhood
critique	positive and negative **critique** of the book
metropolis	millions of people living in the **metropolis**
regiment	many soldiers in a **regiment**
judicious	careful, **judicious** decision about the future
critical	overly **critical** of new players
jury	found guilty by the **jury**
regime	overthrew the dictator for a new **regime**
perjury	untruthful witness committing **perjury**
regal	a **regal** necklace, fit for a princess
epidemic	a flu **epidemic** in several states
regional	a **regional** flood control plan
hypocrite	**hypocrite** who never says what he means

■ **DISCOVER** These words are related to people and the law. Words with **jud, jur,** and **jus** come from Latin words meaning "law" or "judge." Words with **crit** and **reg** come from Greek and Latin words meaning "to judge" and "to guide." Words with **dem** and **pol** come from Greek words meaning "people" and "city."

CHALLENGE!

prejudicial
acropolis
megalopolis
hypercritical
regalia

■ **WRITE**
- six words with **jud, jur,** or **jus**
- three words with **crit**
- five words with **reg**
- six words with **pol** or **dem**

SYNONYMS Write the list word that means the same as each word or phrase below.

1. royal
2. false testimony
3. big city
4. sophisticated
5. evaluation

6. ordinary
7. phony
8. disapproving
9. plan of action
10. military unit

CONTEXT CLUES Write the list word that matches each clue.

11. Our school was struck with an ___ of chicken pox.
12. The ___ delivered a verdict of "not guilty."
13. In the ___ study, the scientists studied changes in where people of different backgrounds live.
14. In a ___ , the people have a say in their government.
15. The Supreme Court is the ___ branch of our government.
16. The old government was overthrown, and the country is now ruled by a new ___ .
17. Lee tried to ___ her mistake by saying it was Jim's fault.
18. The ___ teacher thought carefully before deciding.
19. The local police could not arrest the speeder because he was out of their ____ .
20. A ___ agency handles all calls in our region.

STRATEGIC SPELLING

Seeing Meaning Connections

regulate
regularly
regular
irregular

The words in the box, including the list word **regular,** are related in spelling and meaning. Complete the sentences with these words.

A _(21)_ , healthy pulse rate is between 50 and 100 steady beats per minute. An _(22)_ heartbeat can be dangerous, but there are some things a doctor can do to _(23)_ the rhythm and pace of the heart so that it is beating _(24)_ again.

> **Did You Know?**
> An **epidemic** of plague, known as the *Black Death,* killed about a fourth of the European population in the mid-1300s.

≡	Make a capital.
/	Make a small letter.
∧	Add something.
ℯ	Take out something.
⊙	Add a period.
⌿	New paragraph

PROOFREAD FOR CARELESS ERRORS

Proofread carefully so you don't repeat or drop words when you write. For example:

Fasten your seat belt to ~~to~~ prepare ^for^ takeoff.

Check for Repeated and Dropped Words Write any repeated or dropped words. Write "Correct" if the sentence is correct.

1. Keep luggage under seats or in overhead compartments.
2. Keep your belt fastened until the light on the panel goes off.
3. Let flight attendants know if you ordered a a special meal.
4. Ask flight attendants for magazines or or newspapers.
5. After landing, stay seated until the plane is the gate.

PROOFREAD A SIGN

Find the five misspelled words in this sign and write them correctly. Some may be words you learned before. Fix three repeated or dropped words too.

Store Hours and Policies

- Our reguler weekday hours are 9–6; Saturday hours 10–5.
- It store policie to refund money for returned items only if the customer can can justafy the return.
- Exchanges are allways possible.
- We will prasecute shoplifters.

WRITE A SIGN

Write a sign about a school policy that might be posted in a hallway at your school. Try to use three list words and a personal word.

Word List

judicial	cosmopolitan	regiment	perjury
democracy	jurisdiction	judicious	regal
regular	demographic	critical	epidemic
justify	critique	jury	regional
policy	metropolis	regime	hypocrite

Personal Words 1.___ 2.___

CONTEXT: DEFINITIONS AND EXPLANATIONS

Suppose you read: "For a metropolis to thrive, both the central city and its surrounding communities must work together to provide housing and jobs." You can get the meaning of *metropolis* from the **context,** or words around it. The words "central city and its surrounding communities" explain what a metropolis is.

Read the passage and use the context to write what the numbered words mean. The definition or explanation may not be in the same sentence as the word.

> Suburbanization contributed to the development of metropolitan areas by expanding cities beyond their official boundaries and creating suburbs. Many suburbs were almost completely residential. However, the urbanity, or easy and refined living, of the suburbs had a price. Since most people resided but did not work there, they had to commute, or travel by train, car, or bus to their jobs in the cities.
>
> Suburbs grew as large as cities and small businesses moved in, making them places where people could live and work. In the meantime, some suburbanites moved back to the central cities as revitalization programs helped construct and restore buildings and neighborhoods that were attractive and safe.

1. suburbanization
2. residential
3. urbanity
4. commute
5. revitalization

ENRICHMENT Pick one.

Pros and Cons
Do you live in a metropolitan area, or would you like to? Why or why not? Write a pro and con list of what you think are the good and bad aspects of living in a metropolis.

Revitalize!
In a small group, brainstorm some of the problems metropolitan areas face. Then choose one of those issues to target in an urban revitalization program. Outline the steps of your plan.

In a popular comic book, Metropolis is the name of the city in which the action takes place. Create your own comic book. Give the city in your comic a name that ends in *polis.*

Suffixes -able, -ible, -ance, -ence

■ **FOCUS** Read each word and notice its suffix. Then read the meaning phrase.

occurrence	events listed in order of **occurrence**
endurance	test my **endurance** by running ten miles
deductible	**deductible** from the original price
convenience	the **convenience** of a TV remote control
flammable	**flammable** material that burned up
resemblance	a close **resemblance** between the brothers
reference	a **reference** book on mummies
knowledgeable	**knowledgeable** about basketball
compatible	**compatible** roommates who don't argue
vengeance	swore **vengeance** against their enemy
noticeable	a barely **noticeable** catsup spot
intelligence	a puzzle to test your **intelligence**
collectible	**collectible** dolls and baseball cards
elegance	the **elegance** of jewels and satin
divisible	**divisible** into three equal parts
charitable	a **charitable** contribution to a good cause
edible	unusual but **edible** vegetables in a soup
attendance	few people in **attendance** at the game
available	only a few tickets still **available**
competence	having **competence** to get the job done

■ **DISCOVER** There are no rules or sound clues to help you choose between these suffix pairs: **-able** or **-ible, -ance** or **-ence.** You must remember how the word is spelled. You must also remember which base words change spelling. What happens to **occur** when **-ence** is added?

■ **WRITE**
- five words with **-able**
- five words with **-ible**
- five words with **-ance**
- five words with **-ence**

CHALLENGE!

foreseeable
imperceptible
unpronounceable
perseverance
effervescence

WORD FORMS   Write the list words that come from these base words.

1. flame
2. eat
3. divide
4. attend
5. endure
6. collect
7. charity
8. occur
9. resemble
10. refer
11. deduct
12. knowledge

CONTEXT CLUES   Write the list word that completes each sentence.

13. The mansion's ___ was due as much to the rich and tasteful furnishings as it was to the marble floors.
14. That style of purse is no longer ___, so please choose another.
15. Martin showed some ___ in leading the group but not in solving problems.
16. Even though Charisse and Sylvia get along well now, they aren't sure if they would be ___ as roommates.
17. Knowledge and good judgment are signs of ___.
18. Andrew vowed ___ for the wrong that was done to him.
19. If I move, I will miss the ___ of having a grocery store only one block away.
20. That old ink stain on the tablecloth is barely ___ now.

Building New Words

Add the suffix **-able** or **-ible** to the following base words: *rely, sense, resist, manage, envy, corrupt.* Use your Spelling Dictionary if you need help.

Add -able	**Add -ible**
21.____	24.____
22.____	25.____
23.____	26.____

Take a Hint
You can spell **reference** with ease. Spell it with e's: r<u>e</u>f<u>e</u>r<u>e</u>nce.

≡	Make a capital.
/	Make a small letter.
∧	Add something.
ℯ	Take out something.
⊙	Add a period.
⁋	New paragraph

PROOFREAD FOR PUNCTUATION Put quotation marks around direct quotations and capitalize the first word of the quotation.

Before operating, Dr. Ornaf explained, "this is a new surgical procedure."

Check for Quotation Marks and Capitals Correct the mistakes in these sentences from a news item by writing the word and the quotation mark that should come before or after it. Make sure all words are correctly capitalized.

Mrs. Flores replied, we're thrilled that this new procedure is available. She also noted, "Willy never gave up hope; his courage kept us going. Her husband quickly added, our friends and neighbors have been very supportive.

PROOFREAD A NEWS ITEM Find the five misspelled words and write them correctly. Some may be words you learned before. Also fix the mistakes in the direct quotations.

> Teenager Luz Ruiz organized a neighborhood fund-raiser to help pay for Willy Flores's operation. Luz said, "I no I cant do much myself, but all of us together can. One of Ruiz's neighbors remarked, that girl's compatance, endurence, and charitible heart inspired us all.

WRITE A NEWS ITEM Plan and write a news item about a recent school event. Use three list words and a personal word.

Word List

occurrence	resemblance	noticeable	charitable
endurance	reference	intelligence	edible
deductible	knowledgeable	collectible	attendance
convenience	compatible	elegance	available
flammable	vengeance	divisible	competence

Personal Words 1.___ 2.___

GREEK AND LATIN ROOTS: _vindicare_ The list word
vengeance comes from the Latin root _vindicare,_ which means
"avenge." The words in the box have different meanings, but
because they all come from _vindicare,_ their meanings have
something to do with revenge.

vengeance	vendetta	avenger	vindictive	avenge

Write the _vindicare_ word from the box for each definition below.
Use your Spelling Dictionary if you need help.

1. one who takes revenge
2. a bitter feud based on getting revenge
3. take revenge for or on behalf of
4. punishment in return for a wrong; great force or violence
5. feeling a strong tendency toward revenge

Now that you know what the _vindicare_ words mean, use them to
complete the news flash below.

Smalltown's anonymous _(6)_ , Masked Max, is planning to
_(7)_ the kidnapping of his faithful sidekick Rex, the Amazing
Canine Crusader. The _(8)_ veterinarian, Dr. Vance Vicious,
(who for years has been involved in a _(9)_ with Masked Max)
is thought to be Rex's kidnapper. One can only shudder at the
_(10)_ that will be displayed if Rex is not turned over soon.

ENRICHMENT Pick one.

What Next?
What do you think will
happen to Rex, Masked
Max, and Dr. Vance
Vicious? Write a
follow-up news
flash. You
might want to
illustrate it too.

Help Wanted
With a partner, create
your own superhero who
can right wrongs. Draw
a sketch of the superhero
and write a brief
résumé for him or her.
Hint: A résumé lists
a person's education,
job history, and
accomplishments.

CHALLENGE!
Revenge and _avenge_
mean almost, but not
quite, the same thing. Use
your Spelling Dictionary
to discover the subtle
difference between the
two words. Then
write two scenes
involving Masked
Max and
Dr. Vance
Vicious that
help explain
the difference.

One Word or Two?

■ **FOCUS** Look at the list words. Notice which are one word and which are two words. Then read the meaning phrases.

kind of	**kind of** nervous about public speaking
supposed to	are **supposed to** go home immediately
going to ♻	am **going to** make a spectacular costume
have to	don't **have to** take the quiz
all together	stood **all together** for a picture
altogether	**altogether** too much noise
all ready	were **all ready** to start working
already	finished the test **already**
a part	bought **a part** for the car
apart	took the clock **apart** piece by piece
a lot ♻	want **a lot** of recognition
allot	will **allot** two pencils per person
every day	fed their pets **every day**
everyday	normal, **everyday** low prices
may be	a jacket that **may be** yours
maybe ♻	**maybe** will go to the mall
any more	too full to eat **any more** pizza
anymore	doesn't go to school here **anymore**
any way	can't find **any way** to win
anyway	went **anyway**, in spite of her fear

■ **DISCOVER** Words like **kind of** and **going to** are always two words. For other words, like **a part** and **apart,** you have to think about their meanings before using them in sentences. What you mean determines which sound-alike word you need. **All ready** and **already** aren't interchangeable because they have different meanings. What about **any more** and **anymore?**

CHALLENGE!

à la carte
all-American
breathtaking
foreword
afterwards

■ **WRITE** Sort the list words by writing
■ those that are two words
■ those that are one word

SYNONYMS   Write the list word that means the same as the words in each group below.

1. sort of, in a way, ___
2. intending to, planning to, ___
3. ought to, expected to, ___
4. must, required to, ___

CONTEXT CLUES   Write the list words that complete the sentences. Choose from the words in parentheses.

5. I don't want (anymore, any more) peas.
6. Lenka doesn't live here (anymore, any more).
7. Well, (maybe, may be) you can go next time.
8. It (maybe, may be) a long time before we're through.
9. I saw a movie (everyday, every day) this week.
10. These are my (everyday, every day) clothes.
11. Rami has (allot, a lot) of spare time these days.
12. How much did you (allot, a lot) for each person?
13. That is (altogether, all together) too difficult for my little sister.
14. We were (altogether, all together) when Mom found us.
15. I (already, all ready) finished cleaning my room.
16. The others were (already, all ready) to go when I arrived.
17. Were you able to get (apart, a part) to fix your bike?
18. Ali likes to take things (apart, a part) so she can put them back together.
19. Why don't I go to the park (anyway, any way)?
20. I can't find (anyway, any way) to finish before the deadline.

STRATEGIC SPELLING

Seeing Meaning Connections

Words with _part_
apart
apartheid
partake
partnership

Write the words from the box that fit the definitions. One is a list word.

21. take or have a share
22. in separate parts
23. joint association
24. racial segregation

RECYCLED WORDS

Regardless of how you say it, **going to** is always written as two words.

≡	Make a capital.
/	Make a small letter.
∧	Add something.
ℯ	Take out something.
⊙	Add a period.
⌗	New paragraph

PROOFREAD FOR USAGE Avoid sentence fragments. Make sure each sentence has a subject and verb and makes sense.

I love sports./Because I'm from a family of athletes.

Check for Sentence Fragments Read each item below. If it is a fragment, write "F." If it is a complete sentence, write "Correct."

1. My favorite thing to watch on TV is sports.
2. Especially football and hockey.
3. Because they're action-packed.
4. Basketball is kind of fun to watch too.
5. During the playoffs.

PROOFREAD A PERSONAL NARRATIVE Find the five misspelled words in Alex's personal narrative. Some may be words you learned before. Also correct three sentence fragments.

> My day begins at 7:00. I eat a lot at breakfast everyday. I often hafta run for the bus. Because I'm late. My buddies and I all ways tell jokes at lunch. Play football out side after school. In the evening, I do my homework. See if there's anyway to bug my sister.

WRITE A PERSONAL NARRATIVE Write a personal narrative describing a really good day for you. Try to use three list words and a personal word. Proofread your paragraph.

Word List

kind of	altogether	a lot	maybe
supposed to	all ready	allot	any more
going to	already	every day	anymore
have to	a part	everyday	any way
all together	apart	may be	anyway

Personal Words 1._____ 2._____

SYNONYMS If you say *a lot of* apples, you are using
a synonym for *many.* Words that have the same or similar
meanings are called **synonyms.** Think about using synonyms
to make your writing more interesting and precise.

Write each synonym under the list word where it belongs:
possibly, separate, before, previously, perhaps, unconnected.
Then add a synonym of your own for each of the three words.

apart	maybe	already
1.____	4.____	7.____
2.____	5.____	8.____
3.____	6.____	9.____

The synonyms you chose above have very close meanings.
Sometimes one synonym is clearly better in a sentence than any
others, but other times synonyms can be used interchangeably.
In the paragraph below, replace each use of *everyday* with the
synonym from the box that you think works best.

familiar	ordinary	usual	customary	regular

One **(10) everyday** practice that ensures a healthy smile is
brushing our teeth. The **(11) everyday** times we should brush
are morning and evening. The **(12) everyday** method of
brushing involves vertical or circular movements of the
toothbrush. Flossing is another **(13) everyday** addition to proper
dental hygiene. Modifying **(14) everyday** eating habits is
important too, such as avoiding sugary foods and gum.

ENRICHMENT Pick one.

The Appropriate Words
Use the list of synonyms
for *apart, maybe,* or
already to write a
paragraph in which you
use the list word and
each of its synonyms.

Subtle Differences
With a partner, discuss
the subtle differences
among the synonyms
you listed for *apart.* Act
out the differences.

CHALLENGE!

Keep a journal for one
day, recording the
details of your everyday
routine, even the most
mundane things like
which shoe you put
on first. Compare
everyday routines
with a classmate.

Homophones

23

■ **FOCUS** Say each word and read each phrase. Notice which spelling is used in each meaning phrase.

aisle	rolled the cart down each **aisle**
isle	wrecked ship on a tropical **isle**
symbol	a flag as a **symbol** of a nation
cymbal	crashed one **cymbal** against the other
bizarre	stared at the weird, **bizarre** clothing
bazaar	a church **bazaar** to raise money
assistance	gave **assistance** to the injured bird
assistants	the magician's two **assistants**
suite	a **suite** of rooms at a hotel
sweet	**sweet** strawberry sauce on the cake
allowed ♻	is **allowed** to drive a car
aloud	can read your story **aloud** to us
overdue	owed a quarter on the **overdue** book
overdo	careful not to **overdo** the meat
ascent	slow **ascent** up the rickety stairs
assent	finally gave his **assent** to our request
canvas	painted a water lily on the **canvas**
canvass	**canvass** local stores while looking for work
colonel	a regiment led by its **colonel**
kernel	every sweet, yellow **kernel** of corn

■ **DISCOVER** Homophones such as **allowed** and **aloud** are words that sound alike but have different spellings and different meanings. They cannot be substituted for each other. To use homophones correctly, know what they mean and in which situations to use them. What is the difference between asking for a **sweet** and a **suite?**

CHALLENGE!

bouillon
bullion
cue
queue
callous
callus

■ **WRITE** First write the homophone groups that are most confusing for you. Then write the rest of the homophones.

HOMOPHONE SENTENCES Write the homophone pairs that complete each sentence.

You are not (1) to read (2) in the library.

Let my two (3) know if you need (4) .

The army (5) broke a tooth on a (6) of popcorn.

They were selling many (7) items at the neighborhood (8) .

It was (9) of you to let us use your (10) of rooms for our meeting.

WORD CHOICE Write the correct list word for each sentence.

11. This book is (overdue, overdo) at the library.
12. Try not to (overdue, overdo) running games on a hot day.
13. Please keep the center (aisle, isle) clear so people can leave.
14. We took a rowboat to the (aisle, isle) in the middle of the lake.
15. The handle on my (symbol, cymbal) broke, and I had to get it fixed before the concert.
16. The memorial is a (symbol, cymbal) of military service.
17. Drew will (canvas, canvass) the area before the election.
18. The oil painting on (canvas, canvass) was beautiful.
19. Yvette will (ascent, assent) to the plan if you do.
20. The (ascent, assent) of the balloons was a colorful sight.

STRATEGIC SPELLING

Using the Memory Tricks Strategy

Use memory tricks to help you use homophones correctly. Create homophone sentences for each of the pairs below.

21. ascent—assent
22. overdue—overdo
23. symbol—cymbal

RECYCLED WORDS

Think of this sentence when spelling **allowed:**
Mom <u>owed</u> me a favor, so I was all<u>owed</u> to go.

≡	Make a capital.
/	Make a small letter.
∧	Add something.
ℯ	Take out something.
⊙	Add a period.
¶	New paragraph

PROOFREAD FOR CAPITALIZATION

Use capitals correctly in the heading, inside address, greeting, and closing of a business letter. For example:

2855 rockdale road

Virginia Beach, VA 23452

april 18, 19--

Check Capitalization Fix the capitalization errors in these parts of an inside address and greeting. Write the words correctly.

1. Ms. akemi Shigota
2. York Conference center
3. 986 Washington boulevard
4. scottsdale, AZ 85245
5. Dear Ms. shigota:

PROOFREAD A BUSINESS LETTER Find five misspelled
words in the body of the letter and write them correctly. Some may be words you learned before. Fix three capitalization errors.

> I'd appreciate assistence in obtaining a sweet for our regionel conference. I'll also need a lectern and chairs set up with an aile in the center. Please let me know if thats possible for November 28–30.
>
> very truly yours,
> donald rourke

WRITE A BUSINESS LETTER Write to a company
requesting information about their products. Use three list words and a personal word. For correct letter form, see page 245.

Word List

aisle	bazaar	allowed	assent
isle	assistance	aloud	canvas
symbol	assistants	overdue	canvass
cymbal	suite	overdo	colonel
bizarre	sweet	ascent	kernel

Personal Words 1.___ 2.___

MULTICULTURAL CONNECTION: FOODS We can buy fresh herbs and spices at supermarkets, farmer's markets, and roadside stands. People in other countries can also buy such things at **bazaars.** A few herbs and spices you might find at bazaars are listed in the first box.

thyme
caraway
saffron
cinnamon

Write the word from the box that fits each definition. Use your Spelling Dictionary if you need help.

1. from the Arabic *za'farān,* an orange-yellow coloring and flavoring that comes from the dried stigmas of a crocus
2. from the Greek *kinnamon,* a spice made from the dried, reddish-brown inner bark of a laurel tree of the East Indies
3. a spicy seed used to flavor bread, rolls, and cakes, from a plant whose name comes from the Arabic *karawyā*
4. leaves used for seasoning from a variety of plants in the mint family, from the Greek *thymon*

We associate some foods with particular cultures because that is where they originated. Write the food from the box that fits each item below. Use your Spelling Dictionary if you need help.

borsch
couscous
parmigiana
goulash

5. A dish whose name comes from *Parma,* a city in Italy, is made with eggplant or veal and parmesan cheese.
6. This Russian soup is made with meat stock, cabbage, and onions. Its red color comes from beet juice.
7. *Gulyás* is a highly seasoned Hungarian stew made of beef or veal and vegetables.
8. A North African dish made with coarsely ground hard wheat comes from the Arabic *kaskasa,* meaning "to grind."

ENRICHMENT Pick one.

Menu Madness
Plan a day's menu you might find in a culture other than your own. Perhaps choose a culture you have studied in school. Write it up to look like a real menu. Decorate your menu if you'd like.

What Was Served?
Think about the things your family celebrates— birthdays, holidays, and the like. What foods are traditionally served? In a small group, describe your most favorite and least favorite "celebration" foods.

CHALLENGE!
Spices and herbs add flavor to foods. Research one of these: *ginger, cumin, fennel, paprika.* Find out where the spice or herb is grown, what part of the plant or tree is used, and what it is used for.

111

Review

Look back at the word lists in Lessons 19–23 and think about how you are doing in spelling.

1. Which types of words are hardest for you to spell?
   ❑ words that have silent letters
   ❑ words like **allowed** and **aloud**
   ❑ words like **camouflage** that have unusual letter combinations

2. If someone asked me how to remember when to use **already** and **all ready,** I would tell them ____.

3. You learned that it helps to divide words that are hard to spell into syllables. Have you used this strategy?   **Yes   No   Sometimes**

4. I try to use words I am learning to spell in my writing.
   Yes   No   Sometimes

5. The most interesting word that I have learned to spell is ____.

▨ PROOFREADING

Find the spelling errors in each passage and write the words correctly. All passages have seven errors except the last one, which has eight.

PROOFREAD A NOTICE

For the convence of our riders, the Safety Transit Company is gonna follow a new policie beginning November 1. Passengers asking for charitible contributions on the buses or train will forfit their right to ride. Such requests have become a nusence to other riders and are not compatable with our pledge to provide safe and comfortable service to all. This ruling will be enforced.

PROOFREAD A REVIEW OF A PLAY

Art Attack

Mystery fans will enjoy *Art Attack,* in which a museum is robbed of priceless porcelin, paintings, and precious jewels, including a turkose necklace dating from ancient times. An archaeloge student (Ruth Harris) is a suspect and so is an aging connoissur of art (Werner Schatz), a daily visitor to the museum. The slueth who solves the case is played by Dirk Hamilton, and in one funny scene he discovers a jewel in his breakfast cantalope. Performances are nightly at 7:20 at the Rialto. There is a Sunday matinae at 3:00.

PROOFREAD A FEATURE STORY

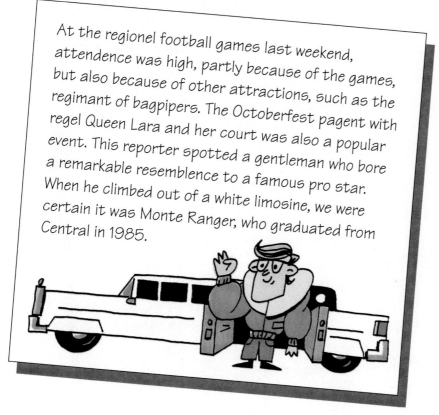

At the regionel football games last weekend, attendence was high, partly because of the games, but also because of other attractions, such as the regimant of bagpipers. The Octoberfest pagent with regel Queen Lara and her court was also a popular event. This reporter spotted a gentleman who bore a remarkable resemblence to a famous pro star. When he climbed out of a white limosine, we were certain it was Monte Ranger, who graduated from Central in 1985.

PROOFREAD A CLASSIFIED AD

I need a job. Do you need assisstence with long over due lawn work this fall? I am knowlagable and avalable and can work everyday after school. I will rake, bag, and do general clean-up. I garenty all work and can provide a referance. Call Steve at 555-1102 and leave a message.

PROOFREAD A BOOK REVIEW

Going Home by Boris Gorchoff is about the experiences of a young Russian boy during the breakup of the Soviet regeem and the criticle events that led to attempts to establish damocracy through the former Soviet Union. The author writes of the every day hardships and the endurence of Moscow citizens who had all ready known food shortages. Gorchoff had not been aloud to emigrate but is now in the United States. This book gives an insider's view of the turmoil the Russians faced during those fateful days.

PROOFREAD A LETTER TO THE EDITOR

The right to a speedy trial

Your editorial about the jurey who convicted a former official of perjary was a good criteke of what's wrong with the judishal system. The intelligance of the jurors should not be questioned, however. What should be questioned is the epedemic of lawsuits that prevent citizens from getting a speedy trial. Although the former official maybe guilty, it shouldn't have taken three years to convict her.

Dallas Young

PROOFREAD A DESCRIPTIVE PARAGRAPH

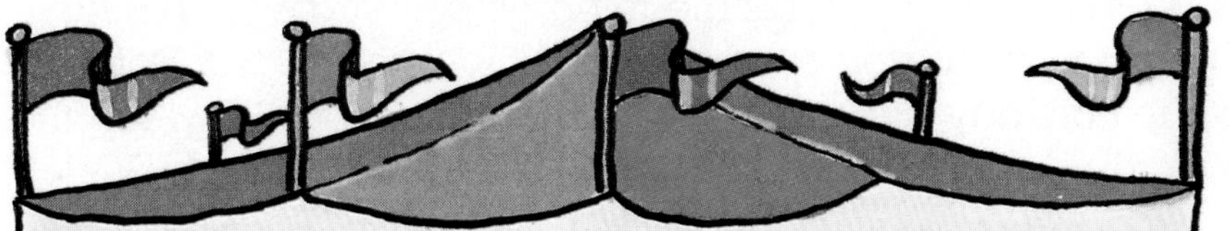

Before television, movies, or radio, the arrival of the circus was an eagerly awaited occurance. When the huge canvass tent was unloaded from the circus train, life seemed alot more interesting than it had the day before. Going to the circus meant the thrill of watching the assent of the trapeze artists and admiring the elagence of the bareback riders. It meant the sweat smell of cotton candy. It meant hearing the reguler beat of a circus band and the calls of the barkers in front of the bizaare sideshows outside the big top.

Using Meaning Helpers

DISCOVER THE STRATEGY   Word pairs like *attend* and *attendance* are related in spelling and meaning. You can use the shorter word as a **meaning helper**—a reminder of how to spell the longer word. For example:

Longer Word	Helper	Clue
attendance	attend	attend + ance
charitable	charity	charity - y + able

✝ **TRY IT OUT**   Now try this meaning helpers strategy. Tell how the helper reminds you of how to spell the longer word. Don't forget to note any spelling changes that take place between the two words.

Longer Word	Helper	Clue
1. luckily	lucky	____
2. vocalize	vocal	____
3. noticeable	notice	____
4. resemblance	resemble	____
5. commission	commit	____
6. invasion	invade	____

Some meaning helpers give you extra help by reminding you of how a tricky sound is spelled in the longer word. For example:

Longer Word	Helper	Clue
moisture	moist	The sound of the **t** in *moist* reminds me that *moisture* is also spelled with a **t**.
narrative	narrate	The long **a** in *narrate* reminds me that the second vowel sound in *narrative* is spelled with an **a**.

Tell how the helper gives a sound clue for the longer word. Be sure to note any spelling changes.

Longer Word	Helper	Clue
7. expression	express	____
8. spacious	space	____
9. protection	protect	____
10. pressure	press	____

LOOK AHEAD Look ahead at the next five lessons for list words that you might use this strategy with. Find two words and write them down. Then write a meaning helper for each word. Use this strategy when you study those words.

Suffixes -ous, -ment, -ness

25

■ **FOCUS** Read the words in each column. Notice what happens to the base word when a suffix is added.

courage + ous	=	**courageous**
outrage + ous	=	**outrageous**
suspicion + ous	=	**suspicious**
ridicule + ous	=	**ridiculous**
miscellany + ous	=	**miscellaneous**
hazard + ous	=	**hazardous**
acknowledge + ment	=	**acknowledgment**
argue + ment	=	**argument**
judge + ment	=	**judgment**
engage + ment	=	**engagement**
excite + ment	=	**excitement**
improve + ment	=	**improvement**
arrange + ment	=	**arrangement**
refresh + ment	=	**refreshment**
even + ness	=	**evenness**
stubborn + ness	=	**stubbornness**
open + ness	=	**openness**
cleanly + ness	=	**cleanliness**
sleepy + ness	=	**sleepiness**
gentle + ness	=	**gentleness**

■ **DISCOVER** Sometimes when suffixes are added to words ending in a consonant or **e**, the spelling of the base word doesn't change: **hazard, hazardous; improve, improvement**. Other times, it does change: **ridicule, ridiculous; sleepy, sleepiness**. What letter is dropped when **-ment** is added to **judge?**

CHALLENGE!

advantageous
conscientious
outspokenness
encouragement
achievement

■ **WRITE**
• Alphabetize the six words with **-ous.**
• Alphabetize the eight words with **-ment.**
• Alphabetize the six words with **-ness.**

WORD FORMS Write the list word that has each meaning and ending indicated below.

1. flat + ness =
2. to decide + ment =
3. not shut + ness =
4. make better + ment =
5. make fun of + ous =
6. not harsh + ness =
7. a mixed selection + ous =
8. to admit you know + ment =
9. hard to deal with + ness =
10. promise to marry + ment =
11. freshen + ment =
12. organize + ment =
13. disagree + ment =

ANTONYMS Write the list word that completes each phrase.

14. not wakefulness, but ___
15. not inoffensive, but ___
16. not cowardly, but ___
17. not dirtiness, but ___
18. not trusting, but ___
19. not boredom, but ___
20. not safe, but ___

STRATEGIC SPELLING
Using the Meaning Helpers Strategy

21.–24. Write four list words that are hard for you. Write a meaning helper below each one and underline the matching letters. Notice any spelling changes between each pair of words.

> **Did You Know?**
> The word **miscellaneous** comes from a Latin word that means "to mix." Then why isn't it *mixcellaneous?*

☰	Make a capital.
/	Make a small letter.
∧	Add something.
ℓ	Take out something.
⊙	Add a period.
¶	New paragraph

PROOFREAD FOR CARELESS ERRORS

Proofread carefully so you don't misspell words by reversing letters. For example:

              mediocre
There are no ~~mediocer~~ players on this team.

Check for Reversed Letters Write correctly any words with reversed letters. Write "Correct" if the sentence is correct.

1. Never before has our team gotten this close to a pennant.
2. The team's termendous strength has been its pitching.
3. Tickets to the playoff games are available thourgh Friday.
4. Stores are selling out of T-shirts and caps.
5. Fans are ready to cheer thier team to victory.

PROOFREAD A SPORTS REPORT Find the eight

misspelled words in this sports report and write them correctly. Some may be words you learned before. Three of the misspellings are with reversed letters.

> *Pennant Fever Hits*
>
> Be perpared for the wierd and wild excitment of the pennant race. Count on rediculous behavior and outragues outfits in the stands. Watch out for hazordous leaping as fans try to catch foul balls. Dont expect good judgment to reign becuase fans are catching pennant fever.

WRITE A SPORTS REPORT Write a sports report about a

game you've seen or a team you follow. Use three list words and a personal word.

Word List

courageous	hazardous	excitement	stubbornness
outrageous	acknowledgment	improvement	openness
suspicious	argument	arrangement	cleanliness
ridiculous	judgment	refreshment	sleepiness
miscellaneous	engagement	evenness	gentleness

Personal Words 1.____ 2.____

MULTICULTURAL CONNECTION: LANGUAGES There are more than 800 **African languages.** The language spoken often helps identify the speaker as a member of a particular ethnic group. Some English words come from words used by speakers of African languages. One of these words names the carrier of a disease causing sleepiness: *tsetse fly.* Some English words originating from African languages are listed in the box.

tsetse fly
impala
gumbo
okra
yam
jazz
gnu

Write the word from the box that fits each definition below. Use your Spelling Dictionary if you need help.

1. a large African antelope; also called a wildebeest
2. soup made with chicken and rice
3. a root like a sweet potato
4. pods of a tall plant, used as a vegetable in gumbo
5. a medium-sized African antelope with long, pointed horns
6. music developed from African American spirituals
7. an African fly that transmits certain diseases

Now that you know what these words mean, use them to complete each sentence.

8. Many people come to New Orleans to hear ___.
9. Can you tell the difference between a sweet potato and a ___?
10.–11. A professional photographer might go on a safari to capture an ___ or a ___ on film.
12.–13. One of the main ingredients of ___ is ___.
14. Scientists study the ___ in order to learn more about the transmission of disease.

ENRICHMENT Pick one.

Sensing Jazz
You can hear jazz, but what if you could also see, smell, taste, and touch it? Use your imagination to describe in writing how jazz might look, smell, taste, and feel.

Out of Africa
With a partner, prepare a menu of food items that come originally from Africa. For information, look in books on African cultures or the encyclopedia. Include recipes if possible. You might want to decorate your menu or recipes in an African motif.

CHALLENGE!
I is for impala, **O** is for okra. Write a children's ABC book using words from Africa. Use an encyclopedia to find out more about the people, plants, and animals of Africa.

Latin Roots 2

■ **FOCUS** Read each word and meaning phrase. Notice that some words have similar parts.

emancipate	to **emancipate,** or free, the slaves
centipede	the many feet of a wormlike **centipede**
manipulate	**manipulate** clay into different shapes
corporation	owns stock in the large **corporation**
pedestal	Ben Franklin's statue on a **pedestal**
perspiration	wiped the **perspiration** off her face
management	good **management** by the president
incorporate	can **incorporate** your ideas into the plan
pedigree	list of ancestors on a show dog's **pedigree**
manufacture	will **manufacture** a better mousetrap
pedometer	a **pedometer** to show how far I walk
respiration	her rate of **respiration,** or breathing
corpse	the **corpse,** peaceful in the casket
manicure	beautiful nails after the **manicure**
conspire	**conspire** with you to plan a surprise
corporal	an army private promoted to **corporal**
expire	license that will **expire** in one month
impede	can **impede** us but can't stop us
spiritual	a **spiritual** hymn, sung in church
corps	a **corps** of army engineers

■ **DISCOVER** These words all have to do with Latin roots for parts of the body. The root *manus* means "hand." What is the meaning of **manipulate?** *Ped* or *pedem* means "foot." What does **pedometer** mean? *Spirare* means "breathe." What is the meaning of **respiration?** *Corpus* means "body." What does **corps** mean?

CHALLENGE!

manipulative
corpuscle
impediment
conspirator
manacle

■ **WRITE**
- five words from *corpus*
- five words from *ped* or *pedem*
- five words from *manus*
- five words from *spirare*

CLASSIFYING   Write a list word that belongs in each group.

1. company, business, ___
2. barometer, speedometer, ___
3. block, hold back, ___
4. produce, make, ___
5. earthworm, caterpillar, ___
6. fingernails, pedicure, ___
7. easel, stand, ___
8. ventilation, inhalation, ___
9. body, dead, ___
10. scheme, plan, ___

CONTEXT CLUES   Write the list word that fits in each sentence.

11. My mom's driver's license will ___ on her birthday.
12. A ___ of nurses was sent to tend to those injured in the battle.
13. The pet owner used a ___ to prove the value of his dog.
14. Our apartment building's ___ company handles repairs.
15. The bank officer tried to ___ the bank's accounts to hide the fact that he had been stealing.
16. When did the owners ___ the slaves?
17. He was drenched with ___ after running five miles.
18. I will ___ your ideas with mine to come up with one proposal for the guidelines.
19. We learned a ___ at choir practice last night.
20. The ___ is hoping to be promoted to sergeant soon.

STRATEGIC SPELLING

Building New Words

The prefixes **in-** and **en-** often mean "in" or "into." Add **in-** or **en-** to each of the following base words to make new words: *born, flame, danger, put, close, vision.* Use your Spelling Dictionary if you need help.

Add in-

21. ____
22. ____
23. ____

Add en-

24. ____
25. ____
26. ____

Did You Know?
The word **centipede** literally means "one hundred feet."

☰	Make a capital.
/	Make a small letter.
∧	Add something.
ℓ	Take out something.
⊙	Add a period.
¶	New paragraph

PROOFREAD FOR USAGE Use the adjective *good* to modify a noun or pronoun. Use the adverb *well* to modify a verb.

I'll be a *good* employee who works *well* with others.

Check for *good* and *well* Write "Incorrect" if *good* or *well* is used incorrectly. Write "Correct" if *good* or *well* is used correctly.

1. I'll do good in college.
2. Being conscientious will help me succeed good in life.
3. I'll be a good influence on others too.
4. I have always been able to set goals good.
5. That's why I predict I'll perform well in college and beyond.

PROOFREAD A PREDICTION Find five misspelled words in Bonita's prediction of her future. Some may be words you've learned before. Also fix two mistakes with *good* and *well*.

> After high school I will go to a good business college. I will join a corperation and work good enough to become part of managment. I will than be able to incorperate my ideas and show that I work good with people. I predict nothing will impede my rise to the top. My image in bronze will be placed on a pedistol in the corporate offices.

WRITE A PREDICTION Write a prediction about your own future. Use three list words and a personal word.

Word List

emancipate	perspiration	pedometer	corporal
centipede	management	respiration	expire
manipulate	incorporate	corpse	impede
corporation	pedigree	manicure	spiritual
pedestal	manufacture	conspire	corps

Personal Words 1.___ 2.___

METAPHORS AND SIMILES Writers use metaphors and similes to enliven their writing. A **metaphor** is a comparison that describes one thing by vividly saying it is another. For example: "The successful *corporation* is a *fortress* that protects our town's economy."

> icicles
> campfires
> hurricane
> waiters
> eel

Use the words from the box to complete these metaphors.

1. The shining stars are ___ in the hot night sky.
2. When Charlie runs fast he is a ___.
3. Penguins are ___ in their tuxedos.
4. Marcus's hands are ___ when he comes in from the cold.
5. The submarine is an ___, gliding silently through the water.

A **simile** also compares two unlike things, but uses *like* or *as* to make the comparison: "My baby *brother* crawls about <u>like</u> a *centipede*."

Write your own simile to complete each sentence below. Don't forget to use *like* or *as*.

6. The cold, dark cave was ___
7. The snowflakes fall ___
8. The train's whistle ___

ENRICHMENT Pick one

My Love Is Like a Red, Red Rose
Write a poem or verse in which you compare two unlike things, using either a simile or a metaphor.

What Am I Like?
In a small group, take turns answering questions like these: "Are you more like a swimsuit or a sweatsuit? a baseball or a football? a sneaker or a black leather loafer? jazz or country music?" Explain your answers. To continue, make up more questions.

CHALLENGE!
Over the course of a week, search for similes and metaphors in current literature. Look through magazines, novels, popular lyrics— even advertisements. List your findings and then mark the most unusual comparison in each list.

Prefixes anti-, inter-, intra-, pro-

■ **FOCUS** Notice the prefix in each word as you read it. Then read the meaning phrase.

intermediate	not high, not low, but **intermediate**
antifreeze	**antifreeze** in the car for winter
intramural	eighth-grade **intramural** basketball league
intervene	will **intervene** to settle the argument
prologue	a **prologue** to introduce the play
intersection	crossed at the **intersection** of two streets
antiseptic	cleaned a cut with an **antiseptic** cream
intravenous	**intravenous** feedings through a tube
international	**international** students from Kenya
antisocial	acts **antisocial** around other people
promote	will **promote** me to the ninth grade
intrastate	**intrastate** trading within Missouri
antidote	a lifesaving **antidote** for the poison
progress	steady **progress** from start to finish
intercept	**intercept** a message meant for her
profound	fell into a **profound,** or very deep, sleep
antibody	an **antibody** in blood to fight germs
interfere	won't **interfere** and spoil your plans
proclaim	loudly **proclaim,** or declare, the winner
antibiotic	took an **antibiotic** for an infection

■ **DISCOVER** Adding prefixes to base words changes their meanings. **Anti-** means "against or not," so **antisocial** means "not social." **Pro-** means "before," so **prologue** can mean "before a literary work." **Intra-** means "within" and **inter-** means "between or among." What do **intrastate** and **international** mean?

CHALLENGE!

antihistamine
proclamation
interdisciplinary
intramuscular
interchangeable

■ **WRITE**
- six words with **anti-**
- five words with **pro-**
- six words with **inter-**
- three words with **intra-**

WORD BUILDING   Add prefixes to these words to make list words.

1. social
2. claim
3. freeze
4. state
5. venous

6. national
7. body
8. mediate
9. septic
10. section

DEFINITIONS   Write the list word that is described by each clue.

11. Use this **pro-** word to say you're getting better and better.
12. Use this **inter-** word to describe when you catch a ball before it gets to the intended player.
13. Use this **pro-** word to describe deep feelings.
14. This **intra-** word describes games within the walls of a school.
15. Use this **pro-** word to say you're moving on to the next grade.
16. This **anti-** word names a substance that counteracts the effects of poison.
17. Use this **inter-** word to say you'll come between two sides and separate them, often to settle an argument.
18. This **anti-** word names a protein substance that helps our bodies fight infection.
19. This **pro-** word names the introduction to a play or novel.
20. This **inter-** word describes meddling or getting in the way.

STRATEGIC SPELLING

Building New Words

Add the prefix **inter-** or **anti-** to the following base words to make new words: *mingle, personal, aircraft, trust, connect, missile.*

Add inter-	Add anti-
21. _____	24. _____
22. _____	25. _____
23. _____	26. _____

Take a Hint
There is an **e** in the prefix **inter-** and in its meaning, "between." **International** means "between or among nations."

≡	Make a capital.
/	Make a small letter.
∧	Add something.
℮	Take out something.
⊙	Add a period.
⁋	New paragraph

March

8:00 AM
9:00 AM
10:00 AM
11:00 AM
Noon
1:00 PM
2:00 PM
3:00 PM
4:00 PM
5:00 PM
6:00 PM

PROOFREAD FOR PUNCTUATION Use a comma or commas to set off an appositive, a word or phrase that follows a noun to identify or explain it. For example:

7:00 Make an appointment with Hal, our regional manager.

8:00 Schedule a meeting with Sue the consultant at noon.

Check for Commas Read each sentence. Write the word or words that should be followed by a comma.

1. 9:00 Fly to Cincinnati company headquarters.
2. 11:00 Interview Ms. Waters the new sales representative.
3. 2:00 Ask Ted the head custodian to fix the alarm.
4. 5:00 Watch Del Turner a company president on TV.

PROOFREAD AN APPOINTMENT CALENDAR Find five misspelled words in Mr. Eakins's appointment calendar and write them correctly. Fix three comma errors too.

9:00	Meet with Dave Eastern regional sales manager to permote Cindy.
10:00	Sales Conference—Don't interfear with there meeting.
11:00	Go over progres of ad campaign.
12:00	Lunch with Del Turner a president.
3:00	Meet with grievance committee—interveen if necessary.

WRITE AN APPOINTMENT CALENDAR Write a daily appointment calendar for a busy executive. Use three list words and a personal word.

Word List

intermediate	intersection	promote	profound
antifreeze	antiseptic	intrastate	antibody
intramural	intravenous	antidote	interfere
intervene	international	progress	proclaim
prologue	antisocial	intercept	antibiotic

Personal Words 1.___ 2.___

GREEK AND LATIN ROOTS: SPEAKING   The list
word **prologue** comes from the Greek root *logos,* which means
"speech." The Latin root *vocare* has a similar meaning, "to call."
The words in the box come from these two roots.

vocational	dialogue	provoke	eulogy	apology

Write the word that fits each definition below. Use your Spelling
Dictionary if you need help.

1. speech in praise of a deceased person
2. words of regret
3. to stir up or call to action
4. having to do with a business, occupation, or calling
5. conversation between two people

Now that you know what the *logos* and *vocare* words mean, use
them to complete these sentences.

6. The ___ between the two characters in the play was very
   humorous.
7. Albert's mother gave a beautiful ___ at Uncle Pete's funeral.
8. We are trying to ___ Katie to make her angry enough to
   change her mind.
9. Will you accept my ___ for forgetting your birthday?
10. Cecile will continue her ___ training in the field of carpentry.

ENRICHMENT   Pick one.

Develop Dialogue

Write a *dialogue*
between yourself and
one of your favorite
characters from a book,
movie, or TV show.
What would you talk
about? What would
you ask this person?
How would the
character respond?

When I Grow Up

What do you think
your *vocational* choice
will be? With a partner
who's interested in the
same field, develop
questions you have
about that job. Then
interview someone
who holds that job.
Report what you
learned about the
job to your class.

CHALLENGE!

Prologue comes from
logos and can mean
"introduction to a
literary work." *Epilogue*
also comes from *logos.*
What does it mean?
Find a few prologues
and epilogues to read,
and then write a
prologue or epilogue
to one of your favorite
stories or poems.

Vowels in Unstressed Syllables

28

■ **FOCUS** Say each word and notice the underlined vowel sounds. Then read each meaning phrase.

miracle	a **miracle** that can't be explained
irritate	can **irritate** my ears with loud drumming
accuracy	will use a stopwatch for perfect **accuracy**
evidence	no **evidence** to prove his innocence
ambulance	an **ambulance** to take her to the hospital
discipline	to **discipline** her for bad behavior
gullible	easily tricked their **gullible** friend
magnificent	the castle's **magnificent** grand ballroom
usually ♻	**usually** starts on time, but not always
extravagant	too much spent on **extravagant** presents
investigate	will **investigate** the theft of the money
article	a magazine **article** about cats
versatile	**versatile** athlete, able to play many sports
telethon	raised funds with a **telethon** on Channel 2
finally ♻	**finally** arrived with the pizza
hesitate	shouldn't **hesitate** to ask for help
memorable	the most **memorable** day of my life
inevitable	**inevitable** tears from the death of a pet
aggravate	**aggravate** a problem by spreading rumors
marathon	street closed for the **marathon** run

■ **DISCOVER** The vowel sound called *schwa, /ə/,* may be spelled with any vowel. This same sound is spelled **e** in **telethon** and **i** in **hesitate.** The underlined letters within the list words represent sounds that can be spelled with any vowel. Words such as **article** end with the sound /əl/. This final sound is often spelled **le.** What letters spell the schwa sound in **memorable?**

belligerent
contemporary
jeopardize
predicament
justification

■ **WRITE** First write the words that you think are easy to spell. Then write the words that you think are difficult to spell. Underline any vowels in these words that give you trouble.

CLASSIFYING Write the list word that belongs in each group.

1. at last, at the end, ___
2. footrace, 26 miles and 385 yards, ___
3. fact, clue, proof, ___
4. easily fooled, easily cheated, believing everything, ___
5. worth remembering, unforgettable, ___
6. TV program, telephones, fund-raiser, ___
7. unavoidable, has to happen, ___
8. having many talents, having a variety of uses, ___
9. control, order, punish, ___
10. luxurious, extreme, excessive, ___

CONTEXT CLUES Write the list word that completes each sentence.

11. I can't use that strong soap because it will ___ my skin.
12. Disobeying the rules will only ___ an already tense situation.
13. Don't ___ to ask for help if you need it.
14. She was awestruck by the queen's ___ collection of jewelry.
15. He ___ does his homework before supper but couldn't tonight.
16. We called for an ___ as soon as we saw the accident.
17. According to this ___ in the newspaper, taxes will increase.
18. That secretary's typing shows a high level of ___.
19. The reporter decided to ___ the rumors of corruption.
20. They feel it's a ___ that the tornado missed their house.

STRATEGIC SPELLING

The Divide and Conquer Strategy

21.–24. Study long words piece by piece. Write four list words that are hard for you. Draw lines to break them into smaller parts. Study the parts.

RECYCLED WORDS

Remember to find <u>all</u> in **fin<u>all</u>y** to spell it correctly.

≡	Make a capital.
/	Make a small letter.
∧	Add something.
℮	Take out something.
⊙	Add a period.
¶	New paragraph

PROOFREAD FOR USAGE When you make comparisons using *good, bad, much,* or *little,* don't add **-er** or *more* to comparative forms or **-est** or *most* to superlative forms.

This is the ~~worstest~~ worst blizzard in ten years, but there is ~~more~~ better news in tomorrow's forecast.

Check Comparatives and Superlatives Read each sentence. Correct mistakes with comparisons.

1. We will have lesser snow tomorrow.
2. The bestest news is that the winds will be calm.
3. Midweek looks more better, with milder temperatures.
4. There will be plenty of sun and lesser precipitation.
5. Conditions will change and get worser at week's end.

PROOFREAD A WEATHER REPORT Find five misspelled words and write them correctly. Some may be words you learned before. Fix three incorrect comparisons too.

> The cold snap will go from bad to more worse. There's evedience of another cold front headed our way. The worstest weather usualy hits on weekends, and this front will too. Strong winds allways make temperatures seem worser, so don't hesatate to bundle up. It's better to be safe then sorry in this winter weather.

WRITE A WEATHER REPORT Report on the weather in your area. Try to use three list words and a personal word.

Word List

miracle	discipline	investigate	hesitate
irritate	gullible	article	memorable
accuracy	magnificent	versatile	inevitable
evidence	usually	telethon	aggravate
ambulance	extravagant	finally	marathon

Personal Words 1.____ 2.____

DICTIONARY: SYNONYM STUDIES   Some dictionary entries include **synonym studies** that explain the difference between words that are closely related in meaning. Illustrative sentences show each word used in context. Below is the synonym study that appears at the end of the entry for the word *evidence*.

> **Syn.** *n.* **1 Evidence, testimony, proof** mean that which tends to demonstrate the truth or falsity of something. **Evidence** applies to facts that indicate, without fully proving, that something is so: *Running away was evidence of his guilt.* **Testimony** applies to any speech or action which serves as evidence of something: *Her testimony contradicted that of the preceding witness.* **Proof** means evidence so full and convincing as to leave no doubt or little doubt: *The signed receipt is proof that the letter was delivered.*

Write the synonyms that best complete the paragraphs. Use the synonym study to help you decide which words work best.

The defense attorney planned to present (1) at the trial that she hoped would convince the jury of her client's innocence. She also expected that a character witness's (2) would help. Further (3) would be the dated receipts that showed her client to be out of town on the day of the crime.

The prosecuting attorney felt that the (4) of a psychiatrist would show a different side of the defendant's character. To further persuade the jury, the prosecutor planned to use the defendant's criminal record as (5) . The final (6) would be fingerprints at the crime scene.

ENRICHMENT   Pick one.

What's the Verdict?
Based on the information you've been given above, write who you think has the better case, the defense or the prosecution. Support your response.

It's a Crime!
In a small group discuss what you think happened. What crime was committed? What were the facts and details surrounding the crime? After you've established the crime scene, stage a mock trial.

CHALLENGE!
Create a synonym study for the list word *irritate*. Use *irritate* and two of the following four words in your synonym study: *aggravate, annoy, exasperate, provoke.*

Using Just Enough Letters

■ **FOCUS** Read each word. Notice how it looks and sounds and how many letters it has. Then read the meaning phrase.

mischievous	a mess made by that **mischievous** cat
refrigerator	will put the milk in the **refrigerator**
remembrance	in **remembrance** of our war veterans
especially	an **especially** good meal
presidency	during the Lincoln **presidency**
disastrous	the **disastrous** day the flood wall broke
existence	discovered the **existence** of a hidden cave
hindrance	ice causing a **hindrance** on roads
monstrous	was a **monstrous** villain in the movie
regardless	will run **regardless** of the pain
motocross	dust and noise of the **motocross** race
pastime	his favorite **pastime** of playing chess
exercise	must get daily **exercise** for her health
allergic	is **allergic** to dust and ragweed
grievous	the **grievous** crime of murder
tuxedo	the groom wearing a **tuxedo**
awkward	the seal's **awkward** way of walking
scientist	a **scientist** using a microscope
drowned	almost **drowned** in the icy waters
assembly	a famous speaker at the school **assembly**

■ **DISCOVER** Don't add extra letters when you spell these words. Pronouncing words correctly—**mo-to-cross,** not mo-tor-cross—and picturing them in your mind will help you spell them with just the right number of letters.

■ **WRITE** First, write the words that are easiest for you to spell correctly. Then write the words that are the most difficult for you to spell correctly. Underline the parts of any words that cause you problems.

CHALLENGE!

ambidextrous
instinctive
rambunctious
colossal
prestige

MAKING INFERENCES Write the list word that is missing from each person's statement.

1. Athlete: "The way to stay fit is to ___ regularly."
2. Principal: "The mayor has agreed to speak at our next ___."
3. Baby-sitter: "That ___ little girl really kept me on my toes."
4. Bridegroom: "The tailor says my ___ will be ready in time."
5. Vice-president: "I plan to run for the ___ next term."
6. Student: "I plan to become a ___ who studies DNA."
7. Homeowner: "My ___ needs fixing; it's just not cold enough."
8. Shopper: "I never buy cheese because I'm ___ to milk."
9. Lifeguard: "No one has ever ___ in this pool."
10. Soldier: "I'm ___ glad to be going home for the holidays."

DEFINITIONS Write the list word that fits each definition.

11. causing grief
12. a pleasant way of passing time
13. bringing disaster
14. not graceful
15. a keepsake or souvenir
16. being somewhere; having life
17. extremely large; enormous
18. a motorcycle race over cross-country trails
19. person or thing that gets in the way
20. without regard; in spite of what happens

> **Did You Know?**
> The **tuxedo** got its name from Tuxedo Park, New York, the site of the country club where the suit was first worn.

STRATEGIC SPELLING

Seeing Meaning Connections

Words with *time*
daytime
meantime
lifetime
pastime

The words in the box, including the list word *pastime,* are related in spelling and meaning. Complete the sentences with these words.

After a (21) of work, Grandmother will retire next year. She says she enjoyed her work, but is looking forward to being outdoors in the (22) , so she can pursue her favorite (23) , gardening. In the (24) , we're planning a retirement party for her.

≡	Make a capital.
/	Make a small letter.
∧	Add something.
ℯ	Take out something.
⊙	Add a period.
¶	New paragraph

PROOFREAD FOR PUNCTUATION Put quotation marks around the titles of songs, stories, poems, articles, and book chapters. Capitalize the first word, the last word, and all important words in a title. For example:

A recently published article is "Exercise for busy People."

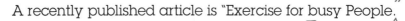

Check for Quotation Marks and Capitals Correct the mistakes in these sentences from a want ad by writing the word and the quotation mark that should come before or after it. Also write words that need to be capitalized.

Writer needs someone to proofread his work. Topics vary widely, so you must be knowledgeable in many subject areas. For instance, two articles in progress are the best Diners in the South and Motocross Celebrities. If qualified, contact James at 555–7770.

PROOFREAD A WANT AD Find the five misspelled words. Write them correctly. Some may be words you learned before. Also fix three mistakes with quotation marks and capitals.

> Student whose pasttime is writing country songs is especialy anxious to hook up with a musician who loves country music to. Call Judd at 555–1893 to request copies of two new songs: "my Grievious Heart and Love's a Hinderance."

WRITE A WANT AD Plan and write a want ad for something you'd like to buy. Try to use three list words and a personal word.

Word List

mischievous	disastrous	motocross	tuxedo
refrigerator	existence	pastime	awkward
remembrance	hindrance	exercise	scientist
especially	monstrous	allergic	drowned
presidency	regardless	grievous	assembly

Personal Words 1.___ 2.___

EXPLORING LANGUAGE: BLENDS A **blend** is a word that is made by combining, or blending, parts of two words. The list word *motocross* is a blend of *motorcycle* and *cross-country*. *Motocross* means "a motorcycle race run over cross-country trails rather than on a paved track." For each blend underlined in the sentences below, write the two words it came from. Use your Spelling Dictionary if you need help.

1. A <u>moped</u> can reach speeds of up to thirty miles an hour.
2. My little sister has figured out how to <u>squiggle</u> out of her highchair without hurting herself.
3. The president's <u>motorcade</u> passed by our school on the way to the airport.
4. A <u>transistor</u> is a tiny electronic device.
5. The word <u>*chortle*</u> was coined by author Lewis Carroll, the man who wrote *Alice in Wonderland.*
6. <u>Gasohol</u> is a fuel used in internal-combustion engines.
7. The candidates' speeches were <u>simulcast</u> on radio and television.
8. Jeremy likes to <u>slosh</u> in the rain, mud, and slush.
9. To enter the field of <u>bionics</u>, you have to know a lot about anatomy, physiology, and electronics.
10. The <u>sportscast</u> was interrupted by a special news report.

ENRICHMENT Pick one

Blend Me a Poem
Use your Spelling Dictionary to find out what words the blends *splatter* and *galumph* came from. Then use those words and two of the blends above to write a poem.

Sports Moves
The blends *chortle*, *slosh*, and *squiggle* are action words. With a partner, discuss some of the moves your favorite athletes make on the courts and fields. Make up three new blends for these actions. Example: slide + run = slun

CHALLENGE!

Do sitcoms make you chortle? Use your Spelling Dictionary to find out what two words *sitcom* came from. Then write a summary of a sitcom you would like to see on TV.

Review

30

HOW AM I DOING?

Look back at the word lists in Lessons 25–29 and think about how you are doing in spelling.

1. The hardest words for me to spell were ____ ____ ____

2. You learned that it helps to divide words that are hard to spell into syllables. Did you use this strategy?   **Yes   No   Sometimes**

3. I try to use words that I am learning to spell in my writing.
   Yes   No   Sometimes

4. I think that I am getting to be a better speller.
   Yes   No   Sometimes

5. The most interesting word that I have learned to spell is ____.

■ PROOFREADING

Find the spelling errors in each passage and write the words correctly. All passages have seven errors except the last one, which has eight.

PROOFREAD A LETTER TO THE EDITOR

Collision at Fourth and Grand

Once again there has been a collision at the hazordous intrasection of Fourth and Grand Streets. It was inevitible, but it is also ridiculus that there are no stop signs on Grand. In my judgement this outragues situation should not be allowed to continue, especialy so near a playground.

PROOFREAD A FRIENDLY LETTER

April 12, 19--

Dear Letitia,

I wanted to tell you that last weekend we used the pedameter you gave me for my birthday. Terry and I hiked fifteen miles, and though we were drenched in persperation because of the humidity, we were determined to let nothing impeed our hike. Unfortunately, I am somewhat alergic to insect bites, but by some miricle I had my medicine with me, so the mosquitoes didn't seriously interfear with our weekend. After dinner, sleepyness quickly overcame us!

Your friend,
Martina

PROOFREAD A CHARACTER SKETCH

My older sister is planning to run in the marethon next week. She started working up to this three years ago when she began an excercise program. It wasn't long until she was able to progres to running every day. Then she started to compete in intermurial relays. Soon, running was more than a pasttime. She had the disipline to run every day and to keep pushing herself reguardless of how she felt. My whole family and I are very proud of her. You see, three years ago, she was recovering from an accident, and doctors thought she would not walk at all.

PROOFREAD A MEMO

To: Sam Tyler

From: Fred Estevez

    The following items should be stocked on the shelves: antifreez, light bulbs, antiseptick bandages, toothpaste, and film. (Film is in the refridgerator.) You made a big improvment in the arangement of hardware supplies. Thanks! Do not hesatate to ask questions of Mr. Jackson, who will be taking over managment of the store while I am away.

PROOFREAD A REPORT

Vincent van Gogh

    Vincent van Gogh was a painter for ten years only. Before that he was a dealer in pictures, a bookseller, and an evangelist. It was not until he was twenty-seven, in 1880, that he finaly made the courages decision to become an artist. It was a decision that resulted in some magnifecent paintings and some grevious times for the artist. Lack of money was usally a hindrence to his very existance. We know of his trials from his letters to Theo, the brother who supported him. Vincent died penniless in 1890. I copied one of his self-portraits for this report.

PROOFREAD A NEWS STORY

Alicia Foster was practicing for the intarstate
swim meet between the northeastern and
southeastern districts of the state when
she complained of dizziness last Thursday.
A rumor that someone had drownded spread
quickly through a school assembaly. In the
excitment an ambulence was called to the
itermidiate gym. Paramedics monitored
her resparation and pulse but could find
nothing wrong.

PROOFREAD A BROCHURE

Do you need an antedote to winter?

Why not investigat one of our Movable
Mystery Tours? Participants board a
train and try to solve a monstrus "crime"
committed on board. Not only are there
a lot of suspicous characters, but evedience
at the crime scene is baffling. You won't find
a real coarpse, but we will conspir to make
your trip a memerable one.

STRATEGY WORKSHOP

Choosing the Best Strategy

DISCOVER THE STRATEGY Remember to use this strategy to study new words:

Steps for Spelling	
1. Look at the word and say it.	4. Picture it.
2. Spell it aloud.	5. Look and write.
3. Think about it.	6. Cover, write, and check it.

For words that give you special problems, try these strategies. For each hard word, choose the strategy that works best for you.

Strategies	How to Use Them
Developing Spelling Consciousness	Dont overlook familiar words when you proofread. (Did you catch the mistake in that last sentence?)
Pronouncing for Spelling	Pronounce the word correctly, (**"fi-nal-ly"**) or make up a secret pronunciation. (**"ve-hi-cle"**)
Divide and Conquer	Divide the word into smaller parts: **grand/daughter** **re/construct/ion** **i/den/ti/fy**
Creating Memory Tricks	Link the word with a memory helper that has the same problem letters. (**Tell these mosquitoes to quit biting!**)

Strategies	How to Use Them
Using Meaning Helpers	Pair the word with a shorter, familiar word that's related in spelling and meaning: **attendance—attend** **narrative—narrate**

TRY IT OUT Tell each speller which strategy you think would work best to help solve each problem.

1. I always miss the silent **t** in *mortgage.*
2. I wish I could remember how to spell the **ough** in *thoroughly.*
3. I forget the **l** in *calves* because it's silent.
4. I spell *expression* this way: **expreshion.**
5. New words give me problems. I don't know how to study them.
6. I keep spelling *moisture* with a **ch** instead of a **t.**
7. I wish I could remember the double **m** and **s** in *commission.*
8. *Chronological* is too long for me to remember.
9. I wish I could stop misspelling little words like *which* and *let's*—words I really do know how to spell.
10. *Catastrophe* is a catastrophe for me to spell. It's so long!

LOOK AHEAD Look ahead at the next five lessons for list words that might give you problems. Write four of them. Then decide which strategy you will use to help you remember how to spell each word, and write it next to the word.

Including All the Letters

31

■ **FOCUS** Read each word. Notice how it looks and sounds and how many letters it has. Then read the meaning phrase.

veterinarian	took their sick dog to the **veterinarian**
beginning ♻	missed the **beginning** of the movie
acquaintance	an **acquaintance**, not a close friend
extraordinary	an amazing, **extraordinary** feat
conscience	a guilty **conscience** after the cruel prank
susceptible	**susceptible** to flattery because he's so vain
something ♻	said **something** that I couldn't hear
comparable	**comparable**, or similar, gifts for them
respiratory	**respiratory** problems from the smoky air
disintegrate	will **disintegrate** into tiny pieces
peculiar	an odd, **peculiar** color for a house
alcohol	clean the cut with rubbing **alcohol**
clothes ♻	wears **clothes** that don't match
sophomore	**sophomore** year following freshman year
overrated	a boring, **overrated** movie
arctic	seals and polar bears in the **arctic** region
basically	**basically** the same, just a few differences
liberal	a **liberal** politician, pushing for changes
rendezvous	will **rendezvous** at noon for our meeting
adjourn	will **adjourn** the trial until tomorrow

■ **DISCOVER** Sometimes we leave letters out of a word because we don't hear them when we say the word. Often all we have to do is say the word correctly to spell it right. Other times exaggerating the pronunciation of problem letters will help. What letter don't you hear in **adjourn?**

CHALLENGE!

paraphernalia
vaudeville
undoubtedly
chrysanthemum
grammatically

■ **WRITE** Look over the list words carefully. First write the words that you are most likely to use in your writing. Then write the rest of the words. Underline letters you might leave out.

ANALOGIES   Write the list word that completes each analogy.

1. Right is to left as conservative is to ___.
2. Junior is to senior as freshman is to ___.
3. First is to last as ___ is to ending.
4. Pediatrician is to child as ___ is to pet.
5. South Pole is to antarctic as North Pole is to ___.
6. Circulatory system is to heart as ___ system is to lungs.
7. Cabinet is to dishes as closet is to ___.
8. Ordinary is to everyday as odd is to ___.
9. Like is to love as ___ is to friend.

DEFINITIONS   Write the list word that means the same as the underlined word or phrase in each sentence.

10. We used <u>an antiseptic</u> to clean the wound.
11. Let's <u>suspend</u> the meeting now and resume it later.
12. That girl is an <u>exceptionally good</u> pianist for her age.
13. He seems to have <u>a particular thing</u> on his mind.
14. People who brag a lot are often <u>sensitive</u> to flattery.
15. Our apartments are <u>approximately the same</u> in size.
16. I'd say that new movie is <u>regarded too highly</u>.
17. Please try to be on time for our <u>appointment to meet</u>.
18. My <u>sense of right and wrong</u> won't let me lie to them.
19. The final report is <u>fundamentally</u> the same as the first draft.
20. Our birdbath started to <u>break up</u> because it was exposed to rain, snow, and wind.

STRATEGIC SPELLING
Choosing the Best Strategy

21.–22. Write two list words that you find hard to spell. Which strategy could help you spell each word? Name the strategy and tell why you chose it. Then compare choices with a partner. For a list of strategies, see pages 142–143.

RECYCLED WORDS RECYCLED WORDS RECYCLED WORDS RECYCLED

Maybe this will help you get all the letters in **beginning:** At the beginning we stayed at the <u>inn</u>.

≡	Make a capital.
/	Make a small letter.
∧	Add something.
ℓ	Take out something.
⊙	Add a period.
¶	New paragraph

PROOFREAD FOR USAGE Don't use *more* or *most* and don't add **-er** or **-est** when making comparisons with *less, least; better, best;* and *worse, worst.* For example:

Skipping school is the ~~most~~ worst thing I have done lately.

Check Comparisons Read this passage. Write the word that completes each comparison correctly.

I wanted the (best, most best) seats I could get. I thought I was (less, lesser) likely to get caught if I skipped school half a day than if I missed the whole day. Was I wrong! It was the (worst, worstest) day of my life. I feel (worse, more worse) about disappointing my dad than I do about missing the game.

PROOFREAD A PERSUASIVE SPEECH Find five spelling errors in this persuasive speech. Write them correctly. Some may be words you learned before. Fix three comparison errors too.

> Skipping school is overated. Tickets for the most best game of the season went on sale at 1:00. I took of right before lunch to miss the leastest amount of school. My concience bothered me too much so I told my dad. Basicly, I had to return the tickets and do a week of detention. The consaquences were worser than I thought.

WRITE A PERSUASIVE SPEECH Write a speech to persuade your classmates not to break a school rule. Try to use three list words and a personal word.

Word List

veterinarian	susceptible	peculiar	arctic
beginning	something	alcohol	basically
acquaintance	comparable	clothes	liberal
extraordinary	respiratory	sophomore	rendezvous
conscience	disintegrate	overrated	adjourn

Personal Words 1.___ 2.___

MULTICULTURAL CONNECTION: ENVIRONMENT The tie between culture and environment is especially strong in the frigid arctic land—the northernmost region of the world. In an area where the average winter temperature is only -30°F, people's lives cannot be separated from their environment. The words in the box have come into English from the languages of people who have inhabited arctic lands for thousands of years.

Write the word from the box that fits each clue. Use your Spelling Dictionary if you need help.

| parka |
| reindeer |
| mukluk |
| lemming |
| tundra |
| floe |

1. This word of Russian origin describes the treeless plains of the arctic region, where the ground remains frozen even in the summer.
2. This word for a sheet of floating ice is of Norwegian origin.
3. This is a fur jacket with a hood that comes from a word of Russian origin.
4. The name for this deer with branching antlers originally comes from the Old Icelandic language.
5. The name for a waterproof boot often made from sealskin is the Inuit word for "large seal."
6. This rodent, whose name is of Norwegian origin, is one of the few animals that lives in the Arctic all year long.

ENRICHMENT   Pick one.

Getting Cold
Write a story about a person moving to an arctic area from the tropics. How will your character's life change? Some changes to think about are clothing, transportation, and food. Use at least four words from the box in your story.

The Midnight Sun
The Arctic is also called "the land of the midnight sun." With a partner, find out why. Each of you list ways in which the length of days and nights would affect your lives. Compare lists.

CHALLENGE!
Investigate life in your environment. Think about how the year-round weather affects the way you live. Make a list of household items and clothing that are uniquely tied to the environment of your region and explain what makes each one an important part of your daily life.

Latin Roots 3

■ **FOCUS** Read each word and meaning phrase. Notice that some words have similar parts.

advertisement	a TV **advertisement** for sneakers
satisfaction	the **satisfaction** of doing a good job
conventional	**conventional,** or usual, sandwich for lunch
facilitate	a calculator to **facilitate** multiplying
controversy	**controversy** over the referee's call
advent	will welcome the **advent** of summer
eventually	**eventually** finished the long book
diversion	a **diversion** from worries about school
artifact	an **artifact**—a tool from the Stone Age
decompose	will **decompose** on the forest floor
introvert	an **introvert,** alone with her thoughts
prevention	helmets for the **prevention** of head injuries
benefactor	a gift from a kindly **benefactor**
convert	can **convert** this liquid to a gas
circumvent	to **circumvent** the rules by cheating
disposable	threw away the **disposable** plates
faction	one **faction** in the club versus another
proposal	a **proposal** for a new swimming pool
extrovert	an **extrovert,** joking with the crowd
imposing	started **imposing** new rules on us

■ **DISCOVER** These words are from Latin words that suggest action. The word *vertere* means "to turn." What does **convert** mean? *Poser,* from the Latin *pausere,* means "to set." What does **proposal** mean? *Venire* means "to come." What does **advent** mean? *Facere* means "to make." What does **facilitate** mean?

CHALLENGE!

incontrovertible
predisposition
intervention
vice versa
facsimile

■ **WRITE** ▪ six words from *vertere*
▪ five words from *facere*
▪ five words from *venire*
▪ four words from *poser*

ETYMOLOGIES   Write the list word that matches each etymology.

1. [< Latin *artem* art + *factum* made]
2. [< *extro-* outside + Latin *vertere* to turn]
3. [< Latin *adventum* < *ad-* to + *venire* come]
4. [< Latin *controversia* < *contra-* against + *versum* turned]
5. [< *intro-* within + Latin *vertere* to turn]
6. [< Latin *benefactum* befitted < *bene* well + *facere* do]
7. [< Latin *circumventum* circumvented < *circum* around + *venire* come]
8. [< Latin *convertere* < *com-* around + *vertere* to turn]

WORD MEANINGS   Write the list word that fits each definition.

9. a group of persons having a common purpose
10. usual or customary
11. able to be thrown away after use
12. to make something easier
13. a public notice recommending some product or service
14. the stopping of progress
15. a distraction from work or worry
16. a feeling of being contented or fulfilled
17. a plan, scheme, or suggestion
18. impressive because of size, appearance, or dignity
19. to break apart or decay
20. in the end

STRATEGIC SPELLING
Building New Words

Add the prefix **extra-** to these words to make new words. Remember to keep all the letters of the base word when adding a prefix.

21. curricular
22. sensory
23. terrestrial

> **Did You Know?**
> In the United States, people call **advertisements** *ads* for short, but in Great Britain the short form is *adverts,* with the accent on the first syllable.

SAVE THE EARTH

GLASS   PLASTIC
RECYCLE

≡	Make a capital.
/	Make a small letter.
∧	Add something.
ℰ	Take out something.
⊙	Add a period.
¶	New paragraph

PROOFREAD FOR USAGE When a sentence starts with *here* or *there*, the subject often comes after the verb, but the two still need to agree. For example:

There ~~is~~ ^are^ many things we can do to save our planet.

Check Subject-Verb Agreement Read each sentence. If the verb is correct, write "Correct." If not, write the correct verb.

1. Here is some ideas that we might propose.
2. There is a chance that we could use recycled paper here.
3. There are a lot of paper wasted in the office.
4. There is an attendance slip from each teacher each period.
5. There is certainly even more things we can do to help.

PROOFREAD A PROPOSAL Find six misspelled words in this proposal and write them correctly. Some may be words you learned before. Fix three errors with subject-verb agreement too.

> There is many things to improve in our school. My proposul is to convert from plastic cups to glass ones. There are proof that it is better for our enviroment. Eventualy, lets stop using disposible items. There is not enough landfills, and it takes plastic a long time to de compose.

WRITE A PROPOSAL Write a proposal suggesting a project to improve your school or community. Use three list words and a personal word.

Word List

advertisement	advent	introvert	disposable
satisfaction	eventually	prevention	faction
conventional	diversion	benefactor	proposal
facilitate	artifact	convert	extrovert
controversy	decompose	circumvent	imposing

Personal Words 1.___ 2.___

SYNONYMS The sentence "My father is a big man" gives a picture of the father, but this sentence gives a better picture: "My father is an imposing man." Why? Because *big* just means "large," but the synonym *imposing* means "impressively large." Use **synonyms**—words that mean almost but not quite the same—to help you express yourself more clearly in your writing.

Sort the words in the box into two groups of synonyms. Use your Spelling Dictionary if you need help.

bashful	
reserved	
distraction	
entertainment	
guarded	
pastime	

Synonyms for *introverted*

1.____
2.____
3.____

Synonyms for *diversion*

4.____
5.____
6.____

Write the synonym from the box you think is best to replace *introverted* or *diversion* in each sentence. Use your Spelling Dictionary if you need help.

Because I'm so **(7) introverted,** it's hard for me to give speeches. In language arts class I had to give a speech about my favorite **(8) diversion,** baking pies. I didn't want my class to notice my shyness, so I brought in fresh apple and blueberry pies as a **(9) diversion.** My teacher, who is usually quiet and **(10) introverted,** laughed out loud when I explained why I brought the pies.

ENRICHMENT Pick one.

A Tantalizing Tale
Elephantine, gargantuan, and *titanic* are all synonyms for *big.* Think of interesting synonyms for some other common words such as *small, run,* and *tired.* Make a list for each. Write a story using as many of the more interesting words from your list as you can.

Don't Yell!
With a partner list as many synonyms for *talk* as you can. Then take a sentence like "I want you to sit here" and take turns saying it the way you would for each different synonym of *talk.* Keep going until you have gone through your entire list.

CHALLENGE!
Choose five or six interesting synonyms for *suddenly.* Write an adventure story in which things happen *suddenly,* and use your synonyms instead of *suddenly.* Make a copy of your story, omitting the synonyms for *suddenly.* Have your classmates decide which synonym best fits each blank.

Prefixes ab-, ad-, co-, com-, con-

■ **FOCUS** Notice the prefix in each word as you read it. Then read the meaning phrases.

abbreviate	should **abbreviate** Texas as TX
absorb	will **absorb** the water with a sponge
abduct	did **abduct** the prize poodle for ransom
abolish	wants to **abolish** hunger forever
abnormal	an **abnormal** 400-pound pumpkin
adjacent	a thin wall between **adjacent** rooms
advantage	the **advantage** of an extra player
addition	the **addition** of a family room to a house
adhesive	**adhesive** to seal the envelope
coordination	a dancer with balance and **coordination**
cohesive	shaped us into a **cohesive** group
cooperate	will **cooperate** to reach our goal
coexist	can **coexist** in spite of disagreements
complicate	obstacles that **complicate** the problem
compound	the **compound** word *bookcase*
compete	will **compete** for the trophy
community	a **community** of students and teachers
confession	the thief's **confession** to the police
concert	tickets for tonight's band **concert**
conservation	**conservation** of our natural resources

■ **DISCOVER** The prefix **ad-** means "to" or "toward," so **adhesive** means "to stick to." **Ab-** can be a variation of **ad-**, as in **abbreviate,** meaning "to shorten," but **ab-** can also mean "away from" or "off." What does **abduct** mean? The prefixes **co-** and **con-** are variations of **com-**, which means "with" or "together." What does **community** mean?

CHALLENGE!

commendation
condemnation
coeducational
abrasive
adversity

■ **WRITE**
- Alphabetize five words with **ab-**.
- Alphabetize four words with **ad-**.
- Alphabetize eleven words with forms of **com-**.

MAKING INFERENCES   Write the list word that fits each clue.

1. A job-seeker with skills and experience has this over a job seeker with no experience.
2. You and your neighbors are all part of this.
3. Two people may do this to get a job done faster.
4. You may attend this to hear your favorite band.
5. "Two plus two" is an example of this.
6. Faced with the evidence, a guilty person may blurt this out.
7. You do this when you participate in a race.
8. This is what kidnappers do.
9. A sponge will do this to your spilled milk.
10. People practice this when they reuse and recycle.
11. You may do this to save time when addressing envelopes.

SENTENCE COMPLETION   Write the list word that completes each sentence.

12. Water is a chemical ____ made of hydrogen and oxygen.
13. It was once considered ____ for a girl to want a career.
14. A new family moved into the apartment ____ to ours.
15. He wants to simplify his life, not ____ it.
16. The therapist suggested exercises to improve my ____.
17. You need a piece of ____ tape to hold the bandage in place.
18. We are a ____ group. We stick together through anything.
19. They want to ____ the use of animals in experiments.
20. Although they disagree politically, the nations ____ in peace.

STRATEGIC SPELLING

Seeing Meaning Connections

| adhesion |
| adhere |
| adherent |

The list word *adhesive* is related to the words in the box in spelling and meaning. Write the word from the box that fits each definition. Use your Spelling Dictionary if you need help.

21. an ____ of that religion
22. will ____ to your fingers
23. the ____ of the bandage to the skin

Take a Hint
They sound almost alike, but don't confuse **addition** with its sound-alike: *edition*. Remember that you <u>add</u> when you do <u>add</u>ition.

≡	Make a capital.
/	Make a small letter.
∧	Add something.
ℓ	Take out something.
⊙	Add a period.
¶	New paragraph

PROOFREAD FOR USAGE Be sure to use irregular verbs correctly. For example:

Many people ~~taked~~ *took* advantage of the free concert in the park.

Check Irregular Verbs Read each sentence. Correct any mistakes with verbs. If a sentence is correct, write "Correct."

1. The band concert brung many people to the park.
2. Selections were chose from many musical styles.
3. Not rushing, they took their time on the ballads.
4. We appreciate that people singed along with their favorites.
5. Did you notice that no one leaved early?

PROOFREAD AN ANNOUNCEMENT Find six misspelled words in this announcement and write them correctly. Some may be words you learned before. Fix two incorrect verbs too.

> A third concert by the school band was a welcome adition to the schedule. People comed from thruout the comunity and taked advantig of the chance to enjoy good music as the band prepared to compeat in a state contest. There will be a concert every Thursday untill further notice. All are invited to attend.

WRITE AN ANNOUNCEMENT Write an announcement about an upcoming event in your community or school. Try to use three list words and a personal word.

Word List

abbreviate	adjacent	cohesive	compete
absorb	advantage	cooperate	community
abduct	addition	coexist	confession
abolish	adhesive	complicate	concert
abnormal	coordination	compound	conservation

Personal Words 1.___ 2.___

LATIN ROOTS: TIME   The words in the first box are from the Latin root *brevis,* which means "short." Write the word from *brevis* that best completes each sentence. Use your Spelling Dictionary if you need help.

| brief |
| brevity |
| abbreviate |
| abbreviation |

1. I wrote a ____ note to my mom asking her a question.
2. Sometimes my notes are difficult to understand because I ____ a lot of words.
3. My mom thinks that ____ is important in notes because she doesn't want to spend a long time reading them.
4. I asked her: What is the two-letter ____ for Massachusetts?

The words in the second box are from a related Latin root *tempus,* which means "time." Complete each sentence with one of the time words. Use your Spelling Dictionary if you need help.

| tempo |
| temper |
| contemporary |
| temporary |

5. I lost my ____ because there was a problem in my car pool about what music we have to listen to.
6. Cecilia's dad likes to listen to old-time music, but we kids like to listen to music that's a little more ____.
7. Cecilia's dad says that he doesn't like the ____ of our music; it's too fast.
8. We have agreed to alternate days as a ____ solution, but we are still seeking a permanent solution to this problem.

ENRICHMENT   Pick one.

Shortcuts
We *abbreviate* to save time and space, but what kinds of things do we abbreviate? Make a list of as many different abbreviations as you can find and write out what each abbreviation stands for. Good places to look for abbreviations are letters, notes, newspapers, food packages, and street signs.

A Timely Tale
With a partner, write a story about time travel, using as many words from *brevem* and *tempus* as you can. For an added challenge, try to use some of these time words that come from the Latin word *annus,* meaning "year": *annual, centennial, perennial, annuity.*

CHALLENGE!
Cities celebrate centennials every hundred years and bicentennials every two hundred years. Sometimes cities celebrate *quasquicentennials* and *sesquicentennials* too. Find out what these words mean. Then investigate to see if your community has celebrated either one of these and when.

Related Words 3

■ **FOCUS** Say each pair of related words. Notice how the spelling and pronunciation change. Read each meaning phrase.

suspend	will **suspend** the banner from the ceiling
suspension	a **suspension** of work because of rain
publish	will **publish** a school newspaper
publication	read the **publication** from cover to cover
consume	can **consume** three hot dogs for lunch
consumption	a car's efficient **consumption** of fuel
omit	can **omit,** or leave out, the vanilla
omission	the **omission** of sugar in the cake
substance	odd **substance** oozing from the wall
substantial	**substantial** enough to last a long time
prescribe	will **prescribe** an antibiotic for infection
prescription	used the **prescription** as directed
provoke	can **provoke** a fight with an insult
provocative	was angered by the **provocative** remark
conclude	will **conclude** the story tomorrow
conclusion	will write a **conclusion** for the essay
influence	used her **influence** as mayor
influential	the **influential** leaders in town
persuade	can't **persuade** them to come with us
persuasive	**persuasion** with logical arguments

■ **DISCOVER** The words **publish** and **publication** are similar in spelling and meaning but are pronounced differently. Say **omit** and **omission**. Which letter changes between the base word and the related word?

CHALLENGE!

presume
presumption
reprehend
reprehension
circumstance
circumstantial

■ **WRITE** ▪ three pairs of words in which **d** changes to **s**
▪ two pairs of words in which **c** changes to **t**
▪ two pairs of words in which **sh** or **k** changes to **c**
▪ two pairs of words in which **t** or **b** changes to **ss** or **p**
▪ one pair of words in which a **p** is added

MAKING CONNECTIONS Write the list word that completes each unfinished sentence in the letter.

Dear Aspiring Author,

We are pleased to inform you that we plan to _(1)_ your article, "How to Survive Junior High," in the spring issue of our _(2)_, *American Teen*. We found the article _(3)_ and humorous, and we think it will _(4)_ a strong response in our readers as well. However, we want to suggest a few changes to shorten and improve it. First, we'd like you to _(5)_ the introduction; readers will never notice the _(6)_. We'd also like you to edit the _(7)_ to make the article _(8)_ on a more upbeat note. Most importantly, we want to _(9)_ you to rewrite the entire article in the first person. To be _(10)_, we are offering an additional fee of ten percent. Please respond to this proposal as soon as possible. Thank you.

Sincerely,

The Editors of *American Teen*

WORD RELATIONSHIPS Write the list word that matches each clue. Then write the list word that is related to it.

11.–12. to order or direct
13.–14. having great prestige or importance
15.–16. to hang down from something high
17.–18. what something is made up of
19.–20. to use up or expend

STRATEGIC SPELLING

Building New Words

Add the suffix **-ive** to each base word from the list to make a new word. Circle any words with spelling changes. Use your Spelling Dictionary if you need help.

21. persuade
22. conclude
23. permit
24. destroy

Did You Know?
Rx, the symbol for medical **prescription,** is an abbreviation of the Latin word *recipe,* which means "take."

≡	Make a capital.
/	Make a small letter.
∧	Add something.
ℓ	Take out something.
⊙	Add a period.
⁋	New paragraph

PROOFREAD FOR CARELESS ERRORS

If you divide a word at the end of a line, divide between syllables. For example:

For people new in town, I'd like to ~~reco~~ recom-
~~mmend~~ mend a fantastic restaurant.

Check Hyphenation Write three words that are incorrectly divided and draw a line to show where the hyphen should be. Use your Spelling Dictionary if you need help.

I don't mean to influence you too much, but I'd like to tell you about my favorite restaurant, Si's Roost. If knowing that everything is made fresh daily doesn't persuade you, the tantalizing aroma of his apple pie will. Si's Roost is the best restaurant in town.

PROOFREAD A RECOMMENDATION

Find the five misspelled words and write them correctly. Some may be words you learned before. Fix three incorrectly hyphenated words too.

> Don't hesatate to stop for the most subst-
> antial meal in town at Si's Roost. First, concume
> as much chicken as you can. Then let the ow-
> ner, Si, persuiade you to try his homemade pie.
> Theres also Si's world famous potato salad that
> you must try. Si's waitresses even pubulish a we-
> ekly newsletter about the specials.

WRITE A RECOMMENDATION

Write a recommendation for a restaurant. Use three list words and a personal word.

Word List

suspend	consumption	prescribe	conclusion
suspension	omit	prescription	influence
publish	omission	provoke	influential
publication	substance	provocative	persuade
consume	substantial	conclude	persuasive

Personal Words 1.___ 2.___

USING EXACT WORDS In this sentence, "I sat in that sticky substance on the chair," *substance* is a vague word. What could that sticky substance have been? Was it recently chewed bubble gum, sap from the nearby maple tree, or even tar dripped from the roofer's brush? Try any one of those in the sentence. Being more exact helps you express your ideas more precisely.

> algae
> lipstick
> marshmallow
> lemonade
> pea soup

Replace *substance* in each sentence with a more exact word from the box above. Use your Spelling Dictionary if you need to.

1. The substance on that graham cracker looks gooey.
2. Some substance leaked from that thermos and ruined the paper plates.
3. How did that substance get on the letter? Did you kiss it?
4. Slurp that substance once more and I'll take away your bowl!
5. The green substance on top of the pond makes it difficult to see the bottom.

We tend to use *said* a lot when we write dialogue. Usually we could choose a more exact word. Use one of the words from the box to replace *said* in each sentence.

> exclaimed
> murmured
> repeated
> swore
> warned

6. He said the directions so softly that I couldn't hear him.
7. As the tomato soup spilled on the tablecloth, Grandma said, "Quick! Let's try to clean that up before it leaves a stain!"
8. Our neighbor said, "You have a headlight out on your car."
9. I said that I would never borrow any of my sister's things again without asking.
10. Promise me that you haven't said my secret to anyone else.

ENRICHMENT Pick one.

Say it Differently
Write a science fiction story about scientists inventing strange and powerful substances. Use *substance* at least five times. Then go back and replace each *substance* with a more exact word. Do not use any exact word for *substance* more than one time.

Ate or Chomped?
Start with a sentence like "I ate green eggs and ham for breakfast." With a partner, alternate substituting a more exact word like *devoured* or *chomped* for *ate*. See how many times you can substitute a more exact word in the sentence.

CHALLENGE!
Vague words are common in our everyday conversation. Ask a friend or relative about a book, movie, or TV show that he or she liked. Keep a list of vague words the person uses. Then ask for more specific words and list the new words.

Words from Many Cultures 2

■ **FOCUS** Say each word and read the meaning phrase that goes with it.

cafeteria	lined up for lunch in the **cafeteria**
anchor	dropped the boat's **anchor** and fished
suede	will waterproof the **suede** shoes
gingham	red and white **gingham** dresses
mattress	a new **mattress** for her bed
kimono	a Japanese **kimono** instead of a dress
catamaran	will sail on the flat-decked **catamaran**
bungalow	a small yard around the tiny **bungalow**
yacht	a party and cruise on their **yacht**
pajamas	wore red flannel **pajamas** to bed
gondola	poled the **gondola** through the canal
pueblo	flat-roofed houses of the Hopi **pueblo**
admiral	should salute the **admiral** of the navy
sequin	sewed on one shiny **sequin** at a time
bureau	storing your shirts and socks in the **bureau**
poncho	put on a **poncho** when the rain started
kayak	paddled the icy waters in a **kayak**
estate	a mansion, stable, and lake on the **estate**
indigo	a blue dye called **indigo**
khaki	a dull brown cloth called **khaki**

■ **DISCOVER** Words come into the English language in many different ways. We commonly borrow words from other languages and make them part of our language. The words in this list are all borrowed from other languages.

CHALLENGE!

marimba
maraca
accordion
castanet
timpani

■ **WRITE** Sort the list words by writing
- six words about boats and the sea
- eight words about textiles and clothing
- six words about buildings and their contents

CONCLUSIONS   Write the list word that fits each clue.

1. I am from a Mexican Spanish word for coffee shop.
2. I'm a loose Japanese garment.
3. I am a Hindustani word for a small house.
4. I am from a Greek word; I hold your boat in one place.
5. From an Arabic word for "the cushion," I am used on a bed.
6. From a Spanish word, I'm a coat that slips over your head.
7. I am from a French word for a large piece of land.
8. From an Arabic word meaning "the chief," I am the commander of a ship.
9. I'm a dull brown fabric from a Persian word for dust.
10. I am a boat with two hulls, from a Tamil word for tied tree. (Tamil is a language of the people of India and Sri Lanka.)
11. I am an Italian boat found in the canals of Venice.

DEFINITIONS   Write the list word that fits each definition.

12. a cotton cloth of colored threads, from a Malay word for striped
13. an Inuit canoe made of skins stretched over a frame with an opening in the middle for a person
14. from an Arabic word, a small, sparkling disk for decorating clothes
15. from a French word for desk, a chest of drawers or dresser
16. from the French word for Sweden, a velvety-soft leather
17. from a Spanish word meaning "people or community," an Indian village with homes made of adobe and stone
18. from a Spanish word, a blue dye
19. from a Dutch word, a ship used for pleasure or racing
20. sleeping garments, originally from a Persian word

STRATEGIC SPELLING

Using the Memory Tricks Strategy

21.–22. Use memory tricks to help you spell. Create memory tricks for two list words that are hard for you. Underline the matching letters in the list words and helpers.

Did You Know?
Suede became the name of the soft leather because of the French phrase *gants de Suède*, which means "gloves of Sweden."

	Make a capital.
/	Make a small letter.
∧	Add something.
ℯ	Take out something.
⊙	Add a period.
¶	New paragraph

PROOFREAD FOR USAGE The verb pairs *bring/take* and *borrow/lend* are often used incorrectly. Don't use one when you mean the other. For example:

Mom has me ~~bring~~ ^take^ my little sister to school every day.

Check Verbs If the wrong verb from the pair is used, write the correct one. If the verb in a sentence is correct, write "Correct."

1. She also has me stop at the store so I can bring home milk.
2. In addition, I bring out the garbage every day.
3. In return, she lets me borrow her things.
4. She borrowed me her silk pajamas for a slumber party.
5. She got mad when I forgot to bring them home with me.

PROOFREAD A SELF-PORTRAIT Find the five misspelled words in Kim's self-portrait. Write them correctly. Some may be words you learned before. Fix three errors with verbs too.

> I'm a kaki pants person—no sequins or suade for me! If I need a dress, my sister borrows me one. Mom knows were to find me at home. I'm in my pagamas, sitting in my chair reading. I like to take my friends home so they can meet my family. I like to bring my family when I go places. One time we took a cruise on a yaght.

WRITE A SELF-PORTRAIT Write about yourself in a self-portrait. Try to use three list words and a personal word.

Word List

cafeteria	kimono	gondola	poncho
anchor	catamaran	pueblo	kayak
suede	bungalow	admiral	estate
gingham	yacht	sequin	indigo
mattress	pajamas	bureau	khaki

Personal Words 1.___ 2.___

EXPLORING LANGUAGE: ANALOGIES Remember that an **analogy** shows how two pairs of words are related. In the analogy **admiral : ship :: teacher : classroom,** the first word is a worker and the second is a workplace. The analogy is read, "admiral is to ship as teacher is to classroom." Some other types of analogies, besides *Worker and Workplace,* are *Synonym*—**humorous : funny :: present : gift**—and *Antonym*—**lost : found :: right : wrong.**

Label each analogy as *Worker and Workplace, Synonym,* or *Antonym.*

1. fierce : ferocious :: fragile : delicate
2. teller : bank :: actor : theater
3. whisper : shout :: oppose : agree
4. brave : cowardly :: heavy : light
5. newscaster : TV studio :: waiter : restaurant

Now that you know some types of analogies, use these words to complete the analogies below: *courageous, cafeteria, laboratory, interesting, inevitable.*

6. university : college :: lunchroom : ____
7. casual : formal :: boring : ____
8. examine : study :: brave : ____
9. sorrow : happiness :: avoidable : ____
10. nurse : hospital :: chemist : ____

ENRICHMENT Pick one.

Who Works Here?
Think of a worker who works at each of these places: *post office, beach, the White House, kitchen, library, department store.* Then write analogies using the workers and workplaces. For an extra challenge, think of some more worker and workplace analogies on your own.

Alike, Only Better!
Wet and *drenched* have similar meanings, but drenched means more wet than wet, just as freezing is more cold than cold. These are synonyms, but one is more intense than the other. Write five analogies like this: **cold : freezing :: wet : ____.** Have your partner complete your analogies.

CHALLENGE!
Some other kinds of analogies are *Manner*—**mumble : speak :: strut : walk** and *Cause and Effect*—**rain : flood :: tension : headache.** Try your hand at writing these kinds of analogies. Prepare an analogy challenge for your classmates and have them complete your analogies.

Review

Look back at the word lists in Lessons 31–35 and think about how you are doing in spelling.

1. The hardest words for me to spell were ____ ____ ____

2. You learned that it helps to divide long words that are hard to spell into syllables. Did you use this strategy?
   Yes   No   Sometimes

3. I try to use words that I am learning in my writing.
   Yes   No   Sometimes

4. I think that I am getting to be a better speller.
   Yes   No   Sometimes

5. The most interesting word that I have learned to spell is ____.

■ PROOFREADING

Find the spelling errors in each passage and write the words correctly. All passages have seven errors except the last one, which has eight.

PROOFREAD A NOTICE

As a result of a proposul by parent organizations, begining next week the cafateria will pubulish the daily lunch menus in the local paper. This will not only fasilitate meal planning for parents but will assure the comunity that students can take advantig of nutritious choices and that tax money is being well-spent.

PROOFREAD A QUESTIONNAIRE

As you may know, the television series *Billy and Pete* has generated some controvoursy. Please take the time to register your opinions about the show.

1. Have you seen an advetisement for the show?
   Yes   No

2. Have you seen the show?   Yes   No

3. Please circle the words that most nearly describe your reaction to the show.
   overated   offensive   pretty good
   provokative   extrordinary

4. If you have not seen the show, do you plan to watch it eventualy?   Yes   No

5. Circle the phrase that most nearly describes your reason for watching television.
   as a divirsion   for education
   for companionship   for current events

PROOFREAD A COMPLAINT

Last week I received a suade vest, a ponsho, and an air matress that I ordered from your catalog. There was substancial damage to the vest when I pulled off an adhesiv sticker that was evidently put there by the manufacturer. Since you guarantee satisifaction on all items, I am hoping to persuaide you to send me a new vest.

PROOFREAD A TELEPHONE MESSAGE

Ben,

The veternarian called to say that Bubbles has a respitory infection. He is going to perscribe some medicine, and you can pick up the perscription when you pick up Bubbles. He says that basicly Bubbles is fine but very suseptible to infection. He did remark that Bubbles seems to be quite an extravert despite her illness.

Shana

PROOFREAD A MOVIE REVIEW

Dr. Danger

The flick of the week is *Dr. Danger* starring Vincent Morello as the doctor and Dawn Blythe as his assistant. Dr. Danger lives on an imposeing astate next to a posh yaught club, but they won't let him join because he's too weird. I guess they think a guy who wears a kamono when he paddles his kiyak doesn't fit in. What they don't realize is that Dr. Danger is pretty good at making things disinegrate. His assistant tries to complecate what plot there is with no success. Send this one out to sea.

PROOFREAD A SOCIAL STUDIES REPORT

In 1847 Frederick Douglass started a publucation, *The North Star,* in Rochester, New York. The newspaper was influencial in helping to abolsh slavery and segregation. In adition, Douglass strongly supported women's rights and strongly opposed consumtion of alchol. In his later life, he made the aquaintance of President Lincoln and served as ambassador to Haiti.

PROOFREAD A NARRATIVE PARAGRAPH

The Day the Squirrel Got In

Last week when Dad went to take our family's clean cloths out of the dryer, he heard an abnorml noise. He thought somthing pecuilar was in there, but what? When he opened the dryer, the pagamas seemed to be moving all by themselves! Suddenly, out popped a squirrel trailing a pair of kakhi pants and some underwear. Dad opened the back door, but the squirrel refused to coroperate. Instead, he ran around the laundry room one way while Dad ran around the other. To conclud, we had to call the animal control truck, and two men managed to capture one very scared animal. I mean the squirrel, not Dad.

Cross-Curricular Lessons

- WORDS FROM SOCIAL STUDIES
- WORDS FROM HEALTH
- WORDS FROM SCIENCE
- WORDS FROM READING
- WORDS FROM MATHEMATICS
- WORDS FOR WORK AND PLAY

Cross-Curricular Lessons

import
naval
grievances
protest
Boston Massacre
redcoats
surrenders
minutemen
proclaims
Declaration of
 Independence

The American Revolution

The American Revolution transformed thirteen British colonies into
a new, independent nation. The list words tell about this event,
one of the most important in world history. Add two words of your
own to the list. Then do the activity. Use your Spelling Dictionary
if you need help.

■ GETTING AT MEANING

Time Line Complete the time line with list words.

1770

1767

The British
Parliament passes
the Townshend
Acts, calling for
(1) taxes on
certain goods
coming into the
American colonies
from Britain.

As a result of
mounting tensions,
British soldiers panic
and fire on a mob of
angry colonists, killing
several of them, in an
event that becomes
known as the (2).

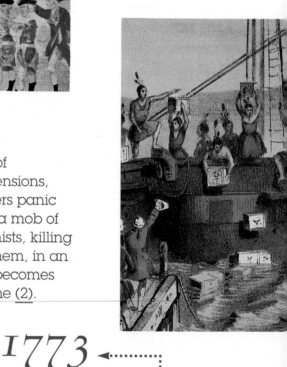

1773

To (3) against the
hated tea tax,
colonists disguised
as Indians dump
crates of British tea
into Boston Harbor.

| 1767 | 1768 | 1769 | 1770 | 1771 | 1772 | 1773 | 1774 |

1775

Colonial citizen-soldiers, known as (4) because of their readiness to fight at a moment's notice, fight British troops, known as (5) because of their bright uniforms, at Lexington and Concord.

1776

The (6) is issued. This defiant document lists the colonists' (7) against Britain's King George III and (8) the united colonies free and independent of British rule.

John Hancock

Choose Sides

Imagine you live in colonial America. Pair up with a partner and choose sides, American and British. If you chose the American side, write some reasons why you should revolt. If you chose the British side, write some reasons why you should remain loyal to Britain. Use your notes as you and your partner discuss the issues, trying to convince each other that your position is the correct one.

1781

A cornered British army (10) to the Americans at Yorktown, ending the Revolutionary War.

1779

American Captain John Paul Jones defeats the British warship *Serapis* in an important (9) battle off the coast of England. Badly damaged, Jones's own ship sinks two days later.

| 1775 | 1776 | 1777 | 1778 | 1779 | 1780 | 1781 |

The Lewis and Clark Expedition

Columbia River
Thomas Jefferson
claim
co-leaders
journals
settlement
Canadian
keelboat
Louisiana
 Purchase
observations

Where did Lewis and Clark explore? What did they find?
The list words tell about their famous expedition. Add two words
of your own. Then do the activity. Use your Spelling Dictionary
if you need help.

■ GETTING AT MEANING

Using a Map Use the map and the pictures to help complete the
sentences with list words.

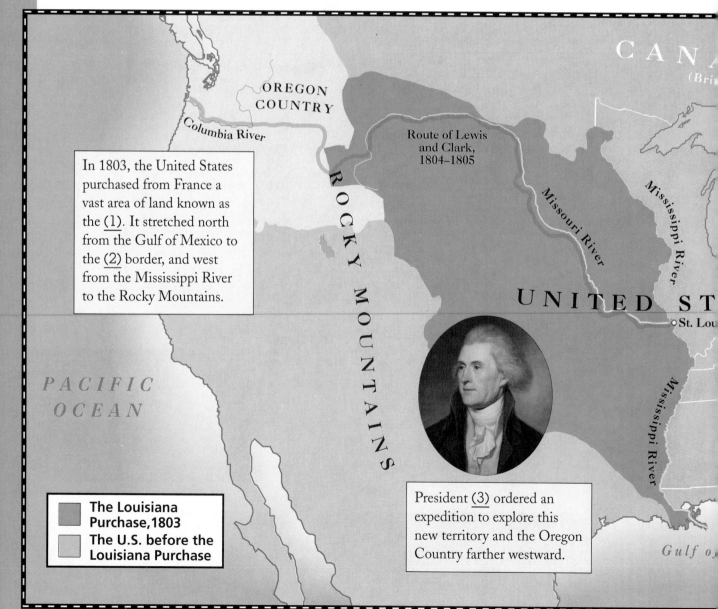

OREGON COUNTRY

Columbia River

Route of Lewis
and Clark,
1804–1805

Missouri River

Mississippi River

CANA
(Bri

UNITED ST
○St. Lou

Mississippi River

PACIFIC
OCEAN

In 1803, the United States
purchased from France a
vast area of land known as
the (1). It stretched north
from the Gulf of Mexico to
the (2) border, and west
from the Mississippi River
to the Rocky Mountains.

■ The Louisiana
  Purchase, 1803
□ The U.S. before the
  Louisiana Purchase

President (3) ordered an
expedition to explore this
new territory and the Oregon
Country farther westward.

Gulf o

Meriwether Lewis and William Clark became the expedition's (4).

In May of 1804, the expedition of about forty-five people set out across the Mississippi from St. Louis in two dugout canoes and a flat-bottomed craft called a (5).

In November of 1805, they reached their westward journey's end at the mouth of the (6). Their return trip took six months.

Lewis and Clark made careful (7) of the plants, animals, people, land, and climate along the way, which they recorded in writing in their (8).

This information helped the United States successfully (9) the Oregon Country and played a large part in the eventual (10) of the American West.

Lakes

S

ATLANTIC OCEAN

N
W — E
S

FOR SALE

Did You Know?

For the 827,987 square miles of the Louisiana Purchase, the U.S. government paid only **$15 million!**

(How much is that per square mile?)

The Indian Removal

homelands
Cherokee
settle
barriers
perish
enforcing
tyrant
invaders
removal
Trail of Tears

The list words all deal with President Andrew Jackson's order to remove the Cherokee Indians from their southeastern lands to an area west of the Mississippi River. Although many whites supported the order, others opposed it. Try adding more words to the list, and then do the activity. Use your Spelling Dictionary if you need help.

■ GETTING AT MEANING

For and Against Use the information in the passage to help you complete the speech balloons with list words.

By and large, white pioneers saw American Indians as **barriers** to their goals. The pioneers wanted to **settle** the Indians' lands and, in fact, thought they had the right to do so. The Indians, on the other hand, saw the pioneers as **invaders.** In 1830, President Andrew Jackson sided with the pioneers and ordered the **removal** of the entire **Cherokee** nation from their ancestral **homelands.** Of the fifteen thousand Cherokee forced to move, about one-fourth would **perish** from disease, starvation, and other hardships during the journey west, which came to be called the **"Trail of Tears."** By **enforcing** his decision to move the Indians, Jackson made some people see him as a **tyrant.**

Our (1) belong to us. The white pioneers are (2) in our territory.

DID YOU KNOW?

THE CHOCTAW, CHICKASAW, CREEK, AND SEMINOLE NATIONS ALSO WERE UPROOTED AND RELOCATED DURING JACKSON'S PRESIDENCY.

overseer
fugitive
Underground Railroad
states' rights
plantations
abolitionist
enslavement
emancipation
secessionist
cotton gin

Slavery

By 1861, disagreement about slavery had helped bring about the American Civil War between the North and the South. The list words tell about slavery and the controversy it caused. Add two more words about slavery to the list. Then do the activities. Use your Spelling Dictionary if you need it.

■ GETTING AT MEANING

Who Said It? For each statement, write the list word that tells who might have said it in the years before the Civil War. Use the definitions in the box for help.

abolitionist
▼
a person who wants to see an institution or custom done away with

fugitive
▼
a person fleeing from danger, an enemy, or justice

overseer
▼
a person who directs workers and their work

secessionist
▼
a person who favors seceding, or withdrawing, from an organization

1. *"Those slaves don't work nearly hard enough. Why, just yesterday, I had to beat one of them when he took too long getting a drink of water."*

2. *"Slavery is the great shame of our country. We must continue to speak against it, write against it, oppose it in every way possible."*

3. *"We left in the darkness—Mama, Papa, and me. For three days now, we've slept by day and run by night. At first, we could hear the master's dogs coming up behind us, but not anymore."*

4. *"No longer can we pretend that the national government has the interests of the southern states at heart. To preserve our rights, our very way of life, we have no choice but to pull away and form our own nation."*

What Is It? Write the list word that each fact describes.

5. Crops such as tobacco, cotton, and sugar cane were planted, tended, and harvested by slaves on these large farms in the South.

6. This mechanical engine, invented by Eli Whitney to separate seeds from fiber, helped make cotton "king" in the South and strengthened the institution of slavery.

7. When this happens, a person's freedom is taken away, and he or she becomes the property of someone else.

8. This secret network of routes and hiding places aided fugitive slaves on their way to freedom in northern states or in Canada.

9. Many southerners used this idea to support their position that individual states, rather than the national government, should have the right to decide whether to allow slavery or not.

10. When this happens, a person is set free from slavery or some other restraint. It comes from the Latin **ex-** (away), **manus** (hand), and **capere** (to take).

PUBLIC SALE!!

AS TRUSTEE FOR JAMES VANMETER, I WILL SELL, ALL OF THE property of James Vanmeter at his residence, known as the Wright place, on the Hornback Mill Road, on Friday the 11th day of September 1863.

CONSISTING OF

THREE SLAVES

Charles, Mary and her child, the man is about 24 years old, a good farm hand, the woman is an excellent cook and washer.

HORSES, MULES, CATTLE, SHEEP, HOGS

AND CROP, CORN IN THE FIELDS,

OATS, WHEAT, TOBACCO

Kitchen Furniture, &c., Farm Implements of every kind. Terms of Sale, a credit of 4 months will be given on all sums of $10, and over carrying interest from day of sale. The purchaser to execute Notes with good security.

JAS. H. O. BUSH, Trustee.

Winchester August 24th 1863.

Handbill (reduced size) of sale of livestock and other property

---

THE LIFE OF A SLAVE

What was slavery like from the slaves' point of view?
To find out, read *To Be a Slave* by Julius Lester (Dial, 1968),
***Now Is Your Time!* by Walter Dean Myers (HarperCollins, 1992),**
or another book that your librarian recommends. Then write about,
or discuss with some classmates, your reactions to the book.

wrangler
longhorn
trail drive
roundup
open range
barbed wire
chuck wagons
lariat
stampede
mustangs

Cowboys

The list words relate to cowboys, people who take care of cattle for ranch owners. The height of the cowboy era lasted from the mid-1860s to the mid-1880s. Add words that you know about cowboys to the list. Then do the activity, using your Spelling Dictionary if you need help.

■ GETTING AT MEANING

A Cowboy Photo Album Use list words to complete the captions for the photographs.

During the height of the cowboy era, most cattle were raised on unfenced grassland known as the (1). Each spring and fall, cowboys held a (2), in which they gathered up the animals, separated the cattle of different ranchers, and branded new calves with their owners' marks.

In a (3), cowboys drove their herds hundreds of miles to railroad stations to ship them to market. At times the cattle would become frightened and rush blindly ahead in a (4), trampling everything in their path.

This is a (7) cow, the kind most commonly raised during the height of the cowboy era. These cattle were hardy animals, well suited to life on the open range and the rigors of trail drives.

During roundups and trail drives, (5) carried the cowboys' food, utensils, and bedrolls. The crew on a trail drive included a (6), from the German word *wrangein*, who looked after the horses. Later, the term came to mean the same as "cowboy."

DID YOU KNOW?

It took strong, independent women to journey west during the 1800s. The few who did became the first cowgirls. Since they were doing the same work men were doing, the cowgirls dressed in the same clothing as the men (boots, Stetson hats, and pants) and worked right alongside them—rounding up, branding, and sending cattle to market.

Cowboys rode horses called (8), from the Spanish word *mestengo*—"untamed." This cowboy posed on his horse, with his most important tool: his (9). The name came from the Spanish words *la reata*, meaning "the rope."

This picture shows a ranch of the early 1900s, when the cowboy era was a thing of the past. To protect their crops from cattle, farmers had been fencing their land with (10) since its invention in the mid-1870s.

The Age of Expansion

empire
manifest destiny
foreign policy
cede
annex
imperialism
purchase
yellow
  journalism
treaty
overseas

During the 1800s, the United States expanded west across the continent and beyond. The list words relate to that expansion. Try to add more words to the list, and then do the activities. Use your Spelling Dictionary for help if you need it.

■ GETTING AT MEANING

Map Captions The map shows the westward growth of the United States in the mid- to late 1800s. Use list words to complete the map captions.

By the 1840s, many Americans believed that expansion across the continent was both destined and morally right. The name they gave to this belief was (1), and they set about achieving it.

Oregon
Country
1846

The United States gained the long-disputed Oregon Country by signing a (2) with Britain.

United States as of 1842

Mexican
Cession
1848

Mexico agreed to give up, or (3), a large part of its territory after its defeat in the Mexican War.

Gadsden
Purchase
1853

Texas
Annexation
1845

The Republic of Texas asked to join the United States. The United States agreed to (4) the area.

Pacific
Ocean

MEXICO

Great Lakes

Gulf of Mexico

The American minister to Mexico, James Gadsden, arranged for the United States to (5) a much smaller area for the sum of $10 million.

180

Letters to the Editor   In 1898, the people of Cuba (an island southeast of the United States) were in revolt against their Spanish rulers. When the U.S. battleship *Maine* sank near Cuba on February 15, many American newspapers called for war against Spain, and their readers responded. Use list words to complete the letters to the editor.

February 18, 1898

Dear Sir:
My heart leapt at your stirring editorial on the sinking of the Maine by the Spanish. This incident proves that we Americans must look (6), beyond our shores, to expand our territory and defend ourselves against attack. Furthermore, the Cubans despise being part of the Spanish (7) and need our support in their struggle for freedom. War is indeed unpleasant, but war it must be.

Washington Gazette

U.S. BATTLESHIP MAINE
SINKS NEAR CUBA

PRESIDENT McK

$50.00
REWA

February 18, 1898

Dear Sir:
I was horrified by your newspaper's response to the sinking of the Maine. Your unproven accusation that it was an act of sabotage by Spain is yet another example of American journalists resorting to the outrageous tactics of (8). We must remember that they are citizens of a foreign country. We must not follow a (9) of interference in their affairs. I know there are those, like you, who believe in the kingly practices of expansionism and (10)—who secretly wish to replace the Spanish empire with an American one. But the very idea violates all that our nation stands for!

MAPPING THE AMERICAN EMPIRE

BEGINNING IN THE MID-1800S, THE UNITED STATES ACQUIRED VARIOUS POSSESSIONS OVERSEAS. WORK WITH SOME CLASSMATES TO FIND OUT WHEN AND HOW THE UNITED STATES ACQUIRED THOSE POSSESSIONS. THEN MAKE OR OBTAIN A LARGE WORLD MAP AND ATTACH IT TO A BULLETIN BOARD. WRITE A LABEL FOR EACH POSSESSION, BASED ON WHAT YOU HAVE LEARNED.

181

The Roaring Twenties

flappers
Jazz Age
Harlem
speakeasies
Prohibition
skyscrapers
racketeers
Art Deco
Charleston
bootleggers

After World War I ended in 1918, Americans wanted to relax, have fun, and enjoy their prosperity. The list words relate to the 1920s, an era that came to be called the Roaring Twenties. If you can, add more words about the 1920s to the list. Then do the activity, using your Spelling Dictionary if you need it.

■ GETTING AT MEANING

What's in a Name? The Roaring Twenties got that nickname because they were noisy, energetic, daring years. Use the pictures and captions to help you write the list word that each sentence describes.

During the Roaring Twenties, flappers shocked their elders by rolling down their stockings, raising their hemlines, cutting their hair short, and dancing wild new dances like the Charleston.

1 These outlaws got their name from pickpockets in England who started noisy disturbances to distract their victims.

2 This lively dance of the 1920s, in which the knees twisted in and the heels swung out with every step, takes its name from a city in South Carolina named after an English king.

3 This era of American history, which included the 1920s, takes its name from a word meaning "to forbid."

4 These places were named for the quiet way that customers asked to be let in, so as not to attract attention from neighbors or police officers.

The Twenties was part of the Prohibition era when the manufacture and sale of alcoholic beverages were forbidden by law. To get around this law, bars and clubs known as speakeasies sold illegal liquor supplied by bootleggers. Gangsters and racketeers fought for control of these illegal enterprises.

Jazz originated among black musicians in the South and spread to northern cities. One major center of jazz was Harlem, an African American community in New York City.

5 This center of African American music, literature, and art in New York City was named for the Dutch city of Haarlem.

 6 These women were nicknamed for one of their unusual items of clothing: galoshes worn with the buckles unfastened so they flopped back and forth.

 7 The name of this distinctive style of design came from the *Exposition Internationale des Arts Décoratifs et Industriels Modernes,* an exposition of decorative and industrial arts held in Paris, France, in 1925.

 8 The name for these people, who found all sorts of unusual ways to transport illegal liquor, comes from the early American practice of smuggling bottles inside one's footwear.

9 These buildings, which became increasingly popular in the 1920s, got their name from the topmost sail of clipper ships.

 10 This other nickname for the Roaring Twenties grew out of the popularity of a new kind of music that developed from African American spirituals.

In the 1920s the value of urban land skyrocketed. To save land and money, architects designed skyscrapers. Some, such as New York's Chrysler Building, reflected Art Deco, a new style of design that relied on streamlined forms and geometric shapes.

NAME YOUR DECADE

Think about the decade that you live in. What nickname would you give it, and why? Write a paragraph or create a poster that explains and supports the nickname you have chosen.

7

6

5

4

3

2

1

0

0

World War II

neutrality
aggression
dictators
Allies
liberation
isolationists
Axis
concentration
 camps
victory
invades

World War II began on September 1, 1939, when Germany invaded Poland. The war ended when Japan formally surrendered on September 2, 1945. The list words relate to the war and the events that led to it. Add words of your own. Use your Spelling Dictionary if you need help with the activity.

■ GETTING AT MEANING

Newspaper Headlines Use the context clues in the news stories to complete the headlines with list words. (Don't forget to capitalize the words as needed.)

World War II Issue

This is the Enemy

(1) Now Rule Germany, Italy, Soviet Union

August 3, 1934 Adolf Hitler has seized complete control of the German government. With this move, Hitler joins the ranks of rulers with total authority over their nations, including Benito Mussolini of Italy and Joseph Stalin of the Soviet Union.

U.S. Continues Policy of (2)! (3) Are Pleased

August 31, 1935 Congress has voted to ban weapons sales to nations at war in order to avoid involvement in foreign wars. One supporter of the ban stated, "What happens in Europe is the concern of Europeans, not Americans."

GERMANY (4) POLAND!
British, French Response to Act of (5) Expected

September 1, 1939 Yesterday, German forces swarmed into Poland without warning and without provocation. Pledged to defend Poland, Britain and France are expected to respond to the attack by declaring war on Germany.

WAR★CHRONICLES

World War II Issue

U.S. Joins (6) in War Against (7)

December 12, 1941 Following Congress's declaration of war on Japan, Germany and Italy yesterday declared war on the United States. Mussolini once stated that the line between Berlin and Rome would be the axis on which the world would turn. That line now extends to Tokyo. The United States now joins Britain, the Soviet Union, and other nations allied against Japan, Germany, and Italy.

Soldiers Discover Nazis' Victims in (9)

April 30, 1945 With the war in Europe all but over, American and British soldiers moving across Germany have discovered camp after camp with half-dead prisoners waiting for release. It is becoming clear that the Nazis system-atically imprisoned, tortured, starved, and mur-dered millions of civilians, including Jews, Poles, and Russians.

LIFE ON THE HOME FRONT

Once committed, the American people supported the war effort wholeheartedly. Interview a family member, neighbor, or someone else who was alive during World War II. Ask what the person remembers about such things as "Rosie the Riveter," rationing, war bonds, and scrap drives. Share what you learn with your classmates.

Allies Complete (8) of France

August 27, 1944 One month after breaking through German lines and driving the Germans back across the French countryside, Allied troops rode triumphantly through Paris yester-day. After four years of occupation by Germany, a joyful France and its capital have been freed from Nazi rule.

War Ends in (10) for Allies

September 3, 1945 Yesterday, the war ended as Japan for-mally surrendered to the Allies, approximately four months after Germany's surrender. The final blows to Japan were struck on August 6 and 9, when American planes dropped atomic bombs on the cities of Hiroshima and Nagasaki.

Gaining Civil Rights

minority groups
nonviolence
demonstrations
civil disobedience
segregation
affirmative action
boycott
desegregation
franchise
discrimination

Civil rights are the rights that a citizen has, such as the right to fair and equal treatment. In the United States, African Americans and certain other groups have had to struggle to gain their civil rights. The list words relate to that struggle. Try adding other words to the list. Then do the activity. Use your Spelling Dictionary if you need help.

■ GETTING AT MEANING

Using a Time Line Use the time line to help you answer the questions with list words.

1. A nineteenth-century Supreme Court ruling upheld the idea of "separate but equal." What is separation of one racial group from another called?

2. Black people refused to ride the buses in Montgomery, Alabama, to protest segregation. What is this protest method?

3. Martin Luther King, Jr., urged black people to protest unjust civil laws by refusing to obey them. What is this protest method?

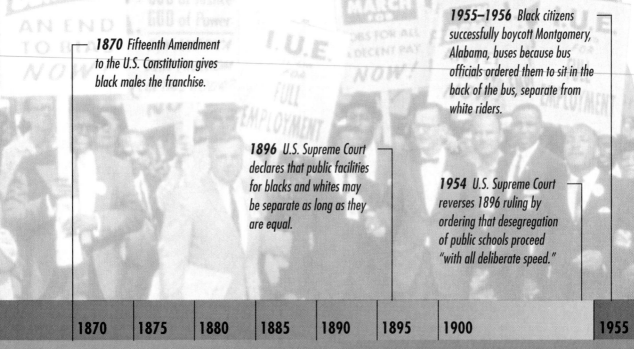

1870 Fifteenth Amendment to the U.S. Constitution gives black males the franchise.

1896 U.S. Supreme Court declares that public facilities for blacks and whites may be separate as long as they are equal.

1955–1956 Black citizens successfully boycott Montgomery, Alabama, buses because bus officials ordered them to sit in the back of the bus, separate from white riders.

1954 U.S. Supreme Court reverses 1896 ruling by ordering that desegregation of public schools proceed "with all deliberate speed."

| 1870 | 1875 | 1880 | 1885 | 1890 | 1895 | 1900 | 1955 |

4. The Fifteenth Amendment gave black males the right to vote. What is another word for "right to vote"?

5. The Civil Rights Act of 1964 stated that businesses must serve all people without regard to race. What is the act of refusing to serve someone because of race?

6. African Americans and other people who differ from the majority of the population in terms of race, religion, or national origin are members of what kinds of groups?

7. When the Supreme Court ordered public schools to stop separating racial groups in 1954, what was it calling for?

8. Martin Luther King, Jr., and his Southern Christian Leadership Conference believed in using only peaceful methods to achieve racial equality. What word describes these methods?

9. Special job training for minority workers is an example of what kind of program?

10. In giving its award to Martin Luther King, Jr., in 1964, the Nobel Peace Prize committee cited the peaceful marches he had led to protest racial injustice. What is another name for protest marches, rallies, and similar gatherings?

1957 SCLC is formed by Martin Luther King, Jr., who urges people to commit acts of civil disobedience to protest racial injustice.

1964 Martin Luther King, Jr., wins Nobel Peace Prize for leading peaceful civil rights demonstrations. Civil Rights Act barring discrimination in public places and by employers becomes law.

1970s To compensate for past discrimination, affirmative action programs set goals for hiring and educating members of minority groups.

1960

1965

1970

Physical Fitness

balance
energetic
oxygen
injure
extending
elastic
bounces
strenuous
discipline
muscular
  strength

Dance is one road to physical fitness. What other words come to mind when you think of dance as a form of exercise? Add two words to the list. Use your Spelling Dictionary if you need help with the activity.

■ GETTING AT MEANING

Dance and Fitness Use context clues and your own knowledge to fill in the blanks with list words.

WELCOME TO THE DANCE

These dancers are serious about their work. They eat right and practice every day. This kind of life takes a great deal of (1), but they're up to the task. They begin with breathing exercises to help them use (2) efficiently and not run short of breath.

Next, they do exercises to stretch their muscles and build up their (3). If they didn't stretch, they could easily (4) themselves while dancing.

One dancer bends and stretches as she holds on to her partner. Her body is so flexible, you'd think it was made of (5)!

Another dancer (6) all around on springy legs.

Some dancers have so much energy they seem ready to burst. In fact, they're so (7) that it almost makes you tired just watching them!

One dancer practices (8) his arms and lifting his partner overhead.

Another dancer holds steady on one foot for minutes at a time to improve his (9).

Dancing is hard work! After a (10) day's workout, the classes cool down and then relax for a while.

STUDIO

READY, SET, DANCE

Alone or with a partner, choose a favorite piece of music and create a new dance. As you make up your dance, think about how its different parts or steps benefit you. Do they help your endurance? balance? agility? strength? If you play a sport, how will this exercise help you play it better?

Personal Care

farsighted
iris
calculus
caries
melanin
plaque
mole
sebaceous
 glands
sebum
wart

The words in the list are all about personal health care.
Add more words to the list. Then do the activities. Use your
Spelling Dictionary if you need help.

■ GETTING AT MEANING

Word Origins Use the word origins to help you fill in the blanks
with list words.

Our bodies have ways of protecting themselves. An oil in the
skin, called (1), helps keep our skin from drying out. This oil is
secreted by the (2).

From the Greek word meaning "black" comes (3), the coloring
agent in our skin that helps protect us against the sun's
harmful rays.

Things can go wrong with our bodies too. We can get a (4) on our
skin. But don't be fooled by that old superstition. This is caused by
a virus, not by touching a toad!

When the inside of a tooth decays, (5) can form, leaving
a cavity.

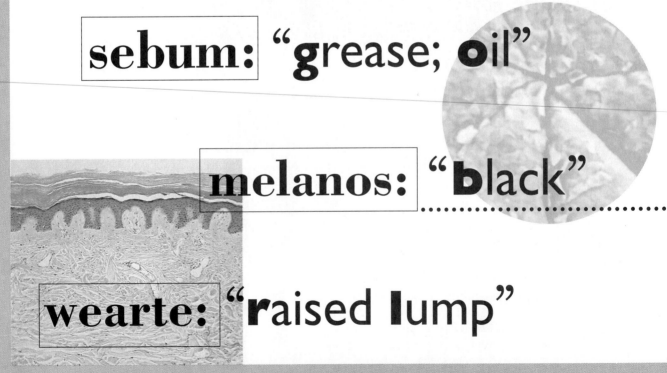

sebum: "grease; oil"

melanos: "black"

wearte: "raised lump"

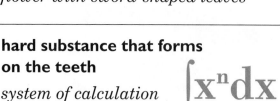

Multiple Meanings Write the list word that each pair of phrases describes.

6 **part of the eye that controls the amount of light coming in**
flower with sword-shaped leaves

7 **hard substance that forms on the teeth**
system of calculation $\int x^n dx$

8 **dark spot or lump on the skin**
small furry animal that lives underground

9 **thin film on the surface of the teeth**
award for extraordinary achievement

10 **eye disorder in which you see distant things more clearly than things that are near**
thinking ahead and planning wisely

caries: "decay"

breathing
prevent
shock
artificial
  respiration
smoke detectors
pedestrians
reflective
emergency
helmet
fire extinguisher

First Aid and Safety

What would you do in an emergency situation? Add two words about first aid or safety to the list. Then complete the activities. Use your Spelling Dictionary if you need help.

■ GETTING AT MEANING

First-Aid Tips Use list words to complete this passage from a first-aid manual.

Resuscitation

A medical (1) calls for clear thinking and quick action. First, check the victim's (2), since a lack of oxygen can cause serious harm. If necessary, use mouth-to-mouth resuscitation—a method of (3)—to force air into the victim's lungs. Keep the victim warm and in a stable, comfortable position until help arrives. This is to keep the victim from going into (4).

FIRST AID

Home Safety Tips Complete these safety tips with words from the list.

SAFETY FIRST *Find out*

what kinds of protective clothing and accessories people should wear during certain jobs, sports, or activities. (Your local sporting goods store might be able to help.) Share what you learned in a demonstration speech or in a booklet of safety tips.

SAFETY TIPS

Fire Safety

Be prepared to (5) fires from causing serious damage in your home. Keep a (6) in your kitchen in case of a cooking fire. Since breathing smoke from a fire can cause serious injury or death, install (7) in your home.

Outdoor Safety Tips Complete these safety tips with words from the list.

Be safe outdoors too, whether you're walking or riding. Bike riders and (8) should obey all traffic lights and signals. Protect your head from serious injury by wearing a (9) when you ride. At night, put (10) tape on your clothing and bicycle to let drivers know where you are.

Physicians

radiologist
dermatologist
podiatrist
cardiologist
orthopedist
pediatrician
surgeon
neurologist
obstetrician
ophthalmologist

All of the list words name different kinds of physicians. Can you think of two more? Add them to the list and then do the activities. Use your Spelling Dictionary if you need help.

■ GETTING AT MEANING

What Am I? Use a list word to describe each kind of physician.

1. My name comes from the Greek word **kardia,** meaning "heart." I specialize in taking care of the heart and blood vessels. What am I?

2. I deal with the structure, functions, and diseases of people's eyes. My name comes from the Greek word **ophthalmos,** meaning "eye." What am I?

3. My name comes from the Greek words **paidos,** meaning "child," and **iatros,** meaning "physician." I take care of babies and children. What am I?

4. I study X rays in order to diagnose and treat medical problems. My name comes from the Latin word **radius,** meaning "ray." What am I?

5. I treat people's skin problems. My name comes from the Greek word **dermatos,** meaning "skin." What am I?

194

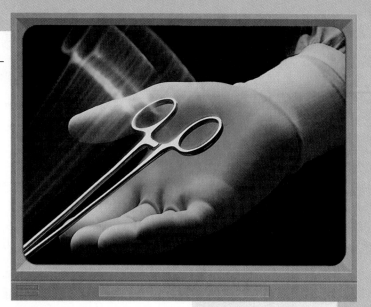

6. My name comes from the Old French word **cirurgien,** meaning "hand work." I perform operations, or surgeries. What am I?

7. My name comes from the Latin word **obstetrica,** meaning "midwife." I treat pregnant women and deliver their babies. What am I?

8. I try to correct the deformities and diseases of bones and joints, especially in children. My name comes from the Greek words **ortho,** meaning "straight"; "correct" and **paidos,** meaning "child." What am I?

9. When people have problems with their feet, they come to. see me. My name comes from the Greek word **podos,** meaning "foot." What am I?

A MEDICAL PLOT

Imagine that you're a writer for a TV series that takes place in a hospital. Write a plot outline for a half-hour fictional drama. Tell who, what, where, why, and when. Center your plot on a medical crisis that's resolved by people who work at the hospital—doctors, nurses, etc. You may need to do some medical research for your plot.

DID YOU KNOW?

Wilhelm Roentgen discovered the X ray in 1895. Within a few months doctors were using this original imaging device to look at broken bones, and they still use Roentgen's X rays today.

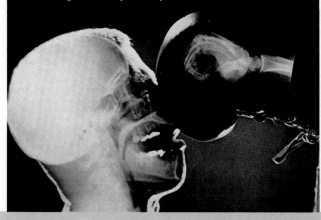

10. I treat diseases of the nervous system. My name comes from the Greek word **neuron,** meaning "nerve." What am I?

DIRECTOR

rolling friction
sliding friction
static friction
relative motion
distance
speed
velocity
acceleration
momentum
force

Force and Motion

Every day, people and things move around you. All motion is caused by force, but not all forces cause motion. Add two force and motion words to the list. Use your Spelling Dictionary if you need help with the activities.

■ GETTING AT MEANING

Which Kind of Friction? Use the drawing to help you decide which kind of friction each item describes.

(1) It occurs as the bowler approaches the foul line and slides his shoes across the floorboards. Rubbing your hands together produces the same kind of friction.

(2) It occurs as the ball rolls along the alley after the bowler has released it. A wheel rolling along a road produces the same kind of friction.

(3) It occurs where the bottom of each pin touches the alley. This kind of friction holds the pins in place, keeps them still, until the ball hits them.

Context Clues
Use the drawing
and the definitions
to help you complete
each fact with one
of the list words
defined at
the right.

4 As the bowler throws the ball, he uses ___ to propel it down the alley.

5 The fact that the ball is moving at 46 miles per hour is a measure of its ___.

6 The fact that the ball is moving at 46 miles per hour due north is a measure of its ___.

7 The measure of how fast the ball's speed and direction are changing is called ___.

8 The measure of how far the ball travels down the alley is called ___.

9 The change in position of the moving ball in relation to the pins is called ___.

10 How heavy the ball is plus how fast and in what direction it travels is a measure of its ___.

relative motion
↓
change in position of a moving object in relation to an object that is not moving

distance
↓
space between two points

speed
↓
distance/time

velocity
↓
speed + direction

momentum
↓
mass + velocity

acceleration
↓
how fast an object's velocity is changing

force
↓
any action that accelerates an object

TWIST AND SHOUT

Sit in a chair that rotates. Hold a heavy object in each hand, with your arms outstretched. Have someone rotate you slowly and then let you go and move away. Quickly pull the objects inward. What happens? Compare this with what happens when a figure skater makes similar movements.

The Atom

atom
electron
proton
neutron
nucleus
atomic number
periodic table
radiation
Geiger counter
nuclear fission

The eyes that are reading these words are made up of atoms. So is the brain that is interpreting what the eyes see. In fact, most everything you can think of is made up of atoms. Add two more words about atoms to the list. Then do the activities.

▉ GETTING AT MEANING

Interpreting a Diagram Use the paragraph to help you label the diagram with list words.

An **atom** is the smallest bit of an element that has all the characteristics of that element. At the atom's core is the **nucleus.** This nucleus is usually made up of **protons,** which are positively charged, and **neutrons,** which have no charge. Outside of the nucleus are negatively charged particles called **electrons.**

DIAGRAM OF AN **1** ___

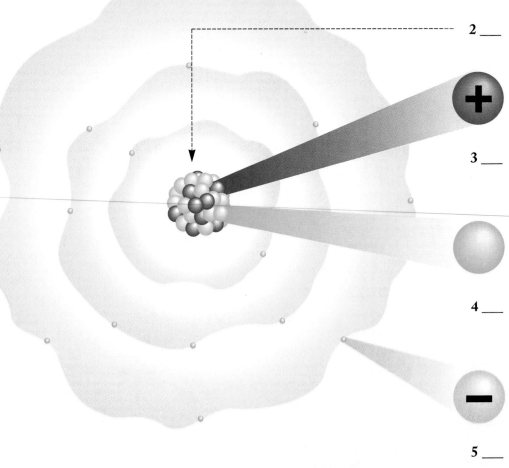

2 ___

3 ___

4 ___

5 ___

Inventors and Their Inventions Read each sentence carefully.
Complete it with the correct word or phrase from the box below.

atomic number   Geiger counter   nuclear fission
radiation   periodic table

6. In 1895 an X ray, a kind of ___ that could penetrate the human body, was discovered.

7. In 1912, Hans Geiger invented the first instrument to detect radioactivity. It was called the ___.

8. In 1939, scientists discovered that certain heavy nuclei split into lighter nuclei when they absorb certain neutrons. They called this process ___.

9. Russian chemist Dmitri Mendeleev helped develop a systematic arrangement of known chemical elements in the form of a table, which is called the ___ of the elements.

10. In this arrangement, each element is placed according to its ___, from low to high.

ПЕРИОДИЧЕСКАЯ СИ СТЕМА ЭЛЕМЕН

24
Cr
Chromium
51.996

These radioactive elements were named for certain people, places, or things. Find out how some of these elements got their names and report your findings on a table or chart.

43 Technetium	86 Radon	90 Thorium	94 Plutonium	98 Californium
61 Promethium	87 Francium	91 Protactinium	95 Americium	99 Einsteinium
84 Polonium	88 Radium	92 Uranium	96 Curium	100 Fermium
85 Astatine	89 Actinium	93 Neptunium	97 Berkelium	101 Mendelevium

Compounds and Mixtures

compound
mixture
chemical
  formula
suspension
emulsifier
solution
solvent
solute
diluted
concentrated

The air you breathe, the food you eat, even your own body—they're all made of compounds and mixtures. Try adding two more words about compounds and mixtures to the list. Then do the activity.

■ GETTING AT MEANING

Cause and Effect Use the definitions above each cause and effect statement to complete it with list words.

mixture   two or more substances that are mixed together but not chemically combined

compound   substance formed when two or more elements are chemically combined

chemical formula   a shorthand way of showing which elements, and how many atoms of each, make up a chemical compound

compound

chemical formula

NaCl

C A U S E When one atom of sodium and one atom of chlorine chemically combine,   **E F F E C T** a molecule of the (1) known as salt forms. Salt has the (2) NaCl.

C A U S E When onion, garlic, oregano, and tomato sauce are put together,   **E F F E C T** a (3) known as spaghetti sauce results.

mixture

200

suspension

suspension mixture in which the particles of one substance are scattered in another without dissolving

emulsifier a substance that keeps the particles of one liquid mixed into another liquid

solution mixture in which one substance dissolves in another

emulsifier

MAYONNAISE

solution

CAUSE	EFFECT
When sugar is dissolved in a mixture of water and lemon juice,	the (4) known as lemonade results.
When drops of oil are scattered in vinegar but not dissolved,	a (5) that is used on salads results.
When egg yolk is added to vinegar and oil,	the vinegar and oil are kept from separating. The yolk acts as an (6), and mayonnaise is formed.

solvent substance that dissolves other substances

solute the substance being dissolved

diluted weakened or thinned by the addition of liquid

concentrated made stronger by the addition of a solute

concentrated

GRAPE JUICE

diluted

CAUSE	EFFECT
When extra sugar is added to grape juice,	the grape juice becomes more (7).
When extra water is added to grape juice,	the grape juice becomes (8). Since the water dissolves the sugar, the water acts as a (9), while the sugar is a (10).

solvent

solute

SUGAR

TRY THIS EXPERIMENT

Which is a better solvent, cold water or hot? Prepare two clear glasses, one half-full of cold tap water, the other half-full of hot tap water. Stir a teaspoonful of salt into each glass. Does the salt dissolve more quickly in one glass than the other? What can you conclude about hot water versus cold water as a solvent?

contract
temperature
solar collectors
expand
transferred
thermometer
ventilate
insulation
thermostat
heat sources

Heat and Temperature

"It sure is a hot one today!" "Won't it ever cool off?" You hear comments like these every summer, but heat is around you all the time—summer and winter, indoors and out. Add heat words to the list. Use your Spelling Dictionary if you need help with the activity.

■ GETTING AT MEANING

Picture Clues Use the pictures to help you fill in the blanks with list words.

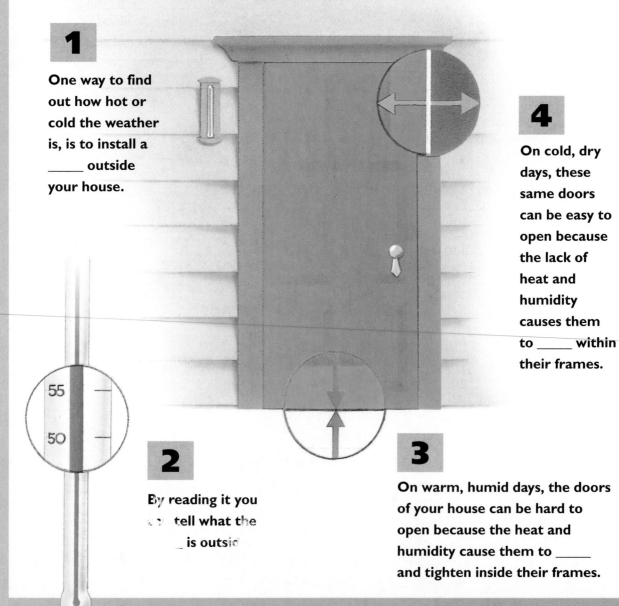

1

One way to find out how hot or cold the weather is, is to install a _____ outside your house.

4

On cold, dry days, these same doors can be easy to open because the lack of heat and humidity causes them to _____ within their frames.

2

By reading it you can tell what the _____ is outside.

3

On warm, humid days, the doors of your house can be hard to open because the heat and humidity cause them to _____ and tighten inside their frames.

202

10 To heat their homes, people also use _____, which gather and store energy from the sun.

5 To help keep their houses cool in summer and warm in winter, people install _____ inside walls and floors.

9 In mild weather, people leave their windows open to _____ their houses with a steady supply of fresh air.

6 Heat is _____ from the furnace to the rooms above by means of convection.

7 In cold weather, people use furnaces, fireplaces, and wood-burning stoves as _____ to warm their houses.

8 The furnace can be controlled by setting the _____.

white light
intensity
luminous
visible spectrum
prism
shadow
opaque
reflects
transparent
translucent

Light

The list words are all about light: what it's made of and what it does. Add two more words about light to the list. Then do the activities.

■ GETTING AT MEANING

Light Facts Write the list words from the passage below that facts 1–4 tell about.

Something that gives off its own light is **luminous.**
Intensity is the strength of light falling on an area.
When something turns back light, it **reflects** it.
When something blocks light, a **shadow** forms.

1 The moon does this to sunlight to make moonlight.

2 The farther you move from the source of light, the less of this there is.

3 To tell time from a sundial, you look at this.

4 The sun is. The moon isn't.

Diagram Write the list words from the caption below that numbers 5–7 refer to.

White light, such as sunlight, is a blend of visible colors. A **prism** spreads this blend into the separate colors of the **visible spectrum**—the small range of electromagnetic wavelengths that we can see.

Something that lets all light pass through it is **transparent.**

Something that lets some light pass through it is **translucent.**

Something that lets no light pass through it is **opaque.**

Categorizing Use the definitions of **transparent, translucent,** and **opaque** above to complete the sentences below.

8. Sandwich bags, window glass, clean air, and clear nail polish are all _____.

9. Aluminum foil, apples, your hand, and an elephant are all _____.

10. Waxed paper, fog, lime gelatin, sunglasses, and tissue paper are all _____.

DID YOU KNOW?
The human eye is incredibly sensitive to light! If you were to stand on a mountain on a very clear night, you would be able to see someone lighting a match almost fifty miles away?

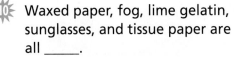

Electricity

electric current
batteries
voltage
generator
conductor
insulator
resistance
parallel circuits
series circuits
circuit breaker

Think about all the things that stop working during a power outage. We rely on electricity more than we usually realize. Add two more words to the list. Then do the activities. Use your Spelling Dictionary if you need help.

■ GETTING AT MEANING

The Basics of Electricity Use the drawings and information to help you complete the passages in purple.

Flip on a light switch. An **electric current** starts moving through copper wires in your wall. Metal is a good **conductor** of electricity. A plastic coating around the wires acts as an **insulator** to keep the electricity safely inside the wires.

Some appliances use power from electrical outlets. These outlets are connected to wires that eventually connect to a **generator** at a power plant that converts other kinds of energy into electricity. Anything that slows or stops the electric current acts as a **resistance.**

Turning on the light starts the flow of (1). The wire acts as a (2). The plastic (3) is a safety device.

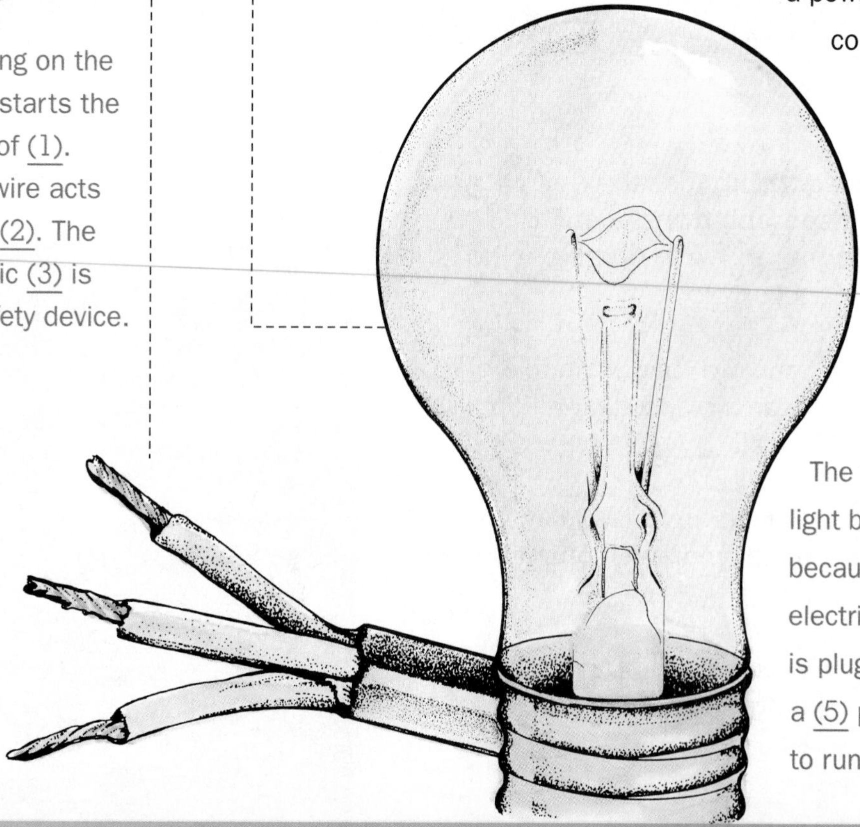

The thin wires in this light bulb glow brightly because of their (4) to electricity. When a lamp is plugged into an outlet, a (5) provides the power to run the light.

Houses are wired in **parallel circuits** instead of **series circuits** so that appliances and lights can be operated independently of each other. A **circuit breaker** automatically stops the electric current to an overloaded circuit.

Suppose the toaster burns out but the clock and TV keep running. Then this house is wired in (6). If too many appliances are running at once, a (7) will kick in to prevent a fire. If this house were wired in (8), then all the appliances and lights would have to be on at once or none of them would work.

Batteries turn chemical fuel into electrical energy. The energy a battery gives to the electric current is the **voltage.**

If this radio did not run on (9), you'd have to plug it in to run it. Its low-(10) battery uses very little energy.

MAKE A SIMPLE ELECTRIC CIRCUIT

You need a low-voltage dry cell battery, two insulated wires with ends stripped, and a light bulb in a socket. Connect the battery to the light with the two wires. When the circuit is complete, the bulb will light up.

chips
inputting
outputting
CPU
hardware
software
programs
floppy disk
keyboard
personal
  computer

Computers

Computers coordinate traffic lights, help people find books in libraries, and read the bar codes at supermarket checkout lines. Add other words about computers to the list. Then do the activities. Use your Spelling Dictionary for help.

▮ GETTING AT MEANING

Diagrams Use the diagram and information below to help you fill in the passages on the next page with list words.

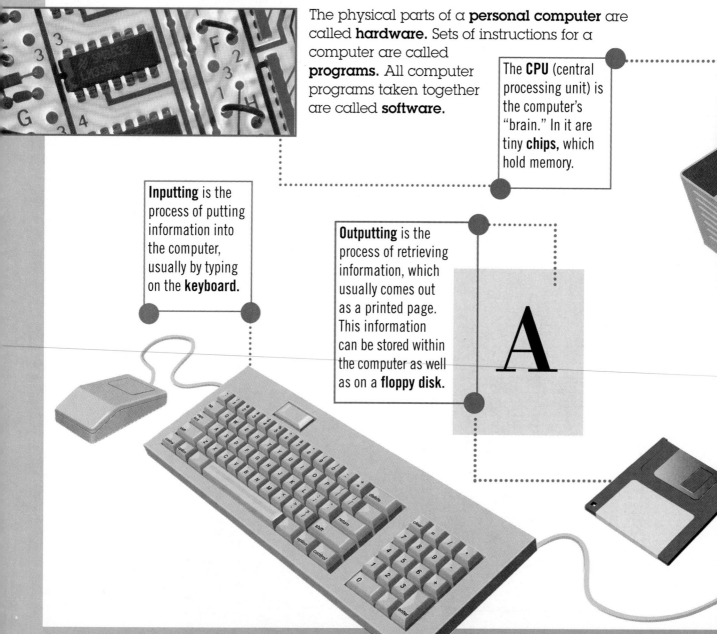

The physical parts of a **personal computer** are called **hardware.** Sets of instructions for a computer are called **programs.** All computer programs taken together are called **software.**

The **CPU** (central processing unit) is the computer's "brain." In it are tiny **chips,** which hold memory.

Inputting is the process of putting information into the computer, usually by typing on the **keyboard.**

Outputting is the process of retrieving information, which usually comes out as a printed page. This information can be stored within the computer as well as on a **floppy disk.**

Stan has twelve computer programs. Nine are games, two are writing programs, and one is a program for composing music. Together, these twelve programs make up Stan's (1) library.

Stan runs these programs on his (2), which consists of a monitor with a screen, a (3) for typing in information, and a Central Processing Unit called a (4), which Stan has nicknamed Brainiac. Stan has taken Brainiac apart to look at the (5) that hold its memory.

Stan works after school at a computer store. He sells both (6), such as monitors and mice, and software. His favorite software (7) are *Babe Ruth's Big League Baseball* and *The Marvelous Mathemagician.*

Stan has bought a new writing program for his computer. It comes on a single (8), which he slides into his computer's disk drive. Seconds later, it's ready to use. Stan begins (9) a story he must write for a composition class. Two hours later he begins (10) his story on his printer; then he settles back to read it.

DID YOU KNOW? One of the first computer programmers was Rear Admiral Grace Murray Hopper. One day in the 1940s, she found a moth caught in the wires of a computer that had stopped working. Her team pasted the moth in a notebook. It was the first computer "bug." Ever since, the word *bug* has meant a computer problem.

The Stars

dwarf
double stars
nebula
neutron star
nuclear fusion
black hole
red giant
white dwarfs
supergiants
supernova

Stars are born; they mature, age, and die. Names have been given to their various stages of life. Add other words about stars to the list. Then do the activities. Use your Spelling Dictionary for help.

■ GETTING AT MEANING

A Star Is Born . . . and Dies Read the photo captions on these pages. Then use them and the clues in the sentences to help you fill in the blanks with list words.

New stars are forming through nuclear fusion in this cloud of gas and dust called a nebula.

1 Large amounts of gas and dust begin to draw together to form new stars in a ____.

5 Some stars then lose their outer layers and collapse inward. These small, pale stars are called ____. Though they're dead, they won't cool completely for billions of years!

2 When the pressure and density get very great, the extremely hot gas and dust combine through ____, and a star is born.

4 As the star ages, it gets bigger and brighter and its outer layers get cooler. When it begins to give off a red light, it is called a ____.

3 The star soon begins to shine. It then enters a long middle age. During this time it is called a ____.

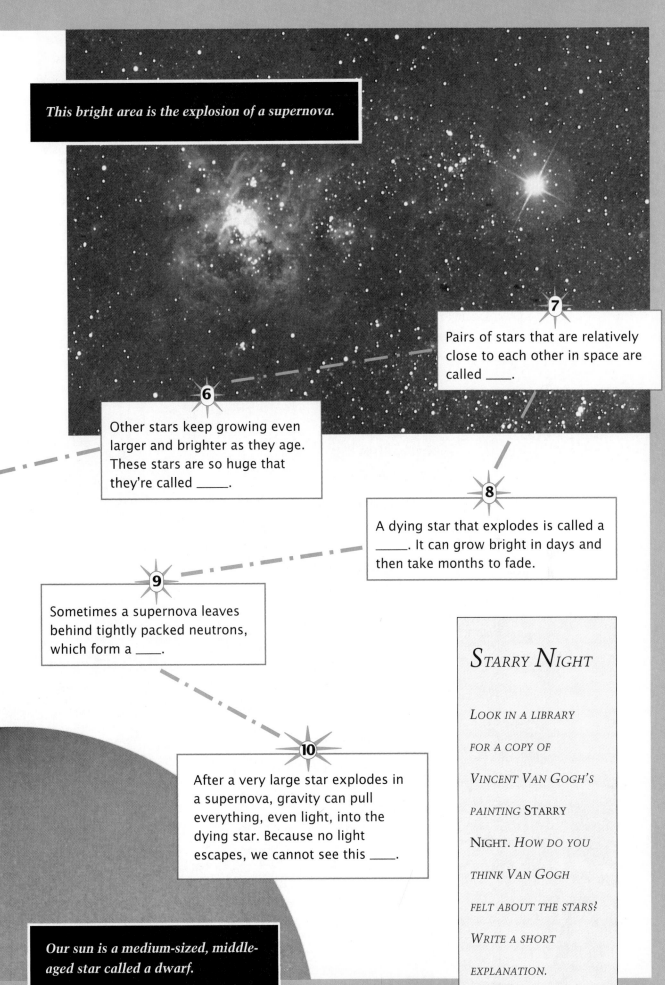

This bright area is the explosion of a supernova.

7

Pairs of stars that are relatively close to each other in space are called ____.

6

Other stars keep growing even larger and brighter as they age. These stars are so huge that they're called ____.

8

A dying star that explodes is called a ____. It can grow bright in days and then take months to fade.

9

Sometimes a supernova leaves behind tightly packed neutrons, which form a ____.

10

After a very large star explodes in a supernova, gravity can pull everything, even light, into the dying star. Because no light escapes, we cannot see this ____.

STARRY NIGHT

LOOK IN A LIBRARY FOR A COPY OF VINCENT VAN GOGH'S PAINTING STARRY NIGHT. HOW DO YOU THINK VAN GOGH FELT ABOUT THE STARS? WRITE A SHORT EXPLANATION.

Our sun is a medium-sized, middle-aged star called a dwarf.

Looking at Yourself

resolved
positive
sympathetic
timid
strain
objectives
self-image
outgoing
candid
seriously

The list words describe feelings and issues that many adolescents deal with every day. Think of two more words and add them to the list. Then do the activities. Use your Spelling Dictionary for help.

■ GETTING AT MEANING

Dear Friend, . . . Complete each letter with words from the list.

October 15

Dear Jenna,

Moving to a new state can be hard on a person. I've been under some real (1) lately. I'm still the new kid in school, so I haven't made any close friends yet. (You know me—I'm not outspoken and (2) like you are.) I am determined to keep an upbeat, (3) outlook, though, so I've set some definite (4) for myself. What do you think of them?

#1: Don't be so (5)! Put yourself out there and make yourself talk to one new person each day.

#2: Don't take things so (6). Lighten up and laugh more often—especially at yourself.

#3: Like yourself. Maintain a good (7). Accept yourself for who you are, even if other people don't!

So, Jen, write soon and tell me what you honestly think of my objectives.

Take care,
Cassandra

October 22

Dear Cass,

Sorry things are a bit rocky for you there, but they'll get better. You asked what I think of your objectives. Well, since you asked for my (8) opinion . . . I think they're great! I've (9) to use them myself, and I've added one more:

#4: Try to be kind to others and share their feelings—be (10). It may be just as hard for them to make new friends as it is for you!

Write and tell me how things are going.

Keep your chin up,

Jenna

ON BEING FRIENDS

With your classmates, compile a list (or a book) of serious, sarcastic, and humorous quotes on friendship. Here are a few to get you started:

"If you have one true friend you have more than your share."
—Thomas Fuller

"Treat your friends as you do your pictures, and place them in their best light."
—Jennie Jerome Churchill

"Animals are such agreeable friends—they ask no questions, they pass no criticisms."
—George Eliot

"A friend is one who dislikes the same people you dislike."
—Anonymous

Meeting Challenges

Many books and articles tell of people meeting challenges. Add two more words about challenges to the list. Use your Spelling Dictionary if you need help with the activity.

overwhelming
perilous
feat
pitfalls
liberate
surviving
suspense
thrive
undaunted
genuine

■ GETTING AT MEANING

At the Movies Complete the interview with list words. Use the captions to help you.

Guy Nosey: I'm talking with famous film spy Jane Bond on the set of *Taking the Plunge* as she prepares to plunge into this tank, (1) herself from her chains, and swim to safety before the sharks can make a snack of her. Tell us, Jane, why aren't you using a stunt double to accomplish this (2) of daring? It's extremely (3), isn't it?

Jane: Well, Guy, I've practiced this stunt so often that I'm prepared for any of the many (4) that I might encounter. I'm confident my attempt will be an (5) success.

Thrown into shark-infested waters . . .

. . . Jane remains undaunted by this perilous predicament.

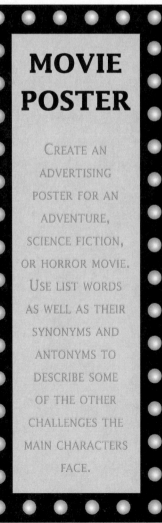

Jane: *(whispering)* Uh, don't tell anyone, but the sharks are mechanical. I'm not in any (6) danger.

GN: So, in spite of the death-defying odds, you're confident of (7) this hazardous stunt?

Will she liberate herself and make it to safety?

Jane: As always, I remain (8) in the face of peril. Actually, I (9) on it! *(whispering)* I also could use the publicity. It's good for my career!

GN: Well, ladies and gentleman, there you have it. Now, I don't know about you, but the (10) is killing me. Will Jane be successful, or will she be shark food? I can't wait to see what happens next.

MOVIE POSTER

CREATE AN ADVERTISING POSTER FOR AN ADVENTURE, SCIENCE FICTION, OR HORROR MOVIE. USE LIST WORDS AS WELL AS THEIR SYNONYMS AND ANTONYMS TO DESCRIBE SOME OF THE OTHER CHALLENGES THE MAIN CHARACTERS FACE.

quest
traditional
obstacle
persevered
suitors
expectations
reunion
understanding
melancholy
despair

Searching for Who You Are

Many stories tell of a quest. A man or woman goes in search of something, faces obstacles, and in the end is rewarded. Can you recognize the typical patterns of such a story? Think of two words to add to the list. Use your Spelling Dictionary if you need help with the activity.

■ **GETTING AT MEANING**

Understanding Traditional Tales
Use the list words to complete this legend.

In Guatemala, this tale has been told for two thousand years. Since the Mayas pass it on by word of mouth to each new generation, it is a (1) tale.

Long ago, a king noticed that his daughter Moonlight was silent and (2). Nothing he did made her smile. Finally the king announced that any man who could make his daughter happy could marry her.

Among the (3) who flocked to the palace was Black Feather. He had great hopes and (4) of marrying the princess, but he was poor. All he could offer was a song.

The princess smiled. "Your voice is beautiful," Moonlight said. "But I prefer the songs of the birds. If you could sing like the birds, then I would marry you." Black Feather felt he could overcome any (5) to win the princess's love. So he set out on a (6) to learn how to sing like the birds.

Black Feather listened to the songs of hundreds of birds, but he could not sing like them. He began to (7) of ever completing his task.

It was then that the Great Spirit of the Woods appeared. "I have watched your struggle," the Great Spirit said. "Because you have (8) and have not given up, I will help you." The Great Spirit hollowed out a tree branch, cut holes in it, and gave it to the young man. "This is a chirimia," the Great Spirit said. "Learn to play it well." Black Feather practiced until he had gained a complete (9) of how to play the flute.

When Black Feather returned to the palace, the princess heard his chirimia. It was filled with the songs of the birds. Black Feather and the princess had a joyful (10) and were soon married. Today in Guatemala, you can still hear the sweet sounds of the chirimia.

MODERN QUESTS

THINK OF A STORY YOU HAVE READ THAT TELLS OF A QUEST.

THE STORY COULD BE MODERN REALISTIC FICTION OR IT COULD BE A TRADITIONAL TALE. MAKE UP A BOOK JACKET THAT HIGHLIGHTS THE QUEST ASPECTS OF THE STORY.

Stories About America

historical fiction
setting
harsh
petition
emigrates
represents
traditions
Civil War
looms
civil rights

Is there a period in American history you're curious about? Historical fiction, fiction based on historical fact, will show you what it was like to live during a time in the past. Think of two more words about historical fiction to add to the word list. Use your Spelling Dictionary if you need help with the activity.

GETTING AT MEANING

Plot Summaries Use list words to complete the description of each book. Then think about which book you would most enjoy reading.

[CALIFORNIA]

[NEBRASKA]

Willa Cather
My Ántonia

A Czech family struggles to farm despite the rugged, (1) conditions on the Nebraska prairie. Antonia's quiet strength (2) the spirit of all the farmers who first cultivated the soil of the American heartland.

[OKLAHOMA]

Rifles for Watie
HAROLD KEITH

A young Union soldier becomes a spy and briefly joins the Cherokee Indian rebels who fought for the South in the American (5). There is suspense and a realistic view of war in this book of (6).

Laurence Yep
Dragonwings
A Newbery Honor Book

The San Francisco earthquake of 1906 is only one of the things Moon Shadow copes with when he (3) from China to California to join his father. Moon Shadow is sustained in a hostile new world by the beliefs and values that make up the rich (4) of the Chinese community.

The mill town of Lowell, Massachusetts, seems to offer independence for poor farm girls in the 1840s. But as a factory girl working the huge mechanical (7) that weave cloth for the textile factories, Lyddie faces long hours, low pay, and dangerous work. Should she sign the workers' (8) demanding better conditions, or will that only make things worse?

[MASSACHUSETTS]

North Carolina in 1963 is the (9) of this book. When her Uncle Pete joins the freedom riders, Sheryl realizes that she also wants to help in the (10) movement that is spreading across the country.

[NORTH CAROLINA]

FACTFACTFACTFACTFACT

TURN HISTORY INTO FICTION

FIND AN INFORMATIONAL ARTICLE ON A PERIOD IN U.S. HISTORY YOU'RE INTERESTED IN. HOW COULD YOU TURN THE INFORMATION INTO A FICTIONAL STORY? OUTLINE THE STORY; DESCRIBE THE MAIN CHARACTERS, THE SETTING, AND THE BEGINNING OF THE PLOT.

FICTIONFICTIONFICTION

Consumer Topics

simple interest
compound interest
principal
unit prices
commission
percent of increase
percent of decrease
credit
installments
budget

For consumers, good money management involves spending and saving in ways that make the most of their earnings. The list words are related to consumer concerns. Add other words that you know, and then do the activity. Use your Spelling Dictionary for help if you need it.

GETTING AT MEANING

Clipping Clues Use the newspaper clippings to complete the paragraphs with list words.

Stan recently graduated from college and started a sales job with a base salary plus a 2 percent (1). Because he wants to make the best use of his money, he prepared a detailed (2) in which he listed his income and expenses. As part of his expenses, he included the monthly payments, or (3), that he makes on the car he purchased on (4) last year.

HELP WANTED SALES

Enthusiastic person wanted for fast-paced sales position. Base salary plus 2 percent **commission** and benefits.

Incredible Deals at Buy-Now Auto Dealership

Special prices on 1,000 new and used cars.
Instant **credit** available with **installments** that will fit your **budget.** Don't miss this chance!

Earn More at Save-Quick Bank

*Don't settle for **simple interest!** Come to Save-Quick Bank and watch your **principal** grow fast with the best **compound interest** plan in town! Earn the maximum interest on interest!*

Smart Shoppers Save $$

By shopping wisely, using coupons, and comparing **unit prices** of competing brands, some shoppers have experienced a **percent of decrease** in their spending even during a time when prices have shown a **percent of increase.**

Stan shops for food carefully, always checking the (5) of all the items he buys. When he noticed prices rising during the last few months, he computed the (6) and found it to be 2 percent. In spite of this, by using coupons and watching ads for sale prices, Stan experienced a $1\frac{1}{2}$ (7) in his own spending during the same period.

With his first paycheck, Stan opened a savings account with a (8) of $100. He chose an account that offered (9) because his savings would increase faster than they would with (10).

The Real Number System

The numbers we deal with in everyday life are in the real number system. The list contains math terminology used to describe real numbers. If you can, add more words to the list. Then do the activities. Use your Spelling Dictionary if you need help.

▉ GETTING AT MEANING

Conversation Clues Study the number line and the five characters' conversation. Then complete the sentences with list words. (Use the number line for items 1–5.)

$$3.45 \times 10^{-2}$$

"THE THREE OF US ARE RATIONAL NUMBERS."

I AM A NUMBER WRITTEN AS **SCIENTIFIC NOTATION.** MY **STANDARD FORM** IS 0.0345.

-0.3̄

I AM A **REPEATING DECIMAL.** I CAN ALSO BE WRITTEN AS THE FRACTION $-\frac{1}{3}$.

0.5

I AM A **TERMINATING DECIMAL.** I CAN ALSO BE WRITTEN AS THE FRACTION $\frac{1}{2}$.

Number line:
A at $-\sqrt{2}$, B at -1, C at $-\frac{2}{3}$, D at $-\frac{1}{2}$, $-\frac{1}{3}$, E at 0 (0.0345), F at $\frac{1}{4}$, G at $\frac{1}{2}$, $\frac{5}{8}$, H at 1; also -2 marked.

"WE'RE ALL R[

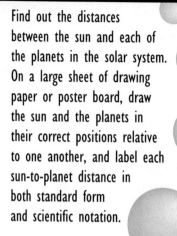

1. ALL THE POINTS ON THE NUMBER LINE REPRESENT _____.

2. POINTS A AND J EACH REPRESENT AN _____.

3. IN ITS DECIMAL FORM, POINT C REPRESENTS A _____.

4. EACH OF THE LABELED POINTS EXCEPT A AND J REPRESENTS A _____.

5. IN ITS DECIMAL FORM, POINT G REPRESENTS A _____.

6. SINCE THE SQUARE ROOT OF 64 IS 8, 64 IS A _____.

7. IN 8^3, 8 IS THE _____.

8. SINCE $10^2 = 100$, THE _____ OF 100 IS 10.

Find out the distances between the sun and each of the planets in the solar system. On a large sheet of drawing paper or poster board, draw the sun and the planets in their correct positions relative to one another, and label each sun-to-planet distance in both standard form and scientific notation.

Using a Chart Study the chart. Then use it to complete the sentences with list words.

STANDARD FORM	SCIENTIFIC NOTATION
0.0015	1.5×10^{-3}
3,800,000	3.8×10^6
9	9.0×10^0

9. THE MAXIMUM DISTANCE FROM THE EARTH TO THE SUN IS NINETY-FOUR MILLION FIVE HUNDRED THOUSAND MILES. THAT NUMBER, WRITTEN IN _____, IS 9.45×10^7.

10. IN _____ THAT NUMBER IS WRITTEN 94,500,000.

I AM AN **IRRATIONAL NUMBER.** I CANNOT BE WRITTEN AS A FRACTION. MY DECIMAL FORM DOES NOT REPEAT OR TERMINATE.

$$\sqrt{2}$$

I AM A **PERFECT SQUARE.** MY **SQUARE ROOT** IS 4 BECAUSE $4^2 = 16$. THE **BASE** IN THE NUMBER 4^2 IS 4.

I   J

$1.\overline{3}$ $\sqrt{3}$ 2   3   4

AL NUMBERS."

Geometry

rectangular
  prism
triangular prism
surface area
volume
formula
three-
  dimensional
pyramid
cylinder
cone
sphere

Three-dimensional geometric figures can be seen all around us. The word list contains the names of some of these figures and various terms used in measuring them. Add more words. Use your Spelling Dictionary if you need help with the activity.

■ GETTING AT MEANING

Diagrams Study the diagrams on both pages and then complete the sentences on the next page with list words.

TO FIND HOW MANY CUBIC UNITS FIT INSIDE A **THREE-DIMENSIONAL** FIGURE, COMPUTE ITS **VOLUME.** TO FIND THE VOLUME OF A RECTANGULAR PRISM, USE THIS **FORMULA:**

$$V = LWH$$

TO FIND HOW MUCH MATERIAL IS NEEDED TO COVER THE OUTSIDE OF A FIGURE, COMPUTE ITS **SURFACE AREA.** TO FIND THE SURFACE AREA OF A **RECTANGULAR PRISM,** USE THIS FORMULA:

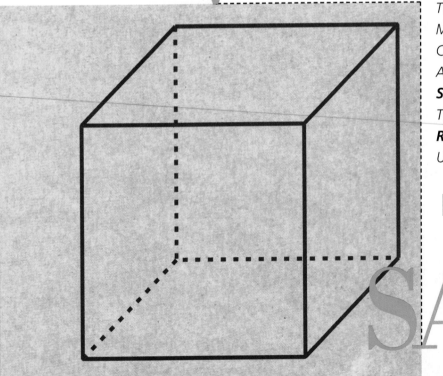

$$SA = \begin{array}{r} 2HL \\ 2HW \\ + 2LW \end{array}$$

OTHER THREE-DIMENSIONAL FIGURES

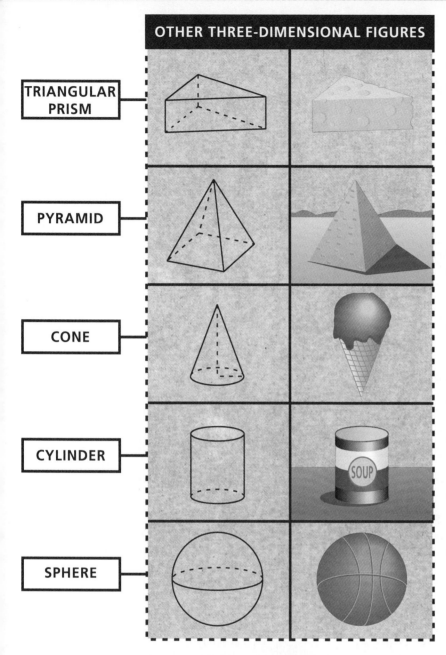

TRIANGULAR PRISM

PYRAMID

CONE

CYLINDER

SPHERE

A SHOEBOX HAS THE SHAPE OF A (1).

THE LEAST AMOUNT OF PAPER NEEDED TO WRAP A GIFT BOX IS THE SAME AS THE (2) OF THE BOX.

THE BASES OF A (3) EACH HAVE THREE SIDES.

A SOUP CAN HAS THE SHAPE OF A (4).

WHEN PACKING A CRATE WITH BOXES, IT WOULD HELP TO KNOW THE (5) OF THE CRATE.

CYLINDERS, PRISMS, AND PYRAMIDS ARE ALL (6) FIGURES.

FOLLOWING A RECIPE IS LIKE USING A (7).

A BASKETBALL HAS THE SHAPE OF A (8).

A (9) AND A (10) EACH HAVE ONLY ONE BASE.

AMAZING**ARCHITECTURE**

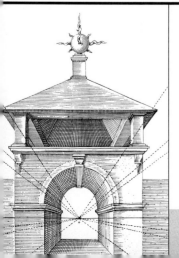

Most buildings are in the shape of a rectangular prism. However, architects sometimes use unusual shapes in their designs. Draw your own design of a building that uses at least three different shapes besides rectangular prisms. Use magazines or books to get ideas. Label each part of the building with its geometric name.

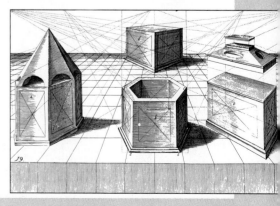

225

Algebra

evaluate
variable
solve
equation
inequality
solution
mathematical
  expression
parentheses
grouping
  symbols
order of
  operations

Algebra expresses mathematical ideas using numbers, symbols, and variables. The words in the list are important in algebra. Add more words to the list. Use your Spelling Dictionary if you need help with the activities.

■ GETTING AT MEANING

Sentence Completion Read the story carefully. Then choose the correct list word from each pair of list words in brackets on the next page.

Derrick's school is competing in an academic contest. Derrick is on the math team. For the first practice problem, the team must **evaluate** the **mathematical expression** $5x + (x - 4)$ when $x = -9$. First a team member substitutes -9 for the **variable** x. Then another member does the subtraction within the **parentheses**. Since there are no other **grouping symbols**, the team members then do the multiplication and addition, using the standard **order of operations**. Another problem requires the team to **solve** the equation $x - 17 = 24$. Their answer, $x = 41$, is correct because $41 - 17 = 24$. Another problem involved finding out if -5 is a **solution** for the **inequality** $x + 4 < -24$. The team's answer was "no" because substituting -5 for x does not make the sentence true.

The ____1____ [equation, mathematical expression] $2x + 3$ does not have any ____2____ [grouping symbols, variables].

The sentence $3x = -12$ is an ____3____ [equation, inequality]. If you ____4____ [evaluate, solve] it correctly, you will find that $x = -4$.

To ____5____ [evaluate, solve] $8 - 3(x + 5)$, substitute a number for the ____6____ [solution, variable], compute within the ____7____ [parentheses, order of operations], and follow the standard ____8____ [order of operations, grouping symbols].

The ____9____ [equation, inequality] $3x + 1 < 9$ has more than one ____10____ [solution, variable].

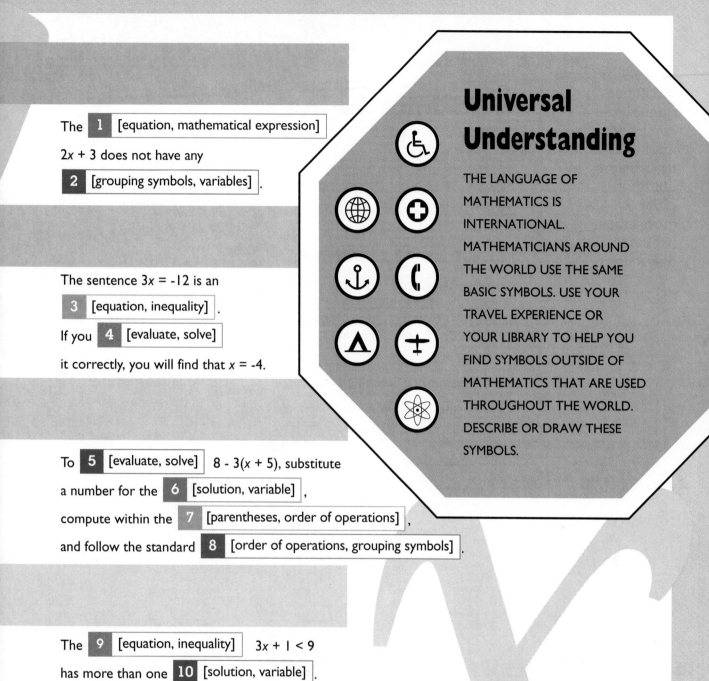

Universal Understanding

THE LANGUAGE OF MATHEMATICS IS INTERNATIONAL. MATHEMATICIANS AROUND THE WORLD USE THE SAME BASIC SYMBOLS. USE YOUR TRAVEL EXPERIENCE OR YOUR LIBRARY TO HELP YOU FIND SYMBOLS OUTSIDE OF MATHEMATICS THAT ARE USED THROUGHOUT THE WORLD. DESCRIBE OR DRAW THESE SYMBOLS.

DID YOU KNOW?

Algebra is generally considered to have begun in 1591. In that year Francois Vieté, a French mathematician, first used variables to describe patterns. Vieté's work quickly led to a great deal more mathematics being invented.

Consumer Topics 2

outstanding
   balance
annual rate
comparison
finance charge
investment
utility
profit
gross income
net income
deductions

Most consumers earn, spend, save, and invest money. The list contains words related to these activities. Add other words, using your Spelling Dictionary if you need help with this activity.

▇ GETTING AT MEANING

Family Finances The Matthews family keeps a family income summary, along with some helpful newspaper articles. Study the items from this file and then fill each blank with a list word.

Susan Matthews is learning good financial habits from her parents, Ceretha and Max. When deciding how much she could afford for apartment rent, she knew that she couldn't consider her total salary, or (1), as being available.

She had to subtract (2) first, and then consider the result: her (3).

The Home Mart

MINIMUM DUE	NEW BALANCE	AMOUNT PAID
20.00	175.98	
20.00	175.98	

37009-KB

ADDRESS

CITY   ST   ZIP

PHONE #

PLEASE INDICATE ANY
ADDRESS OR PHONE #
CHANGES ABOVE

BILLING DATE 11/15/94
ACCOUNT NUMBER 111-333-411

The Home Mart
100 South Mall Plaza
Chicago, IL 60606

Ceretha Matthews
1245 Chestnut Street
APT 14
Chicago, IL 60610

MAIL THIS PORTION WITH YOUR PAYMENT

1000100040583949944000048396

DATE	REFERENCE	STORE/DEPT	DESCRIPTION	AMOUNT
10/26	01028726	17-48	GOURMET	26.09
11/09	01023455	17-48	APPLIANCES	124.99
11/14	01028911	15-56	HOME ACCENTS	24.90

Smith-Harris Motors, Inc.

Ceretha Matthews 3627501
1245 Chestnut Street
APT 14
Chicago, Illinois 60610
Check Date 11/11/94

TAX INFORMATION	CURRENT
F.I.T.	182.66
FICA	116.78
State	44.98
Life	4.07

Pay Rate	Regular	Taxes	$344.42	Net Pay
Total Hours	75.00	Other	$ 4.07	
Total Earnings	$2244.27	Total Deductions	$348.49	

Comparison Shopping Is Worth the Time, Experts Say

Results of a study just release[d] composed of financial expert[s] indicate that in the long run, [it] helps consumers save substa[ntial] purchases.

Investment in Local Utility Pays Off!

Municipal Electric Company's increase in **profit** means investors will receive a $0.02 per share increase in dividend. After a somewhat sluggish start, Municipal Electric's market activity appears to have been taking a consistent upward swing. Investors who have been with Municipal Electric from the beginning are really seeing their investments multiply!

Susan also needs to consider other expenses, like (4) bills. Even in applying for charge accounts, Susan makes a careful (5) of the (6) of interest charged by each company. Susan knows that she can avoid a (7) if she pays the new balance each month and never has an (8). Susan recently made an (9) in some stock. If the company she invested in makes a (10), then the value of her stock should increase.

COMPARING CREDIT

Gather data about three different credit cards from department stores, gasoline companies, or banks. Ask about the annual rate, the credit limit, the payment schedule, and the minimum payment required. Also find out if an annual fee is charged and if special discounts are available with the card. Then write a report about your findings.

Writer's Handbook

INTRODUCTION

Spelling is an important part of writing. Since writing is a form of communication, if your spelling is unclear, your communication could be unclear also. This handbook will tell you some of the other things you need to know in order to become a better writer.

CONTENTS

The Writing Process

Producing a polished piece of writing takes several steps: **prewriting, drafting, revising, proofreading,** and **presenting.** This section answers questions you might have about those steps.

1. PREWRITING

What should I do before I begin writing?

Just as it's easier to see in the dark if you have a flashlight, it's easier to write something if you have a plan to guide you. Before you begin writing, take some time and plan ahead.

- **Decide what to write about.** Are you having trouble coming up with a good topic? You might find some ideas by going through your writing journal and rereading your thoughts, feelings, and observations. You also might try looking through books, magazines, or newspapers for ideas.
- **Determine your purpose and audience.** What is your purpose for writing? Do you want to express feelings or opinions? describe or explain something? inform, persuade, or entertain? Who will be your audience? Will you address a certain person or group, or are you writing only for yourself?
- **Narrow your topic.** Make sure all your ideas really do focus on a specific topic. To do this, you might create a web, develop a written outline, write down questions, or logically group words or phrases that pertain to the topic you've chosen.
- **Gather information about your topic.** Depending on what you're writing about, you might take notes from different sources; conduct interviews; list points you want to make; arrange events on a time line; or note how things look, sound, smell, taste, and feel.
- **Organize your information.** Depending on your type of writing and your purpose for writing, you will need to organize by time order, spatial order, or order of importance.

2. DRAFTING

How do I actually begin writing?

Gather up your materials and find a quiet, comfortable place with good lighting. Plan on writing for at least twenty minutes. If you have trouble getting started, these strategies might help:

- **Set a goal.** Promise yourself you'll write a certain amount, or for a certain length of time, and then keep your promise.
- **Tune out distractions,** such as radio, TV, or conversations. Concentrate on the task at hand.
- **Review your resources.** Examine your notes or journal to come up with an idea for a good opening line or paragraph.
- **Get started!** Set aside all concerns about perfect spelling, punctuation, or capitalization during this drafting stage. You will work on them later, at the proofreading stage. For now, just begin with a sentence that is direct and interesting and that states your main idea. Then let your ideas flow freely.

3. REVISING

How do I revise my writing?

When you revise, you reread what you have written, looking for ways to improve it. To begin revising, you might do the following:

- **Read your draft to yourself** to catch such errors as unclear or unnecessary parts, or ideas that are out of order.
- **Discuss your writing** with other students or with your teacher. Read your draft aloud and ask for reactions. Do your listeners understand what you wrote? Can they suggest ways to improve your draft?

What kinds of questions should I ask?

That depends on your purpose, audience, and type of writing. Here are some points to consider:

Ask these questions!

- Does my writing have a clear beginning, middle, and end?
- Does each paragraph have a topic sentence that sets up or states its main idea?
- Do all my details, events, or reasons support this main idea?
- Are they all in the right order?
- Are there any extra or inexact words I should delete or replace?
- Should I delete any information that doesn't relate to the topic?
- Do I need to add or rearrange information?
- Are all my facts and figures correct?
- Have I used language appropriate for my audience and type of writing?

≡	Make a capital.
/	Make a small letter.
∧	Add something.
ℯ	Take out something.
⊙	Add a period.
⁋	New paragraph

What kinds of changes should I make?

To clarify your writing, try making these changes:

- **Add or subtract** words or ideas.
- **Move** words, sentences, or paragraphs.
- **Replace** words or ideas that are unclear or inexact.

4. PROOFREADING

Why should I proofread, and when and how should I do it?

After revising your first draft, you should proofread it for errors in grammar, usage, punctuation, capitalization, and spelling. Proofread once after revising your first draft. Then, after finishing your final draft, proofread it one last time.

Use proofreading symbols such as the ones on this page to clearly indicate any corrections needed.

What kinds of things should I look for when I proofread?

Here are some suggestions:

- Did I capitalize the first word of each sentence?
- Did I capitalize all proper nouns and proper adjectives?
- Is each sentence correctly punctuated?
- Have I avoided fragments and run-on sentences?
- Did I stick to the correct verb tense throughout?
- Do all my subjects and verbs agree?
- Did I check the spellings of unfamiliar words?
- Did I indent every paragraph?
- If there is a special format for this kind of writing, have I followed it?
- Is my handwriting clear and legible?

Check for these possible errors!

5. PRESENTING

How should I present my final work?

For regular assignments, try following these steps:

- Copy your final draft neatly on one side of white, lined paper.
- If you are using a computer, make final corrections to your rough draft and print out a new, clean version.
- Put your name, subject, and date in the top right-hand corner.
- Skip a line (or add an extra return) and write or type the title of your piece. Center it on the line.
- Leave an inch margin on the sides and bottom of the paper.

Special ways to present your writing include displaying it on a bulletin board, binding it in an illustrated book or newspaper, or performing it as a play.

Taking Writing Tests

These tips should help make the task of taking writing tests easier.

GENERAL GUIDELINES FOR WRITING TESTS

- **Follow instructions carefully.** Listen closely to find out how much time you have, what you should use to write (pen, pencil, computer, etc.), when you should begin and end, and any special instructions.
- **Read the assignment and identify the key words.** Before you begin writing, make sure you clearly understand what the directions are asking you to do. Here are some key words that often appear in test directions:

Look for these key words!

Categorize or Classify: Sort ideas or facts into groups.
Compare and Contrast: Point out similarities (compare) and differences (contrast).
Defend: Give evidence to show why a view is right.
Define: Tell what something is or means.
Describe: Create a word picture with details and examples.
Discuss: State your ideas about what something means.
Evaluate: Give your opinion, with support, on whether an idea is good or bad, right or wrong.
Explain: Clarify through reasons, examples, or steps.
Summarize: State main points, or retell important parts of a story.

- **Plan how you'll use your time.** Allot some time at the start to plan out what you will write. Save time at the end to reread and catch any errors.
- **Write a strong opening** to catch your readers' attention. Be sure it specifically addresses the topic of the assignment.
- **Use specific facts and details** to help develop your ideas. Be sure to put them into the proper order or form.
- **Take time to wrap things up.** Don't stop writing just because your time is up. Use the last few minutes to write a strong conclusion that pulls things together.

WRITING A DESCRIPTION

Writers create different moods by describing how things look, sound, smell, taste, or feel in different settings.

KEY WORDS IN ASSIGNMENTS
- "**Describe** the **setting** and tell what **mood** it conveys . . ."
- "Tell what things **look, smell, taste, sound,** and **feel** like . . ."

SAMPLE ASSIGNMENTS
- You are walking down a long corridor, and you come to a door. You open the door and slowly walk through it. Use sensory details to describe the sights, sounds, feelings, smells, and tastes that you experience when you step through the door. Also describe the mood that these things convey.
- You're late for school, and you just spilled orange juice down the front of your T-shirt. You can't find your books, and the dog has eaten your lunch. . . . And this is just the beginning! Write a description of the scene around you. Use sensory details to help convey the mood.

A PLAN OF ATTACK
- Before you write, visualize your setting and list as many sensory details as you can to describe it. Then list words and phrases that help describe the mood that the setting conveys.
- Begin your writing with a strong opening that immediately draws your readers (or listeners) into the setting and conveys the mood.
- Use **spatial order** to describe your setting, proceeding from left to right, near to far, or top to bottom.
- Use words and phrases that signal spatial order, such as *to the left, behind, around, above,* and *near.*
- Use sensory details, figurative language, and exact words to describe the setting and convey the mood as clearly as possible.

FOLLOW-UP CHECKLIST
- Does your opening grab your audience's attention?
- Have you used strong sensory details and spatial order?
- Does your description convey a strong mood to your audience?
- Is the focal point of your composition a description of a moment in time rather than a series of moments?
- Is all your capitalization, punctuation, and spelling correct?

WRITING COMPARISON/CONTRAST

Comparing and contrasting helps writers tell how two things or viewpoints are alike and different.

KEY WORDS IN ASSIGNMENTS

- "Tell how these two things (or viewpoints) are **alike and different.**"
- "Write a description that **compares and contrasts** . . ."

SAMPLE ASSIGNMENTS

- Although most households in the United States have at least one TV set, not everyone in the house may feel the same about watching it. Compare and contrast how people feel about watching TV by listing some of its advantages and disadvantages.
- Bicycles and airplanes are two ways of getting around. Compare and contrast these two modes of transportation by describing their likenesses and differences.

A PLAN OF ATTACK

- Before you write, make a comparison/contrast chart. On one side, list how the two things or viewpoints are alike—for example: *both take you places.* On the other side, list how the two things are different—for example: *planes usually take you to far-away places; bicycles usually take you to local places.*
- Consider organizing your writing into two paragraphs, based on your chart. For the first assignment, describe the advantages of TV viewing in one paragraph and the disadvantages in the other. For the second assignment, use the first paragraph to tell how bicycles and planes are alike and the second to tell how they are different.
- Begin each paragraph with a topic sentence that explains what you will be describing, comparing, or contrasting.
- Use words that help signal your comparisons and contrasts, such as *both, alike, similar; each, different, although, on the other hand.*

FOLLOW-UP CHECKLIST

- Does each of your topic sentences clearly state what you are comparing or contrasting?
- Do all the details relate to the main idea of the paragraph?
- Have you used appropriate words and phrases to signal comparisons or contrasts?

WRITE A DETAILED EXPLANATION

A detailed explanation uses related details to explain a main idea. Often these related details are made up of examples or reasons.

KEY WORDS IN ASSIGNMENTS

- "Explain the **reasons why** . . ."
- "Tell **how** the . . ."
- "Give **examples** to explain how . . ."

SAMPLE ASSIGNMENTS

- Sometimes life can be boring. Think of times you've been bored, and things you've done to relieve your boredom. Use these examples to help you write an explanation of how to relieve boredom.
- Some people are scared of insects, even the harmless variety. What is it about certain insects that scares some people? Write an explanation of why some people are scared of insects. Use reasons and examples to make your explanation clear.

A PLAN OF ATTACK

- Before you write, list as many examples and reasons as you can think of to explain how life can be boring or why people are scared of insects.
- Organize your reasons and examples by **order of importance.** Make them build from least important (weakest) to most important (strongest) or from most important to least important.
- Begin with a topic sentence that clearly states what you plan to explain. Then cite your reasons or examples, one at a time, in the order of importance you have chosen.
- Use words and phrases that signal each new reason or example, such as *for example, for this reason, this is why, because, this shows.*

FOLLOW-UP CHECKLIST

- Have you stated your main idea in a topic sentence?
- Do all your reasons and examples help support the main idea?
- Have you kept to the pattern of organization you've chosen?
- Have you used words and phrases that signal new reasons or examples?
- Are your punctuation, capitalization, spelling, and usage correct?

WRITING INSTRUCTIONS

Instructions are step-by-step directions that tell readers how to accomplish a task. The steps are arranged in a specific order so that readers can follow them easily and correctly.

KEY WORDS IN ASSIGNMENTS

- "Explain **how to** . . ."
- "**List the steps** to follow to . . ."
- "Tell what you **need** to . . ."

SAMPLE ASSIGNMENTS

- You've got to pack a picnic basket for an outing with friends. Write the materials you will need and the steps you will follow to pack the basket, ensuring that the cold food stays cold, the warm food stays warm, and *everything* you pack stays fresh—and fits in the basket!
- Your school is having a kite-building contest, and you've decided to enter. Write step-by-step instructions for the kite you plan to build. Be sure to include the materials you will use.

A PLAN OF ATTACK

- Before you write, think through each step of the instructions. Then list the steps in order, making sure to include any materials required.
- When you begin writing, start with a topic sentence that states what your instructions are for. Then tell what materials you will need.
- Organize the steps in **sequential order**. Tell what you will do first, next, and so on.
- Use clue words and phrases such as *first, next, then, when, as soon as, after that,* and *finally* to make the sequential order clear.

FOLLOW-UP CHECKLIST

- Does your topic sentence tell what the instructions are for?
- Are your steps arranged in the proper sequence, or order?
- Have you used clue words and phrases to help signal that order?
- Have you included all the materials?
- Are your capitalization, punctuation, spelling, and usage correct?

WRITING A PERSONAL NARRATIVE

A personal narrative is a true account of something you have done, felt, or experienced.

KEY WORDS IN ASSIGNMENTS

- "What did you **do** when . . . ?"
- "Write how you **felt** when . . ."
- "Tell **what happened** when . . ."

SAMPLE ASSIGNMENTS

- What has been the proudest moment of your life so far? What made it so? Give a detailed account of your experience, including what you did, how you felt, and what you said at that moment.
- Think about the scariest experience you have ever had. What happened? Where were you, and who was with you? Tell about your experience. Be sure to include what you were thinking and feeling.

A PLAN OF ATTACK

- Before you write, narrow your topic to one particular proud moment or scary experience that you want to tell your readers about.
- Next, relive the experience in your mind and jot down some words and phrases that explain exactly what you were doing, thinking, and feeling at the time.
- Then use the words and phrases to help you write a rough outline for your narrative. Be sure to include a beginning, a middle, and an end.
- As you write your narrative, keep your readers in mind. Imagine you are introducing yourself to them as you relate your story.

FOLLOW-UP CHECKLIST

- Does your narrative have a clear beginning, middle, and end?
- Does the beginning grab your readers' attention and tell them what you will be writing about?
- Did you "capture the moment" by using exact words and phrases to describe your thoughts and feelings?
- Will readers know you better after reading your personal narrative?

WRITING A PERSUASIVE LETTER

When you write a persuasive letter, you are trying to convince someone to agree with your opinion or point of view on an issue.

KEY WORDS IN ASSIGNMENTS

- "Try to **persuade** someone to . . . "
- "**Convince** others to agree with your opinion on . . . "

SAMPLE ASSIGNMENTS

- You and two other students are running for class president. You think you are the best candidate for the office, and you want to convince others to agree with you. Write a letter that you will read to your class, persuading them to vote for you. Cite several strong reasons or examples that prove your qualifications.
- You want to go on an overnight field trip. Write your parents a letter, persuading them that the trip will be a beneficial learning experience. Give several reasons or examples to support your opinion.

A PLAN OF ATTACK

- Before you write, list several reasons that you can use to persuade your classmates to vote for you, or to persuade your parents that the trip will be beneficial. Look over your reasons and make sure they really do support your point of view. Cross out any that don't.
- Begin with a topic sentence that states your point of view. Then list examples or reasons that support it.
- Organize your examples or reasons by **order of importance.** Make them build from least important (weakest) to most important (strongest) or from most important to least important.
- Use words and phrases that signal each new reason or example, such as *for example, for this reason, this is why, because, this proves.*

FOLLOW-UP CHECKLIST

- Does your topic sentence clearly state your opinion or point of view?
- Do your reasons strongly support your opinion and persuade others to agree with you?
- Do they keep to your pattern of organization?
- Have you included only information that is relevant to your argument?

Rules, Guidelines, and Models

CAPITALIZATION

Capitalize the following in your writing:

Names, initials, and titles used with names:

    Capt. Anthony Roberts, Sr.   Mrs. Michelle J. Bennett

Proper adjectives:

    Greek mythology   French bread
    Scandinavian furniture

The pronoun *I:*

    My parents and I threw a surprise party for my sister.

Names of cities, states, countries, continents:

    El Paso   Rhode Island   Italy   Antarctica

Names of bodies of water, mountains, structures, organizations:

    Mediterranean Sea   Empire State Building
    Mt. Rushmore   Salvation Army

Names of streets and street abbreviations:

    Sinclair Ave.   Geneva Street   Euclid Blvd.   Glen Road

Days, months, holidays, special events:

    Friday   Sun.   March   Jan.
    Labor Day   Thanksgiving   Winter Carnival

First, last, and all important words in movie, book, story, play, and TV show titles:

    The Sword in the Stone   Where the Sidewalk Ends
    "The Minister's Black Veil"   All in the Family

First word in the greeting and closing of a letter:

    Dear cousin,   Yours truly,

First word in a sentence:

    Could Jack give me a ride to school?

First word inside quotation marks:

    Jack replied, "Yes, but I won't be leaving until later."

First word of each main topic and subtopic in an outline:

    I. Caring for a pet puppy
      A. What to feed it
      B. How to groom it

Both letters of the United States Postal Service state abbreviations:

State abbreviations:

AL (Alabama)	**LA** (Louisiana)	**OH** (Ohio)
AK (Alaska)	**ME** (Maine)	**OK** (Oklahoma)
AZ (Arizona)	**MD** (Maryland)	**OR** (Oregon)
AR (Arkansas)	**MA** (Massachusetts)	**PA** (Pennsylvania)
CA (California)	**MI** (Michigan)	**RI** (Rhode Island)
CO (Colorado)	**MN** (Minnesota)	**SC** (South Carolina)
CT (Connecticut)	**MS** (Mississippi)	**SD** (South Dakota)
DE (Delaware)	**MO** (Missouri)	**TN** (Tennessee)
FL (Florida)	**MT** (Montana)	**TX** (Texas)
GA (Georgia)	**NE** (Nebraska)	**UT** (Utah)
HI (Hawaii)	**NV** (Nevada)	**VT** (Vermont)
ID (Idaho)	**NH** (New Hampshire)	**VA** (Virginia)
IL (Illinois)	**NJ** (New Jersey)	**WA** (Washington)
IN (Indiana)	**NM** (New Mexico)	**WV** (West Virginia)
IA (Iowa)	**NY** (New York)	**WI** (Wisconsin)
KS (Kansas)	**NC** (North Carolina)	**WY** (Wyoming)
KY (Kentucky)	**ND** (North Dakota)	

PUNCTUATION

Use **periods**

- to end declarative or imperative sentences:

    This spaghetti sauce is delicious.
    Please let me have your recipe.

- after most abbreviations:

    Sr.   Mr.   P.M.   Dec.   Dr.   Sgt.

Use **exclamation marks**

- after exclamatory sentences:

    It's freezing cold outside!

Use **question marks**

- after interrogative sentences:

    Where are your gloves and scarf?

Use **commas**

- between the day and the year in a date:

  April 1, 2001

- between the day and the month in a date:

  Tuesday, November 30

- to set off a date from the rest of a sentence:

  On June 12, 1991, Julie graduated from college.

  We plan to leave for vacation on Saturday, July 8.

- between the name of a city and state:

  Orlando, Florida

- to set off an address from the rest of a sentence:

  I sent the letter to 16 Oak Street, Tupelo, Mississippi,
  last Monday.

- after the greeting and closing of a friendly letter:

  Dear Mom,   Your daughter,

- between a series of words in a sentence:

  I had orange juice, cereal, and a bagel for breakfast.

- before the conjunction that joins a compound sentence:

  I like to read in my spare time, but Sue likes to
  listen to music.

  We pitched the tent, and Dad built the fire.

- after introductory words or phrases:

  Unfortunately, the picnic was cancelled because of rain.

  Of course, we'll try to schedule it for another weekend.

- to set off interrupting words or phrases:

  Next Saturday, by the way, is not a good day
  to reschedule.

- to separate the noun of address from the rest of a sentence:

  Would you like to join us, Andrew?

  Thanks for the invitation, everyone, but I was just leaving.

- before quotation marks or inside the end quotation marks:

  Neil asked, "Did you see where I put my catcher's mitt?"

  "I've got a game in a few minutes," he added.

- to set off appositives (words or phrases that identify or explain nouns):

> My favorite store, Oak Street Market, was having a sale on fruit.
>
> I bought some peaches and apples, my two favorites.

- after mild interjections (words that express feeling):

> Wow, look at that storm.

Use **quotation marks**

- around the exact words someone used when speaking:

> "You two are my best friends," said Jackson.

- around titles of stories, poems, songs, and articles:

> "The Tortoise and the Hare"   "Dream Dust"
> "Knock on Wood"

Underline or **italicize** titles of books and movies:

> Last of the Mohicans   Groundhog Day

Use **apostrophes**

- to form the possessive of a noun:

> principal's   friends'   class's

- in contractions in place of dropped letters.

> don't (do not)   it's (it has)   I've (I have)

Use **colons**

- between hours and minutes to indicate time:

> 6:25   11:10

- after the greeting in a business letter:

> To whom it may concern: Dear Officer Holmes:

BUSINESS LETTER FORM

Business letters ask for information about particular products or services, or they give opinions and suggestions about products, services, or situations.

Since you usually write business letters to people you don't know, your tone should be rather formal, and you should be as brief and to-the-point as possible.

Study the business letter below. Notice its five parts and how each of those parts is capitalized and punctuated.

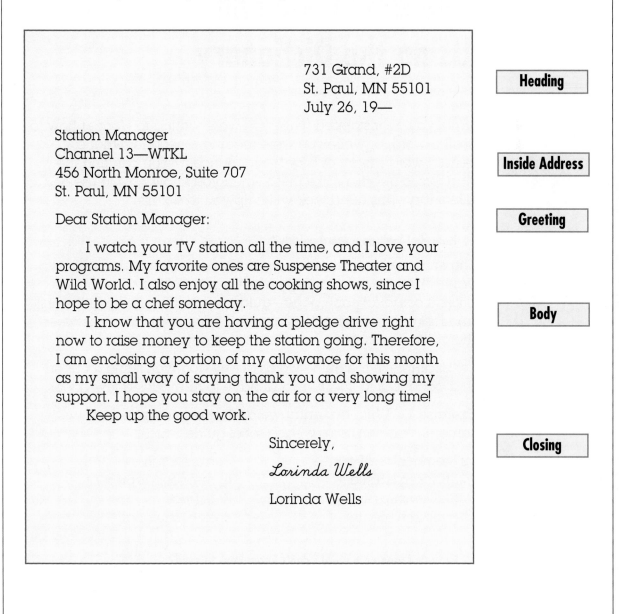

731 Grand, #2D
St. Paul, MN 55101
July 26, 19—

Heading

Station Manager
Channel 13—WTKL
456 North Monroe, Suite 707
St. Paul, MN 55101

Inside Address

Dear Station Manager:

Greeting

   I watch your TV station all the time, and I love your programs. My favorite ones are Suspense Theater and Wild World. I also enjoy all the cooking shows, since I hope to be a chef someday.
   I know that you are having a pledge drive right now to raise money to keep the station going. Therefore, I am enclosing a portion of my allowance for this month as my small way of saying thank you and showing my support. I hope you stay on the air for a very long time!
   Keep up the good work.

Body

Sincerely,

Lorinda Wells

Lorinda Wells

Closing

Dictionary Handbook

Understanding and Using the Dictionary

Have you ever stopped while you were writing to wonder how to spell a word, or while you were reading to wonder what a certain word meant or how to pronounce it? You can find the answers to questions like these when you know how to use a dictionary. This handbook will help you to do this.

1. How do I look up a word quickly?

The **entry words** in a dictionary are arranged in alphabetical order. To find a word quickly, use the pairs of words at the top outside corner of each page—**guide words.** They tell you the first and last entry words on that page. If your word falls in-between the guide words, then you know it's somewhere on that page.

For example, if the guide words are **fly I fog,** you'll find *focus* on that page, but to find *fish* you'll have to turn back a few pages.

Exercise 1   Write two entry words that would appear on the same dictionary page as each set of guide words.

1. remodel I saffron
2. thicken I thistle
3. fellowship I formula
4. captain I center
5. able I arch
6. reindeer I represent
7. fit I foot
8. sick I snowball

2. How do I look up a word I don't know how to spell?

The key is finding out how the word begins. For example, suppose you need to correct this misspelling: "He wanted to become a *sitizen*." How else might the word begin? Think about what letters could make the sound /s/ at the beginning of this word. You know that the letters **s** and **c** are common spellings of this sound, so you try them out.

First, you try *sitizen*. You look through the **guide words** until you find the page headed **sir l size**, but *sitizen* isn't there. So you try *citizen*, and there it is on the page headed **cistern l civilize.**

Exercise 2   Use your Spelling Dictionary to find out which word in each pair is spelled correctly. Write the correct spelling and the guide words from the dictionary page where each is found.

1. dilute—delute
2. engagement—ingagement
3. fenomenon—phenomenon
4. cronicle—chronicle
5. sculpture—skulpture
6. sentennial—centennial

3. What do I do if I still can't find the word?

Most dictionaries have a spelling chart that shows all the possible spellings for each English sound. The part of the chart for the sound /k/ is shown.

k   **c**oat, **k**ind, ba**ck**, e**ch**o, a**ch**e, **q**uit, a**cc**ount, anti**que**, e**x**cite, a**cq**uire

Notice that there are ten possible spellings for this sound in English. Use the spelling chart if you still can't find a word after you've looked up every spelling you can think of.

Exercise 3   Use the spelling chart called "Spellings of English Sounds" at the beginning of your Spelling Dictionary to answer these questions.

1. How many ways can the sound /f/ be spelled?
2. Which word in the chart has the sound /yü/ spelled the same as in *hue?*
3. Which word in the chart has the sound /zh/ spelled the same as in *treasure?*
4. How many ways can the sound /ə/ be spelled?
5. What are the five ways that the sound /n/ can be spelled?
6. What are the four ways that the sound /r/ can be spelled?

4. How do I know which definition fits my word?

Many words have more than one meaning. In fact, a word like cut has dozens of meanings. You can use the **context** of the word, the **parts of speech** labels, and the **illustrative phrases** and **sentences** provided to help you choose the proper **definition** of your word. What is the definition of the word *fine* in this sentence? "The artist used a single-bristle brush to paint his subject's fine, black eyelashes."

> **fine** (fīn), *adj.* **1** of very high quality; very good; excellent: *a fine view, a fine scholar.* **2** very thin or slender: *fine wire.* **3** sharp: *a tool with a fine edge.* **4** polished; elegant; refined: *fine manners.* **5** subtle: *The law makes fine distinctions.* **6** good-looking; handsome: *a fine young man.* **7** clear; bright: *fine weather.* —**fine′ly,** *adv.* —**fine′ness,** *n.*

From the context of the sentence, you know that the definition you are looking for means "very thin." Reading the definitions, you can see that the one you want is definition 2: very thin or slender.

Exercise 4   Write the part of speech and the number of the definition that fits the italicized word in each sentence. Use your Spelling Dictionary.

1. Our church held a *bazaar* to raise money for the fire victims.
2. Dotted *lines* separated the four lanes of the highway.
3. To everyone's relief, Alice's tumor turned out to be *benign.*
4. We knew just the right *accessories* to go with Jay's suit.
5. We sat on the shore and watched the *outgoing* tide.

5. How can I find out how to pronounce a word?

The entry word is broken into **syllables.** Right after it comes the pronunciation, enclosed in parentheses: **mix▪ture** (miks′chər). The **accent mark** tells you which syllable to emphasize.

The **pronunciation key,** which appears on every page in most dictionaries, shows how to sound out the pronunciations.

Some words can be said in more than one way. For example, two pronunciations are given in your Spelling Dictionary for *advertisement* (ad′vər tīz′mənt or ad vėr′tis mənt). The pronunciation (ad′vər tīz′mənt) is given first, not because it is more correct than (ad vėr′tis mənt), but because it is used by more people. If you say (ad vėr′tis mənt), you are just as correct as those people who say (ad′vər tīz′mənt).

Exercise 5 Write the word that each pronunciation represents. Use the pronunciation key below to help you.

1. (slüth)
2. (ang′kər)
3. (pol′ə se)
4. (ek′sər sīz)
5. (reb′əl or ri bel′)

6. (nō wun)
7. (byùr′ō)
8. (mag′nit)
9. (kwest)
10. (lug′ij)

a	hat	ī	ice	ù	put	ə	stands for
ā	age	o	not	ü	rule	a	in about
ä	far, calm	ō	open	ch	child	e	in taken
âr	care	ȯ	saw	ng	long	i	in pencil
e	let	ô	order	sh	she	o	in lemon
ē	equal	oi	oil	th	thin	u	in circus
ėr	term	ou	out	ᵺ	then		
i	it	u	cup	zh	measure		

6. How do I find the correct spelling for a word that is not an entry word?

Sometimes when you add endings such as **-ed, -ing, -s,** and **-es** to words, the spelling changes. These are not listed as entry words. To find the correct spellings of these forms, look up the base word and find the **related forms** in the entry.

Exercise 6 In your Spelling Dictionary, look up the base word of each misspelled related form. Write the related form correctly.

1. manicureist
2. volcanos
3. purchaseable

4. rationaly
5. commutted
6. crisises

7. What if my dictionary lists two ways to spell a word?

Some words may be spelled in more than one way. Sometimes this is shown in a single entry, with the more common spelling first: **R.S.V.P.** or **r.s.v.p.** Other times, different spellings are listed as separate entries, and the definition is given under the more common spelling:

> **ar▪chae▪ol▪o▪gy** (är′kē ol′ə jē), *n.* the scientific study of the people, customs, and life of ancient times. Also, **archeology.**
> **ar▪che▪ol▪o▪gy** (är′kē ol′ə jē), *n.* archaeology.

Exercise 7   Look up these words in your Spelling Dictionary. Write the more common spelling for each word.

1. cuing, cueing
2. teddy bear, Teddy bear
3. extravert, extrovert
4. mah-jongg, mah-jong

8. How do I find out where a word in our language came from originally?

A dictionary also gives you information about how words came into our language. An explanation of a word's origin is called an **etymology.** A word's etymology is usually found at the end of the entry, enclosed in brackets. Read this entry for *calligraphy.*

> **cal·lig·ra·phy** (kə lig′rə fē), *n.* beautiful handwriting. [< Greek *kalligraphia* < *kallos* beauty + *graphein* write]

From the etymology you learn that *calligraphy* came to our language from Greek and means "beautiful writing."

Exercise 8   Use your Spelling Dictionary to find the etymologies of the following words. Write the language, languages, or other source each word came from.

1. liaison
2. mosquito
3. catamaran
4. tycoon
5. okra
6. weird
7. therapy
8. boycott

9. What else can I find in a dictionary entry?

Sometimes an entry is followed by a **synonym study.** These explain subtle differences between words that are closely related in meaning. Look at this entry for the word *revenge:*

> **re·venge** (ri venj′), *n.* harm done in return for a wrong; satisfaction obtained by repayment of an injury, etc.; vengeance: *take revenge, get revenge.* —*v.t.* do harm in return for. See synonym study below
> **Syn.** *v.t.* **Revenge, avenge** mean to punish someone in return for a wrong. **Revenge** applies when it is indulged in to get even: *Gangsters revenge the murder of one of their gang.* **Avenge** applies when the punishment seems just: *They fought to avenge the enemy's invasion of their country.*

Exercise 9   Use **revenge** and **avenge** each in a sentence to illustrate their differences in meaning.

1._____

2._____

10. Why are there two different entries for some words?

These words are homographs. A **homograph** is a word that is spelled the same as another word but has a different origin and meaning. Look at the two entries for *low*.

> **low**[1] (lō), *adj.* **1** not high or tall; short: *low walls, a low hedge.* **2** in a low place: *a low shelf.* **3** small in amount, degree, force, value, etc.; moderate: *a low price.* —*adv.* **1** in, at, or to a low portion, point, degree, etc.: *Supplies are running low.* **2** near the ground, floor, or base: *fly low.* **3** softly; quietly; not loudly. [< Scandinavian (Old Icelandic) *lāgr*].
>
> **low**[2] (lō), *v.i., v.t.* make the sound of a cow; moo. —*n.* the sound a cow makes; mooing. [Old English *hlōwan*]

If you look at the etymologies of the two words, you will see that *low*[1] is originally from the Scandinavian word *lāgr* and *low*[2] is originally from the Old English word *hlōwan*.

Exercise 10 Use a dictionary to look up these homographs. Explain the differences in their origins and meanings. (Note: You won't find these in your Spelling Dictionary.)

1. row[1], row[2]
2. net[1], net[2]
3. league[1], league[2]

4. pro[1], pro[2]
5. hip[1], hip[2], hip[3]
6. rail[1], rail[2], rail[3]

1._____

2._____

3._____

4._____

5._____

6._____

Spelling Dictionary

Parts of a Dictionary Entry

1   2   3   4

↓   ↓   ↓   ↓

heav·y (hev′ē), *adj.,* **heav·i·er,**
heav·i·est, *adv.* —*adj.* **1** hard to lift or
carry; of great weight: *a heavy
load.* See synonym study below.   **5**
2 of great amount, force, or
intensity: *A <u>heavy rain drenched</u>* ←**6**
us. —*adv.* **hang heavy,** pass slowly **7**
and uninterestingly: *The time hung
heavy on my hands.* (Old English ←**8**
hefig < hebban heave) —**heav′i ness,** ←**9**
10   *n.* **Syn.** *adj.* **1 Heavy** and **weighty**
mean of great weight. **Heavy,**
when used figuratively, suggests
something pressing down on the
mind or feelings: *The President has
heavy responsibilities.* **Weighty** is
used chiefly figuratively, applying
to something of great importance:
*She made a weighty
announcement.*

1 Entry word
2 Pronunciation
3 Part-of-speech label
4 Inflected forms
5 Definition
6 Illustrative sentence
7 Idiom
8 Etymology
9 Run-on entry
10 Synonym study

Full Pronunciation Key

a	hat, cap	**i**	it, pin	**p**	paper, cup	**v**	very, save
ā	age, face	**ī**	ice, five	**r**	run, try	**w**	will, woman
ä	father, far			**s**	say, yes	**y**	young, yet
âr	care, hair	**j**	jam, enjoy	**sh**	she, rush	**z**	zero, breeze
		k	kind, seek	**t**	tell, it	**zh**	measure,
b	bad, rob	**l**	land, coal	**th**	thin, both		seizure
ch	child, much	**m**	me, am	**ŦH**	then, smooth		
d	did, red	**n**	no, in			**ə**	represents:
		ng	long, bring	**u**	cup, butter		a in about
e	let, best			**u̇**	full, put		e in taken
ē	equal, be	**o**	hot, rock	**ü**	rule, move		i in pencil
ėr	term, learn	**ō**	open, go				o in lemon
		ȯ	all, saw				u in circus
f	fat, if	**ô**	order, store				
g	go, bag	**oi**	oil, voice				
h	he, how	**ou**	house, out				

Spellings of English Sounds*

Symbol	Spellings	Symbol	Spellings
a	at, plaid, half, laugh	ng	long, ink, handkerchief, tongue
ā	able, aid, say, age, eight, they, break, vein, gauge, crepe, beret	o	odd, honest
ä	father, ah, calm, heart, bazaar, yacht, sergeant	ō	open, oak, toe, own, home, oh, folk, though, bureau, sew, brooch, soul
âr	dare, aerial, fair, prayer, where, pear, their, they're	ȯ	all, author, awful, broad, bought, walk, taught, cough, Utah, Arkansas
b	bad, rabbit	ô	order, board, floor, tore
ch	child, watch, future, question	oi	oil, boy
d	did, add, filled	ou	out, owl, bough, hour
e	end, said, any, bread, says, heifer, leopard, friend, bury	p	pay, happy
		r	run, carry, wrong, rhythm
ē	equal, eat, eel, happy, cities, vehicle, ceiling, receive, key, these, believe, machine, liter, people	s	say, miss, cent, scent, dance, tense, sword, pizza, listen
		sh	she, machine, sure, ocean, special, tension, mission, nation
ėr	stern, earth, urge, first, word, journey	t	tell, button, two, Thomas, stopped, doubt, receipt, pizza
f	fat, effort, laugh, phrase		
g	go, egg, guest, ghost, league	th	thin
		ᴛʜ	then, breathe
gz	example, exhaust	u	up, oven, trouble, does, flood
h	he, who, jai alai, Gila monster	u̇	full, good, wolf, should
hw	wheat	ü	food, junior, rule, blue, who, move, threw, soup, through, shoe, two, fruit, lieutenant
i	it, England, ear, hymn, been, sieve, women, busy, build, weird		
ī	I, ice, lie, sky, type, rye, eye, island, high, eider, aisle, height, buy, coyote	v	very, have, of, Stephen
		w	will, quick
		y	yes, opinion
j	jam, gem, exaggerate, schedule, badger, bridge, soldier, large, allegiance	yü	use, few, cue, view, vacuum
		z	zero, has, buzz, scissors, xylophone
k	coat, kind, back, echo, ache, quit, account, antique, excite, acquire	zh	measure, garage, division
l	land, tell	ə	alone, complete, moment, authority, bargain, April, cautious, circus, pageant, physician, oxygen, dungeon, tortoise
m	me, common, climb, solemn, palm		
n	no, manner, knife, gnaw, pneumonia		

*Not all English spellings of these sounds are included in this list.

A

ab·bre·vi·ate (ə brē′vē āt), *v.t.*, **-at·ed, -at·ing.** shorten (a word or phrase) so that a part stands for the whole: *"Hour" is abbreviated to "hr."* (< Late Latin *abbreviatum* shortened < Latin *ad-* to + *brevis* short.)

ab·bre·vi·a·tion (ə brē′vē ā′shen), *n.* part of a word or phrase standing for the whole; shortened form: *"Dr." is an abbreviation of "Doctor."*

ab·duct (ab dukt′), *v.t.* carry off (a person) by force or by trickery; kidnap. (< Latin *abductum* led away < *ab-* away + *ducere* to lead) **—ab·duc′tion,** *n.*

ab·nor·mal (ab nôr′məl), *adj.* away from the normal; deviating from the ordinary conditions, the standard, or a type. See **irregular** for synonym study.

a·bol·ish (ə bol′ish), *v.t.* do away with completely; put an end to: *Slavery was abolished in the United States in 1865.* (< Middle French *aboliss-*, a form of *abolir* < Latin *abolere* destroy) **—a·bol′ish·a·ble,** *adj.*

ab·o·li·tion·ist (ab′ə lish′ə nist), *n.* **1** person who advocates abolition of any institution or custom. **2 Abolitionist,** person in the 1830s to 1860s who favored the compulsory abolition of slavery.

a·bra·sive (ə brā′siv), *n.* substance that erodes, grinds, or polishes a surface by friction. Sandpaper, pumice, and emery are abrasives. **—a·bra′sive·ness,** *n.*

ab·sorb (ab sôrb′), *v.t.* **1** take in or suck up (a liquid or gas): *The sponge absorbed the spilled milk.* **2** take in and make a part of itself; assimilate: *The U.S. has absorbed millions of immigrants.* (< Latin *absorbere* < *ab-* from + *sorbere* suck in) **—ab·sorb′a·ble,** *adj.*

ab·stain (ab stān′), *v.i.* **1** hold oneself back voluntarily, especially because of one's principles; refrain. **2** refrain from voting. (< Old French *abstenir* < Latin *abstinere* < *abs-* off + *tenere* to hold)

ab·sten·tion (ab sten′shən), *n.* **1** an abstaining; abstinence. **2** fact of not voting: *There were 5 votes in favor, 4 against, and 3 abstentions.*

ac·cel·e·ra·tion (ak sel′ə rā′shən), *n.* rate of change of velocity, expressed in meters/second/second.

acceleration
acceleration of
race cars

ac·ces·so·ry (ak ses′ər ē), *n., pl.* **-sor·ies,** *adj.* **—n. 1** subordinate part or detail; adjunct. **2** Often, **accessories,** *pl.* nonessential but usually desirable additional clothing, equipment, etc. **—adj.** added; extra; additional.

ac·com·pa·ny (ə kum′pə nē), *v.t.*, **-nied, -ny·ing.** go in company with. (< Middle French *accompagner* take as a companion < *a-* to + *compain* companion)

ac·cor·di·on (ə kôr′dē ən), *n.* a portable musical wind instrument played by pressing the keys and the bellows to force air through the reeds. **—adj.** having folds like an accordion: *a skirt with accordion pleats.* (< German *Akkordion*)

ac·cu·mu·late (ə kyü′myə lāt), *v.*, **-lat·ed, -lat·ing. —v.t.** collect little by little. **—v.i.** grow into a heap by degrees; pile up; gather: *Dust had accumulated in the house.* (< Latin *accumulatum* heaped up < *ad-* in addition + *cumulus* a heap)

ac·cu·ra·cy (ak′yər ə sē), *n.* condition of being without errors or mistakes; precise correctness; exactness.

a·chieve·ment (ə chēv′mənt), *n.* something achieved or won by exertion; accomplishment; feat: *Martin Luther King, Jr., won the Nobel Prize for his achievements.*

ac·knowl·edg·ment (ak nol′ij mənt), *n.* **1** something given or done to show that one has received a service, favor, gift, message, etc. **2** act of admitting the existence or truth of anything; admission.

ac·quit·tance (ə kwit′ns), *n.* a written release from a debt or obligation.

a·cre·age (ā′kər ij), *n.* **1** number of acres. **2** land sold by the acre.

a·crop·o·lis (ə krop′ə lis), *n.* **1** the high, fortified part or citadel of an ancient Greek city. **2 the Acropolis,** the citadel of Athens on which the Parthenon was built. (< Greek *akropolis* < *akros* highest part + *polis* city)

ad·di·tion (ə dish′ən), *n.* **1** operation, indicated by the sign +, of collecting separate numbers or quantities into one number or quantity known as the sum. **2** part added to a building.

ad·here (ad hir′), *v.i.*, **-hered, -her·ing.** stick fast; remain firmly attached; cling (*to*). (< Latin *adhaerere* < *ad-* to + *haerere* to stick)

ad·her·ent (ad hir′ent), *n.* a faithful supporter or follower: *an adherent of the conservative party.* —*adj.* sticking fast; attached.

ad·he·sion (ad hē′zhən), *n.* act or condition of adhering; sticking fast. (< Latin *adhaesionem* < *adhaerere.* See ADHERE.)

ad·he·sive (ad hē′siv), *n.* **1** gummed tape used to hold bandages in place; adhesive tape. **2** glue, paste, or other substance for sticking things together. —*adj.* holding fast; adhering easily; sticky. —**ad·he′sive·ly,** *adv.*

ad·ja·cent (ə jā′snt), *adj.* lying near or close; adjoining; next: *The house adjacent to ours has been sold.* (< Latin *adjacentem* < *ad-* near + *jacere* to lie) —**ad·ja′cent·ly,** *adv.*

ad·journ (ə jėrn′), *v.t.* put off until a later time; postpone: *The members of the club voted to adjourn.* —*v.i.* stop business or proceedings for a time; recess: *The court adjourned from Friday until Monday.* (< Old French *ajorner* < *a* to + *jorn* day)

ad·mir·al (ad′mer əl), *n.* **1** the commander of a navy or fleet. **2** officer in the United States Navy ranking next below a fleet admiral and next above a vice-admiral. (earlier *amiral* < Old French < Arabic *amīr al* chief of the)

ad·van·tage (ad van′tij), *n., v.,* **-taged, -tag·ing.** —*n.* a favorable circumstance or condition; any gain resulting from a better or superior position; benefit: *the advantages of good health and a sound education.* See synonym study below. —*v.t.* give an advantage to; help; benefit. (< Old French *advantage* < *avant* before < Latin *abante.*)

Syn. *n.* **1 Advantage, benefit, profit** mean gains of different kinds. **Advantage** applies to a gain resulting from a position of superiority over others: *In most sports, a well-coordinated person has an advantage over those with*

less coordination. **Benefit** applies to gain in personal or social improvement: *The general relaxation of the body is one of the chief benefits of swimming.* While **profit** applies especially to material gain it is also applied to gain in anything valuable: *There is profit even in mistakes.*

ad·van·ta·geous (ad′vən tā′jəs), *adj.* giving an advantage or advantages; favorable; beneficial.

ad·vent (ad′vent), *n.* a coming; arrival: *the advent of the new year, the advent of industrialism.* (< Latin *adventum* < *ad-* to + *venire* come)

ad·ven·tur·ous (ad ven′chər əs), *adj.* enterprising; daring.

ad·ver·si·ty (ad vėr′sə tē), *n., pl.* **-ties.** condition of being in unfavorable circumstances, as financial circumstances.

ad·ver·tise·ment (ad′ver tīz′mənt, ad vėr′tis mənt), *n.* a public notice or announcement, now always paid for, recommending some product or service.

ad·vo·cate (*v.* ad′və kāt; *n.* ad′və kit, ad′və kāt), *v.,* **-cat·ed, -cat·ing,** *n.* —*v.t.* speak or write in favor of. —*n.* person who defends, maintains, or publicly recommends a proposal, belief, etc.; supporter. (< Latin *advocatum* summoned < *ad-* to + *vocare* to call)

aer·i·al (âr′ē əl), *n.* the antenna of a radio, television set, etc. —*adj.* carried out from or done by aircraft: *an aerial photograph.*

aer·o·bics (âr′ō′biks), *n.* a system of physical exercises that adds the body's consumption of oxygen and improves the functioning of the circulatory system. (< *aerob(ic)* + *-ics*)

aes·thet·ic (es thet′ik), *adj.* based on or determined by beauty rather than by practically useful, scientific, or moral considerations. (< Greek *aisthētikos* sensitive, perceptive < *aisthanesthai* perceive) —**aes·thet′i·cal·ly,** *adv.*

af·fec·tive (af′ek tiv), *adj.* having to do with the emotions; emotional.

adversity

adversity caused by a flash flood in Australia

a	hat	**ī**	ice	**u̇**	put	**ə** stands for	
ā	age	**o**	not	**ü**	rule	**a**	in about
ä	far, calm	**ō**	open	**ch**	child	**e**	in taken
âr	care	**ȯ**	saw	**ng**	long	**i**	in pencil
e	let	**ô**	order	**sh**	she	**o**	in lemon
ē	equal	**oi**	oil	**th**	thin	**u**	in circus
ėr	term	**ou**	out	**ŦH**	then		
i	it	**u**	cup	**zh**	measure		

af·firm·a·tive ac·tion (ə fėr′mə tiv ak′shən), a program that encourages the employment of women and minorities in order to compensate for past discrimination.

af·ter·wards (af′tər wərdz), adv. later.

ag·gra·vate (ag′rə vāt), v.t., -vat·ed, -vat·ing. 1 make more burdensome; make worse: The danger was aggravated by rebellion at home. 2 INFORMAL. annoy; irritate; exasperate. (< Latin aggravatum made heavy < ad- on, to + gravis heavy)

ag·gres·sion (ə gresh′ən), n. practice of making assaults or attacks on the rights or territory of others as a method or policy. (< Latin aggressionem < ad- up to + gradi to step)

ag·gres·sive (ə gres′iv), adj. very active; energetic.

aisle (īl), n. passage between rows of seats in a hall, theater, school, etc. (< Middle French ele < Latin ala wing)

à la carte (ä′ lə kärt′), with a stated price for each dish (instead of one price for the whole meal). (< French, according to the bill of fare)

al·co·hol (al′kə hôl), n. the colorless, flammable, volatile liquid in wine, beer, whiskey, gin, and other fermented and distilled liquids that makes them intoxicating. (< Medieval Latin, originally, "fine powder," then "essence" < Arabic al-kuḥl the powdered antimony)

al·gae (al′jē), n.pl. group of related organisms, mostly aquatic and often independently mobile, containing chlorophyll but lacking true stems, roots, or leaves. (< Latin, plural of alga seaweed)

all-A·mer·i·can (ôl′ə mãr′ə kən), adj. made up entirely of Americans or American elements. —n. (in sports) a player who is all-American.

al·ler·gic (ə lėr′jik), adj. having an allergy: allergic to eggs.

Al·lies (al′īz), n.pl. the countries that fought against Germany, Italy, and Japan in World War II.

al·lot (ə lot′), v.t., -lot·ted, -lot·ting. divide and distribute in parts or shares. (< Middle French allotir < a- to + lot lot)

al·low (ə lou′), v., al·lowed, al·low·ing. let (someone) do something; permit: The class was not allowed to leave. (< Old French alouer < Latin allaudare approve < ad- to + laudare to praise)

all read·y (ôl red′ē), completely ready: She was all ready to begin exercising. See already.

all to·geth·er (ôl tə geth′ər), everyone in a group: We were all together for the picnic. See altogether.

al·lude (ə lüd′), v.i., -lud·ed, -lud·ing. refer indirectly (to); I didn't tell him of your decision; I didn't even allude to it. (< Latin alludere < ad- + ludere to play)

a lot (ə lot), very much: She misses her cat a lot.

a·loud (ə loud′), adv. loud enough to be heard; not in a whisper; loudly.

al·read·y (ôl red′ē), adv. 1 before this time: We arrived at noon but you had already left. 2 by this time; even now: Are you finished already? (for all ready)

al·to·geth·er (ôl′tə geth′ər), adv. 1 to the whole extent; completely; entirely: The house was altogether destroyed by fire. 2 on the whole; considering everything: Altogether, I'm sorry it happened. 3 in all: Altogether there were 14 books.

am·a·teur (am′ə chėr, am′ə tėr), n. 1 person who does something for pleasure, not for money or as a profession. 2 person who does something rather poorly. —adj. made or done by amateurs. (< French < Latin amator lover < amare to love)

am·bi·dex·trous (am′bə dek′strəs), adj. able to use both hands equally well.

am·bu·lance (am′byə ləns), n. an automobile, boat, or aircraft equipped to carry sick or injured.

am·phib·i·an (am fib′ē ən), n. any of a class of cold-blooded vertebrates with moist, scaleless skin that, typically, lay eggs in water where the young hatch and go through a larval or tadpole stage, breathing by means of gills. Frogs, toads, newts, and salamanders belong to this class.

a·nal·y·sis (ə nal′ə sis), n., pl. -ses (-sēz′). 1 a breaking up of anything complex into its various simple elements. 2 this process as a method of studying the nature of a thing. (< Greek < analyein loosen up < ana- up + lyein loosen)

an·chor (ang′kər), n. a heavy, shaped piece of iron or steel lowered into the water to hold a ship or boat fixed in a particular place. —v.t. hold in place with an anchor. (Old English ancor < Latin ancora < Greek ankyra)

algae

growing **algae**

amphibian

a long-tailed **amphibian**

an·cient (ān′shənt), *adj.* 1 of or belonging to times long past: *ancient records.* 2 of great age; very old: *the ancient hills.* —*n.* a very old person. (< Old French *ancien* < Late Latin *anteanus* former < Latin *ante* before)

an·nex (*v.* ə neks′; *n.* an′eks), *v.t.* join or add to a larger or more important thing: *The United States annexed Texas in 1845.* —*n.* an addition to an existing building. (< Latin *annexum* bound to < *ad-* to + *nectere* to bind)

an·ni·hi·late (ə nī′ə lāt), *v.t.,* **-lat·ed, -lat·ing.** destroy completely; wipe out of existence: *The flood annihilated over thirty towns and villages.* (< Late Latin *annihilatum* brought to nothing < Latin *ad-* to + *nihil* nothing) —**an·ni·hi·la′tive,** *adj.* —**an·ni·hi·la′tor,** *n.*

an·nu·al (an′yü əl), *adj.* 1 coming once a year: *A birthday is an annual event.* 2 in a year; for a year: *an annual salary of $12,000.* (< Late Latin *annualis* < Latin *annus* year) —**an′nu·al·ly,** *adv.*

an·nu·al rate (an′yü əl rāt), amount of interest charged or earned in a year.

an·nu·i·ty (ə nü′ə tē, ə nyü′ə tē), *n.,* *pl.* **-ties.** sum of money paid every year or at certain regular times. (< Medieval Latin *annuitatem* < Latin *annuus* yearly < *annus* year)

a·no·rak (ä′nə räk′), *n.* a heavy jacket with a fur hood, worn in arctic regions. (< Eskimo (Greenland) *ánorâq* clothing)

an·te·bel·lum (an′ti bel′-əm), *adj.* 1 before the war. 2 before the American Civil War. (< Latin *ante bellum* before the war)

an·ti·air·craft (an′tē âr′kraft′), *adj.* used in defense against enemy aircraft.

an·ti·bi·ot·ic (an′ti bī ot′ik), *n.* substance produced by a living organism, especially a bacterium or a fungus, that destroys or weakens harmful microorganisms.

an·ti·bod·y (an′ti bod′ē), *n., pl.* **-bod·ies.** a protein substance produced in the blood or tissues that destroys or weakens bacteria or neutralizes poisons.

an·ti·dote (an′ti dōt), *n.* medicine or remedy that counteracts the effects of a poison: *Milk is an antidote for some poisons.* (< Greek *antidoton* < *anti-* against + *didonai* give)

an·ti·freeze (an′ti frēz′), *n.* liquid with a low freezing point added to the cooling medium in the radiator of an internal-combustion engine to prevent the system from freezing.

an·ti·his·ta·mine (an′ti his′tə mēn′), *n.* any of various drugs that inhibit or relieve the effects of histamine in the body, used in the treatment of colds and allergies.

an·ti·mis·sile (an′ti mis′əl), *adj.* designed or used to intercept and destroy enemy missiles.

an·ti·sep·tic (an′tə sep′tik), *n.* substance that prevents the growth of germs that cause infection.

an·ti·so·cial (an′ti sō′shəl), *adj.* 1 against the general welfare: *antisocial behavior.* 2 opposed to friendly relationship and normal companionship with others.

an·ti·trust (an′ti trust′), *adj.* opposed to trusts or other business monopolies: *antitrust legislation.*

an·y·more (en′ē môr′, en′ē mōr′), *adv.* at present; now; currently.

an·y more (en′ē môr), more than one has already had: *I am too tired to play any more games with you.*

an·y·way (en′ē wā), *adv.* 1 in any case; at least: *I am coming anyway, no matter what.* 2 in any way whatever. 3 carelessly.

an·y way (en′ē wā), no matter which way: *Any way I go, my dog Ginger finds me.*

a·part (ə pärt′), *adv.* 1 to pieces; in pieces; in separate parts: *Take the watch apart.* 2 away from each other. —*adj.* separate.

a part (ə pärt), thing that helps to make up a whole: *A chapter is a part of a book.*

ancient (def. 1)
ancient ruins in Turkey

a	hat	**ī**	ice	**u̇**	put		**ə** stands for	
ā	age	**o**	not	**ü**	rule		**a**	in about
ä	far, calm	**ō**	open	**ch**	child		**e**	in taken
âr	care	**ȯ**	saw	**ng**	long		**i**	in pencil
e	let	**ô**	order	**sh**	she		**o**	in lemon
ē	equal	**oi**	oil	**th**	thin		**u**	in circus
ėr	term	**ou**	out	**ᴛʜ**	then			
i	it	**u**	cup	**zh**	measure			

a·part·heid (ə pärt′hāt, ə pärt′hīt), *n.* racial segregation, especially as practiced by law in the Republic of South Africa. (< Afrikaans, separateness)

a·pol·o·gy (ə pol′ə jē), *n., pl.* **-gies.** words of regret for an offense or accident; expressing regret and asking pardon. (< Late Latin *apologia* a speech in defense < Greek < *apo-* + *legein* speak)

ap·pre·hend (ap′ri hend′), *v.t.* formally arrest or seize (a person): *The suspect was apprehended.* (< Latin *apprehendere* < *ad-* upon + *prehendere* seize)

ap·pre·hen·sive (ap′ri hen′siv), *adj.* afraid that some misfortune is about to occur; fearful.

ap·pro·pri·ate (*adj.* ə prō′prē it; *v.* ə prō′prē āt), *adj., v.,* **-at·ed, -at·ing.** *adj.* especially right or proper for the occasion; suitable; fitting: *Plain, simple clothes are appropriate for school wear.* —*v.t.* set apart for a special purpose: *The legislature appropriated a billion dollars for foreign aid.* (< Late Latin *appropriatum* made one's own < Latin *ad-* to + *proprius* one's own) —**ap·pro′pri·ate·ly,** *adv.*

ap·ro·pos (ap′rə pō′), *adv.* fittingly; opportunely. —*adj.* to the point; fitting; suitable. (< French *à propos* to the purpose)

a·rach·no·pho·bi·a (ə rak′nə fō′bē ə), *n.* an abnormal fear of spiders.

ar·chae·ol·o·gy (är′kē ol′ə jē), *n.* the scientific study of the people, customs, and life of ancient times.

ar·chi·pel·a·go (är′kə pel′ə gō, är′chə pel′ə gō), *n., pl.* **-gos,** or **-goes.** group of many islands. (< Italian *arcipelago* < *arci-* chief + *pelago* sea)

ar·chi·tec·ture (är′kə tek′chər), *n.* science or art of planning and designing buildings.

arc·tic (ärk′tik, är′tik), *adj.* at or near the North Pole: *the arctic fox.* (< Greek *arktikos* of the Bear (constellation) < *arktos* bear)

ar·gu·ment (är′gyə mənt), *n.* discussion by persons who disagree.

ar·ma·dil·lo (är′mə dil′ō), *n., pl.* **-los.** any of several small, burrowing, chiefly nocturnal mammals ranging from Texas to tropical America. Armadillos are covered with an armorlike shell of small, bony plates. (< Spanish, diminutive of *armado* armed (one) < Latin *armatum* armed)

archaeology
Archaeology helps reconstruct a picture of life in the past.

ar·range·ment (ə rānj′mənt), *n.* **1** a putting or a being put in proper order. **2** something arranged in a particular way.

Art De·co (ärt dā′kō), a decorative style of the 1920s and 1930s which used vivid colors, bold outline, and geometrical forms. (< French *Art Déco,* short for *Arts Décoratifs* Decorative Arts)

ar·ti·cle (är′tə kəl), *n.,* a written composition on a special subject forming part of the contents of a magazine, newspaper, or book. (< Old French < Latin *articulus,* diminutive of *artus* joint)

ar·ti·fact (är′tə fakt), *n.* anything made by human skill or work, especially a tool or weapon. (< Latin *artem* art + *factum* made)

ar·ti·fi·cial in·tel·li·gence (är′tə fish′əl in tel′ ə jəns), ways of making the computer more closely mimic human thinking.

ar·ti·fi·cial res·pi·ra·tion, (är′tə fish′əl res′pə rā′shən), the first-aid procedure used to restore normal breathing to a person who has stopped breathing by forcing air alternately into and out of the lungs.

as·cent (ə sent′), *n.* **1** act of going up; rising: *early balloon ascents.* **2** act of climbing a ladder, mountain.

as·sem·bly (ə sem′blē), *n., pl.* **-blies.** group of people gathered together for some purpose: *The principal addressed the school assembly.*

as·sent (ə sent′), *v.i.* express agreement; agree; consent: *Everyone assented to the plans for the dance.* (< Latin *assentire* < *ad-* along with + *sentire* feel, think)

as·sist·ance (ə sis′təns), *n.* an assisting; help; aid.

as·sist·ant (ə sis′tənt), *n.* person who assists another, especially as a subordinate in some office or work. —*adj.* helping; assisting.

a·sym·met·ri·cal (ā′sə met′rə kəl), *adj.* not symmetrical.

at·om (at′əm), *n.* the smallest particle of an element that has all the characteristics of that element. (< Latin *atomus* < Greek *atomos* indivisible < *a-* not + *tomos* a cutting)

a·tom·ic num·ber (ə tom′ik num′bər), the number of protons in an atom's nucleus.

a·tro·cious (ə trō′shəs), *adj.* monstrously wicked or cruel: *an atrocious crime.* —**a·tro′cious·ly,** *adv.*

a·troc·i·ty (ə tros′ə tē), n., pl. -ties. monstrous wickedness or cruelty. (< Latin *atrocitatem* < *atrox* fierce)

at·tend·ance (ə ten′dəns), n. 1 act of attending. 2 number of people present; persons attending. 3 **take attendance,** call the roll.

aus·pi·cious (ȯ spish′əs), adj. with signs of success; favorable.

au·to·mat·ic (ȯ′tə mat′ik), adj. (of machinery, etc.) moving or acting by itself; regulating itself: *an automatic elevator.* (< Greek *automatos* self-acting) —**au′to·mat′i·cal·ly,** adv.

a·vail·a·ble (ə vā′lə bel), adj. 1 that can be used or secured: *She is not available for the job; she has other work.* 2 that can be had: *All available tickets were sold.*

a·venge (ə venj′), v., **a·venged, a·veng·ing.** —v.t. take revenge for or on behalf of: *Hamlet avenged his father's murder.* See **revenge** for synonym study. —v.i. get revenge. (< Old French *avengier* < *a-* to + *vengier* avenge < Latin *vindicare*) —**a·veng′er,** n.

awk·ward (ȯk′wərd), adj. not graceful or skillful in movement; clumsy: *The seal is awkward on land.* (< obsolete *awk* perversely, in the wrong way < Scandinavian (Old Icelandic) *öfugr* + *-ward*) —**awk′ward·ly,** adv.

ax·is (ak′sis), n., pl. **ax·es. the Axis,** Germany, Italy, Japan, and their allies, during World War II. (< Latin)

B

ba·con (bā′kən), n. 1 salted and smoked meat from the back and sides of a hog. 2 **bring home the bacon, a** succeed; win. **b** earn a living. (< Middle French < Germanic)

bag·gage (bag′ij), n. the trunks, bags, suitcases, etc., that a person takes along when traveling; luggage. (< Old French *baggage* < *bague* bundle)

bal·ance (bal′əns), n., v., **-anced, -anc·ing.** —n. steady condition or position; steadiness. —v.t. keep a steady condition or position. (< Old French < Late Latin *bilancem* two-scaled < Latin *bi-* two + *lanx*)

bam·boo (bam bü′), n., pl. **-boos.** any of various species of woody or treelike tropical or semitropical grasses. (< Dutch *bamboe* < Malay *bambu*)

ban·jo (ban′jō), n., pl. **-jos.** a musical instrument having four or five strings, played by plucking the strings with the fingers. (probably of Bantu origin)

barbed wire (bärbd wīr), wire with sharp points on it every few inches, used for fences.

ba·rom·e·ter (bə rom′ə tər), n. 1 instrument for measuring the pressure of air, used in determining height above sea level and in predicting probable changes in the weather. 2 something that indicates changes: *His newspaper column is a barometer of public opinion.* (< Greek *baros* weight + English *-meter*)

bar·ri·er (bâr′ē ər), n. pl. **bar·ri·ers,** something that stands in the way; obstacle. (< Anglo-French *barrere* < *barre* bar)

base (bās), n. 1 (of an exponent) a number raised to a power. In 4^3, 4 is the base. 2 (geometry) a name used for a side of a polygon or surface of a space figure.

bash·ful (bash′fəl), adj. uneasy in unaccustomed situations or in the presence of others; embarrassed.

ba·sic (bā′sik), adj. of, at, or forming a base; fundamental: *Addition and subtraction are some of the basic processes of arithmetic.* —n. an essential part. —**ba′si·cal·ly,** adv.

ba·tik (bə tēk′), n. method of executing designs on textiles by covering the material with wax in a pattern, dyeing the parts left exposed, and then removing the wax. (< Javanese *mbatik*)

bamboo
Bamboo is a treelike grass that grows in groves.

banjo
A **banjo** has a head and neck like a guitar and a body like a tambourine.

a	hat	ī	ice	u̇	put	ə stands for
ā	age	o	not	ü	rule	a in about
ä	far, calm	ō	open	ch	child	e in taken
âr	care	ȯ	saw	ng	long	i in pencil
e	let	ô	order	sh	she	o in lemon
ē	equal	oi	oil	th	thin	u in circus
ėr	term	ou	out	ᴛH	then	
i	it	u	cup	zh	measure	

bazaar (def. 1)

a **bazaar** for shopping and browsing

bat·ter·y (bat′ər ē), *n., pl.* **-ter·ies. 1** a single electric cell: *a flashlight battery.* **2** set of two or more electric cells connected together for the production of electric current: *a car battery.*

ba·zaar (bə zär′), *n.* **1** (in various countries of Asia) a marketplace consisting of a street or streets full of small shops and booths. **2** sale of articles held for some charity or purpose. (< Persian *bāzār*)

be·cause (bi kòz′), *conj.* for the reason that; since: *Children play ball because it's fun.* —*adv.* **because of,** by reason of; on account of. (Middle English *bi cause* by (the) cause)

be·fore (bi fôr′), *prep.* **1** earlier than: *Come before five o'clock.* **2** in front of; in advance of; ahead of: *Walk before me.* **3** rather than; sooner than: *I will die before giving in.* **4** in the presence of or sight of: *perform before an audience.* —*adv.* **1** earlier; sooner. **2** in front; in advance; ahead: *I went before to see if the road was safe.* **3** until now; in the past: *I didn't know that before.* —*conj.* **1** previously to the time when: *I would like to talk to her before she goes.* **2** rather than; sooner than: *I will die before I give in.* (Old English *beforan*)

be·gin·ning (bi gin′ing), *n.* **1** a start: *make a good beginning.* **2** first part. —*adj.* that begins.

be·lieve (bi lēv′), *v.*, **-lieved, -liev·ing.** —*v.t.* accept as true or real: *We all believe that the earth is round.* —*v.i.* have faith (in a person or thing); trust: *We believe in our friends.* (Old English *belēfan*)

bel·li·cose (bel′ə kōs), *adj.* fond of fighting and quarreling; warlike. (< Latin *bellicosus* < *bellum* war)

bel·lig·er·ent (bə lij′ər ənt), *adj.* fond of fighting; tending or inclined to war. —*n.* person engaged in fighting with another person. (< Latin *belligerantem* < *bellum* war + *gerere* to wage)

ben·e·fac·tor (ben′ə fak′tər), *n.* person who has helped others, either by gifts or some kind act. (< Late Latin < Latin *benefactum* befitted < *bene* well + *facere* do)

ben·e·fi·cial (ben′ə fish′əl), *adj.* producing good; favorable; helpful: *Sunshine is beneficial.*

ben·e·fi·ci·ar·y (ben′ə fish′ē är′ē), *n., pl.* **-ar·ies.** person who receives or is to receive money or property from an insurance policy, a will.

ben·e·fit (ben′ə fit), *n.* anything which is for the good of a person or thing; advantage; help. See **advantage** for synonym study. —*v.t.* give benefit to; be good for: *Rest will benefit a sick person.* (< Anglo-French *benfet* < Latin *benefactum* good deed < *bene* well + *facere* do)

be·nev·o·lent (bə nev′ə lənt), *adj.* wishing or intended to promote the happiness of others; charitable.

be·nign (bi nīn′), *adj.* **1** kindly in feeling; benevolent; gracious: *a benign old woman.* **2** not dangerous to health; not malignant: *a benign tumor.* (< Latin *benignus* < *bene* well + *-gnus* born)

bi·o·chem·ist (bī′ō kem′ ist), *n.* an expert in the science that deals with the chemical processes of living matter; biological chemistry.

bi·og·ra·pher (bē ŏg′rē fər), *n.* person who writes a biography.

bi·og·ra·phy (bī og′rə fē), *n., pl.* **-phies.** an account of a person's life.

bi·ol·o·gy (bī ol′ə jē), *n.* the scientific study of living organisms, including their origins, structures, activities, and distribution. Botany and zoology are branches of biology.

bi·on·ic (bī on′ik), *adj.* having both biological and electronic parts.

bi·on·ics (bī on′iks), *n.* study of the anatomy and physiology of animals as a basis for new or improved electronic devices. (< bio(logy) + (electro)nics)

bi·op·sy (bī′op sē), *n., pl.* **-sies.** examination of cells or tissues taken from a living body, for diagnosis. (< *bio-* + Greek *opsis* a viewing)

bi·zarre (bə zär′), *adj.* strikingly odd in appearance or style. (< French < Spanish *bizarro* brave < Italian *bizzarro* angry < *bizza* anger)

black hole (blak hōl), region of space in which so much mass is concentrated that nothing, not even light, can escape; the result of the death of massive stars.

BLT, abbreviation for a kind of sandwich: bacon, lettuce, and tomato.

boc·cie (boch′ē), *n.* an Italian form of the game of bowls, played outdoors on a narrow, enclosed court. (< Italian *bocce*, plural of *boccia* ball)

book·keep·er (bùk′kē′pər), *n.* person who keeps a record of accounts.

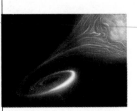

black hole

a mysterious **black hole** in space

boom (büm), *n.* a long pole or beam, used to extend the bottom of a sail.

boot·leg·ger (büt′leg′ər), *n., pl.* **boot·leg·gers.** person who sells, transports, or makes goods (especially alcoholic liquor) unlawfully. (from practice of smuggling liquor in boot legs)

borsch (bôrsh), *n.* a Russian soup consisting of meat stock, cabbage, and onions, colored red with beet juice and served with sour cream. (< Russian *borshch*)

Bos·ton Mas·sa·cre (bò′stən mas′ə kər), violent encounter between American colonists and British soldiers in Boston, March 5, 1770.

bouil·lon (bùl′yon), *n.* a clear, thin soup. (< French < *bouillir* to boil)

bounce (bouns), *v.,* **bounces, bounced, bounc·ing,** *v.i.* spring into the air like a rubber ball. —*n.* a springing back; bound; rebound. (Middle English *bunsen*)

boy·cott (boi′kot), *v.t.* combine against (a person, business, nation, etc.) in agreement not to buy from, sell to, or associate with and try to keep others from doing so. (< Captain Charles C. *Boycott,* 1832-1897, English land agent in Ireland whose tenants and neighbors boycotted him when he refused to lower rents)

breath·ing (brē′ŦHing), *n.* respiration. —*adj.* living.

breath·tak·ing (breth′tā′king), *adj.* thrilling; exciting.

brev·i·ty (brev′ə tē), *n., pl.* **-ties.** shortness in speech or writing. (< Latin *brevitatem* < *brevis* short)

brief (brēf), *adj.* using few words; concise. —*n.* a short statement; summary. (< Old French *bref* < Latin *brevem* short.) —**brief′ly,** *adv.*

budg·et (buj′it), *n.* estimate of the amount of money that will probably be received and spent for various purposes in a given time. —*v.i.* draw up or prepare a budget. (< Middle French *bougette,* diminutive of *bouge* bag < Latin *bulga*)

bul·lion (bùl′yən), *n.* gold or silver in the form of ingots or bars. (< Anglo-French < Old French *bouillir* to boil; influenced by Old French *billon* debased metal)

bun·ga·low (bung′gə lō), *n.* a small house, usually of one story or a story and a half, with low, sweeping lines.

bur·eau (byùr′ō), *n., pl.* **bur·eaus** (byùr′ōz). chest of drawers for clothes, often having a mirror; dresser. (< French, desk (originally cloth-covered) < Old French *burel,* diminutive of *bure* coarse woolen cloth < Late Latin *burra*)

bur·eau·crat (byùr′ə krat), *n.* official in a bureaucracy.

C

caf·e·ter·i·a (kaf′ə tir′ē ə), *n.* restaurant where people wait on themselves. (< Mexican Spanish *cafetería* coffee shop < *café* coffee)

cake (kāk), *n.* **1** a baked mixture of flour, sugar, eggs, flavoring, and other things. **2 take the cake,** SLANG. **a** win first prize. **b** excel. (probably < Scandinavian (Old Icelandic) *kaka*)

cal·cu·lus (kal′kyə ləs), *n., pl.* **-li** (-lī), **-lus·es.** plaque that has hardened on the teeth; called tartar.

cal·lig·ra·phy (kə lig′rə fē), *n.* beautiful handwriting. (< Greek *kalligraphia* < *kallos* beauty + *graphein* write)

cal·lous (kal′əs), *adj.* hard or hardened, as parts of the skin that are exposed to constant pressure.

cal·lus (kal′əs), *n.* a hard, thickened place on the skin. (< Latin)

cam·ou·flage (kam′ə fläzh), *n., v.,* **-flaged, -flag·ing.** —*n.* a disguise or false appearance serving to conceal. The white fur of a polar bear is a natural camouflage. —*v.t.* give a false appearance to in order to conceal; disguise. (< French < *camoufler* to disguise)

calligraphy
an inscription in **calligraphy**

a	hat	**ī**	ice	**u̇**	put	**ə**	stands for
ā	age	**o**	not	**ü**	rule	**a**	in about
ä	far, calm	**ō**	open	**ch**	child	**e**	in taken
âr	care	**ȯ**	saw	**ng**	long	**i**	in pencil
e	let	**ô**	order	**sh**	she	**o**	in lemon
ē	equal	**oi**	oil	**th**	thin	**u**	in circus
ėr	term	**ou**	out	**ŦH**	then		
i	it	**u**	cup	**zh**	measure		

Ca·na·di·an (kə nā′dē ən), *adj.* of Canada or its people. —*n.* native or inhabitant of Canada.

ca·nas·ta (kə nas′tə), *n.* a card game similar to rummy, played with two decks of cards plus four jokers. (< Spanish, literally, basket, ultimately < Latin *canistrum*.)

can·cel·la·tion (kan′sə lā′shən), *n.* **1** a canceling. **2** a being canceled.

can·did (kan′did), *adj.* saying openly what one really thinks; frank and sincere; outspoken: *a candid reply.* (< Latin *candidus* white < *candere* to shine) —**can′did·ness**, *n.*

can·ta·loupe (kan′tl ōp), *n.* kind of muskmelon with a hard, rough rind and sweet, juicy, orange flesh. (< French *cantaloup* < Italian *Cantalupo* papal estate near Rome where first cultivated)

can·vas (kan′vəs), *n.* piece of canvas on which an oil painting is painted. —*adj.* made of canvas. (< Old French *canevas* < Latin *cannabis* hemp)

can·vass (kan′vəs), *v.t.* go through (a city, district, etc.) asking for votes, orders, donations. —*n.* act or process of canvassing. (< obsolete verb *canvass* toss (someone) in a sheet, (later) shake out, discuss < *canvas*) —**can′vass·er**, *n.*

cap·i·tal·ism (kap′ə tə liz′əm), *n.* an economic system based on the ownership of land, factories, and other productions by private individuals or groups of individuals who compete with one another.

cap·ture (kap′chər), *v.,* **-tured, -tur·ing.** *n.* —*v.t.* make a prisoner of; take by force, skill, or trickery; seize. —*n.* capturing. (< Latin *captura* a taking < *capere* take)

car·a·way (kar′ə wā), *n.* plant of the same family as parsley that yields fragrant, spicy seeds which are used to flavor bread, rolls, cakes, etc. (< Arabic *karawyā*)

car·di·ol·o·gist (kär′dē ol′ə jist), *n.* an expert in cardiology, a branch of medicine dealing with the heart and the diagnosis and treatment of its diseases.

car·i·ca·ture (kar′ə kə chùr), *n., v.,* **-tured, -tur·ing.** —*n.* picture, cartoon, or description that exaggerates the peculiarities of a person or the defects of a thing. —*v.t.* make a caricature of. (< French < Italian *caricatura* < *caricare* overload, exaggerate < Late Latin *carricare* to load < Latin *carrus* wagon)

car·ies (kãr′ēz, kãr′ē ēz), *n., pl.* **car·ies. 1** decay of teeth or bones. **2** cavity formed in a tooth by such decay. (< Latin)

car·tog·ra·pher (kär tog′rə fər), *n.* maker of maps or charts.

cas·ta·net (kas′tə net′), *n.* one of a pair of instruments held in the hand and clicked together to beat time for dancing or music. (< Spanish *castañeta* < Latin *castanea*.)

cat·a·ma·ran (kat′ə mə ran′), *n.* boat with two hulls side by side joined by crosspieces. (< Tamil *kattamaram* tied tree)

ca·tas·tro·phe (kə tas′trə fē), *n.* a sudden, widespread, or extraordinary disaster; great calamity or misfortune. (< Greek *katastrophē* an overturning < *kata-* down + *strephein* to turn)

cau·cus (kȯ kəs), *n.* a meeting of members or leaders of a political party to choose candidates, etc. —*v.i.* hold a caucus. (probably of Algonquian origin)

cede (sēd), *v.t.,* **ced·ed, ced·ing.** give up; surrender; hand over to another: *Spain ceded the Philippines to the United States.* (< Latin *cedere* yield, go)

cen·ten·ni·al (sen ten′ē əl), *adj.* **1** of or having to do with 100 years or the 100th anniversary. **2** 100 years old. —*n.* **1** a 100th anniversary: **2** celebration of the 100th anniversary. (< Latin *centum* hundred + English *(bi)ennial*)

cen·ter·board (sen′tər bôrd′), *n.* a movable keel of a sailboat. It is lowered through a slot in the bottom of a boat to prevent drifting to leeward.

cen·ti·me·ter (sen′tə mē′tər), *n.* unit of length equal to ¹⁄₁₀₀ of a meter.

cen·ti·pede (sen′tə pēd′), *n.* any of a class of flat, wormlike arthropods with many pairs of legs, the front pair of which are clawlike and contain poison glands. (< Latin *centipeda* < *centum* hundred + *pedem* foot)

chal·lenge (chal′ənj), *v.,* **-lenged, -leng·ing,** *n.* —*v.t.* call to a game or contest. —*n.* a call to a game or contest. (< Old French *chalenger* < Latin *calumniari* to slander < *calumnia* false accusation.) —**chal′leng·er**, *n.*

char·i·ta·ble (chãr′ə tə bəl), *adj.* **1** generous in giving to poor, sick, or helpless people. **2** of or for charity.

cantaloupe

a **cantaloupe** cut into halves

catastrophe

the **catastrophe** of Hurricane Camille in Louisiana, 1969

Charles·ton (chärlz′tən), *n.* a lively ballroom dance, especially popular in the 1920s.

chem·i·cal for·mu·la (kem′ə kəl fôr′myə lə), expression showing by chemical symbols the composition of a compound, such as H_2O.

Cher·o·kee (châr′ə kē), *n., pl.* **-kee** or **-kees.** member of a tribe of Iroquois Indians of the southern Appalachians, now living mostly in Oklahoma.

chip (chip), *n., pl.* **chips.** in electronics: **a** a small piece of semiconductor material, usually silicon, which holds an integrated circuit. **b** an integrated circuit.

chop su·ey (chop′ sü′ē), fried or stewed meat and vegetables cut up and cooked in a sauce. It is served with rice. (< Chinese (Canton) *tsap sui* odds and ends)

cho·re·o·graph (kôr′ē ə graf), *v.t.* arrange or design dancing for.

chor·tle (chôr′tl), *v.,* **-tled, -tling,** *n.* —*v.i., v.t.* chuckle or snort with glee. —*n.* a gleeful chuckle or snort. (blend of *chuckle* and *snort;* coined by Lewis Carroll) —**chor′tler,** *n.*

chron·ic (kron′ik), *adj.* **1** lasting a long time: *Rheumatism is often a chronic disease.* **2** suffering long from an illness: *a chronic invalid.* **3** never stopping; constant; habitual: *a chronic liar.* (< Greek *chronikos* of time < *chronos* time) —**chron′i·cal·ly,** *adv.*

chron·i·cle (kron′ə kəl), *n., v.,* **-cled, -cling.** —*n.* record of events in the order in which they took place; history; story. —*v.t.* write the history of; tell the story of.

chron·o·graph (kron′ə graf), *n.* instrument for measuring very short intervals of time accurately, such as a stopwatch. (< Greek *chronos* time + English *-graph*)

chron·o·log·i·cal (kron′ə loj′ə kəl), *adj.* of or in accordance with chronology; arranged in the order in which the events happened. —**chron′o·log′i·cal·ly,** *adv.*

chry·san·the·mum (krə san′thə məm), *n.* any of a genus of plants of the composite family that have many-petaled round flowers of various colors and that bloom in the fall. (< Latin < Greek *chrysanthemon* < *chrysos* gold + *anthemon* flower)

chuck wag·ons (chuk wag′ənz), (in the western United States) wagons or trucks, that carry food and cooking equipment for workers.

cin·na·mon (sin′ə mən), *n.* spice made from the dried, reddish-brown inner bark of a laurel tree of the East Indies. (< Latin < Greek *kinnamon;* of Semitic origin)

cir·cuit break·er (sèr′kit brā′kər), safety device that switches off when too much current flows in a circuit.

cir·cum·lo·cu·tion (sèr′kəm lō kyü′shən), *n.* use of several or many words instead of one or a few.

cir·cum·scribe (sèr′kəm skrīb′), *v.t.* **-scribed, -scrib·ing.** draw a line around; mark the boundaries of; bound. (< Latin *circumscribere* < *circum* around + *scribere* write)

cir·cum·stance (sèr′kəm stans), *n.* condition that accompanies an act or event. (< Latin *circumstantia* < *circumstare* surround < *circum* around + *stare* stand)

cir·cum·stan·tial (sèk′kəm stan′shəl), *adj.* depending on or based on circumstances: *Stolen jewels found in a person's possession are circumstantial evidence.*

cir·cum·vent (sèr′kəm vent′), *v.t.* **1** get the better of or defeat by trickery; outwit: *circumvent the law.* **2** go around. (< Latin *circumventum* circumvented < *circum* around + *venire* come) —**cir′cum·ven′tion,** *n.*

civ·il dis·o·be·di·ence (siv′əl dis′ə bē′dē əns), deliberate, public refusal to obey a law that one considers unjust. Civil disobedience is often used as a form of protest.

cinnamon
different forms of the spice **cinnamon**

a	hat	**ī**	ice
ā	age	**o**	not
ä	far, calm	**ō**	open
âr	care	**ȯ**	saw
e	let	**ô**	order
ē	equal	**oi**	oil
èr	term	**ou**	out
i	it	**u**	cup

u̇	put	**ə stands for**	
ü	rule	**a**	in about
ch	child	**e**	in taken
ng	long	**i**	in pencil
sh	she	**o**	in lemon
th	thin	**u**	in circus
ᴛʜ	then		
zh	measure		

Civil War

Christian Fleetwood, an honored soldier from the **Civil War**

civ·il rights (siv′əl rīts), the rights of a citizen, guaranteed to all citizens of the United States, regardless of race, color, religion, or sex.

Civ·il War (siv′əl wôr), war between the northern and southern states of the United States from 1861 to 1865; War Between the States.

claim (klām), v.t. say one has (a right, title, possession, etc.) and demand that others recognize it; assert one's right to: *claim a tract of land.* —n. something that is claimed. (< Old French *claimer, clamer* < Latin *clamare* call, proclaim) —**claim′a·ble**, adj.

clean·li·ness (klen′lē nis), n. cleanness; habitual cleanness.

clothes (klōz, klōᴛʜz), n.pl. coverings for a person's body; clothing.

co·ed·u·ca·tion·al (kō′ej ə kā′shə nəl), adj. educating boys and girls or men and women together in the same school or classes.

co·ex·ist (kō′ig zist′), v.i. exist together or at the same time.

co·he·sive (kō hē′siv), adj. tending to hold together; sticking together. —**co·he′sive·ly**, adv. —**co·he′sive·ness**, n.

co·lead·ers (cō lē′dərs), two or more people who together assume the responsibilities of leadership.

col·lage (kə läzh′), n. picture made by pasting on a background such things as parts of photographs and newspapers, fabric, and string. (< French, pasting, gluing < Greek *kolla* glue)

col·lapse (kə laps′), v., **-lapsed, -laps·ing**, n. —v.i. break down; fail suddenly. —n. a falling or caving in; sudden shrinking together. (< Latin *collapsum* fallen completely < *com-* completely + *labi* to fall)

col·lect·i·ble (kə lek′tə bəl), adj. able to be collected. —n. anything that is collected, especially unusual or dated objects having little worth.

col·lege (kol′ij), n. institution of higher learning that gives degrees.

col·lo·qui·al (kə lō′kwē əl), adj. used in everyday, informal talk, but not in formal speech or writing.

colo·nel (kėr′nl), n. a commissioned officer in the army, air force, or Marine Corps ranking next above a lieutenant colonel and next below a brigadier general. (< Middle French *coronel, colonel* < Italian *colonello* commander of a regiment < *colonna* military column < Latin *columna* column)

co·los·sal (kə los′əl), adj. of huge size.

Co·lum·bi·a Riv·er (kə lum′bē ə riv′ər), river flowing from British Columbia through E Washington and between Washington and Oregon into the Pacific. 1214 mi.

com·mand (kə mand′), v.t. **1** give an order to; direct. **2** have authority or power over; be in control of; govern: *to command a ship.* **3** have a position of control over; rise high above; overlook: *A hilltop commands the plain around it.* —n. **1** an order; direction: *The admiral obeyed the queen's command.* **2** authority; power; control: *The rebels are now in command of the government.* (< Old French *comander* < Popular Latin *commandare,* alteration of Latin *commendare.*)

com·mand·er (kə man′dər), n. **1** person who commands. **2** officer in charge of an army or a part of an army. **3** a navy officer ranking next below a captain and next above a lieutenant commander.

com·man·do (kə man′dō), n., pl. **com·man·dos. 1** soldier trained to make brief surprise raids in enemy territory. **2** group of such soldiers. (< Afrikaans *kommando*)

com·mem·o·rate (kə mem′ə rāt′), v., **-rat·ed, -rat·ing.** preserve or honor the memory of. (< Latin *commemoratum* remembered < *com-* + *memorare* bring to mind)

com·men·da·tion (kom′ən dā′shən), n. praise; approval.

com·mis·e·rate (kə miz′ə rāt′), v.t., v.i., **-rat·ed, -rat·ing.** feel or express sorrow for another's suffering or trouble; sympathize with. (< Latin *commiseratum* pitied < *com-* + *miser* wretched) —**com·mis′e·ra′tion**, n.

com·mis·sion (kə mish′ən), n. percentage of the amount of business done, paid to the agent who does it. (< Latin *commissionem* < *committere* commit)

com·mit (kə mit′), v.t., **-mit·ted, -mit·ting. 1** do or perform (usually something wrong): *commit a crime.* **2** hand over for safekeeping; deliver. **3** send to prison or an asylum. **4** give over; carry over; transfer: *commit a poem to memory.* **5** reveal (one's opinion). **6** involve; pledge. (< Latin *committere* < *com-* with + *mittere* send, put) —**com·mit′ta·ble**, adj.

com·mu·ni·ty (kə myü′nə tē), *n., pl.* **-ties.** all the people living in the same place and subject to the same laws; people of any town.

com·mute (kə myüt′), *v.,* **-mut·ed, -mut·ing,** *n.* —*v.i.* travel regularly to and from work especially between suburb and downtown. —*n.* the distance ordinarily traveled by a commuter. (< Latin *commutare* < *com-* + *mutare* to change)

com·par·a·ble (kom′pər ə bəl), *adj.* able to be compared.

com·par·i·son (kəm pâr′ə sən), *n.* act or process of comparing; finding the likenesses and differences.

com·pas·sion·ate (kəm pash′ə nit), *adj.* desiring to relieve another's suffering; sympathetic.
—**com·pas′sion·ate·ly,** *adv.*

com·pat·i·ble (kəm pat′ə bəl), *adj.* able to exist well together. (< Medieval Latin *compatibilem* < Latin *compati* suffer with.)
—**com·pat′i·bil′i·ty,** *n.*

com·pete (kəm pēt′), *v.i.,* **-pet·ed, -pet·ing.** **1** try hard to obtain something wanted by others; be rivals. **2** take part (in a contest). (< Latin *competere* < *com-* together + *petere* seek)

com·pe·tence (kom′pə təns), *n.* ability; fitness.

com·pli·cate (kom′plə kāt), *v.t.,* **-cat·ed, -cat·ing.** make hard to understand, settle, cure, etc.; mix up; make complex. (< Latin *complicatum* folded together < *com-* together + *plicare* to fold)

com·po·sure (kəm pō′zhər), *n.* calmness; quietness; self-control.

com·pound (*adj.* kom′pound; *n.* kom′pound), *adj.* formed by the joining of two or more words. "Steamship," "high school," and "hit-and-run" are compound words. —*n.* substance formed by chemical combination of two or more elements in definite proportions by weight. (< Old French *compondre* put together < Latin *componere* < *com-* together + *ponere* put)

com·pound in·ter·est (kom′pound in′tər ist), interest paid on both the original sum of money borrowed or invested and interest added to it.

com·pre·hend (kom′pri hend′), *v.t.* understand the meaning of: *He comprehends the theory.* (< Latin *comprehendere* < *com-* + *prehendere* seize)

com·pre·hen·sion (kom′pri hen′shən), *n.* act or power of understanding; ability to get the meaning.

con·cen·trat·ed (kon′sən trā′tid), *adj.* (of liquids and solutions) made strong or stronger: *concentrated orange juice.*

con·cen·tra·tion camps (kon′sən trā′shən kamps), camps where political enemies, prisoners of war, or members of minority groups are held by government order.

con·cert (kon′sərt), *n.* a musical performance in which several musicians or singers take part. (< French < Italian *concerto* < Latin *concertare* strive with < *com-* with + *certare* strive.)

con·clude (kən klüd′), *v.t.,* **-clud·ed, -clud·ing.** bring to an end; finish. (< Latin *concludere* < *com-* up + *claudere* to close)

con·clu·sion (kən klü′zhən), *n.* final part; end. (< Latin *conclusionem* < *concludere.*)

con·clu·sive (kən klü′siv), *adj.* decisive; convincing; final.
—**con·clu′sive·ly,** *adv.*
—**con·clu′sive·ness,** *n.*

con·dem·na·tion (kon′dem nā′shən), *n.* **1** a condemning: *the condemnation of an unsafe bridge.* **2** a being condemned: *His condemnation made him an outcast.*

con·duc·tor (kən duk′tər), *n.* thing that transmits heat, electricity, light, sound, etc. Copper is a good conductor of heat and electricity.

cone (kōn), *n.* a solid figure formed by connecting a circle to a point not in the plane of the circle. (< Latin *conus* < Greek *konos* pine cone, cone)

concert
young clarinetists
playing a **concert**

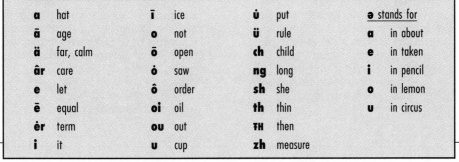

a	hat	**ī**	ice	**u̇**	put	**ə** stands for	
ā	age	**o**	not	**ü**	rule	**a**	in about
ä	far, calm	**ō**	open	**ch**	child	**e**	in taken
âr	care	**ȯ**	saw	**ng**	long	**i**	in pencil
e	let	**ô**	order	**sh**	she	**o**	in lemon
ē	equal	**oi**	oil	**th**	thin	**u**	in circus
ėr	term	**ou**	out	**ᴛʜ**	then		
i	it	**u**	cup	**zh**	measure		

con·fer·ence (kon'fer əns), *n.*
1 meeting of interested persons to discuss a particular subject.
2 association of schools, churches, etc., joined together for some special purpose.

con·fes·sion (kən fesh'ən), *n.* **1** an owning up; acknowledgment; admission. **2** admission of guilt.

con·ges·tion (kən jes'chən), *n.* an overcrowded condition.

con·grat·u·late (kən grach'ə lāt), *v.t.*, **-lat·ed, -lat·ing.** express one's pleasure at the happiness or good fortune of. (< Latin *congratulatum* congratulated < *com-* + *gratus* pleasing)

con·grat·u·la·tion (kən grach'ə lā'shən), *n.* **1** a congratulating. **2 congratulations,** *pl.* expression of pleasure at another's happiness.

con·nois·seur (kon'ə sėr'), *n.* a critical judge of art or of matters of taste; expert. (< Old French < *connoistre* know < Latin *cognoscere*.)

con·science (kon'shəns), *n.* sense of right and wrong; ideas and feelings within a person that warn of what is wrong. (< Latin *conscientia* < *conscire*.)

con·sci·en·tious (kon'shē en'shəs), *adj.* careful to do what one knows is right; controlled by conscience.

con·sen·sus (kən sen'səs), *n.* general agreement; opinion of all or most of the people consulted. (< Latin < *consentire*.)

con·sent (kən sent'), *v.i.* give approval or permission; agree. —*n.* approval; permission; assent. (< Latin *consentire* < *com-* with + *sentire* feel, think) —**con·sent'er,** *n.*

con·se·quence (kon'sə kwens), *n. pl.,* **con·se·quenc·es.** result or effect; outcome.

con·ser·va·tion (kon'sər vā'shən), *n.* a preserving from harm or decay; protecting from loss or from being used up: *the conservation of forests.*

con·spir·a·tor (kən spir'ə tər), *n.* person who conspires; plotter.

con·spire (kən spīr'), *v.,* **-spired, -spir·ing.** —*v.i.* **1** plan secretly with others to do something unlawful or wrong; plot. **2** act together: *All things conspired to make her birthday a happy one.* —*v.t.* plot (something evil or unlawful). (< Latin *conspirare,* originally, breathe together < *com-* + *spirare* breathe) —**con·spir'er,** *n.*

constellation

Sagittarius is a southern **constellation** between Scorpio and Capricorn.

con·stel·la·tion (kon'stə lā'shən), *n.* group of stars usually having a recognized shape. The Big Dipper is the easiest constellation to locate. (< Late Latin *constellationem* < Latin *com-* together + *stella* star)

con·struc·tion (kən struk'shən), *n.* **1** act of constructing; building. **2** thing constructed; building.

con·sume (kən süm'), *v.t.,* **-sumed, -sum·ing. 1** use up; spend: **2** eat or drink up. (< Latin *consumere* < *com-* + *sumere* take up)

con·sump·tion (kən sump'shən), *n.* **1** a consuming; using up; use: *We took along some food for consumption on our trip.* **2** amount used up: *The consumption of fuel oil is much greater in winter.* (< Latin *consumptionem* < *consumere.*)

con·tem·po·rar·y (kən tem'pə rar'ē), *adj., n., pl.* **-rar·ies.** —*adj.* **1** belonging to or living in the same period of time: *Walt Whitman and Emily Dickinson were contemporary poets.* **2** of or having to do with the present time; modern: *contemporary literature.* —*n.* person living in the same period of time as another or others. (< *con-* together + Latin *temporarius* belonging to time < *tempus* time)

con·tract (kən trakt'), *v.t.* draw together; make shorter, narrower, or smaller: *contract a muscle. The earthworm contracted its body.* (< Latin *contractum* drawn together < *com-* + *trahere* to draw)

con·tro·ver·sy (kon'trə vėr'sē), *n., pl.* **-sies. 1** an arguing a question about which differences of opinion exist. **2** quarrel; wrangle. (< Latin *controversia* < *contra-* against + *versum* turned)

con·ven·ience (kən vē'nyəns), *n.* **1** fact or quality of being convenient: *The convenience of packaged goods increases their sale.* **2** comfort; advantage; accommodation.

con·ven·tion·al (kən ven'shə nəl), *adj.* **1** depending on conventions; customary: *"Good morning" is a conventional greeting.* **2** acting or behaving according to commonly accepted and approved ways. **3** of the usual type or design; commonly used or seen: *conventional furniture.*
—**con·ven'·tion·al·ly,** *adv.*

con·vert (kən vėrt′), *v.t.* turn to another use; change into an object or material of a different form, character, or function: *These machines convert cotton into cloth.* (< Latin *convertere* < *com-* around + *vertere* to turn)

con·vict (*v.* kən vikt′; *n.* kon′vikt), *v.t.* prove guilty. —*n.* person serving a prison sentence for some crime. (< Latin *convictum* overcome, defeated < *com-* + *vincere* conquer)

con·vince (kən vins′), *v.t.,* **-vinced, -vinc·ing.** make a (person) feel sure; cause to believe; persuade by argument or proof: *The mistakes you made convinced me you had not studied your lesson.* (< Latin *convincere* < *com-* + *vincere* conquer) **—con·vin′ci·ble,** *adj.*

co·op·e·rate (kō op′ə rāt′), *v.i.,* **-rat·ed, -rat·ing.** work together; unite in producing a result. (< Late Latin *cooperatum* worked together < *co-* + *operari* to work)

co·or·di·na·tion (kō ôrd′n ā′shən), *n.* harmonious adjustment or working together.

cor·por·al (kôr′pər əl), *n.* the lowest-ranking noncommissioned officer in the army, ranking next below a sergeant and next above a private first class, usually in charge of a squad.

cor·po·ra·tion (kôr′pə rā′shən), *n.* group of persons with authority to act as a single person.

corps (kôr), *n., pl.* **corps** (kôrz). **1** branch of specialized military service: *the Army Medical Corps.* **2** group of people with special training, organized for working together: *a corps of nurses.* (< French < Latin *corpus* body. Doublet of CORPSE, CORPUS.)

corpse (kôrps), *n.* a dead human body. (< Old French *corps, cors* < Latin *corpus* body.)

cor·pus·cle (kôr′pus′əl), *n.* any of the cells that form a large part of the blood, lymph, etc. (< Latin *corpusculum,* diminutive of *corpus* body)

cor·rupt (kə rupt′), *adj.* **1** influenced by bribes; dishonest: *a corrupt judge.* **2** morally bad; evil; wicked. —*v.t.* **1** bribe. **2** make evil or wicked. (< Latin *corruptum* corrupted, broken < *com-* + *rumpere* to break) **—cor·rupt′ly,** *adv.* **—cor·rupt′ness,** *n.*

cor·rupt·i·ble (kə rup′tə bəl), *adj.* that can be corrupted.

cos·mo·pol·i·tan (koz′mə pol′ə tən), *adj.* **1** free from national or local prejudices; feeling at home in all parts of the world. **2** belonging to all parts of the world; not limited to any one country or its inhabitants. —*n.* a person who feels at home all over.

cot·ton gin (kot′n jin), machine for separating the fibers of cotton from the seeds; gin.

coun·ter·feit (koun′tər fit), *v.t.* copy (money, handwriting, pictures, etc.) in order to deceive or defraud; forge. —*n.* copy made to deceive or defraud and passed as genuine; forgery. **—count′er·feit′er,** *n.*

cou·ra·geous (kə rā′jəs), *adj.* full of courage; brave; fearless. **—cou·ra′geous·ly,** *adv.*

cous·cous (küs′küs′), *n.* a North African dish consisting of coarsely ground hard wheat that has been soaked in water and steamed in broth. (< French, ultimately < Arabic *kaskasa* to grind, pound)

CPU, central processing unit, part of a computer which interprets and carries out instructions, and in which data are processed.

cred·it (kred′it), *n.* **1** delayed payment; time allowed for delayed payment. **2 on credit,** on a promise to pay later. (< Middle French *crédit* < Italian *credito* < Latin *creditum* a loan < *credere* trust, entrust, believe)

cri·sis (krī′sis), *n., pl.* **cri·ses.** (-sēz′). a deciding event. (< Latin < Greek *krisis* < *krinein* decide)

cri·ter·i·on (krī tir′ē ən), *n., pl.* **cri·ter·i·a.** rule or standard for making a judgment; test. (< Greek *kritērion* < *krinein* decide, judge)

coordination
The gymnast exhibits
coordination on
the balance beam.

cotton gin
Eli Whitney's
cotton gin

a	hat	**ī**	ice	**u̇**	put	**ə** stands for	
ā	age	**o**	not	**ü**	rule	**a**	in about
ä	far, calm	**ō**	open	**ch**	child	**e**	in taken
âr	care	**ȯ**	saw	**ng**	long	**i**	in pencil
e	let	**ô**	order	**sh**	she	**o**	in lemon
ē	equal	**oi**	oil	**th**	thin	**u**	in circus
ėr	term	**ou**	out	**ᴛʜ**	then		
i	it	**u**	cup	**zh**	measure		

crit·i·cal (krit′ə kəl), *adj.* 1 inclined to find fault or disapprove: *a critical disposition.* 2 full of danger or difficulty: *The patient was critical.* —**crit′i·cal·ly**, *adv.*

crit·i·cism (krit′ə siz′əm), *n.* unfavorable remarks or judgments; disapproval; faultfinding: *I am the object of your criticism.*

cri·tique (kri tēk′), *n., v.,* -**tiqued, -tiqu·ing.** —*n.* a critical essay or review. —*v.t.* write a review of; criticize. (< French)

cro·quet (krō kā′), *n.* an outdoor game played by driving wooden balls through wickets with mallets. (< French, dialectal variant of *crochet.*)

cue (kyü), *n., v.,* **cued, cue·ing** or **cu·ing.** —*n.* action, speech, or word which gives the signal for an actor, singer, musician, etc., to enter or to begin. —*v.t.* provide (a person) with a cue or hint.

cul·tur·al (kul′chər əl), *adj.* of or having to do with culture: *Music and art are cultural studies.* —**cul′tur·al·ly**, *adv.*

cus·tom·ar·y (kus′tə mâr′ē), *adj.* 1 according to custom; as a habit; usual; habitual: *customary greetings.* 2 holding or held by custom; established by custom. —**cus′tom·ar′i·ly**, *adv.*

cyl·in·der (sil′ən dər), *n.* a solid figure with two circular bases that are parallel and congruent. (< Latin *cylindrus* < Greek *kylindros* < *kylindein* to roll)

cym·bal (sim′bəl), *n.* one of a pair of brass or bronze plates, used as a musical instrument. Cymbals make a loud, ringing sound. (Old English *cimbal* < Latin *cymbalum* < Greek *kymbalon* < *kymbē* hollow of a vessel) —**cym′bal·ist**, *n.*

Declaration of Independence
The **Declaration of Independence** helped establish our country's freedom from Great Britain.

D

day·dream (dā′drēm′), *n.* 1 dreamy thinking about pleasant things. 2 something imagined but not likely to come true. —*v.i.* think dreamily about pleasant things. —**day′dream′er**, *n.*

day·light-sav·ing time (dā′līt′sā′ving tīm′), time that is one hour ahead of standard time. Clocks are set ahead one hour in the spring and back one hour in the fall.

day·time (dā′tīm′), *n.* time when it is day and not night.

de·ceit·ful (di sēt′fəl), *adj.* 1 ready or willing to deceive. 2 meant to deceive; deceiving; misleading. —**de·ceit′ful·ness**, *n.*

Dec·la·ra·tion of In·de·pend·ence (dek′lə rā′shən of in′di pen′dəns), the public statement adopted by the Second Continental Congress on July 4, 1776, in which the American colonies declared themselves free and independent of Great Britain.

de·com·pose (dē′kəm pōz′), *v.,* -**posed, -pos·ing.** —*v.t.* rot; decay. —*v.i.* become rotten; decay. —**de′·com·pos′a·ble**, *adj.*

de·duct·i·ble (di duk′tə bəl), *adj.* that can be deducted.

de·duc·tion (di duk′shən), *n., pl.* **de·duc·tions.** 1 act of deducting; subtraction. 2 amount deducted.

de·fen·si·ble (di fen′sə bəl), *adj.* 1 that can be defended. 2 justifiable. —**de·fen′si·bil′i·ty**, *n.* —**de·fen′si·bly**, *adv.*

de·fine (di fīn′), *v.t.,* -**fined, -fin·ing.** make clear the meaning of; explain: *A dictionary defines words.* (< Latin *definire* to limit < *de-* down + *finis* end) —**de·fin′a·ble**, *adj.*

def·i·ni·tion (def′ə nish′ən), *n.* statement that makes clear the meaning of a word.

de·hy·drate (dē hī′drāt), *v.,* **de·hy·drat·ed, de·hy·drat·ing.** —*v.t.* take water or moisture from; dry: *dehydrate vegetables.* —*v.i.* lose water or moisture. (< *de-* remove + Greek *hydōr* water) —**de′hy·dra′·tion**, *n.*

del·i·cate (del′ə kit), *adj.* of fine weave, quality, or make; easily torn; thin. (< Latin *delicatus* pampered) —**del′i·cate·ly**, *adv.* —**del′i·cate·ness**, *n.*

del·i·ca·tes·sen (del′ə kə tes′n), *n.* 1 *sing. in use.* store that sells prepared foods, such as cooked meats, smoked fish, cheese, salads, pickles, sandwiches, etc. 2 *pl. in use.* the foods sold at such a store. (< German *Delikatessen*, plural of *Delikatesse* delicacy)

de·mand (di mand′), *v.t.* 1 ask for as a right: *The accused demanded a trial by jury.* 2 ask for with authority: *The teacher demanded quiet during the exam.* 3 ask to know or to be told: *demand an answer.* 4 call for; require; need: *Training a puppy demands patience.* (< Latin *demandare* < *de-* + *mandare* to order)

de·moc·ra·cy (di mok′rə sē), *n., pl.* **-cies.** 1 government that is run by the people who live under it. 2 country, state, or community having such a government. (< Greek *dēmokratia* < *dēmos* people + *kratos* rule)

de·mo·graph·ic (dē′mə graf′ik, dem′ə graf′ik), *adj.* of or having to do with demography.

de·mog·ra·phy (di mog′rə fē), *n.* science dealing with statistics of human populations, including size, diseases, number of births, deaths, etc. (< Greek *dēmos* people)

dem·on·stra·tion (dem′ən strā′shən), *n., pl.* **dem·on·stra·tions.** parade or meeting to protest or to make demands: *The tenants held a demonstration against the rent.*

de·pend·ent (di pen′dənt), *adj.* relying on another for help, support, etc.: *A child is dependent on its parents.* —*n.* person who is supported by another. —**de·pend′ent·ly,** *adv.*

der·ma·tol·o·gist (der′mə tol′ə jist), *n.* a doctor who specializes in dermatology, a branch of medicine that deals with the skin, its structure, and its diseases.

de·scribe (di skrīb′), *v.t.,* **-scribed, -scrib·ing.** tell or write about; give a picture or an account of in words. (< Latin *describere* < *de-* + *scribere* write) —**de·scrib′a·ble,** *adj.*

de·seg·re·gate (dē seg′rə gāt), *v.,* **-gat·ed, -gat·ing.** —*v.t.* abolish racial segregation in: *desegregate a public school.* —*v.i.* become desegregated. —**de·seg′re·ga′tion,** *n.*

de·spair (di spâr′), *n.* loss of hope; a being without hope; a feeling that nothing good can happen to one; helplessness. —*v.i.* lose hope; be without hope. (< Old French *desperer* lose hope < Latin *desperare* < *de-* out of, without + *sperare* to hope)

de·struc·tive (di struk′tiv), *adj.* destroying; causing destruction. —**de·struc′tive·ness,** *n.*

de·tain (di tān′), *v.t.* 1 keep from going; hold back. 2 keep from going away; hold as a prisoner. 3 withhold. (< Old French *detenir* < Latin *detinere* < *de-* + *tenere* to hold) —**de·tain′ment,** *n.*

de·ten·tion (di ten′shən), *n.* 1 act of detaining; holding back. 2 a keeping in custody; confinement. (< Late Latin *detentionem* < Latin *detinere.*)

di·ag·no·sis (dī′əg nō′sis), *n., pl.* **di·ag·no·ses** (-sēz′). 1 act or process of identifying a disease by careful investigation of its symptoms. 2 conclusion reached after a careful study of symptoms or facts. (< Greek < *dia-* apart + *gignoskein* know)

di·a·logue (dī′ə lôg), *n.* 1 conversation between two or more persons. 2 conversation in a play, novel, story, etc. (< Greek *dialogos* < *dia-* between + *logos* speech)

di·am·e·ter (dī am′ə tər), *n.* 1 a line segment passing from one side through the center of a circle, sphere, etc., to the other side. 2 the length of such a line segment; measurement from one side to the other through the center. (< Greek *diametros* < *dia-* + *metron* measure)

dic·ta·tor (dik′tā tər), *n., pl.* **dic·ta·tors.** person exercising absolute authority, without having any claim, seizes control of a government.

dif·fer·ent (dif′ər ent), *adj.* 1 not alike; not like; unlike: *A boat is different from an automobile.* 2 not the same; separate; distinct. —**dif′fer·ent·ly,** *adv.*

dif·fe·ren·ti·ate (dif′ə ren′shē āt), *v.t.,* **-at·ed, -at·ing.** make different; cause to have differences.

di·lem·ma (də lem′ə), *n.* situation requiring a choice between two alternatives, which are or appear equally unfavorable; difficult choice. (< Greek *dilēmma* < *di-* two + *lēmma* premise)

despair
a look of **despair** on a young man's face

dialogue (def. 1) performers involved in a **dialogue**

a	hat	**ī**	ice	**ù**	put	**ə stands for**	
ā	age	**o**	not	**ü**	rule	**a**	in about
ä	far, calm	**ō**	open	**ch**	child	**e**	in taken
âr	care	**ò**	saw	**ng**	long	**i**	in pencil
e	let	**ô**	order	**sh**	she	**o**	in lemon
ē	equal	**oi**	oil	**th**	thin	**u**	in circus
ėr	term	**ou**	out	**ᴛʜ**	then		
i	it	**u**	cup	**zh**	measure		

discipline

Training a horse requires patience and **discipline.**

distance

a mountain in the far **distance**

di·lute (də lüt′, dī lüt′), v., **di·lut·ed, di·lut·ing,** adj. —v.t. make weaker or thinner by adding water or some other liquid. —adj. weakened or thinned by the addition of water or some other liquid. (< Latin *dilutum* washed away < *dis-* + *luere* to wash)

dis·as·trous (də zas′trəs), adj. bringing disaster; causing much suffering or loss. —**dis·as′trous·ness,** n.

dis·ci·pline (dis′ə plin), n., v., **-plined, -plin·ing.** —n. training, especially training of the mind or character. —v.t. bring to a condition of order and obedience; bring under control; train. (< Latin *disciplina* < *discipulus* pupil) —**dis′ci·plin·er,** n.

dis·crim·i·na·tion (dis krim′ə nā′shən), n. a difference in attitude or treatment shown to a particular person, class, etc.: *racial discrimination.*

dis·in·te·grate (dis in′tə grāt), v., **-grat·ed, -grat·ing.** —v.t. break up; separate into small parts or bits. —v.i. become disintegrated; break up. —**dis·in′te·gra′tor,** n.

dis·miss (dis mis′), v.t., **dis·missed, dis·miss·ing, 1** send away; allow to go: *At noon the teacher dismissed the class.* **2** put out of mind; stop thinking about: *Dismiss your troubles.* (< Latin *dismissum* sent away < *dis-* + *mittere* to send)

dis·pos·a·ble (dis pō′zə bel), adj. **1** that can be disposed of after use. **2** at one's disposal; available.

dis·tance (dis′təns), n. length of a path over which an object travels, usually expressed in meters or kilometers.

dis·trac·tion (dis trak′shən), n. act of turning aside or drawing away the mind, attention, etc.

dis·trib·ute (dis trib′yüt), v.t., **-ut·ed, -ut·ing.** give some of to each; divide and give out in shares; deal out: *distribute candy.* (< Latin *distributum* divided < *dis-* apart, individually + *tribuere* assign)

di·ver·sion (də vėr′zhən), n. distraction from work, care, etc.; amusement; entertainment; pastime: *Baseball is my favorite diversion.*

di·vis·i·ble (də viz′ə bel), adj. **1** capable of being divided. **2** capable of being divided without leaving a remainder. —**di·vis′i·bly,** adv.

does·n't (duz′nt), does not.

dou·ble stars (dub′əl stärz), two stars so close together that they look like one to the naked eye.

drown (droun), v.i. die under water or other liquid because of lack of air to breathe. (Old English *druncnian.*)

dwarf (dwôrf), n., pl. **dwarfs** n. any of a class of stars of small size and luminosity, including the sun.

E

e·co·nom·ic (ē′kə nom′ik, ek′ə nom′ik), adj. of or having to do with economics. Economic problems have to do with the production, distribution, and consumption of goods and services.

ed·i·ble (ed′ə bel), adj. fit to eat; eatable. —n. **edibles,** pl. things fit to eat; food. (< Late Latin *edibilis* < Latin *edere* eat)

ef·fec·tive (ə fek′tiv), adj. **1** able to produce an effect: *an effective order.* **2** producing the desired effect; getting results: *an effective medicine.* —**ef·fec′tive·ly,** adv. —**ef·fec′tive·ness,** n.

ef·fer·ves·cence (ef′ər ves′ns), n. **1** act or process of bubbling. **2** liveliness and gaiety.

ef·fi·cient (ə fish′ənt), adj. able to produce the effect wanted without waste of time, energy. (< Latin *efficientem* < *ex-* + *facere* do, make) —**ef·fi′cient·ly,** adv.

egg (eg), n. **1** the round or oval body, covered with a shell or membrane, laid by the female of birds, reptiles, amphibians, fishes, insects, etc., that do not bring forth living young. **2 walk on eggs,** proceed or act cautiously. (< Scandinavian (Old Icelandic)) —**egg′like′,** adj.

e·las·tic (i las′tik), adj. **1** having the quality of returning to its original size, shape, or position after being stretched, squeezed, bent. **2** springing back; springy: *an elastic step.* —n. tape, cloth, cord, etc., woven partly of rubber. (< New Latin *elasticus* < Greek *elastos* ductile, driven < *elaunein* to drive) —**e·las′ti·cal·ly,** adv.

e·lec·tric cur·rent (i lek′trik kėr′ənt), the flow of electric charge, expressed in amperes.

e·lec·tron (i lek′tron), n. a negatively charged particle, often found in an atom, that usually moves around a nucleus. (< *electr(ic)* + *-on*)

el·e·gance (el′ə gəns), *n.* **1** good taste; refined grace and richness; luxurious beauty. **2** elegant.

el·o·quence (el′ə kwəns), *n.* flow of speech that has grace and force.

el·o·quent (el′ə kwənt), *adj.* **1** having eloquence. **2** very expressive: *eloquent eyes.* (< Latin *eloquentem* speaking out < *ex-* out + *loqui* speak) **—el′o·quent·ly,** *adv.*

e·lude (i lüd′), *v.t.,* **e·lud·ed, e·lud·ing.** avoid or escape by cleverness, quickness, etc.; slip away from; evade. (< Latin *eludere* < *ex-* out + *ludere* to play)

e·man·ci·pate (i man′sə pāt), *v.t.,* **-pat·ed, -pat·ing.** release from slavery or restraint; set free. (< Latin *emancipatum* set free < *ex-* away + *manus* hand + *capere* to take) **—e·man′ci·pa′tor,** *n.*

e·man·ci·pa·tion (i man′sə pā′shən), *n.* a release from slavery or restraint.

em·bar·go (em bär′gō), *n., pl.* **em·bar·goes. 1** an order of a government forbidding merchant ships to enter or leave its ports. **2** any restriction put on commerce by law. (< Spanish < *embargar* restrain, ultimately < Latin *in-* + Popular Latin *barra* bar)

em·bar·rass·ment (em bär′əs mənt), *n.* **1** act of embarrassing. **2** condition of being embarrassed.

e·mer·gen·cy (i mėr′jen sē), *n., pl.* **-cies,** *adj.* **—***n.* a sudden need for immediate action. **—***adj.* for a time of sudden need: *an emergency brake.*

em·i·grant (em′ə grənt), *n. pl.,* **em·i·grants,** *adj.* **—***n.* person who leaves his or her own country or region to settle in another. **—***adj.* leaving one's country to settle in another.

em·i·grate (em′ə grāt), *v.i.,* **em·i·grates, em·i·grat·ed, em·i·grat·ing.** leave one's own country or region to settle in another. (< Latin *emigratum* moved out < *ex-* out + *migrare* to move)

em·i·nent (em′ə nənt), *adj.* **1** above all or most others; outstanding; distinguished. **2** conspicuous; noteworthy. **3** standing out above other things; prominent. (< Latin *eminentem* standing out, prominent < *ex-* out + *minere* jut) **—em′i·nent·ly,** *adv.*

e·mo·tion·al (i mō′shə nəl), *adj.* **1** showing emotion: *an emotional reaction.* **2** appealing to the emotions. **—e·mo′tion·al·ly,** *adv.*

em·pire (em′pīr), *n.* group of countries or states under one ruler or government: *The Roman Empire consisted of many separate territories.* (< Old French < Latin *imperium* < *imperare*.)

e·mul·si·fi·er (i mul′ sə fī ər), *n.* substance that keeps the particles of one liquid mixed in another liquid.

en·close (en klōz′), *v.t.,* **-closed, -clos·ing. 1** shut in on all sides; surround. **2** put a wall or fence around. **3** place in an envelope or package along with something else: *She enclosed a check.*

en·clo·sure (en klō′zhər), *n.* **1** a space that is enclosed. **2** thing that encloses. A wall or fence is an enclosure.

en·core (äng′kôr, än′kôr), *interj., n.,* **—***interj.* once more; again. **—***n.* a demand by the audience for the repetition of a song, etc., or for another appearance of the performer or performers. (< French)

en·cour·age·ment (en kėr′ij mənt), *n.* **1** condition of being or feeling encouraged. **2** something that encourages. **3** act of encouraging.

en·dan·ger (en dān′jer), *v.t.* cause danger to; expose to loss or injury.

en·dur·ance (en dùr′əns, en dyùr′əns), *n.* **1** power to last and to withstand hard wear: *A runner must have great endurance.* **2** power to put up with.

en·er·get·ic (en′ər jet′ik), *adj.* full of energy; eager to work.

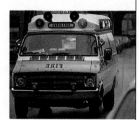

emergency
an ambulance rushing
to an **emergency**

a	hat	ī	ice	u̇	put		ə stands for
ā	age	o	not	ü	rule	a	in about
ä	far, calm	ō	open	ch	child	e	in taken
âr	care	ȯ	saw	ng	long	i	in pencil
e	let	ô	order	sh	she	o	in lemon
ē	equal	oi	oil	th	thin	u	in circus
ėr	term	ou	out	ᴛʜ	then		
i	it	u	cup	zh	measure		

en·force (en fôrs′, en fōrs′), *v.t.*, **en·forced, en·forc·ing.** force obedience to; cause to be carried out; execute; administer: *Monitors help enforce school regulations.* —**en·forc′er**, *n.*

en·gage·ment (en gāj′mənt), *n.* **1** a promise or pledge to marry; betrothal. **2** appointment made to meet someone at a certain time.

en·slave (en slāv′), *v.t.*, **-slaved, -slav·ing.** make a slave or slaves of; take away freedom from. —**en·slave′ment**, *n.*

en·ter·tain·ment (en′tər tān′mənt), *n.* thing that interests, pleases, or amuses. A show or a circus is an entertainment.

en·tre·pre·neur (än′ trə prə nėr′), *n.* person who organizes and manages a business or industrial enterprise, attempting to make a profit but taking the risk of a loss. (< French < *entreprendre* undertake)

en·vel·op (en vel′əp), *v.t.* **1** wrap or cover; enfold. **2** hide; conceal: *Fog enveloped the village.* (< Old French *enveloper* < *en-* in + *voloper* to wrap) —**en·vel′op·er**, *n.*

en·ve·lope (en′və lōp, än′və lōp), *n.* a paper cover in which a letter or anything flat can be mailed, filed, etc. It can usually be folded over and sealed by wetting a gummed edge.

en·vi·a·ble (en′vē ə bəl), *adj.* to be envied; worth having; desirable.

en·vi·ron·ment (en vī′rən mənt), *n.* **1** all the surrounding things, conditions, and influences affecting the development of living things. **2** condition of the air, water, soil, etc.; natural surroundings. —**en·vi·ron·men′tal**, *adj.*

en·vi·sion (en vizh′ən), *v.t.* picture in one's mind.

en·vy (en′vē), *n., pl.* **-vies,** *v.,* **-vied, -vy·ing.** —*n.* feeling of discontent, dislike, or desire because another has what one wants. —*v.t.* envy toward. (< Old French *envie* < Latin *invidia*, ultimately < *invidere* look with enmity at < *in-* against + *videre* see)

ep·i·dem·ic (ep′ə dem′ik), *n.* the rapid spread of a disease so that many people have it at the same time. (< Greek *epidēmia* a stay, visit, prevalence (of a disease) < *epi-* among + *dēmos* people)

ep·i·logue (ep′ə lóg), *n.* **1** a concluding section added to a novel, poem, etc., that rounds out or interprets the work. **2** speech or poem, addressed to the audience by one of the actors at the end of a play. (< Greek *epilogos*, ultimately < *epi-* above + *legein* speak)

e·qua·tion (i kwā′zhən), *n.* a mathematical sentence that states the equality of expressions.

es·pe·cial·ly (e spesh′ə lē), *adv.* more than others; specially; chiefly.

es·tate (e stāt′), *n.* **1** a large piece of land belonging to a person; landed property: *a beautiful estate with a country house.* **2** that which a person owns; property; possessions: *When she died, her estate was divided up.*

eu·lo·gy (yü′lə jē), *n., pl.* **-gies.** speech or writing in praise of a person or thing, especially a deceased person. (< Greek *eulogia* < *eu-* well + *legein* speak)

e·val·u·ate (i val′yü āt), *v.t.*, **-at·ed, -at·ing.** find out the value or the amount of; estimate the worth or importance of; appraise.

e·ven (ē′vən), *adj.* **1** having the same height everywhere; level; flat; smooth: *Even country has no hills.* **2** at the same level; in the same plane or line. —*v.t.* make level or equal; make even: *She evened the edges by trimming them.* —*adv.* in an even manner. —**e′ven·ly**, *adv.* —**e′ven·ness**, *n.*

e·ven·tu·al·ly (i ven′chü ə lē), *adv.* in the end; finally.

eve·ry day (ev′rē dā), all the days: *Every day is better than the last.*

eve·ry·day (ev′rē dā′), *adj.* **1** of every day; daily: *Accidents are everyday occurrences.* **2** for every ordinary day; not for Sundays or holidays: *She wears everyday clothes to work.* **3** not exciting.

eve·ry·thing (ev′rē thing), *pron.* every thing; all things. —*n.* something extremely important.

ev·i·dence (ev′ə dəns), *n.* **1** anything that shows what is true and what is not; facts; proof: *The evidence showed that he had not been near the place.* See synonym study below. **2** indication; sign: *A smile gives evidence of pleasure.*
Syn. *n.* **1 Evidence, testimony, proof** mean that which tends to demonstrate the truth or falsity of something. **Evidence** applies to facts that indicate, without fully proving, that something is so:

entertainment

entertainment by the Morris Dancers in Covent Garden, England

Running away was evidence of his guilt. **Testimony** applies to any speech or action which serves as evidence of something: *Her testimony contradicted that of the preceding witness.* **Proof** means evidence so full and convincing as to leave no doubt or little doubt: *The signed receipt is proof that the letter was delivered.*

ex·ag·ge·rate (eg zaj′ə rāt′), *v.,* **-rat·ed, -rat·ing.** —*v.t.* make (something) greater than it is. (< Latin *exaggeratum* heaped up < *ex-* up + *agger* to heap)

ex·cel·lent (ek′sə lənt), *adj.* of unusually good quality; better than others. —**ex′cel·lent·ly,** *adv.*

ex·cep·tion·al (ek sep′shə nəl), *adj.* out of the ordinary; unusual. —**ex·cep′tion·al·ly,** *adv.*

ex·cite·ment (ek sīt′mənt), *n.* **1** an excited condition. **2** thing that excites. **3** an exciting; arousing.

ex·claim (ek sklām′), *v.i., v.t.* say or speak suddenly in surprise or strong feeling; cry out. (< Latin *exclamare* < *ex-* out + *clamare* cry out) —**ex·claim′er,** *n.*

ex·cla·ma·tion (ek′sklə mā′shən), *n.* something exclaimed; interjection. *Ah!* and *oh!* are exclamations.

ex·er·cise (ek′sər sīz), *n., v.,* **-cised, -cis·ing.** —*n.* **1** active use of the body or mind for their improvement or as a means of training for any kind of activity. **2** something that gives practice and training or causes improvement. —*v.i.* take exercise; go through exercises. (< Old French *exercice* < Latin *exercitium* < *exercere* keep busy < *ex-* out + *arcere* prevent)

ex·ist·ence (eg zis′təns), *n.* **1** being. **2** occurrence; presence.

ex·pand (ek spand′), *v.t.* **1** make larger; increase in size; enlarge. **2** spread out; open out; unfold. —*v.i.* grow or become larger. (< Latin *expandere* < *ex-* out + *pandere* to spread.) —**ex·pand′a·ble,** *adj.*

ex·pec·ta·tion (ek′spek tā′shən), *n., pl.* **ex·pec·ta·tions.** an expecting; anticipation.

ex·pire (ek spīr′), *v.,* **-pired, -pir·ing.** —*v.i.* **1** come to an end: *You must obtain a new license when your old one expires.* **2** die. —*v.t.* breathe out (air). (< Latin *exspirare* < *ex-* out + *spirare* breathe)

ex·pres·sion (ek spresh′ən), *n.* **1** a putting into words; expressing: *the expression of an idea.* **2** word or group of words used as a unit: *"Shake a leg" is a slang expression.* **3** indication of feeling, spirit, character; look that shows feeling. —**ex·pres′sion·less,** *adj.*

ex·tend (ek stend′), *v.t.,* **ex·tend·ed, ex·tend·ing. 1** stretch out: *extend your hand.* **2** continue or prolong in time, space, or direction. (< Latin *extendere* < *ex-* out + *tendere* to stretch)

ex·tra·cur·ric·u·lar (ek′strə kə rik′yə lər), *adj.* outside the regular course of study: *Football and debating are extracurricular activities.*

ex·traor·di·nar·y (ek strôr′də nâr′ē), *adj.* beyond what is ordinary; very unusual or remarkable; exceptional. —**ex·traor′di·nar′i·ly,** *adv.*

ex·tra·sen·sor·y (ek′strə sen′sər ē), *adj.* beyond the normal range of the senses.

ex·tra·ter·res·tri·al (ek′strə tə res′trē əl), *adj.* outside the earth or its atmosphere.

ex·trav·a·gant (ek strav′ə gənt), *adj.* **1** spending carelessly and lavishly; wasteful. **2** beyond the bounds of reason; excessive: *an extravagant price.* (< Medieval Latin *extravagantem* < Latin *extra-* outside + *vagari* to wander) —**ex·trav′a·gant·ly,** *adv.*

ex·tro·vert (ek′strə vėrt′), *n.* person tending to act rather than think. Extroverts are more interested in what is going on around them than in their own thoughts. Also, **extravert.** (< *extro-* outside (variant of *extra-*) + Latin *vertere* to turn)

exercise (def. 1)
participating in a road race for **exercise**

expression (def. 3)
a cheerful **expression**

a	hat	**ī**	ice	**u̇**	put	**ə** stands for	
ā	age	**o**	not	**ü**	rule	**a**	in about
ä	far, calm	**ō**	open	**ch**	child	**e**	in taken
âr	care	**ȯ**	saw	**ng**	long	**i**	in pencil
e	let	**ô**	order	**sh**	she	**o**	in lemon
ē	equal	**oi**	oil	**th**	thin	**u**	in circus
ėr	term	**ou**	out	**ᴛʜ**	then		
i	it	**u**	cup	**zh**	measure		

F

fa·cil·i·tate (fə sil′ə tāt), *v.t.,* **-tat·ed, -tat·ing.** make easy; lessen the labor of: *A computer facilitates many tasks.* —**fa·cil′i·ta′tor,** *n.*

fac·sim·i·le (fak sim′ə lē), *n.* an exact copy or likeness; perfect reproduction. (< Latin *fac* make + *simile* similar, like)

fac·tion (fak′shən), *n.* group of persons in a political party, church, club, etc., acting together or having a common purpose. (< Latin *factionem* party, class, originally, a doing < *facere* do.)

fail·ure (fā′lyər), *n.* a being unable to do or become what is wanted, expected; not succeeding.

fa·mil·iar (fə mil′yər), *adj.* **1** known from constant association; well-known: *a familiar face.* **2** of everyday use; common; ordinary. **3** well-acquainted; versed: *He is familiar with French.* (< Latin *familiaris* < *familia.*)

far·sight·ed (fär′sī′tid), *adj.* seeing distant things more clearly than near ones because the parallel light rays entering the eye come to a focus behind, rather than on, the retina. —**far′sight′ed·ness,** *n.*

fat (fat), *n.* **1** a white or yellow oily substance formed in animal tissue, made up chiefly of carbon, hydrogen, and oxygen. **2 chew the fat,** SLANG. talk, especially in an idle fashion; chat. (Old English *fǣtt*)

fa·vor·ite (fā′vər it), *adj.* liked better than others. —*n.* person or thing preferred above others.

feat (fēt), *n.* a great or unusual deed; act showing great skill, strength, or daring; achievement. (< Old French *fait* < Latin *factum* (thing) done.)

fe·ro·cious (fə rō′shəs), *adj.* savagely cruel or destructive; fierce. (< Latin *ferocem* fierce) —**fe·ro′cious·ly,** *adv.* —**fe·ro′cious·ness,** *n.*

fe·roc·i·ty (fə ros′ə tē), *n., pl.* **-ties.** savage cruelty; fierceness.

Fer·ris wheel (fer′is hwēl), a large, upright wheel rotating about a fixed axis, with swinging seats hanging from its rim. (< George W. G. *Ferris,* 1859–1896, American engineer, the inventor)

fer·ti·lize (fėr′tl īz), *v.t.,* **-lized, -liz·ing.** put fertilizer on.

fi·nal·ly (fī′nl ē), *adv.* **1** at the end; at last. **2** in such a way as to decide or settle the question.

fi·nance charge (fī′nans chärj), amount of interest charged to borrow money, usually in percent.

fin·ger (fing′gər), *n.* **1** one of the five slender divisions that end the hand, especially the four excluding the thumb. **2 have a finger in the pie, a** take part or share in a project; help to do something. **b** interfere or meddle. (Old English) —**fin′ger·like′,** *adj.*

fire ex·tin·guish·er (fīr ek sting′gwish ər), a portable container filled with chemicals which can be sprayed on a fire to put it out.

flam·boy·ant (flam boi′ent), *adj.* **1** gorgeously brilliant; flaming; showily striking: *flamboyant colors.* **2** very ornate; much decorated; florid: *flamboyant architecture.* **3** given to display; ostentatious; showy. **4** having wavy lines or flamelike curves: *flamboyant designs.* (< French) —**flam·boy′ant·ly,** *adv.*

flam·ma·ble (flam′ə bəl), *adj.* easily set on fire; inflammable.

flap·per (flap′ər), *n., pl.* **flap·pers.** a young woman of the 1920s who dressed unconventionally and behaved with some freedom.

floe (flō), *n.* **1** field or sheet of floating ice. **2** a floating piece broken off from such a field or sheet. (< Scandinavian (Norwegian) *flo*)

flop·py disk (flop′ē disk), a flexible plastic disk with a magnetic surface, used for computer data storage.

flo·ri·cul·ture (flôr′ə kul′chər), *n.* cultivation of flowers or flowering plants, especially ornamental plants. —**flo′ri·cul′tur·ist,** *n.*

for·bid·den (fər bid′n), *adj.* not allowed; against the law or rules; prohibited. —*v.* a pp. of **forbid.**

force (fôrs), *n.* any action that accelerates an object, expressed in newtons. (< Old French, ultimately < Latin *fortis* strong) —**force′less,** *adj.* —**forc′er,** *n.*

fo·reign pol·i·cy (fôr′ən pol′ə sē), plan of action adopted as tactically or strategically best by a government for managing affairs with other nations.

fore·see (fôr sē′), *v.,* **-saw, -seen, -see·ing.** —*v.t.* see or know beforehand; anticipate. —*v.i.* use foresight. —**fore·se′er,** *n.*

fore·word (fôr′wėrd′), *n.* a brief introduction or preface to a book, speech, etc.

floe (def. 2)
an ice **floe**

floriculture
beautiful **floriculture**
at the Kew Gardens
in London

for·feit (fôr′fit), *v.t.* lose or have to give up by one's own act, neglect, or fault. —*n.* loss or giving up of something as a penalty. (< Old French *forfait* a forfeit < *forfaire* transgress, do wrong) —**for′feit·er,** *n.*

for·mu·la (fôr′myə lə), *n., pl.* **-las** or **-lae.** an equation that states a general fact or rule by using variables. (< Latin, diminutive of *forma* form)

for·syth·i·a (fôr sith′ē ə), *n.* any of a genus of shrubs of the olive family, having many bell-shaped, yellow flowers. (< New Latin < William *Forsyth,* 1737–1804, British horticulturist)

found·ry (foun′drē), *n., pl.* **-ries.** place where metal is melted and molded; place where things are made of molten metal.

fran·chise (fran′chīz), *n.* right to vote: *The United States gave women the franchise in 1920.* (< Old French < *franc* free.)

fu·gi·tive (fyü′jə tiv), *n.* person who is fleeing or who has fled from danger, an enemy, justice, etc. (< Latin *fugitivus* < *fugere* flee)

fun·nel (fun′l), *n.* **1** a tapering utensil with a wide, cone-shaped mouth ending in a tube, used to prevent spilling in pouring liquids, powder, grain, etc., into containers with small openings. **2** anything shaped like a funnel. (< Old French *fonel,* ultimately < Late Latin *fundibulum* < Latin *infundibulum* < *in-* in + *fundere* pour)

fuse (fyüz), *n., v.,* **fused, fus·ing.** —*n.* wire or strip of easily fusible metal inserted in an electric circuit that melts and breaks the connection when the current becomes dangerously strong. —*v.t.* join together by melting; melt. —*v.i.* become melted; melt together: *Copper and zinc fuse to make brass.* (< Latin *fusum* poured, melted < *fundere* pour, melt) —**fuse′less,** *adj.*

G

ga·lumph (gə lumf′), *v.i.* gallop in a clumsy way: *cows galumphing home.* (perhaps blend of *gallop* and *triumph;* coined by Lewis Carroll)

gas·o·hol (gas′ə hȯl), *n.* a fuel for internal-combustion engines, composed of ninety percent unleaded gasoline and ten percent ethyl alcohol. (blend of *gasoline* and *alcohol*)

Gei·ger count·er (gī′gər koun′tər), an instrument used to detect radiation from radioactive material. (< Hans *Geiger,* 1882–1947, German physicist)

gen·e·ra·tor (jen′ə rā′tər), *n.* a device that uses electromagnetic induction to change mechanical energy into electricity.

gen·tle (jen′tl), *adj.,* **-tler, -tlest. 1** not severe, rough; mild. **2** soft; low. (< Old French *gentil* < Latin *gentilis* of the (same) family, national < *gentem* family, nation.)

gen·u·ine (jen′yü ən), *adj.* **1** actually being what it seems or is claimed to be; real; true. **2** without pretense; sincere; frank. (< Latin *genuinus* native, natural, ultimately < *gignere* beget)

ge·og·ra·phy (jē og′rə fē), *n., pl.* **-phies. 1** study of the earth's surface, climate, continents, etc. **2** the surface features of a place or region: *the geography of Ohio.* (< Greek *geōgraphia* < *gē* earth + *graphein* describe)

ge·om·e·try (jē om′ə trē), *n., pl.* **-tries.** branch of mathematics which studies the relationship of points, lines, angles, and surfaces of figures in space; the mathematics of space. (< Greek *geōmetria* < *gē* earth + *-metria* measuring)

ghet·to (get′ō), *n., pl.* **ghet·tos. 1** part of a city where any racial group or nationality lives. **2** (formerly) a part of a city in Europe where Jews were required to live. (< Italian)

funnel (def. 2) the **funnel** of a tornado approaching Enid, Oklahoma

a	hat	**ī**	ice	**u̇**	put	**ə**	stands for
ā	age	**o**	not	**ü**	rule	**a**	in about
ä	far, calm	**ō**	open	**ch**	child	**e**	in taken
âr	care	**ȯ**	saw	**ng**	long	**i**	in pencil
e	let	**ô**	order	**sh**	she	**o**	in lemon
ē	equal	**oi**	oil	**th**	thin	**u**	in circus
ėr	term	**ou**	out	**ᴛʜ**	then		
i	it	**u**	cup	**zh**	measure		

ging·ham (ging′əm), *n.* a cotton cloth made from colored threads. Its patterns are usually in stripes, plaids, or checks. (< French *guingan* < Malay *ginggang* striped)

gi·raffe (jə raf′), *n.* a large African mammal that chews its cud and has a very long neck, long legs, and a spotted skin. Giraffes are the tallest living animals. (< Italian *giraffa* < Arabic *zarāfah*)

glimpse (glimps), *n.*, *v.*, **glimpsed,** **glimps·ing.** —*n.* **1** a short, quick view or look. **2** a short, faint appearance. —*v.t.* catch a short, quick view of. (Middle English *glimsen.*)

gnu (nü, nyü), *n.*, *pl.* **gnus** or **gnu.** a large African antelope with an oxlike head, curved horns, high shoulders, and a long tail; wildebeest. (< Kaffir *nqu*)

go·ing to (gō′ing tü), intend to, plan to: *I am going to read this novel.*

gon·do·la (gon′dl ə), *n.* a long, narrow boat with a high peak at each end, rowed or poled by a single oar. It is used on the canals of Venice. (< Italian)

gou·lash (gü′läsh), *n.* stew made of beef or veal and vegetables. (< Hungarian *gulyás (hús)* herdsman's (meat))

gov·ern·ment (guv′ərn mənt, guv′ər mənt), *n.* rule or authority over a country, state, district, etc.; authoritative direction of the affairs of state.

grad·u·ate (*v.* graj′ü āt; *n.*, *adj.* graj′ü it), *v.*, **-at·ed, -at·ing,** *n.*, *adj.* —*v.i.* finish a course of study at a school, college, or university and receive a diploma or other document saying so. —*n.* person who had graduated and has a diploma. —*adj.* that has graduated. (< Medieval Latin *graduatum* graduated < Latin *gradus* step, degree)

grad·u·a·tion (graj′ü ā′shən), *n.* **1** a graduating from a school, college, or university. **2** ceremony of graduating; graduating exercises.

gra·ham crackers (grā′əm krak′ərs), *n.* crackers made from whole-wheat flour, including all the bran. (< Sylvester *Graham,* 1794–1851, American minister and dietary reformer, who advocated the use of this flour)

gram·mat·i·cal·ly (grə mat′ik lē), *adv.* according to the rules and principles of grammar.

granddaughter
granddaughters and grandmother sharing some affection

grand·daugh·ter (grand′dô′tər), *n.* daughter of one's son or daughter.

graph·ic (graf′ik), *adj.* **1** producing by words the effect of a picture; lifelike; vivid: *a graphic description of a battle.* **2** of or about graphs and their use. —*n.* an etching, drawing, lithograph, etc.; any work of the graphic arts. (< Latin *graphicus* < Greek *graphikos* < *graphein* write) —**graph′ic·ly,** *adv.*

great-aunt (grāt′ant′), *n.* grandaunt.

great-grand·moth·er (grāt′grand′muᴛʜ′ər), *n.* grandmother of one's father or mother.

griev·ance (grē′vəns), *n.*, *pl.* **griev·an·ces.** a real or imagined wrong; reason for being angry or annoyed; cause for complaint.

griev·ous (grē′vəs), *adj.* **1** hard to bear; causing great pain or suffering; severe: *grievous cruelty.* **2** very evil or offensive; outrageous: —**griev′ous·ly,** *adv.*

gross in·come (grōs in′kum′), the total amount of money earned.

group·ing sym·bols (grü′ping sim′bəls), symbols such as parentheses and brackets and fraction bars that group numbers and/or variables together.

guar·an·tee (gar′ən tē′), *n.*, *v.*, **-teed, -tee·ing.** —*n.* a promise or pledge to replace or repair a purchased product, return the money paid, etc., if the product is not as represented. —*v.t.* stand back of; give a guarantee for.

guard·ed (gär′did), *adj.* kept safe; carefully watched over; defended; protected. —**guard′ed·ly,** *adv.* —**guard′ed·ness,** *n.*

Gua·te·ma·la (gwä′tə mä′lə), *n.* country in NW Central America. 6,817,000 pop.; 42,000 sq. mi. (108,800 sq. km.) *Capital:* Guatemala City. —**Gua′te·ma′lan,** *adj.*, *n.*

gul·li·ble (gul′ə bəl), *adj.* easily deceived or cheated.

gum·bo (gum′bō), *n.*, *pl.* **-bos. 1** the okra plant. **2** its sticky pods. **3** soup usually made of chicken and rice and thickened with these pods. (of Bantu origin)

gun (gun), *n.* weapon with a metal tube for shooting bullets or shells. **jump the gun, a** start too soon; start before the signal to do so. **b** get a head start on one's opposition. (< Scandinavian (Old Icelandic) *Gunnhildr,* woman's name)

H

half·way (haf′wā′), *adv.* half the way; half the required distance: *The rope reached only halfway around the tree.* —*adj.* midway.

ham·mock (ham′ək), *n.* a hanging bed or couch made of canvas, netted cord, etc., suspended by cords or ropes at both ends. (< Spanish *hamaca* < Taino)

hand·cuff (hand′kuf′), *n.* one of a pair of metal rings joined by a short chain and locked around the wrists of a prisoner. —*v.t.* put handcuffs on.

hard·ware (härd′wâr′, härd′wâr′), *n.* the mechanical parts of a computer, teaching machine, nuclear reactor, etc.

har·dy (här′dē), *adj.*, **-di·er, -di·est.** able to bear hard treatment, fatigue, etc.; strong; robust: *hardy frontier settlers.* —**har′di·ly**, *adv.* —**har′di·ness**, *n.*

Har·lem (här′ləm), *n.* northern section of Manhattan, bordering the Harlem and East rivers.

harsh (härsh), *adj.* rugged; bleak: *a harsh coast.* (Middle English *harsk* < Scandinavian (Danish) *harsk* rancid) —**harsh′ly**, *adv.* —**harsh′ness**, *n.*

have to (hav tü), required to, must: *You have to be on time.*

haz·ard·ous (haz′ər dəs), *adj.* full of risk; dangerous; perilous.

heart·y (här′tē), *adj.*, **heart·i·er, heart·i·est**, *n., pl.* **heart·ies.** —*adj.* 1 warm and friendly; genuine; sincere. 2 strong and well; vigorous. —*n.* a brave and good comrade.

heat sources (hēt sôr sez), anything that can give off heat because its temperature is higher than that of its surroundings.

hel·i·cop·ter (hel′ə kop′tər), *n.* type of aircraft without wings, lifted from the ground and supported in the air by one or more horizontal propellers or rotors. (< French *hélicoptère* < Greek *helix, helikos* spiral + *pteron* wing)

hel·met (hel′mit), *n.* a covering made of steel, leather, plastic, or some other sturdy material, worn to protect the head. (< Old French; of Germanic origin)

he·ro·ic (hi rō′ik), *adj.* 1 of, like, or suitable for a hero, his deeds, or his qualities; brave, great, or noble. 2 of or about heroes and their deeds; epic. 3 unusually daring or bold. —**he·ro′i·cal·ly**, *adv.*

her·o·ism (her′ō iz′əm), *n.* 1 actions and qualities of a hero or heroine; great bravery; daring courage. 2 a doing something noble at great cost to oneself; a very brave act.

hes·i·tate (hez′ə tāt), *v.i.*, **-tat·ed, -tat·ing.** 1 feel that perhaps one should not; be unwilling; not want: *I hesitated to interrupt you.* 2 stop for an instant; pause. (< Latin *haesitatum* stuck fast < *haerere* stick fast) —**hes′i·tat′er**

hick·or·y (hik′ər ē), *n., pl.* **-or·ies.** any of a genus of North American trees of the same family as the walnut, bearing a hard nut with an edible, sweet kernel. (alteration of earlier *pohickery;* of Algonquian origin)

hid·e·ous (hid′ē əs), *adj.* very ugly; frightful; horrible. (< Old French *hideus* < *hide* fear, horror) —**hid′e·ous·ness**, *n.*

hin·drance (hin′drəns), *n.* 1 person or thing that hinders. 2 act of hindering. See **obstacle** for synonym study.

his·to·ri·cal fic·tion (hi stôr′ə kəl fik′shən), novels, plays, and other prose writings about imaginary people and happenings that take place in the past.

ho·gan (hō′gän′), *n.* dwelling used by the Navajos. Hogans are built with logs and mounded over with earth. (< Navajo *hoghan* house)

home·land (hōm′land′), *n., pl.* **home·lands.** country that is one's home; one's native land.

hom·i·ny (hom′ə nē), *n.* whole or coarsely ground hulled corn, usually eaten boiled.

hazardous
hazardous barrels of toxic waste

helicopter

a	hat	**ī**	ice	**u̇**	put	**ə** stands for	
ā	age	**o**	not	**ü**	rule	**a**	in about
ä	far, calm	**ō**	open	**ch**	child	**e**	in taken
âr	care	**ȯ**	saw	**ng**	long	**i**	in pencil
e	let	**ô**	order	**sh**	she	**o**	in lemon
ē	equal	**oi**	oil	**th**	thin	**u**	in circus
ėr	term	**ou**	out	**ᴛʜ**	then		
i	it	**u**	cup	**zh**	measure		

hors d'oeu·vre (ôr/ dėrv/), *pl.* **hors d'oeu·vres** (ôr/ dėrvz/), **hors d'oeu·vre.** relish, light food, or dainty sandwich served as an appetizer before the regular courses of a meal. (< French, literally, apart from (the main) work)

hy·drant (hī/drənt), *n.* a large, upright cylinder with a valve for drawing water directly from a water main; fireplug.

hy·drau·lic (hī drò/lik), *adj.* **1** having to do with water or other liquids at rest or in motion. **2** operated by the pressure of water or other liquids in motion, especially when forced through an opening or openings. (< Latin *hydraulicus,* ultimately < Greek *hydōr* water + *aulos* pipe)

hy·dro·e·lec·tric (hī/drō i lek/trik), *adj.* of or having to do with the generation of electricity by water power.

hy·dro·gen (hī/drə jən), *n.* a colorless, odorless, gaseous element that burns easily and weighs less than any other element. It combines with oxygen to form water. (< French *hydrogène* < *hydro-* + *-gène* -gen)

hy·dro·pho·bi·a (hī/drə fō/bē ə), *n.* an abnormal fear of water.

hy·per·crit·i·cal (hī/pər krit/ə kəl), *adj.* too critical.

hyp·o·crite (hip/ə krit), *n.* **1** person who pretends to be very good or religious. **2** person who is not sincere; pretender. (< Greek *hypokritēs* actor < *hypo-* under + *kritēs* a judge)

igloo

Inuit youngsters in an **igloo**

I

i·den·ti·fy (ī den/tə fī), *v.t.,* **-fied, -fy·ing.** recognize as being, or show to be, a particular person or thing; prove to be the same. —**i·den/ti·fi·a·ble,** *adj.* —**i·den/ti·fi·a·bly,** *adv.*

ig·loo (ig/lü), *n., pl.* **-loos.** a dome-shaped hut used by Eskimos, often built of blocks of hard snow. (< Eskimo *igdlu* house)

im·me·di·ate·ly (i mē/dē it lē), *adv.* at once; without delay.

im·mi·grant (im/ə grənt), *n., pl.* **im·mi·grants.** person who comes into a foreign country or region to live there: *Canada has many immigrants from Europe.*

im·mi·grate (im/ə grāt), *v.i.,* **-grat·ed, -grat·ing.** come into a foreign country or region to live there.

im·mi·gra·tion (im/ə grā/shən), *n.* **1** a coming into a foreign country or region to live there. **2** the persons who immigrate; immigrants.

im·mi·nent (im/ə nənt), *adj.* likely to happen soon; about to occur: *Black clouds show rain is imminent.* (< Latin *imminentem* overhanging, threatening) —**im/·mi·nent·ly,** *adv.*

im·mune (i myün/), *adj.* protected from disease, poison, etc.; having immunity: *Vaccination makes a person practically immune to polio.* (< Latin *immunis,* originally, free from obligation < *in-* not + *munia* duties, services)

im·mu·nize (im/yə nīz), *v.t.,* **-nized, -niz·ing.** give immunity to; make immune: *Vaccination immunizes people against smallpox.* —**im/mu·ni·za/tion,** *n.*

im·pa·la (im pä/lə, im pal/ə), *n.* a medium-sized reddish-brown antelope, found in eastern and southern Africa and noted for long leaps. The male has long curved horns. (< Zulu)

im·pede (im pēd/), *v.t.,* **-ped·ed, -ped·ing.** stand in the way of; hinder; obstruct. (< Latin *impedire* < *in-* on + *pedem* foot)

im·ped·i·ment (im ped/ə mənt), *n.* **1** hindrance; obstruction. **2** some physical defect, a speech defect.

im·per·cep·ti·ble (im/pər sep/tə bəl), *adj.* that cannot be perceived or felt; very slight. —**im/per·cep/ti·bly,** *adv.*

im·per·i·al·ism (im pir/ē ə liz/əm), *n.* policy of extending the rule or authority of one country over other countries and colonies.

im·port (*v.* im pôrt/; *n.* im/pôrt), *v.t.* bring in from a foreign country for sale or use: *The United States imports coffee from Brazil.* —*n.* article imported: *Rubber is a useful import.* (< Latin *importare* < *in-* in + *portare* carry)

im·pos·ing (im pō/zing), *adj.* impressive because of size, appearance, dignity, etc.

im·ply (im plī/), *v.t.,* **-plied, -ply·ing.** mean without saying so; express indirectly; suggest: *Her smile implied that she had forgiven us.* (< Old French *emplier* involve, put (in) < Latin *implicare* < *in-* in + *plicare* to fold.)

immigrant

immigrants on Ellis Island in the 1900s

im·pres·sion (im presh′ən), *n.* **1** effect produced on the senses or mind. **2** effect produced by any operation or activity.

im·prove·ment (im prüv′mənt), *n.* a making better; becoming better.

in·born (in′bôrn′), *adj.* born in a person; instinctive; natural.

in·con·ceiv·a·ble (in′kən sē′və bəl), *adj.* **1** impossible to imagine. **2** hard to believe; incredible. —**in′con·ceiv′a·bly,** *adv.*

in·con·tro·vert·i·ble (in′kon trə vėr′tə bəl), *adj.* that cannot be disputed or denied.

in·cor·po·rate (*v.* in kôr′pə rāt′; *adj.* in kôr′pər it), *v.,* **-rat·ed, -rat·ing,** *adj.* —*v.t.* make (something) a part of something else; join or combine (something) with something else. —*adj.* united; combined; incorporated. (< Latin *incorporatum* formed into a body < *in-* into + *corpus* body)

in·de·struct·i·ble (in′di struk′tə bəl), *adj.* that cannot be destroyed. —**in′de·struct′i·bly,** *adv.*

in·di·go (in′də gō), *n., pl.* **-gos,** *adj.* —*n.* a blue dye formerly obtained from various plants, but now usually made artificially. —*adj.* deep violet-blue. (< Spanish *índigo* < Latin *indicum* < Greek *indikon,* originally adjective, Indian)

in·e·qual·i·ty (in′i kwol′ə tē), *n., pl.* **-ties.** a mathematical sentence with one of the following symbols: $<, >, \le, \ge$.

in·ev·i·ta·ble (in ev′ə tə bəl), *adj.* not to be avoided; sure to happen. (< Latin *inevitabilis* < *in-* not + *evitare* avoid < *ex-* out + *vitare* shun) —**in·ev′i·ta·bly,** *adv.*

in·fer (in fėr′), *v.,* **-ferred, -fer·ring.** —*v.t.* find out by a process of reasoning from something known or assumed; conclude: *People inferred that so able a governor would make a good President.* —*v.i.* draw inferences. (< Latin *inferre* introduce, bring in < *in-* in + *ferre* bring) —**in·fer′a·ble,** *adj.*

in·fer·ence (in′fər əns), *n.* **1** process of inferring. **2** that which is inferred; conclusion.

in·flame (in flām′), *v.t.,* **-flamed, -flam·ing. 1** make more violent; excite: *The stirring speech inflamed the crowd.* **2** make unnaturally hot, red, sore, or swollen. (< Latin *inflammare* < *in-* in + *flamma* flame)

in·flu·ence (in′flü əns), *n., v.,* **-enced, -enc·ing.** —*n.* **1** power of persons or things to act on others, seen only in its effects: *the influence of the moon on the tides.* **2** power to produce an effect without using force or authority. —*v.t.* have an influence on: *The moon influences the tides.* (< Medieval Latin *influentia* emanation from the stars believed to affect human destiny, originally, a flowing in < Latin *in-* in + *fluere* to flow)

in·flu·en·tial (in′flü en′shəl), *adj.* **1** having much influence: *Influential friends helped her to get a job.* **2** using influence; producing results. —**in′flu·en′tial·ly,** *adv.*

i·ni·ti·a·tion (i nish′ē ā′shən), *n.* ceremonies by which one is admitted to a group or society.

in·jure (in′jər), *v.t.,* **-jured, -jur·ing. 1** do damage to; harm; hurt: *I injured my arm while skiing.* **2** be unfair to; do injustice or wrong to.

in·no·cent (in′ə sənt), *adj.* **1** doing no wrong or evil; free from sin or wrong; not guilty. **2** without knowledge of evil: *A baby is innocent.* —*n.* an innocent person. (< Latin *innocentem* < *in-* not + *nocere* to harm) —**in′no·cent·ly,** *adv.*

in·put (in′pu̇t′), *v.,* **in·put, in·put·ting,** *n.* —*v.t.* put in; introduce. —*n.* information or instructions put into a computer.

in·scrip·tion (in skrip′shən), *n.* something inscribed; words, names, letters, etc., written or engraved on stone, metal, paper. (< Latin *inscriptionem* < *inscribere*.)

impression (def. 2) The flood left an **impression** in the mud.

inscription an **inscription** on Thomas Jefferson's gravestone

a	hat	ī	ice	u̇	put	ə stands for	
ā	age	o	not	ü	rule	a	in about
ä	far, calm	ō	open	ch	child	e	in taken
âr	care	ȯ	saw	ng	long	i	in pencil
e	let	ô	order	sh	she	o	in lemon
ē	equal	oi	oil	th	thin	u	in circus
ėr	term	ou	out	ᵺ	then		
i	it	u	cup	zh	measure		

in·sen·si·tive (in sen/sə tiv), *adj.* **1** not sensitive; not able to feel or notice. **2** slow to feel or notice. —**in·sen/si·tive·ly**, *adv.* —**in·sen/si·tive·ness**, *n.*

in·spect (in spekt/), *v.t.* **1** look over carefully; examine: *A dentist inspects my teeth twice a year.* **2** examine formally; look over officially: *All mines are inspected by government officials.* (< Latin *inspectum* looked over < *in-* + *specere* to look) —**in·spect/a·ble**, *adj.*

in·spec·tion (in spek/shən), *n.* an inspecting; examination.

in·stall·ment (in stȯl/mənt), *n., pl.* **in·stall·ments.** part of a sum of money or of a debt to be paid at certain stated times: *The table cost $100; we paid for it in installments.*

in·stinc·tive (in stingk/tiv), *adj.* of or having to do with instinct; caused or done by instinct; born in an animal or person, not learned: *The spinning of webs is instinctive in spiders.* —**in·stinc/tive·ly**, *adv.*

in·struc·tion·al (in struk/shə nəl), *adj.* of or for instruction; educational.

in·struc·tor (in struk/tər), *n.* person who instructs; teacher.

in·suf·fi·cient (in/sə fish/ənt), *adj.* not sufficient; lacking in what is needed; inadequate. —**in/suf·fi/cient·ly**, *adv.*

in·su·late (in/sə lāt), *v.t.*, **-lat·ed, -lat·ing. 1** keep from losing or transferring electricity, heat, sound, etc., especially by covering, packing, or surrounding with a nonconducting material. **2** set apart; separate from others; isolate. (< Latin *insula* island)

in·su·la·tion (in/sə lā/shən), *n.* **1** an insulating. **2** a being insulated. **3** material used in insulating.

in·su·la·tor (in/sə lā/tər), *n.* that which insulates; something that prevents the passage of electricity, heat, or sound; nonconductor.

in·tel·li·gence (in tel/ə jəns), *n.* ability to learn and know; quickness of understanding; mind.

intensity

The **intensity** of the lava from a volcano changes the environment.

in·ten·si·ty (in ten/sə tē), *n., pl.* **-ties.** amount or degree of strength of electricity, heat, light, sound, etc., per unit of area, volume, etc.

in·ter·cept (in/tər sept/), *v.t.* take or seize on the way from one place to another: *intercept a letter, intercept a messenger.* (< Latin *interceptum* caught between, interrupted < *inter-* between + *capere* to take, catch) —**in/ter·cep/tion**, *n.*

in·ter·change·a·ble (in/tər chān/jə bəl), *adj.* **1** capable of being used or put in place of each other. **2** able to change places. —**in/ter·change/a·bly**, *adv.*

in·ter·con·nect (in/tər kə nekt/), *v.t.* connect with each other. —**in/ter·con·nec/tion**, *n.*

in·ter·dis·ci·pli·nar·y (in/tər dis/ə plə när/ē), *adj.* between different fields of study.

in·ter·fere (in/tər fir/), *v.i.*, **-fered, -fer·ing. 1** get in the way of each other; come into opposition; clash. **2** mix in the affairs of others; meddle. (< Old French *entreferir* strike each other < *entre-* between + *ferir* to strike) —**in/ter·fer/er**, *n.*

in·ter·me·di·ate¹ (in/tər mē/dē it), *adj.* being or occurring between; middle: *Gray is intermediate between black and white.* —*n.* person who acts between others to bring about an agreement; mediator. (< Latin *intermedius* < *inter-* between + *medius* in the middle)

in·ter·me·di·ate² (in/tər mē/dē āt), *v.i.*, **-at·ed, -at·ing.** come in to help settle a dispute; mediate. (< *inter-* + *mediate*, verb)

in·ter·min·gle (in/tər ming/gəl), *v.t., v.i.*, **-gled, -gling.** mix together.

in·ter·mis·sion (in/tər mish/ən), *n.* a time between periods of activity; pause: *The band played only with a short intermission at ten.*

in·ter·na·tion·al (in/tər nash/ə nəl), *adj.* **1** between or among nations: *A treaty is an international agreement.* **2** having to do with the relations between nations. —**in/ter·na/tion·al·ly**, *adv.*

in·ter·per·son·al (in/tər pėr/sə nəl), *adj.* between persons.

in·ter·pre·ta·tion (in tėr/prə tā/shən), *n.* an interpreting; explanation.

in·ter·sec·tion (in/tər sek/shən), *n.* point, line, or place where one thing crosses another. —**in/ter·sec/tion·al**, *adj.*

in·ter·vene (in/tər vēn/), *v.i.*, **-vened, -ven·ing.** come between persons or groups to help settle a dispute; act as an intermediary: *The President was asked to intervene in the coal strike.* (< Latin *intervenire* < *inter-* between + *venire* come) —**in/ter·ven/er, in/ter·ve/nor**, *n.*

in·ter·ven·tion (in/tər ven/shən), *n.* **1** an intervening. **2** interference, especially by one nation in the affairs of another.

in·tra·mur·al (in′trə myùr′əl), *adj.*
1 within the walls; inside. **2** carried
on by members of the same school.

in·tra·mus·cu·lar (in′trə mus′kyə lər),
adj. within or into a muscle:
intramuscular injection.

in·tra·state (in′trə stāt′), *adj.* within a
state, especially within a state of
the United States: *intrastate
commerce.*

in·tra·ve·nous (in′trə vē′nəs), *adj.*
1 within a vein or the veins. **2** into
a vein or veins.
—**in′tra·ve′nous·ly**, *adv.*

in·tro·vert (in′trə vėrt′), *n.* person
exhibiting introversion. —*v.t.*
1 direct (one's thoughts, etc.)
inward or upon oneself. **2** turn or
bend inward: *introverted toes.*
(< *intro-* within + Latin *vertere* to
turn)

in·trude (in trüd′), *v.,* **-trud·ed,
-trud·ing.** —*v.i.* force oneself in;
come unasked and unwanted: *If
you are busy, I will not intrude.*
—*v.t.* give unasked and unwanted;
force in: *intrude one's opinions
upon others.* (< Latin *intrudere*
< *in-* in + *trudere* to thrust)
—**in·trud′er**, *n.*

in·tru·sion (in trü′zhən), *n.* act of
intruding; coming unasked and
unwanted.

in·tu·i·tion (in′tü ish′ən, in′tyü
ish′ən), *n.* immediate perception or
understanding of truths, facts, etc.,
without reasoning. (< Late Latin
intuitionem a gazing at < Latin
intueri consider, look upon < *in-* +
tueri to look)

in·tu·i·tive (in tü′ə tiv, in tyü′ə tiv),
adj. perceiving or understanding
by intuition: *an intuitive mind.*
—**in·tu′i·tive·ly**, *adv.*
—**in·tu′i·tive·ness**, *n.*

in·vade (in vād′), *v.,* **in·vades,
in·vad·ed, in·vad·ing.** —*v.t.*
1 enter with force or as an enemy
for conquest or spoils: *Soldiers
invaded the country.* **2** enter as if to
take possession: *Tourists invaded
the city.* **3** interfere with; encroach
upon; violate: *The law punishes*

people who *invade* the rights of
others. —*v.i.* make an invasion.
(< Latin *invadere* < *in-* in +
vadere go, walk)

in·vad·er (in vād ər) *n., pl.* **in·vad·ers.**
person, animal, or thing that enters
as if to take possession.

in·va·sion (in vā′zhən), *n.* an
invading; entering by force or as
an enemy. (< Late Latin
invasionem < *invadere.*)

in·ves·ti·gate (in ves′tə gāt), *v.t.,*
-gat·ed, -gat·ing. look into
thoroughly; examine closely:
investigate a complaint. (< Latin
investigatum traced, searched out
< *in-* in + *vestigare* to track, trace
< *vestigium* footstep, vestige)
—**in·ves′ti·ga·tor**, *n.*

in·vest·ment (in vest′mənt), *n.*
something that is expected to yield
money as income or profit or both.

in·vin·ci·ble (in vin′sə bəl), *adj.*
unable to be conquered;
impossible to overcome: *invincible
courage, an invincible fighter.*
(< Latin *invincibilis* < *in-* not +
vincere conquer) —**in·vin′ci·bly**,
adv.

in·voke (in vōk′), *v.t.,* **-voked,
-vok·ing. 1** call on in prayer;
appeal to for help or protection.
2 ask earnestly for; beg for: *The
condemned criminal invoked the
judge's mercy.* (< Latin *invocare*
< *in-* on + *vocare* to call)
—**in·vok′er**, *n.*

IQ, intelligence quotient.

i·ris (ī′ris), *n.* **1** any of a genus of
plants with sword-shaped leaves
and large, showy flowers most of
which have three upright parts
and three drooping parts;
fleur-de-lis. **2** the flower of any of
these plants. **3** the colored part
around the pupil of the eye. The
iris controls the amount of light
entering the eye. (< Latin, rainbow
< Greek)

ir·ra·tion·al num·ber (i rash′ə nəl
num′bər), a number that cannot
be written as a fraction; a
nonrepeating decimal.

							ə stands for	
a	hat	ī	ice	u̇	put			
ā	age	o	not	ü	rule		a	in about
ä	far, calm	ō	open	ch	child		e	in taken
âr	care	ȯ	saw	ng	long		i	in pencil
e	let	ô	order	sh	she		o	in lemon
ē	equal	oi	oil	th	thin		u	in circus
ėr	term	ou	out	ᴛʜ	then			
i	it	u	cup	zh	measure			

ir·reg·u·lar (i reg′yə lər), *adj.* **1** not regular; not according to rule; out of the usual order or natural way. **2** not according to law or morals: *irregular behavior.* See synonym study below. —**ir·reg′u·lar·ly,** *adv.*
Syn. *adj.* **1,2 Irregular, abnormal** mean out of the usual or natural order or pattern. **Irregular** means not according to the accepted standard: *She has irregular habits.* **Abnormal** means a deviation from what is regarded as normal, average, or typical for the class: *Seven feet is an abnormal height for a person.*

ir·rel·e·vant (i rel′ə vənt), *adj.* not to the point; off the subject: *an irrelevant question.* —**ir·rel′e·vant·ly,** *adv.*

ir·rev·o·ca·ble (i rev′ə kə bəl), *adj.* **1** not able to be revoked; final: *an irrevocable decision.* **2** impossible to call or bring back. —**ir·rev′o·ca·bly,** *adv.*

ir·ri·tate (ir′ə tāt), *v.t.,* **-tat·ed, -tat·ing.** make impatient or angry; annoy; provoke; vex: *Their constant interruptions irritated me.* (< Latin *irritatum* enraged, provoked)

isle (īl), *n.* **1** a small island. **2** island. (< Old French < Latin *insula*)

i·so·la·tion·ist (ī′sə lā′shə nist, is′ə lā′shə nist), *n., pl.* **i·so·la·tion·ists.** person who believes in or favors isolationism. —*adj.* of or having to do with isolationists or isolationism.

journal

a **journal** for personal thoughts

J

jai a·lai (hī′ ä lī′), game similar to handball, played on a walled court with a hard ball, popular in Spain and Latin America; pelota. (< Spanish < Basque < *jai* festival + *alai* merry)

jazz (jaz), *n.* class of music in which melody is subordinate to syncopated rhythms, characterized by improvisation, the use of dissonances, sliding from tone to tone, and the imitation of vocal effects by the instruments. Jazz is native to the United States, and developed from early Afro-American spirituals and folk music. (probably an American Negro word, of west African origin)

Jazz Age (jaz āj), term used to describe the 1920s in the United States, when jazz music first became an important part of American culture.

Jef·fer·son (jef′ər sən), *n.* **Thomas,** (tom′əs), *n.* 1743–1826, American statesman, third president of the United States, from 1801 to 1809. He drafted the Declaration of Independence.

jeop·ar·dize (jep′ər dīz), *v.t.,* **-dized, -diz·ing.** put in danger; risk.

jin·rik·i·sha (jin rik′shə, jin rik′shȯ), *n.* a small, two-wheeled carriage with a folding top, pulled by a runner, formerly used in the Orient. (< Japanese *jinrikisha* < *jin* man + *riki* strength + *sha* cart)

jour·nal (jėr′nl), *n., pl.* **jour·nals.** a daily record of events or occurrences.

jour·nal·ism (jėr′nl iz′əm), *n.* work of writing for, editing, managing, or publishing a newspaper or magazine.

judg·ment (juj′mənt), *n.* **1** result of judging; opinion or estimate. **2** ability to form sound opinions; power to judge well; good sense.

ju·di·cial (jü dish′əl), *adj.* **1** of or by judges; having to do with courts or the administration of justice. **2** of or suitable for a judge; impartial; fair. (< Latin *judicialis* < *judicium* judgment < *judicem* judge)

ju·di·cious (jü dish′əs), *adj.* having, using, or showing good judgment; wise; sensible. —**ju·di′cious·ly,** *adv.*

juke·box (jük′boks′), *n.* an automatic phonograph operated by inserting a coin in a slot. The records to be played are selected by pushing a button. (< Gullah *juke* disorderly, of west African origin + English *box*)

jur·is·dic·tion (jùr′is dik′shən), *n.* **1** right, power, or authority to administer justice or exercise judicial functions. **2** authority; power; control. (< Latin *jurisdictionem* < *jus, juris* law + *dicere* say)

jur·y (jùr′ē), *n., pl.* **jur·ies.** group of persons selected to hear evidence in a court of law and sworn to give a decision in accordance with the evidence presented to them. (< Anglo-French *jurie* < Old French *jurer* swear < Latin *jurare* < *jus, juris* law)

jus·ti·fi·ca·tion (jus′tə fə kā′shən), *n.* **1** a justifying. **2** a being justified.

jus·ti·fy (jus′tə fī), *v.t.,* **-fied, -fy·ing.** show to be just or right; give a good reason for; defend. (< Old French *justifier* < Late Latin *justificare* < Latin *justus* just + *facere* make) —**jus′ti·fi′er,** *n.*

K

ka·lei·do·scope (kə lī′də skōp), *n.* tube containing bits of colored glass and two mirrors. As it is turned, it reflects continually changing patterns. (< Greek *kalos* pretty + *eidos* shape + English -*scope*)

ka·ra·te (kä rä′tē), *n.* a Japanese method of fighting without weapons by striking with the hands, elbows, knees, and feet at certain vulnerable parts of the opponent's body. (< Japanese)

kay·ak (kī′ak), *n.* an Eskimo canoe made of skins stretched over a light frame of wood or bone with an opening in the middle for a person. —*v.i.* go in a kayak. (< Eskimo)

keel (kēl), *n.* the main timber or steel piece that extends the whole length of the bottom of a ship or boat. The whole ship is built up on the keel.

keel·boat (kēl′bōt′), *n.* a large, shallow barge, with a keel and covered deck, formerly used on the Missouri and other rivers.

ker·nel (kér′nl), *n.* **1** the softer part inside the hard shell of a nut or inside the stone of a fruit. **2** grain or seed of wheat, corn, or other cereal plant.

key·board (kē′bôrd′), *n.* the set of keys in a piano, organ, computer.

khak·i (kak′ē, kä′kē), *n.* **1** a dull yellowish brown. **2** a heavy twilled wool or cotton cloth of this color, much used for soldiers' uniforms. **3 khakis,** *pl.* uniform made of this cloth. (< Hindi *khākī*, originally, dusty < Persian *khāk* dust)

ki·mo·no (kə mō′nə), *n., pl.* **-nos. 1** a loose outer garment held in place by a wide sash, worn by Japanese men and women. **2** a woman's loose dressing gown. (< Japanese)

kind of (kīnd ov), sort of, in a way.

knowl·edge·a·ble (nol′i jə bəl), *adj.* well-informed, especially about a particular subject.

kum·quat (kum′kwot), *n.* any of several yellow or orange fruits somewhat like a small orange, having a sour pulp and a sweet rind. Kumquats are used in preserves and candy. (< Chinese (Canton) *kam* golden + *kwat* orange)

L

lar·i·at (lar′ē ət), *n.* **1** rope for fastening horses, mules, to a stake. **2** lasso. (< Spanish *la reata* the rope)

la·ser (lā′zer), *n.* device which generates and amplifies light waves in a narrow and extremely intense beam of light of only one wavelength going in only one direction. Laser beams are used to cut materials and remove diseased body tissues. (< *l(ight) a(mplification by) s(timulated) e(mission of) r(adiation)*)

launch (lônch), *n.* **1** an open motorboat used for pleasure trips, ferrying passengers, etc. **2** the largest boat carried by a warship. (< Spanish and Portuguese *lancha* kind of long boat < Malay *lancharān* < *lanchār* fast)

lee·ward (lē′werd, lü′erd), *adj., adv.* **1** on the side away from the wind. **2** in the direction toward which the wind is blowing.

left field (left fēld), **1** (in baseball) the section of the outfield beyond third base. **2 out in left field,** SLANG. out of contact with reality; unreasonable or improbable. —**left fielder.**

leg·is·la·ture (lej′ə slā′chər), *n.* group of persons that has the duty and power of making laws.

lem·ming (lem′ing), *n.* any of several genera of small, mouselike, arctic rodents, having a short tail and furry feet. (< Norwegian)

lem·on·ade (lem′ə nād′), *n.* drink made of lemon juice, sugar, and water.

kayak
Inuks maneuvering
a **kayak**

left field (def. 1)
a view of **left field**
during a baseball game

a	hat	ī	ice	u̇	put	ə stands for	
ā	age	o	not	ü	rule	a	in about
ä	far, calm	ō	open	ch	child	e	in taken
âr	care	ȯ	saw	ng	long	i	in pencil
e	let	ô	order	sh	she	o	in lemon
ē	equal	oi	oil	th	thin	u	in circus
ér	term	ou	out	ᴛʜ	then		
i	it	u	cup	zh	measure		

loom

Peruvian women working
on a **loom**

le·o·tard (lē′ə tärd), *n.* Usually, **leotards,** *pl.* a tight-fitting one-piece garment, with or without sleeves, worn by dancers, acrobats. (< French *léotard,* < Jules *Léotard,* French aerialist of the 1800's)

li·a·ble (lī′ə bəl), *adj.* **1** subject to the possibility; likely or possible, especially unpleasantly likely: *That glass is liable to break.* **2** exposed to or in danger of something likely.

li·ai·son (lē′ā zon′, lē ā′zon), *n.* **1** connection between military units, branches of a service, etc., to secure proper cooperation. **2** similar connection or communication between civilian bodies, such as companies, etc. (< French < Latin *ligationem* a binding < *ligare* to bind)

li·bel (lī′bəl), *n., v.,* **-beled, -bel·ing** or **-belled, -bel·ling.** —*n.* a written or published statement, picture, etc., tending to damage a person's reputation or subject someone to public ridicule and disgrace. —*v.t.* make false or damaging statements about. (< Old French, a formal written statement < Latin *libellus,* diminutive of *liber* book)

lib·er·al (lib′ər əl), *adj.* **1** giving or given freely; generous. **2** plentiful; abundant; ample: *a liberal supply of food.* **3** not narrow in one's views and ideas; broad-minded. —*n.* person who holds liberal principles. (< Latin *liberalis* befitting free people, honorable, generous < *liber* free) —**lib′er·al·ly,** *adv.* —**lib′er·al·ness,** *n.*

lib·er·ate (lib′ə rāt′), *v.t.,* **-rat·ed, -rat·ing.** set free; free or release from slavery, prison, confinement, etc. (< Latin *liberatum* freed < *liber* free) —**lib′e·ra·tor,** *n.*

lib·e·ra·tion (lib′ə rā′shən), *n.* **1** a setting free. **2** a being set free.

life ex·pect·an·cy (līf ek spek′ tən sē), the average number of remaining years that a person at a given age can expect to live.

life·guard (līf′gärd′), *n.* person trained in lifesaving who is employed on a beach or at a swimming pool to help in case of accident or danger to swimmers.

life in·sur·ance (līf in shùr′əns), **1** insurance by which a specified sum of money is paid to the insured person's survivors at the person's death. **2** sum paid by the insurance company at death.

life jack·et (līf jak′it), a sleeveless jacket filled with a light material, such as kapok, or with compressed air, worn as a life preserver.

life-size (līf′sīz), *adj.* as big as the living person, animal, etc.; equal in size to the original.

life·time (līf′tīm′), *n.* time of being alive; period during which a life lasts. —*adj.* for life.

lim·ou·sine (lim′ə zēn′, lim′ə zēn′), *n.* a large automobile or small bus used to transport passengers to or from an airport, a bus station, etc. (< French < *Limousin,* former French province)

line (līn), *n., v.,* **lined, lin·ing.** —*n.* **1** a long narrow mark. **2** row of persons or things: *a line of trees.* **3 out of line, a** in disagreement. **b** uncalled-for; not suitable or proper. —*v.t.* arrange a line along; form a line along. (fusion of Old English *līne,* line, rope, and Old French *ligne* line, both ultimately < Latin *linea* line, linen thread < *linum* flax)

lip·stick (lip′stik′), *n.* a small stick of a waxlike cosmetic, used for coloring the lips.

long·horn (lòng′hôrn′), *n.* one of a breed of cattle with very long horns, formerly common in the southwestern United States and Mexico.

loom (lüm), *n., pl.* **looms.** frame or machine for weaving yarn or thread into cloth.

lo·qua·cious (lō kwā′shəs), *adj.* talking much; fond of talking. —**lo·qua′cious·ly,** *adv.* —**lo·qua′cious·ness,** *n.*

Lou·i·si·an·a Pur·chase (lù ē′zē an′ə per′chəs), large region that the United States bought from France in 1803. It extended from the Mississippi River to the Rocky Mountains and from Canada to the Gulf of Mexico.

luck·i·ly (luk′ə lē), *adv.* by good luck; fortunately.

luff (luf), *v.i.* turn the bow of a ship toward the wind; sail into the wind. —*n.* **1** act of turning the bow of a ship toward the wind. **2** the forward edge of a fore-and-aft sail.

lug·gage (lug′ij), *n.* baggage, especially of a traveler or passenger; suitcases and the like.

lu·mi·nous (lü′mə nəs), *adj.* shining by its own light: *The sun and stars are luminous bodies.* —**lu′mi·nous·ly,** *adv.* —**lu′mi·nous·ness,** *n.*

M

ma·chet·e (mə shet′ē, mə chet′ē), *n.* a large, heavy knife, used as a tool for cutting brush, sugar cane, etc., and as a weapon. (< Spanish)

mac·ra·mé (mak′rə mā), *n.* a coarse lace or fringe made by knotting thread or cord in patterns. (< French *macramé* < Italian *macramè* < Turkish *makrama* napkin)

mag·nate (mag′nāt), *n.* an important, powerful, person. (< Late Latin *magnatem* < Latin *magnus* great)

mag·net (mag′nit), *n.* **1** stone or piece of metal that has the property of attracting iron or steel. **2** anything that attracts.

mag·nif·i·cent (mag nif′ə sənt), *adj.* **1** richly colored or decorated; splendid; grand; stately. **2** noble; exalted. —**mag·nif′i·cent·ly,** *adv.*

mah-jongg or **mah-jong** (mä′jong′), *n.* game of Chinese origin played by four people with 144 oblong tiles. Each player tries to form winning combinations by drawing or discarding. (< dialectal Chinese *ma chiang*, literally, sparrows (from a design on the pieces))

man·a·cle (man′ə kəl), *n., v.,* **-cled, -cling.** —*n.* **1** Usually, **manacles,** *pl.* fetter for the hands; handcuff. **2** anything that fetters; restraint. —*v.t.* put manacles on. (< Old French *manicle* < Latin *manicula,* diminutive of *manus* hand)

man·age (man′ij), *v.,* **-aged, -ag·ing,** —*v.t.* **1** guide or handle with skill or authority; control; direct. **2** succeed in accomplishing; contrive; arrange. **3** make use of: *manage tools well.* —*v.i.* **1** conduct affairs. **2** get along: *manage on one's income.* (earlier *manege* < Italian *managgiare* handle or train (horses) < *mano* hand < Latin *manus*) —**man′age·a·ble,** *adj.*

man·age·ment (man′ij mənt), *n.* **1** a managing or handling; control; direction. **2** persons that manage a business.

man·date (man′dāt), *n.,* **1** an order or command: *a royal mandate.* **2** order from a higher court or official to a lower one. (< Latin *mandatum* < *mandare* to order)

man·i·cure (man′ə kyùr), *v.,* **-cured, -cur·ing,** *n.* —*v.t., v.i.* care for (the fingernails and hands); trim, clean, and polish (the fingernails). —*n.* the care of the hands. (< French < Latin *manus* hand + *cura* care) —**man′i·cur′ist,** *n.*

man·i·fest des·ti·ny (man′ə fest des′tə nē), the belief in the 1840s in the inevitable territorial expansion of the United States.

ma·nip·u·late (mə nip′yə lāt), *v.t.,* **-lat·ed, -lat·ing.** handle or treat, especially skillfully: *manipulate clay into a pot.* (< Latin *manipulus* handful < *manus* hand + root of *plere* to fill) —**ma·nip′u·la′tion,** *n.* —**ma·nip′u·la′tor,** *n.*

ma·nip·u·la·tive (mə nip′yə lā′tiv), *adj.* of or having to do with manipulation.

man·ne·quin (man′ə kən), *n.* figure of a person used by tailors, artists, stores, etc.

man·ner·ism (man′ə riz′əm), *n.* an odd trick or habit; way of acting.

man·u·fac·ture (man′yə fak′chər), *v.,* **-tured, -tur·ing,** *n.* —*v.t.* make by hand or by machine; produce by human labor, especially in large quantities with the help of machines. —*n.* act or process of manufacturing. (< Middle French < Medieval Latin *manufactura* < Latin *manu facere* make by hand)

man·u·script (man′yə skript), *n.* book or paper written by hand or with a typewriter. Before printing was invented, all books and papers were handwritten manuscripts. —*adj.* written by hand. (< Latin *manu scriptus* written by hand)

ma·ra·ca (mə rä′kə), *n.* a percussion instrument consisting of seeds, pebbles, etc., enclosed in a dry gourd and shaken like a rattle. (< Portuguese < Tupi)

mah-jongg
a winning hand in
mah-jongg

a	hat	**ī**	ice	**u̇**	put	**ə** stands for	
ā	age	**o**	not	**ü**	rule	**a**	in about
ä	far, calm	**ō**	open	**ch**	child	**e**	in taken
âr	care	**ȯ**	saw	**ng**	long	**i**	in pencil
e	let	**ô**	order	**sh**	she	**o**	in lemon
ē	equal	**oi**	oil	**th**	thin	**u**	in circus
ėr	term	**ou**	out	**ŦH**	then		
i	it	**u**	cup	**zh**	measure		

mar·a·thon (mâr′ə thon), *n.* **1** a footrace of 26 miles, 385 yards (42.2 kilometers). **2** any race over a long distance.

ma·rim·ba (mə rim′bə), *n.* a musical instrument somewhat like a xylophone. (of Bantu origin)

marsh·mal·low (märsh′mal′ō, märsh′mel′ō), *n.* a soft, white, spongy candy, covered with powdered sugar, made from corn syrup, sugar, starch, and gelatin.

mar·su·pi·al (mär sü′pē əl), *n.* any of an order of mammals having a pouch covering the mammary glands on the abdomen, in which the female nurses and carries her incompletely developed young. Kangaroos belong to this order.

marsupial

A kangaroo is

a **marsupial.**

mast (mast), *n.* a long pole of wood or metal rising from the keel of a vessel set upright on a ship to support the yards, sails, rigging, etc. (Old English *mæst*)

ma·ter·i·al·ism (mə tir′ē ə liz′əm), *n.* tendency to care too much for the things of this world and to neglect spiritual needs.

math·e·mat·i·cal ex·pres·sion (math′ə mat′ə kəl ek spresh′ən), a mathematical phrase that uses numbers, variables, and operation symbols to represent a value.

mat·i·nee (mat′n ā′), *n.* a dramatic or musical performance held in the afternoon. (< French *matinée* < Old French *matin* morning)

mat·tress (mat′ris), *n.* **1** a covering of strong cloth stuffed with cotton, foam rubber, etc., and sometimes containing springs, used on a bed. **2** air mattress. (< Old French *materas* < Italian *materasso* < Arabic *almaṭrah* the cushion)

Ma·ya (mī′ə, mä′yə), *n., pl.* **Ma·yas** or **Ma·ya** for 1. **1** member of an ancient American Indian people of Central America and Mexico. The Mayas had a highly developed civilization from about A.D. 350 to about A.D. 800. **2** their language. —**Ma′yan,** *adj., n.*

may·be (mā′bē), *adv.* it may be; possibly; perhaps.

→ **maybe, may be.** *Maybe* is an adverb; *may be* is a verb form: *Maybe you'll have better luck next time. He may be the next mayor.*

may be (mā bē), could be, might be: *This may be his last chance.*

mean·time (mēn′tīm′), *n.* time between. —*adv.* **1** in the intervening time; in the time between. **2** at the same time.

me·di·o·cre (mē′dē ō′kər), *adj.* neither good nor bad; of average quality. (< Latin *mediocris,* originally, halfway up < *medius* middle + *ocris* jagged mountain)

meg·a·lop·o·lis (meg′ə lop′ə lis), *n.* a large metropolitan area, often including several cities. (< Greek *megas, megalou* great + *polis* city)

mel·an·chol·y (mel′ən kol′ē), *n., pl.* **-chol·ies,** *adj.* —*n.* condition of sadness and low spirits; gloominess. —*adj.* depressed in spirits; sad. (< Greek *melancholia* < *melanos* black + *cholē* bile)

mel·a·nin (mel′ə nən), *n.* any of a class of dark-brown or black pigments that help protect the skin against sun damage. (< Greek *melanos* black)

me·men·to (mə men′tō), *n., pl.* **me·men·tos** or **me·men·toes.** something serving as a reminder of what is past or gone; souvenir. (< Latin, remember)

mem·or·a·ble (mem′ər ə bəl), *adj.* worth remembering; not to be forgotten; notable: *a memorable trip.* —**mem′or·a·bly,** *adv.*

mem·o·ran·dum (mem′ə ran′dəm), *n., pl.* **mem·o·ran·da** (mem′ə ran′də). a short written statement for future use; note to aid one's memory. (< Latin, (thing) to be remembered)

me·tab·o·lism (mə tab′ə liz′əm), *n.* the sum of the physiological processes by which an organism maintains life. (< Greek *metabolē* change < *meta-* after + *bolē* a throwing)

met·ro·nome (met′rə nōm), *n.* device that can be adjusted to make loud ticking sounds at different speeds. Metronomes are used especially to mark time for persons practicing on musical instruments. (< Greek *metron* measure + *-nomos* regulating < *nemein* regulate)

me·trop·o·lis (mə trop′ə lis), *n.* a large city; important center, especially the center of some activity: *a financial metropolis.* (< Greek *mētropolis* < *mētēr* mother + *polis* city)

mile·age (mī′lij), *n.* **1** miles covered or traveled: *Our car's mileage last year was 10,000 miles.* **2** miles traveled per gallon of gasoline.

milk (milk), *n.* **1** the whitish liquid secreted by the mammary glands of female mammals for the nourishment of their young.

2 cry over spilt milk, to waste sorrow or regret on what has happened and cannot be remedied.

mi·nor·i·ty group (mə nôr′ə tē grüp), *n., pl.* **mi·nor·i·ty groups.** a group of people who differ from the majority of the population in terms of race, religion, or national origin.

min·ute·man (min′it man′), *n., pl.* **min·ute·men.** member of the American militia just before and during the Revolutionary War. They kept themselves ready for military service at a minute's notice.

mi·nu·ti·a (mi nü′shē ə, mi nyü′shē ə), *n.* sing. of **minutiae.**

mi·nu·ti·ae (mi nü′shē ē, mi nyü′shē ē), *n. pl.* very small matters; trifling details. (< Latin, trifles, plural of *minutia* smallness < *minutum.*)

mir·a·cle (mir′ə kəl), *n.* **1** a wonderful happening that is contrary to or independent of the known laws of nature, and is therefore ascribed to God or some supernatural being or power. **2** something marvelous; a wonder. (< Latin *miraculum,* ultimately < *mirus* wonderful)

mis·cel·la·ne·ous (mis′ə lā′nē əs), *adj.* not all of one kind or nature; of mixed composition or character: (< Latin *miscellaneus* < *miscellus* mixed < *miscere* to mix)

mis·chie·vous (mis′chə vəs), *adj.* **1** causing mischief; naughty. **2** full of pranks and teasing fun. —**mis′chie·vous·ly,** *adv.* —**mis′chie·vous·ness,** *n.*

mix·ture (miks′chər), *n.* **1** what has been mixed; product of mixing. **2** two or more substances mixed together but not chemically combined. (< Latin *mixtura* < *miscere* to mix)

moc·ca·sin (mok′ə sən), *n.* a soft leather shoe originally worn by North American Indians, typically without heels; the sole and the sides stitched to the upper part with rawhide. (of Algonquian origin)

mois·ture (mois′chər), *n.* slight wetness. Dew is moisture that collects at night on cool surfaces.

mole (mōl), *n.* a spot or lump on the skin that is usually brown, black, etc.

mo·men·tum (mō men′təm), *n., pl.* **-tums, -ta** (-tə). measure of the strength of an object's motion, depending on both an object's mass and its velocity.

mon·strous (mon′strəs), *adj.* **1** of extremely large size; huge; enormous. **2** shocking; horrible; dreadful. —**mon′strous·ly,** *adv.*

mo·ped (mō′ped), *n.* motorbike which can be pedaled as a vehicle or operated with a motor at up to 30 miles (48 kilometers) an hour. (blend of *motor* and *pedal*)

mort·gage (môr′gij), *n., v.,* **-gaged, -gag·ing.** —*n.* a legal right or claim to a piece of property, given as security in case the loaned money is not repaid when due. —*v.t.* give a lender a claim to (one's property) in case a debt is not paid when due. (< Old French < *mort* dead + *gage* pledge)

mo·sa·ic (mō zā′ik), *n.* decoration made of small pieces of stone, glass, wood, etc., of different colors inlaid to form a picture or design. (< Medieval Latin *mosaicus, musaicus* of the Muses, artistic)

mo·squi·to (mə skē′tō), *n., pl.* **mo·squi·toes.** any of a family of small, slender insects with two wings. The females can pierce the skin of humans and animals and draw blood, causing itching. (< Spanish, diminutive of *mosca* fly < Latin *musca*)

mo·to·cross (mō′tō krôs′), *n.* a motorcycle race run over cross-country trails rather than on a paved track. (< French *moto-cross* < *moto* motorcycle + *cross* (-country) a cross-country race < English *cross-country,* adjective)

mo·tor·cade (mō′tər kād), *n.* procession or long line of automobiles.

mot·to (mot′ō), *n., pl.* **-toes** or **-tos.** a brief sentence adopted as a rule of conduct: *"Think before you speak"* is a good motto.

minuteman
minutemen getting ready to march

a	hat	**ī**	ice	**u̇**	put	**ə** stands for	
ā	age	**o**	not	**ü**	rule	**a**	in about
ä	far, calm	**ō**	open	**ch**	child	**e**	in taken
âr	care	**ȯ**	saw	**ng**	long	**i**	in pencil
e	let	**ô**	order	**sh**	she	**o**	in lemon
ē	equal	**oi**	oil	**th**	thin	**u**	in circus
ėr	term	**ou**	out	**ᴛʜ**	then		
i	it	**u**	cup	**zh**	measure		

natural

a **natural** arch

mug·wump (mug′wump′), *n.* person who is independent in politics. (< Massachuset *mukquomp* chief)

muk·luk (muk′luk), *n.* a high, waterproof boot, often made of sealskin, worn by Eskimos and others in arctic regions. (< Eskimo *muklok* large seal)

mur·mur (mėr′mėr), *n.* **1** a soft, low, indistinct sound that rises and falls a little and goes on without breaks. **2** complaint made under the breath, not aloud. —*v.t.* utter in a murmur. (< Latin)

mus·cu·lar strength (mus′kyə lėr strengkth), *n.* the ability of muscles to put forth force.

musk·rat (musk′rat′), *n., pl.* **-rats** or **-rat.** a water rodent of North America, like a rat, but larger, having webbed hind feet, a glossy coat, and a musky smell.

mus·tang (mus′tang), *n., pl.* **mus·tangs.** a small, wiry, wild or half-wild horse of the North American plains, descended from domesticated Spanish stock. (< Spanish *mestengo* untamed)

N

na·ive (nä ēv′), *adj.* simple in nature; like a child; not sophisticated. (< French *naïve,* feminine of *naïf* < Latin *nativus.*) **na·ive′ly,** *adv.*

na·po·le·on (nə pō′lē ən), *n.* kind of pastry with a custard, cream, or jam filling. (< *Napoleon I*)

nar·rate (nar′āt, na rāt′), *v.t.,* **-rat·ed, -rat·ing.** give an account of; tell (a story, etc.): *narrate an incident.* (< Latin *narratum* made known, told) **—nar′ra·tor,** *n.*

nar·ra·tive (nar′ə tiv), *n.* story or account; tale. —*adj.* that narrates. **—nar′ra·tive·ly,** *adv.*

NAS·A (nas′ə), *n.* National Aeronautics and Space Administration (an agency of the United States government established to direct and aid civilian research and development in aeronautics and aerospace technology).

NA·TO (nā′tō), *n.* North Atlantic Treaty Organization (an alliance of sixteen Western nations providing military cooperation, originally formed in 1949.

nat·ur·al (nach′ėr əl), *adj.* produced by nature; based on some state of things in nature. —*n.* that which is natural. **—nat′ur·al·ness,** *n.*

naval

a **naval** ship at sea

nat·ur·al·ist (nach′ėr ə list), *n.* **1** person who makes a study of living organisms, especially in their native habitats. **2** writer or artist who practices naturalism.

na·ture (nā′chėr), *n.* **1** all things except those made by human beings; the world: *the wonders of nature.* **2** the sum total of the forces at work throughout the universe: *the laws of nature.*

na·val (nā′vəl), *adj.* **1** of or for warships or the navy: *a naval officer.* **2** having a navy.

neb·u·la (neb′yə lə), *n., pl.* **-lae** (-le′), **-las.** mass of dust particles and gases in outer space (**galactic nebula**), which may either be dark or appear as a haze illuminated by stars. (< Latin, mist, cloud)

neck (nek), *n.* **1** the part of the body that connects the head with the shoulders. **2** the part of a garment that fits the neck. **neck and neck, a** abreast. **b** running equal or even in a race or contest. (Old English *hnecca*) **—neck′less,** *adj.*

ne·go·ti·ate (ni gō′shē āt), *v.,* **-at·ed, -at·ing.** —*v.i.* talk over and arrange terms; confer; consult. —*v.t.* arrange for: *They finally negotiated a peace treaty.* (< Latin *negotiatum* engaged in business < *negotium* business < *neg-* not + *otium* ease, leisure) **—ne·go′ti·a′tion,** *n.* **—ne·go′ti·a′tor,** *n.*

net in·come (net in′kum′), the amount of money remaining after deductions.

neu·rol′o·gist (nu rol′ə jist, nyu rol′ə jist), *n.* an expert who studies the nervous system and its diseases.

neu·tral (nü′trəl, nyü′trəl), *adj.* **1** on neither side in a quarrel or war. **2** of or belonging to a neutral country or neutral zone: *a neutral port.* —*n.* a person or country not taking part in a quarrel or war. (< Latin *neutralis* of neuter gender < *neuter*) **—neu′tral·ly,** *adv.*

neu·tral·i·ty (nü tral′ə tē, nyü tral′ə tē), *n.* the attitude or policy of a nation that does not take part directly or indirectly in a war.

neu·tron (nü′tron, nyü′tron), *n.* a particle having no electric charge and found either by itself or in a nucleus. (< *neutr(al)* + *-on*)

neu·tron star (nü′tron or nyü′tron stär), star in which the inward force of gravity is balanced by the outward pressure of packed neutrons.

nom de plume (nom′ də plüm′), *n.,* *pl.* **noms de plume** (nomz′ də plüm′). pen name. (formed in English from French *nom* name, *de* of, *plume* pen)

non·vi·o·lence (non vī′ə ləns), *n.* belief in the use of peaceful methods to achieve any goal.

no one (nō wun), no person; nobody.

nor·mal (nôr′məl), *adj.* of the usual standard; regular; usual: *The normal temperature of the human body is 98.6 degrees.* —**nor′mal·ly,** *adv.*

no·tice·a·ble (nō′ti sə bəl), *adj.* **1** easily seen or noticed; observable. **2** worth noticing; deserving notice. —**no′tice·a·bly,** *adv.*

nu·cle·ar fis·sion (nü′klē ər or nyü′klē ər fish′ən), the splitting of an atomic nucleus into two parts, especially when bombarded by a neutron. Fission is used to induce the chain reaction in an atomic bomb.

nu·cle·ar fu·sion (nü′klē ər or nyü′klē ər fyü′zhən), the combining of two atomic nuclei to produce a nucleus of greater mass. Fusion releases vast amounts of energy and is used to produce the reaction in a hydrogen bomb.

nu·cle·us (nü′klē əs, nyü′klē əs), *n.,* *pl.* **-cle·i** or **-cle·us·es.** the central part of an atom, consisting of a proton or protons, neutrons, and other particles. (< Latin, kernel < *nux, nucis* nut)

nui·sance (nü′sns, nyü′sns), *n.* thing or person that annoys, troubles, offends, or is disagreeable; annoyance. (< Old French < *nuire* to harm < Latin *nocere*)

O

ob·jec·tive (əb jek′tiv), *n.,* *pl.* **ob·jec·tives.** something aimed at; object; goal: *My objective is to play tennis better.* —**ob·jec′tive·ly,** *adv.* —**ob·jec′tive·ness,** *n.*

ob·ser·va·tion (ob′zər vā′shən), *n.* **1** act, habit, or power of seeing and noting. **2** Often, **observations,** *pl.* something seen and noted; data or information secured by observing.

ob·sta·cle (ob′stə kəl), *n.* something that stands in the way or stops progress. (< Latin *obstaculum* < *ob-* in the way of + *stare* to stand) **Syn.** Obstacle, obstruction, hindrance mean something that gets in the way of action or progress. **Obstacle** applies to something that stands in the way and must be moved or overcome before one can continue toward a goal: *A fallen tree across the road was an obstacle to our car.* **Obstruction** applies especially to something that blocks a passage: *The enemy built obstructions in the road.* **Hindrance** applies to something that holds back or makes progress difficult: *Noise is a hindrance to studying.*

ob·ste·tri·cian (ob′stə trish′ən), *n.* doctor who specializes in obstetrics, a branch of medicine concerned with caring for and treating women before, in, and after childbirth. (< Latin *obstetrica* < *obstetrix* midwife < *ob-* by + *stare* to stand)

ob·struc·tion (əb struk′shən), *n.* thing that obstructs; something in the way: *The whirlpool was an obstruction to navigating the river.* See **obstacle** for synonym study.

oc·ca·sion·al (ə kā′zhə nəl), *adj.* happening or coming now and then, or once in a while. —**oc·ca′sion·al·ly,** *adv.*

oc·cur·rence (ə kėr′əns), *n.* **1** an occurring: *The occurrence of storms delayed our trip.* **2** event; happening; incident.

o·kra (ō′krə), *n.* **1** a tall plant of the mallow family, cultivated for its sticky pods, which are used in soups and as a vegetable. **2** the pods. (< a west African word)

o·mis·sion (ō mish′ən), *n.* **1** an omitting. **2** a being omitted.

observation (def. 1) a science **observation** in a laboratory

ɑ	hat	ī	ice	u̇	put	ə stands for	
ā	age	o	not	ü	rule	ɑ	in about
ä	far, calm	ō	open	ch	child	e	in taken
âr	care	ô	saw	ng	long	i	in pencil
e	let	ô	order	sh	she	o	in lemon
ē	equal	oi	oil	th	thin	u	in circus
ėr	term	ou	out	ᴛʜ	then		
i	it	u	cup	zh	measure		

o·mit (ō mit′), *v.t.,* **o·mit·ted, o·mit·ting. 1** leave out. **2** fail to do; neglect: *They omitted making their beds. (< Latin omittere < ob-* by + *mittere* let go)

o·paque (ō pāk′), *adj.* any object which light does not pass through. (< Latin *opacus* dark, shady)

o·pen (ō′pən), *adj.* **1** letting (anyone or anything) in or out; not shut; not closed. **2** not having its door, gate, lid, etc., closed not closed up: *an open box. —v.t.* move or turn away from a shut or closed position to allow passage; give access to. **—o′pen·ly,** *adv.* **—o′pen·ness,** *n.*

open range

o·pen range (ō′pən rānj), large, unfenced area of grassland and water for raising cattle or sheep.

oph·thal·mol·o·gist (of′thal mol′ə jist, op′thal mol′ə jist), *n.* doctor who specializes in ophthalmology, a branch of medicine that deals with the structure, functions, and diseases of the eye.

op·ti·mism (op′tə miz′əm), *n.* **1** tendency to look on the bright side of things. **2** belief that everything will turn out for the best. (< French *optimisme* < Latin *optimus* best)

o·rang·u·tan (ô rang′ù tan′), *n.* a large ape of the forests of Borneo and Sumatra, that has very long arms and long, reddish-brown hair. (< Malay < *orang* man + *utan* of the woods)

or·der of op·e·ra·tions (ôr′dər ov op′ə rā′shəns), in mathematics, the order in which the operations are done within an expression.

or·di·nar·y (ôrd′n er′ē), *adj.* **1** according to habit or custom; usual; regular; normal. **2** not special; common; everyday; average. (< Latin *ordinarius* < *ordinem* order) **—or′di·nar′i·ness,** *n.*

o·ri·ga·mi (ôr′ə gä′mē), *n.* the Japanese art of folding paper to make decorative objects, such as figures of birds and flowers. (< Japanese)

or·tho·pe·dist (ôr′thə pē′dist), *n.* doctor who specializes in orthopedics, a branch of surgery that deals with the deformities and diseases of bones and joints, especially in children. (< *ortho-* + Greek *paidos* child)

out·go·ing (out′gō′ing), *n.* a going out. *—adj.* **1** outward bound; going out; departing. **2** friendly and helpful to others; sociable.

out·put (out′pùt′), *n., v.,* **out·put, out·put·ting.** *—n.* information put out by or delivered by a computer. *—v.t.* deliver information.

out·ra·geous (out rā′jəs), *adj.* very offensive or insulting; shocking. **—out·ra′geous·ly,** *adv.* **—out·ra′geous·ness,** *n.*

out·side (out′sīd′), *n.* **1** side or surface that is out; outer part: *the outside of a house.* **2** space or position that is beyond or not inside. *—adv.* on or to the outside.

out·spo·ken (out′spō′kən), *adj.* not reserved; frank: *an outspoken person.* **—out′spo′ken·ness,** *n.*

out·stand·ing bal·ance (out stan′ding bal′əns), the difference between the amount one owes or has withdrawn from an account and the amount one is owed or deposits in an account.

o·ver·do (ō′vər dü′), *v.t.,* **-did** (-did′), **-done** (-dun′), **-do·ing. 1** do or attempt to do too much: *She overdoes exercise.* **2** cook too much: *The meat is overdone.*

o·ver·due (ō′vər dü′, ō′vər dyü′), *adj.* more than due; due some time ago but not yet arrived, paid, etc.: *The train is overdue.*

o·ver·rate (ō′vər rāt′), *v.t.,* **o·ver·rat·ed, o·ver·rat·ing.** rate or estimate too highly.

o·ver·seas (*adv.* ō′vər sēz′), *adv.* across the sea; abroad.

o·ver·se·er (ō′vər sē′ər), *n.* one who oversees others or their work.

o·ver·whelm·ing (ō′vər hwel′ming), *adj.* too many, too great, or too much to be resisted; overpowering. **—o′ver·whelm′ing·ly,** *adv.*

ox·y·gen (ok′sə jən), *n.* a colorless, odorless, tasteless gaseous element that forms about one fifth of the atmosphere by volume. Animals and plants cannot live, and fire will not burn, without oxygen. (< French *oxygène* < Greek *oxys* sharp + *-genēs* born)

P

pag·eant (paj′ənt), *n.* an elaborate spectacle; procession in costume; pomp; display; show: *The coronation of a new ruler is always a splendid pageant.*

pains·tak·ing (pānz′tā′king), *adj.* **1** very careful; particular; scrupulous. **2** marked or characterized by attentive care. **—pains′tak′ing·ly,** *adv.*

paint·er[1] (pān′tər), *n.* **1** person who paints pictures; artist. **2** person who paints houses, etc. (< Old French *peinteur,* ultimately < Latin *pictorem* < *pingere* to paint)

paint·er[2] (pān′tər), *n.* a rope, usually fastened to the bow of a boat, for tying it to a ship, etc. (probably < Middle French *pentoir* hanging cordage < Latin *pendere* to hang)

pa·ja·mas (pə jä′məz, pə jam′əz), *n.pl.* sleeping or lounging garments consisting of a jacket or blouse and loose trousers. (< Hindustani *pājāmā* < Persian *pāe* leg + *jāmah* garment)

pal·an·quin (pal′ən kēn′), *n.* a covered platform enclosed at the sides, often with a couch, that is carried by poles resting on the shoulders of four or six men, formerly used in the Orient. (< Portuguese *palanquim* < Malay *palangki* couch)

par·a·graph (pâr′ə graf), *n.* group of sentences relating to the same idea or topic and forming a distinct part of a chapter, letter, or other piece of writing. Usually begin a paragraph on a new line and indent. (< Greek *paragraphos* line (in the margin) marking a break in sense < *para-*[1] + *graphein* write)

par·al·lel cir·cuits (pâr′ə lel sėr′kits), the paths of electric current connecting several electrical devices in which the removal of one device does not break the electrical flow to the other devices.

par·a·pher·nal·ia (par′ə fər nā′lyə), *n., pl. or sing.* **1** personal belongings. **2** equipment; outfit. (< Medieval Latin < Greek *parapherna* a woman's personal property besides her dowry < *para-*[1] + *phernē* dowry)

pa·ren·the·sis (pə ren′thə sis), *n., pl.* **pa·ren·the·ses** (-sēz′). **1** word, phrase, sentence, etc., inserted within a sentence to explain or qualify something. **2** either or both of two curved lines () used to set off such an expression.

par·ka (pär′kə), *n.* a fur jacket with a hood, worn in Alaska and in northeastern Asia.

par·lia·ment (pär′lə mənt), *n.* council or congress that is the highest lawmaking body in some countries. (< Old French *parlement* < *parler* speak.)

par·mi·gia·na (pär′mə jä′nə, pär′mə zhä′nə), *adj.* cooked or sprinkled with Parmesan cheese. (< Italian, feminine of *parmigiano* of Parma)

par·take (pär tāk′), *v.i.,* **-took, -tak·en, -tak·ing. 1** eat or drink some; take some. **2** take or have a share; participate.

part·ner·ship (pärt′nər ship), *n.* **1** a being a partner; joint interest; association: *a business partnership.* **2** company or firm with two or more members who share in the risks and profits of the business.

pas·sage (pas′ij), *n.* **1** hall or way through or between parts of a building; passageway; corridor. **2** means of passing; way through.

pas·time (pas′tīm′), *n.* a pleasant way of passing time; amusement; recreation; diversion; games.

pea soup (pē süp), thick soup made with mashed (split) peas, other vegetables, and sometimes ham.

pe·can (pi kän′, pi kan′, pē′kan), *n.* an olive-shaped, edible nut with a smooth, thin shell, that grows on a hickory tree common in the southern and central United States. (< Cree *pakan* hard-shelled nut)

pe·cul·iar (pi kyü′lyər), *adj.* out of the ordinary; strange; odd; unusual. (< Latin *peculiaris* of one's own < *peculium* private property < *pecu* money, cattle) **—pe·cul′iar·ly,** *adv.*

ped·es·tal (ped′i stəl), *n.* **1** base on which a column or a statue stands. **2** any base; support; foundation.

pe·des·tri·an (pə des′trē ən), *n., pl.* **pe·des·tri·ans.** person who goes on foot; walker. **—***adj.* going on foot; walking. (< Latin *pedester* on foot < *pedem* foot)

passage (def. 1)
a **passage** outside the building

a	hat	**ī**	ice	**u̇**	put	**ə stands for**
ā	age	**o**	not	**ü**	rule	**a** in about
ä	far, calm	**ō**	open	**ch**	child	**e** in taken
âr	care	**ȯ**	saw	**ng**	long	**i** in pencil
e	let	**ô**	order	**sh**	she	**o** in lemon
ē	equal	**oi**	oil	**th**	thin	**u** in circus
ėr	term	**ou**	out	**ᴛʜ**	then	
i	it	**u**	cup	**zh**	measure	

pe·di·a·tri·cian (pē′dē ə trish′ən), *n.* doctor who specializes in pediatrics, a branch of medicine dealing with children's diseases and the care of babies and children.

ped·i·gree (ped′ə grē′), *n.* **1** list of ancestors of a person or animal. **2** line of descent; ancestry; lineage. (< Middle French *pie de grue* foot of crane (because a symbol resembling the toes of a bird was used in showing descent))

pe·dom·e·ter (pi dom′ə tər), *n.* instrument for recording the number of steps taken by the person who carries it and thus measuring the distance traveled in walking. (< French *pédomètre* < Latin *pedem* foot + Greek *metron* measure)

personal computer

pem·mi·can (pem′ə kən), *n.* dried, lean meat pounded into a paste with melted fat and pressed into cakes. It was an important food among certain tribes of North American Indians. (< Cree *pimikan*)

per·ceive (pər sēv′), *v.t.*, **-ceived, -ceiv·ing. 1** be aware of through the senses; see, hear, taste, smell, or feel. **2** take in with the mind; observe; understand. (< Old French *perceivre* < Latin *percipere* < *per-* thoroughly + *capere* to grasp) **—per·ceiv′a·ble,** *adj.* **—per·ceiv′er,** *n.*

per·cent of de·crease (pər sent′ ov dē′krēs), amount of decrease expressed as percent.

per·cent of in·crease (pər sent′ ov in′krēs), amount of increase expressed as percent.

per·cep·tion (pər sep′shən), *n.* **1** act of perceiving: *His perception of the change came in a flash.* **2** understanding that is the result of perceiving: *I now have a clear perception of what went wrong.* (< Latin *perceptionem* < *percipere* perceive. See PERCEIVE.)

pe·ren·ni·al (pə ren′ē əl), *adj.* **1** lasting through the whole year: *a perennial stream.* **2** lasting for a very long time; enduring. **3** (of a plant) lasting more than two years. *—n.* a perennial plant. (< Latin *perennis* < *per-* through + *annus* year) **—pe·ren′ni·al·ly,** *adv.*

per·fect square (pėr′fikt skwâr), a number whose square root is a positive or negative whole number, or zero.

per·haps (per haps′), *adv.* it may be; maybe; possibly. (Middle English *per happes* by chances)

per·il·ous (pãr′ə·ləs), *adj.* full of peril; dangerous. **—per′·il·ous·ly,** *adv.* **—per′il·ous·ness,** *n.*

per·i·od·ic ta·ble (pir′ē od′ik tā′bəl), table in which the chemical elements, arranged in the order of their atomic numbers, are shown in related groups.

per·ish (pãr′ish), *v.i.* be destroyed; die: *Soldiers perish in battle.* (< Old French *periss-,* a form of *perir* < Latin *perire* < *per-* to destruction + *ire* go)

per·jur·y (pėr′jer ē), *n., pl.* **-jur·ies.** act or crime of willfully giving false testimony or withholding evidence while under oath.

per·mis·sive (pər mis′iv), *adj.* **1** not forbidding; tending to permit; allowing. **2** permitted; allowed. **—per·mis′sive·ly,** *adv.* **—per·mis′sive·ness,** *n.*

per·pe·trate (pėr′pə trāt), *v.t.,* **-trat·ed, -trat·ing.** do or commit (a crime, fraud, trick, or anything bad or foolish). (< Latin *perpetratum* perpetrated < *per-* thoroughly + *patrare* perform) **—per′pe·tra′tion,** *n.* **—per′pe·tra′tor,** *n.*

per·pet·u·ate (pər pech′ü āt), *v.t.,* **-at·ed, -at·ing.** make perpetual; keep from being forgotton. **—per·pet′u·a′tion,** *n.* **—per·pet′u·a′tor,** *n.*

per·se·cute (pėr′ sə kyüt), *v.t.,* **-cut·ed, -cut·ing. 1** cause to suffer repeatedly; do harm to persistently; oppress. **2** annoy; harrass. **—per′se·cu′tor,** *n.*

per·se·ver·ance (pėr′sə vir′əns), *n.* a sticking to a purpose or an aim; a persevering; tenacity.

per·se·vere (pėr′sə vir′), *v.i.,* **per·se·vered, per·se·ver·ing.** continue steadily in doing something hard; persist. (< Latin *perseverare* < *per-* thoroughly + *severus* strict)

per·sist·ent (pər sis′tənt), *adj.* **1** not giving up, especially in the face of dislike, disapproval, or difficulties; persisting; persevering. **2** going on; continuing; lasting: *a persistent headache that lasted for three days.* **—per·sist′ent·ly,** *adv.*

per·son·al com·put·er (pėr′sə nəl kəm pyü′tər), a small computer for use at home or work which consists of a monitor with a screen, a keyboard, and a CPU.

per·spec·tive (per spek′tiv), *n.* **1** art of picturing objects on a flat surface so as to give the appearance of distance or depth. **2** view of things or facts in which they are in the right relations: *a lack of perspective.* **3** a mental view, outlook, or prospect. (< Medieval Latin *perspectiva (ars)* (science) of optics < Latin *perspicere* look through < *per-* through + *specere* to look) —**per·spec′tive·ly,** *adv.*

per·spi·ra·tion (pėr′spe rā′shen), *n.* the salty fluid secreted by sweat glands through pores of the skin.

per·suade (per swād′), *v.t.,* **-suad·ed, -suad·ing.** win over to do or believe; make willing or sure by urging; convince. (< Latin *persuadere* < *per-* thoroughly + *suadere* to urge) —**per·suad′er,** *n.*

per·sua·sion (per swā′zhen), *n.* a persuading: *All our persuasion was of no use; she would not come here.*

per·sua·sive (per swā′siv), *adj.* able, intended, or fitted to persuade. —**per·sua′sive·ly,** *adv.* —**per·sua′sive·ness,** *n.*

per·tain (per tān′), *v.i.* **1** belong or be connected as a part, possession. **2** have to do with; be related; refer. (< Old French *partenir* < Latin *pertinere* reach through, connect < *per-* through + *tenere* to hold)

per·ti·nent (pėrt′n ent), *adj.* having to do with what is being considered; relating to the matter in hand; to the point. (< Latin *pertinentem* pertaining) —**per′ti·nent·ly,** *adv.*

pe·ti·tion (pe tish′en), *n.* a formal request to a superior or to one in authority for some privilege, right, benefit, etc.: *Many people signed a petition asking the city council for a new library.* (< Latin *petitionem* < *petere* seek)

phe·nom·e·non (fe nom′e non), *n., pl.* **-na** (or **-nons** for 2). **1** fact, event, or circumstance that can be observed. **2** an extraordinary or remarkable person or thing. (< Greek *phainomenon* < *phainesthai* appear)

pho·tog·ra·phy (fe tog′re fē), *n.* process, art, or business of taking photographs.

pic·tur·esque (pik′che resk′), *adj.* quaint or interesting enough to be used as the subject of a picture.

pip·sis·se·wa (pip sis′e we), *n.* any of a genus of low, creeping evergreen plants whose leaves are used in medicine as a tonic, etc. (< Cree *pipisisikweu*)

pis·ta·chi·o (pi stä′shē ō, pi stash′ē ō), *n., pl.* **-chi·os,** *adj.* —*n.* **1** a greenish nut having a flavor that suggests almond. **2** a small tree that it grows on, belonging to the same family as the sumac. —*adj.* light-green. (< Italian *pistacchio,* ultimately < Persian *pistah*)

pit·fall (pit′fol′), *n., pl.* **pit·falls. 1** a hidden pit to catch animals or human beings. **2** any trap or hidden danger.

plan·ta·tion (plan tā′shen), *n., pl.* **plan·ta·tions.** a large farm or estate, especially in a tropical or semitropical region, on which cotton, tobacco, sugar cane, rubber trees, etc., are grown. The work on a plantation is done by laborers who live there.

plaque (plak), *n.* **1** a thin, flat, ornamental plate or tablet of metal, porcelain, etc., usually intended to be hung up as a wall decoration. **2** a thin film of saliva and food particles which forms on the surface of the teeth.

pleas·ure (plezh′er), *n.* a feeling of being pleased; enjoyment; delight.

po·di·a·trist (pe dī′e trist), *n.* person who treats ailments of the human foot; chiropodist.

pol·i·cy (pol′e sē), *n., pl.* **-cies.** plan of action adopted as tactically or strategically best by a government, person, etc.; way of managing affairs so as to achieve some purpose.

po·lit·i·cal (pe lit′e kel), *adj.* of or concerned with politics: *political parties.* —**po·lit′i·cal·ly,** *adv.*

a	hat	**ī**	ice	**u̇**	put	**ə** stands for	
ā	age	**o**	not	**ü**	rule	**a**	in about
ä	far, calm	**ō**	open	**ch**	child	**e**	in taken
âr	care	**ȯ**	saw	**ng**	long	**i**	in pencil
e	let	**ô**	order	**sh**	she	**o**	in lemon
ē	equal	**oi**	oil	**th**	thin	**u**	in circus
ėr	term	**ou**	out	**ᴛʜ**	then		
i	it	**u**	cup	**zh**	measure		

pol·i·tics (pol′ə tiks), *n. sing. or pl.*
1 management of political affairs;
the science and art of government.
2 political principles or opinions.

pon·cho (pon′chō), *n., pl.* **-chos.** a
large piece of cloth, often
waterproof, with a slit in the middle
for the head to go through.
Ponchos are worn in South America
as cloaks. (< Spanish
< Araucanian *pontho*)

por·ce·lain (pôr′sə lin), *n.* **1** a very
fine earthenware, usually having a
translucent white body and a
transparent glaze; china. **2** dish or
other object made of this material.

port (pôrt), *n.* the side of a ship or
aircraft to the left of a person
facing the bow or front. —*adj.* on
the left side of a ship or aircraft.
—*v.t., v.i.* turn or shift to the left
side. (origin uncertain)

port·fo·li·o (pôrt fō′lē ō), *n., pl.* **-li·os.**
1 a portable case for loose papers,
drawings, etc.; briefcase. **2** position
and duties of a cabinet member,
diplomat, or minister of state.
3 holdings in the form of stocks,
bonds, etc. (< Italian *portafoglio*,
ultimately < Latin *portare* carry +
folium sheet, leaf)

pos·i·tive (poz′ə tiv), *adj.* **1** admitting
of no question; without doubt:
positive proof. **2** showing
agreement or approval.
—**pos′i·tive·ly,** *adv.*

pos·ses·sive (pə zes′iv), *adj.*
1 desirous of ownership: *a
possessive nature.* **2** asserting or
claiming ownership: *a possessive
manner.* —**pos·ses′sive·ly,** *adv.*
—**pos·ses′sive·ness,** *n.*

pos·si·ble (pos′ə bəl), *adj.* **1** that can
be; that can be done; that can
happen: *Come if possible.* **2** that
can be true or a fact: *It is possible
that she went.* **3** that can be done,
chosen, etc., properly. —*n.*
something that is possible;
possibility.

post·age (pō′stij), *n.* amount paid on
anything sent by mail.

post·script (pōst′skript), *n.* addition to
a letter, written after the writer's
name has been signed.

pos·ture (pos′chər), *n., v.,* **-tured,
-tur·ing.** —*n.* **1** position of the
body; way of holding the body:
*Good posture is important for
health.* **2** condition; situation; state:
*In the present posture of public
affairs it is difficult to predict what
will happen.* **3** mental or spiritual

attitude. —*v.i.* **1** take a certain
posture: *The dancer postured
before the mirror, bending and
twisting her body.* **2** pose for effect.
—*v.t.* put in a certain posture.
(< French < Italian *postura* < Latin
positura < *ponere* to place)

prec·e·dent (pres′ə dənt), *n.* **1** action
that may serve as an example or
reason for a later action. **2** (in law)
a judicial decision, case, etc., that
serves as a pattern in future
situations that are similar.

pre·dic·a·ment (pri dik′ə mənt), *n.* an
unpleasant, difficult, or dangerous
situation. (< Late Latin
praedicamentum quality, category
< Latin *praedicare* to predicate)

pre·dis·po·si·tion (prē′dis′pə
zish′ən), *n.* previous inclination.

pre·fer (pri fėr′), *v.,* **-ferred, -fer·ring.**
—*v.t.* like better; choose rather:
She prefers reading to sewing.
—*v.i.* have or express a
preference: *I will come later, if you
prefer.* (< Latin *praeferre* put
before < *prae-* pre- + *ferre* carry)

pref·er·a·ble (pref′ər ə bəl), *adj.* to
be preferred; more desirable.
—**pref′er·a·bil′i·ty,** *n.*
—**pref′er·a·ble·ness,** *n.*
—**pref′er·a·bly,** *adv.*

pref·er·en·tial (pref′ə ren′shəl), *adj.*
of, giving, or receiving preference.

prej·u·di·cial (prej′ə dish′əl), *adj.*
causing prejudice or
disadvantage; hurtful; detrimental.
—**prej′u·di′cial·ly,** *adv.*

pre·lim·i·nar·y (pri lim′ə ner′ē), *adj.,
n., pl.* **-nar·ies.** —*adj.* coming
before the main business; leading
to something more important. —*n.*
a preliminary step; something
preparatory.

pre·oc·cu·pa·tion (prē ok′yə
pā′shən), *n.* **1** act of preoccupying.
2 condition of being preoccupied.

pre·pos·ter·ous (pri pos′tər əs), *adj.*
contrary to nature, reason, or
common sense; absurd; senseless.
(< Latin *praeposterus* with the
posterior in front < *prae-* pre- +
posterus coming after, behind)
—**pre·pos′ter·ous·ly,** *adv.*

pre·scribe (pri skrīb′), *v.,* **-scribed,
-scrib·ing.** —*v.t.* **1** lay down as a
rule to be followed; order; direct.
2 order as a remedy or treatment:
The doctor prescribed quinine.
—*v.i.* give medical advice; issue a
prescription. (< Latin *praescribere*
write before < *prae-* pre- +
scribere write)

poncho
wearing **ponchos**
in Bolivia

pre·scrip·tion (pri skrip′shən), *n.* **1** act of prescribing. **2** something prescribed; order; direction. **3** a written direction or order for preparing and using a medicine.

pres·i·den·cy (prez′ə dən sē), *n., pl.* **-cies.** **1** office of president. **2** time in which a president is in office.

pres·sure (presh′ər), *n., v.,* **-sured, -sur·ing.** —*n.* **1** the continued action of a weight or force. **2** force per unit of area: *There is a pressure of 27 pounds to the square inch in this tire.* —*v.t.* force or urge by exerting pressure: *The salesman tried to pressure my father into buying the car.* —**pres′sure·less,** *adj.*

pres·tige (pre stēzh′), *n.* reputation, influence, or distinction based on what is known of one's abilities, achievements, and opportunities. (< Middle French, illusion, magic spell < Latin *praestigiae* tricks)

pre·sume (pri züm′), *v.t.,* **-sumed, -sum·ing.** take for granted without proving; suppose. (< Latin *praesumere* take for granted < *prae-* pre- + *sumere* take)

pre·sump·tion (pri zump′shən), *n.* unpleasant boldness.

pre·vent (pri vent′), *v.t.* **1** stop or keep (from): *I will come if nothing prevents me from doing so.* **2** keep from happening: *Rain prevented the game.* (< Latin *praeventum* forestalled < *prae-* pre- + *venire* come) —**pre·vent′er,** *n.*

pre·ven·tion (pri ven′shən), *n.* a preventing: *the prevention of fire.*

pre·vi·ous (prē′vē əs), *adj.* coming or going before; that came before; earlier. (< Latin *praevius* leading the way < *prae-* pre- + *via* road) —**pre′vi·ous·ly,** *adv.*

prin·ci·pal (prin′sə pəl), *adj.* **1** sum of money on which interest is paid. **2** money or property from which income or interest is received.

prism (priz′əm), *n.* a wedge-shaped transparent object that separates light into its different wavelengths (colors). (< Greek *prisma* something sawed off, prism < *priein* to saw)

prob·a·ble (prob′ə bəl), *adj.* **1** likely to happen: *Cooler weather is probable after this shower.* **2** likely to be true: *Indigestion is the probable cause of your pain.* (< Latin *probabilis* < *probare* to prove) —**prob′a·bly,** *adv.*

pro·claim (prə klām′), *v.t.,* **pro·claims, pro·claimed, pro·claim·ing.** make known publicly and officially; declare publicly. (< Latin *proclamare* < *pro-* forth + *clamare* to shout)

proc·la·ma·tion (prok′lə mā′shən), *n.* an official announcement; public declaration.

prof·it (prof′it), *n.* Often, **profits,** *pl.* the gain from a business; what is left when the cost of goods and of carrying on the business is subtracted from the amount of money taken in. See **advantage** for synonym study. —*v.i.* make a gain from a business; make a profit. (< Old French < Latin *profectus* advance < *proficere* make progress < *pro-* forward + *facere* to make) —**prof′it·er,** *n.*

pro·found (prə found′), *adj.* **1** very deep: *a profound sigh, a profound sleep.* **2** deeply felt; very great: *profound despair, profound sympathy.* (< Latin *profundus* < *pro-* before + *fundus* bottom) —**pro·found′ly,** *adv.*

pro·gram (prō′gram), *n., pl.* **pro·grams.** *v.,* **pro·grams, pro·grammed, pro·gram·ming** or **pro·grams, pro·gramed, pro·gram·ing.** —*n.* set of instructions for an electronic computer or other automatic machine outlining the steps to be performed by the machine in a specific operation. —*v.t.* prepare a set of instructions for (a computer or other automatic machine). (< Greek *programma* proclamation, ultimately < *pro-* forth + *graphein* write)

presidency (def. 1)
the seal from the office of the **presidency**

							ə stands for
a	hat	ī	ice	u̇	put		
ā	age	o	not	ü	rule	a	in about
ä	far, calm	ō	open	ch	child	e	in taken
âr	care	ȯ	saw	ng	long	i	in pencil
e	let	ô	order	sh	she	o	in lemon
ē	equal	oi	oil	th	thin	u	in circus
ėr	term	ou	out	ŦH	then		
i	it	u	cup	zh	measure		

publish (def. 1)
published magazines for distribution

prog·ress (*n.* prog′res; *v.* prə gres′), *n.* **1** an advance or growth; development; improvement: *the progress of science.* **2** a moving forward; going ahead: *make rapid progress on a journey.* —*v.i.* get better; advance; develop.

pro·hi·bi·tion (prō′ə bish′ən), *n.* **1** law or laws against making or selling alcoholic liquors. **2** Often, **Prohibition.** period between 1920 and 1933 when national prohibition was in force in the United States.

pro·logue (prō′lôg), *n.* **1** introduction to a novel, poem, or other literary work. **2** speech or poem addressed to the audience by one of the actors at the beginning of a play. (< Greek *prologos* < *pro-* before + *logos* speech)

pro·mote (prə mōt′), *v.t.,* **-mot·ed, -mot·ing. 1** raise in rank, condition, or importance; elevate: *Pupils who pass the test will be promoted.* **2** help to develop or establish; cause to advance; further. —**pro·mot′a·ble,** *adj.*

proof (prüf), *n.* **1** way or means of showing beyond doubt the truth of something: *Is what you say a guess or have you proof?* See **evidence** for synonym study. **2** establishment of the truth of anything. (< Old French *prouve* < Late Latin *proba* < Latin *probare* prove.)

pro·pos·al (prə pō′zel), *n.* **1** what is proposed; plan, scheme, or suggestion. **2** offer of marriage.

pros·e·cute (pros′ə kyüt), *v.t.,* **-cut·ed, -cut·ing.** bring before a court of law: *Reckless drivers will be prosecuted.* (< Latin *prosecutum* followed after < *pro-* forth + *sequi* follow)

pro·tect (prə tekt′), *v.t.* shield from harm or danger; shelter; defend; guard. (< Latin *protectum* covered up, protected < *pro-* in front + *tegere* to cover)

pro·tec·tion (prə tek′shən), *n.* act of protecting; condition of being kept from harm; defense.

pro·test (*n., adj.* prō′test; *v.* prə test′), *n.* statement that denies or objects strongly: *They yielded only after protest.* —*adj.* characterized by protest; expressing protest or objection against some condition: *a protest movement.* —*v.t.* object to: *protest a decision.* (< Middle French *protester* to protest < Latin *protestari* < *pro-* before + *testis* witness) —**pro·test′a·ble,** *adj.* —**pro·test′er,** *n.*

pueblo

a **pueblo** in the southwest

pro·ton (prō′ton), *n.* a positively charged particle found free or in a nucleus. (< Greek *prōton* first)

pro·voc·a·tive (prə vok′ə tiv), *adj.* **1** irritating; vexing. **2** tending or serving to call forth action, thought, laughter, anger, etc.: *a provocative remark.* —**pro·voc′a·tive·ly,** *adv.* —**pro·voc′a·tive·ness,** *n.*

pro·voke (prə vōk′), *v.t.,* **-voked, -vok·ing. 1** make angry; vex. **2** stir up; excite: *The insult provoked him to anger.* **3** call forth; bring about; start into action; cause. (< Latin *provocare* < *pro-* forth + *vocare* to call)

PS, postscript.

pub·li·ca·tion (pub′lə kā′shen), *n.* book, newspaper, or magazine; anything that is published.

pub·lish (pub′lish), *v.t.* **1** prepare and offer (a book, paper, map, piece of music, etc.) for sale or distribution. **2** bring out the book or books of: *publish an author.* (< Old French *publiss-,* a form of *publier* to publish < Latin *publicare* < *publicus* public) —**pub′lish·a·ble,** *adj.*

pueb·lo (pweb′lō), *n., pl.* **-los.** an Indian village consisting of houses built of adobe and stone, usually with flat roofs and often several stories high. (< Spanish, people, community < Latin *populus*)

punc·tu·al (pungk′chü əl), *adj.* on time; prompt: *be punctual to the minute.* (< Latin *punctum* point) —**punc′tu·al·ly,** *adv.* —**punc′tu·al·ness,** *n.*

pur·chase (pér′chəs), *v.t.,* **-chased, -chas·ing.** get by paying a price; buy: *purchase a new car.* (< Anglo-French *purchacer* pursue < Old French *pur-* forth + *chacier* to chase) —**pur′chas·a·ble,** *adj.* —**pur′chas·er,** *n.*

pyr·a·mid (pir′ə mid), *n.* the solid figure formed by connecting points of a polygon to a point not in the plane of the polygon. (< Greek *pyramidos*) —**pyr′a·mid′ic,** *adj.*

py·ro·pho·bi·a (pī′rə fō′bē ə), *n.* an abnormal fear of fire.

Q

quest (kwest), *n.* **1** a search or hunt. **2** expedition of knights. —*v.t.* search or seek for; hunt. (< Old French *queste* < Popular Latin *quaesita* < Latin *quaerere* seek) —**quest′er,** *n.*

ques·tion·a·ble (kwes′chə nə bəl), *adj.* open to question or dispute; doubtful; uncertain: *a questionable statement.* —**ques′tion·a·bly,** *adv.*

queue (kyü), *n., v.,* **queued, queu·ing** or **queue·ing.** —*n.* 1 braid of hair hanging down from the back of the head. 2 a line of people, automobiles, etc. —*v.i.* form or stand in a long line. (< French < Latin *coda, cauda* tail) —**queu′er,** *n.*

R

rack·et·eer (rak′ə tir′), *n., pl.* **rack·et·eers.** person who extorts money through bribery, by threatening violence, or by some other illegal means. —*v.i.* extort money in this way.

ra·dar (rā′där), *n.* instrument for determining the distance, direction, speed, etc., of unseen objects by the reflection of microwave radio waves. (< *ra(dio) d(etecting) a(nd) r(anging)*)

ra·di·a·tion (rā′dē ā′shən), *n.* 1 a transfer of energy through space in waves. 2 either radiant energy or sub-atomic particles given off during radioactivity or fission.

ra·di·ol·o·gist (rā′dē ol′ə jist), *n.* an expert in radiology, the science dealing with X rays or the rays from radioactive substances, especially for medical diagnosis or treatment.

ra·di·us (rā′dē əs), *n., pl.* **-di·i.** any line segment going straight from the center to the outside of a circle or a sphere. Any spoke in a wheel is a radius. (< Latin, ray, spoke of a wheel)

ram·bunc·tious (ram bungk′shəs), *adj.* wild and noisy; boisterous. —**ram·bunc′tious·ness,** *n.*

ra·tion·al (rash′ə nəl), *adj.* 1 reasoned out; sensible; reasonable. 2 able to think and reason clearly. —**ra′tion·al·ly,** *adv.*

ra·tion·ale (rash′ə nal′), *n.* the fundamental reason. (< Latin, neuter of *rationalis* rational)

ra·tion·al num·ber (rash′ə nəl num′bər), any number that can be written as a fraction; a terminating or repeating decimal.

real estate (rē′əl e stāt′), land together with the buildings, fences, trees, water, minerals, etc., that belong with it.

re·al·ism (rē′ə liz′əm), *n.* 1 thought and action based on realities. 2 (in art and literature) the picturing of life as it actually is.

re·al·ize (rē′ə līz), *v.t.,* **-ized, -iz·ing.** 1 understand clearly; be fully aware of: *She realizes how hard you worked.* 2 make real; bring into actual existence: *Her uncle's present made it possible for her to realize her dream.*

re·al·ly (rē′ə lē), *adv.* 1 actually; truly; in fact: *things as they really are.* 2 indeed: *Oh, really?*

re·al num·ber (rē′əl num′bər), *n., pl.* **re·al num·bers.** any rational or irrational number.

re·as·sure (rē′ə shùr′), *v.t.,* **-sured, -sur·ing.** 1 restore to confidence. 2 assure again or anew. —**re′as·sur′ing·ly,** *adv.*

reb·el (*n., adj.* reb′əl; *v.* ri bel′), *n., adj., v.,* **re·belled, re·bel·ling.** —*n.* person who resists or fights against authority instead of obeying. —*adj.* defying law or authority: *a rebel army.* —*v.i.* resist or fight against law or authority. (< Old French *rebelle* < Latin *rebellem* disorderly < *rebellare* be disorderly, rebel, ultimately < *re-* again + *bellum* war)

re·cede (ri sēd′), *v.i.,* **-ced·ed, -ced·ing.** go or move backward. (< Latin *recedere* < *re-* back + *cedere* go)

re·ces·sion (ri sesh′ən), *n.* period of temporary business reduction, shorter and less extreme than a depression.

real estate

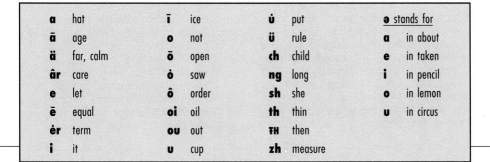

a	hat	**ī**	ice	**ù**	put	**ə** stands for	
ā	age	**o**	not	**ü**	rule	**a**	in about
ä	far, calm	**ō**	open	**ch**	child	**e**	in taken
âr	care	**ò**	saw	**ng**	long	**i**	in pencil
e	let	**ô**	order	**sh**	she	**o**	in lemon
ē	equal	**oi**	oil	**th**	thin	**u**	in circus
ėr	term	**ou**	out	**ᴛʜ**	then		
i	it	**u**	cup	**zh**	measure		

redcoat
the English **redcoats**

re·con·nais·sance (ri kon′ə səns), *n.* examination or survey, especially for military purposes. (< French)

re·con·struct (rē′kən strukt′), *v.t.* construct again; rebuild; make over.

re·cord (*v.* ri kôrd′; *n., adj.* rek′ərd), *v.t.* set down in writing so as to keep for future use. —*n.* **1** anything written and kept. **2 off the record,** not to be recorded or quoted. —*adj.* making or affording a record: *a record wheat crop.* (< Old French *recorder* < Latin *recordari* remember, call to mind < *re-* back + *cordis* heart, mind) —**re·cord′a·ble,** *adj.*

rec·tan·gu·lar prism (rek tang′gyə lər priz′əm), a polyhedron whose congruent and parallel bases are rectangles.

red·coat (red′kōt′), *n., pl.* **red·coats.** (in former times) a British soldier.

red gi·ant (red jī′ənt), first stage of a star as it begins to die; a rather large star that glows slightly reddish, since it is relatively cool.

ref·er·ence (ref′ər əns), *n.* **1** statement, book, etc., referred to. **2** something used for information or help: *A dictionary is a reference.*

re·fer·ral (ri fėr′əl), *n.* **1** act of referring. **2** person who is referred.

re·flect (ri flekt′), *v.t.,* **re·flects, re·flect·ed, re·flect·ing.** turn back or throw back (light, heat, sound, etc.). (< Latin *reflectere* < *re-* back + *flectere* to bend)

re·flec·tive (ri flek′tiv), *adj.* that reflects; reflecting: *the reflective surface of polished metal.* —**re·flec′tive·ly,** *adv.*

re·fresh·ment (ri fresh′mənt), *n.* **1** a refreshing. **2** a being refreshed. **3** thing that refreshes. **4 refreshments,** *pl.* food or drink: *serve refreshments at a party.*

re·frig·er·a·tor (ri frij′ə rā′tər), *n.* box, room, etc., that keeps foods and other items cool, usually by mechanical means.

refreshment (def. 3)
Lemonade is a cool
refreshment.

re·fund (*v.* ri fund′; *n.* rē′fund), *v.t.* make return or restitution of (money received or taken); pay back. —*n.* **1** a return of money paid. **2** the money paid back. (< Latin *refundere* < *re-* back + *fundere* pour) —**re·fund′a·ble,** *adj.*

re·fuse (ri fyüz′), *v.t.,* **-fused, -fus·ing.** say no to; decline to accept; reject: *refuse an offer.* (< Old French *refuser* < Latin *refusum* poured back < *re-* + *fundere* pour) —**re·fus′a·ble,** *adj.* —**re·fus′er,** *n.*

re·gal (rē′gəl), *adj.* **1** belonging to a king or queen; royal. **2** fit for a king or queen; stately; splendid; magnificent. (< Latin *regalis* < *regem* king) —**re′gal·ly,** *adv.*

re·ga·li·a (ri gā′lē ə), *n.pl.* the emblems of royalty. Crowns and scepters are regalia. (< Latin, royal things)

re·gard·less (ri gärd′lis), *adj.* with no heed; careless: *regardless of expense.* —*adv.* in spite of what happens. —**re·gard′less·ly,** *adv.*

re·gime (ri zhēm′), *n.* **1** system, method, or form of government or rule. **2** any prevailing political or social system. (< French *régime* < Latin *regimen*)

reg·i·ment (*n.* rej′ə mənt; *v.* rej′ə ment), *n.* a military unit consisting of several battalions or squadrons, usually commanded by a colonel. —*v.t.* treat in a strict or uniform manner. (< Late Latin *regimentum* rule < Latin *regere* to rule)

re·gion·al (rē′jə nəl), *adj.* of or in a particular region: *a regional storm.*

reg·u·lar (reg′yə lər), *adj.* **1** fixed by custom or rule; usual; ordinary; normal: *Six o'clock was her regular hour of rising.* **2** coming, acting, or done again and again at the same time. —*n.* member of a regularly paid group of any kind: *The fire department was made up of regulars and volunteers.* (< Latin *regularis* < *regula*)

reg·u·lar·ly (reg′yə lər lē), *adv.* **1** in a regular manner. **2** at regular times.

reg·u·late (reg′yə lāt), *v.t.,* **-lat·ed, -lat·ing.** **1** control by rule, principle, or system: *regulate the behavior of students.* **2** keep at some standard: *regulate the air.*

rein·deer (rān′dir′), *n., pl.* **-deer.** a large deer with branching antlers, native to Greenland and northern regions of the Old World, used to pull sleighs and for meat, milk, and hides. (< Scandinavian (Old Icelandic) *hreindȳri* < *hreinn* reindeer + *dȳr* animal)

rel·a·tive mo·tion (rel′ə tiv mō′shən), changing position with respect to the position of another object.

re·li·a·ble (ri lī′ə bəl), *adj.* worthy of trust; that can be depended on. —**re·li′a·bil′i·ty,** *n.*

re·mem·brance (ri mem′brəns), *n.* **1** power to remember; act of remembering; memory. **2** any thing or action that makes one remember a person; keepsake.

re·mote con·trol (ri mōt′ kən trōl′), control from a distance of a machine, operation, etc., usually by electrical impulses or signals.

re·mov·al (ri mü′vəl), *n.* **1** a removing; taking away. **2** a change of place or location.

ren·dez·vous (rän′də vü), *n., pl.* **-vous** (-vüz), *v.,* **-voused** (-vüd), **-vous·ing** (-vü′ing). —*n.* an appointment or engagement to meet at a fixed place or time; meeting by agreement. —*v.t.* bring together (troops, ships, space capsules, etc.) at a fixed place. (< Middle French < *rendez-vous* present yourself!)

re·peat·ed (ri pē′tid), *adj.* said, done, or made more than once. —**re·peat′ed·ly,** *adv.*

re·peat·ing dec·i·mal (ri pēt′ing des′ə mel), decimal in which the same figure or series of figures is repeated indefinitely. EXAMPLES: .3333+, .2323+.

re·per·cus·sion (rē′pər kush′ən), *n.* **1** an indirect influence or reaction from an event: *repercussions of a scandal.* **2** sound flung back; echo.

re·port card (ri pôrt kärd), a report sent regularly by a school to parents or guardians, indicating the quality of a student's work.

rep·re·hend (rep′ri hend′), *v.t.* reprove, rebuke, or blame. (< Latin *reprehendere,* originally, pull back < *re-* back + *prehendere* to grasp)

rep·re·hen·si·ble (rep′ri hen′sə bel), *adj.* deserving reproof, rebuke, or blame. —**rep′re·hen′si·bil′i·ty,** *n.*

rep·re·sent (rep′ri zent′), *v.t.,* **rep·re·sents, rep·re·sent·ed, rep·re·sent·ing. 1** stand for; be a sign or symbol of: *The 50 stars in our flag represent the 50 states.* **2** act in place of; speak and act for.

re·sem·blance (ri zem′bləns), *n.* **1** similar appearance; likeness: *Twins often show great resemblance.* **2** a copy; image.

re·sent·ment (ri zent′mənt), *n.* the feeling that one has at being injured or insulted; indignation.

re·served (ri zėrvd′), *adj.* **1** kept in reserve; kept by special arrangement: *a reserved seat.* **2** set apart: *a reserved section at the stadium.* **3** self-restrained in action or speech. —**re·serv′ed·ly,** *adv.*

res·i·den·tial (rez′ə den′shəl), *adj.* **1** of, having to do with, or suitable for homes or residences: *a residential district.* **2** of or having to do with residence. **3** serving or used as a residence: *a residential building.* —**res′i·den′tial·ly,** *adv.*

re·sist (ri zist′), *v.t.* **1** act against; strive against; oppose: *The window resisted all efforts to open it.* **2** strive successfully against; keep from. (< Latin *resistere* < *re-* back + *sistere* make a stand) —**re·sist′er,** *n.*

re·sist·i·ble (ri zis′tə bel), *adj.* that can be resisted.

re·sist·ance (ri zis′təns), *n.* the measure of how much the flow of electric current is opposed, expressed in ohms.

re·solve (ri zolv′), *v.,* **re·solved, re·solv·ing,** *n.* —*v.t.* make up one's mind; determine; decide: *resolve to do better work in the future.* —*n.* thing determined on. determination. (< Latin *resolvere* < *re-* back + *solvere* to loosen) —**re·solv′a·ble,** *adj.* —**re·solv′er,** *n.*

res·pi·ra·tion (res′pə rā′shən), *n.* act of inhaling and exhaling; breathing.

res·pir·a·to·ry (res′pər ə tôr′ē), *adj.* having to do with or used for respiration. The lungs are respiratory organs.

re·trieve (ri trēv′), *v.t.,* **-trieved, -triev·ing.** get again; recover: *retrieve a lost pocketbook.* —*n.* act of retrieving; recovery. (< Old French *retruev-,* a form of *retrouver* find again < *re-* again + *trouver* to find)

re·un·ion (rē yü′nyən), *n.* **1** a coming together again. **2** a being reunited.

rev·eil·le (rev′ə lē), *n.* a signal on a bugle or drum to waken soldiers or sailors in the morning. (< French *réveillez(-vous)* awaken!)

residential (def. 1)
a **residential** neighborhood

a	hat	**ī**	ice	**u̇**	put	**ə stands for**	
ā	age	**o**	not	**ü**	rule	**a**	in about
ä	far, calm	**ō**	open	**ch**	child	**e**	in taken
âr	care	**ȯ**	saw	**ng**	long	**i**	in pencil
e	let	**ô**	order	**sh**	she	**o**	in lemon
ē	equal	**oi**	oil	**th**	thin	**u**	in circus
ėr	term	**ou**	out	**ᴛʜ**	then		
i	it	**u**	cup	**zh**	measure		

re·venge (ri venj′), *n., v.,* **-venged, -veng·ing.** —*n.* harm done in return for a wrong; satisfaction obtained by repayment of an injury, etc.; vengeance: *take revenge, get revenge.* —*v.t.* do harm in return for. See synonym study below. (< Middle French < *revenger* avenge < Latin *re-* back + *vindicare* avenge)

Syn. *v.t.* **Revenge, avenge** mean to punish someone in return for a wrong. **Revenge** applies when it is indulged in to get even: *Gangsters revenge the murder of one of their gang.* **Avenge** applies when the punishment seems just: *They fought to avenge the enemy's invasion of their country.*

re·vi·tal·ize (rē vī′tə līz), *v.t.,* **-ized, -iz·ing.** restore to vitality; put new life into. —**re·vi′tal·i·za′tion,** *n.*

re·voke (ri vōk′), *v.,* **-voked, -vok·ing,** *n.* —*v.t.* take back; repeal; cancel; withdraw: *revoke a driver's license.* —*n.* (in cards) a failure to follow suit when one can and should; renege. (< Latin *revocare* < *re-* back + *vocare* to call)

ric·o·chet (rik′ə shā′; British rik′ə shet′), *n., v.,* **-cheted** (-shād′), **-chet·ing** (-shā′ing) or **-chet·ted** (-shet′id), **-chet·ting** (-shet′ing). —*n.* the skipping or jumping motion of an object after glancing off a flat surface. —*v.i.* move with a skipping or jumping motion. (< French)

ri·dic·u·lous (ri dik′yə ləs), *adj.* deserving ridicule; laughable; absurd. —**ri·dic′u·lous·ly,** *adv.* —**ri·dic′u·lous·ness,** *n.*

ro·de·o (rō′dē ō, rō dā′ō), *n., pl.* **-de·os.** contest or exhibition of skill in roping cattle, riding horses, etc. (< Spanish < *rodear* go around, ultimately < Latin *rota* wheel)

role mod·el (rōl mod′l), person whose patterns of behavior influence another's attitudes and actions.

roll·ing fric·tion (rōl′ing frik′shən), weak, backwards force that arises as a round object rolls over a surface.

roof (rüf, rùf), *n.* **1** the top covering of a building. **2** something like it: *the roof of a car.* **3 go through the roof** or **hit the roof,** INFORMAL. become very excited. (Old English *hrōf*) —**roof′like′,** *adj.*

round·up (round′up′), *n.* **1** act of driving or bringing cattle together from long distances. **2** the people and horses that do this.

roof (def. 1)
tiled **roofs** in Holland

R.S.V.P. or **r.s.v.p.,** please answer (for French *répondez s'il vous plaît*).

rud·der (rud′ər), *n.* **1** a flat piece of wood or metal hinged vertically to the rear end of a boat or ship and used to steer it. **2** a similar piece on an aircraft. (Old English *rōthor*)

RV, recreational vehicle.

S

sac·char·in (sak′ər ən), *n.* a very sweet crystalline substance obtained from coal tar, used as a substitute for sugar.

sa·fa·ri (sə fär′ē), *n.* **1** journey or hunting expedition in eastern Africa. **2** any long trip or expedition. (< Swahili < Arabic *safar* a journey)

saf·fron (saf′rən), *n.* **1** an autumn crocus with purple flowers having orange-yellow stigmas. **2** an orange-yellow coloring matter obtained from the dried stigmas of this crocus. Saffron is used to color and flavor candy, rice, etc. —*adj.* orange-yellow. (< Old French *safran,* ultimately < Arabic *za′farān*)

sam·pan (sam′pan), *n.* any of various small boats used in the rivers and coastal waters of China, Japan, and southeast Asia. (< Chinese *san pan,* literally, three boards)

sat·is·fac·tion (sat′i sfak′shən), *n.* **1** act of satisfying; fulfillment of conditions or desires. **2** condition of being satisfied, or pleased and contented.

scen·ic (sē′nik, sen′ik), *adj.* **1** of or having to do with natural scenery. **2** having much fine scenery; picturesque: *a scenic highway.* **3** of or having to do with stage scenery or stage effects. —**scen′i·cal·ly,** *adv.*

sci·en·tif·ic no·ta·tion (sī′en tif′ik nō tā′shən), a way to write a number as the product of a power of 10 and a number greater than or equal to 1 and less than 10.

sci·en·tist (sī′en tist), *n.* person who has expert knowledge of some branch of science, especially a physical or natural science.

scrib·ble (skrib′əl), *v.,* **-bled, -bling,** *n.* —*v.t.* write or draw carelessly or hastily. —*v.i.* make marks that do not mean anything. —*n.* something scribbled. (< Medieval Latin *scribillare,* ultimately < Latin *scribere* write)

scu·ba (skü′bə), *n.* portable breathing equipment, including one or more tanks of compressed air, used by underwater swimmers and divers. —*v.i.* swim underwater using this equipment. (< *s(elf) c(ontained) u(nderwater) b(reathing) a(pparatus)*)

sculp·ture (skulp′chər), *n., v.,* **-tured, -tur·ing.** —*n.* **1** art of making figures by carving, modeling, casting, etc. **2** piece of such work. —*v.t.* make (figures) by carving, modeling, casting, etc. (< Latin *sculptura,* variant of *scalptura* < *scalpere* carve)

se·ba·ceous gland (si bā′shəs gland), *n., pl.* **se·ba·ceous glands.** gland in an inner layer of the skin that supplies oil to the skin and hair.

se·bum (sē′bəm), *n.* the fatty secretion of the sebaceous glands. (< Latin, tallow, grease)

se·ces·sion·ist (si sesh′ə nist), *n.* **1** person who favors secession. **2** person who secedes.

seg·re·ga·tion (seg′rə gā′shən), *n.* separation of one racial group from another or from the rest of society, as in schools, housing.

self-es·teem (self′ə stēm′), *n.* thinking well of oneself; self-respect; conceit.

self-im·age (self′im′ij), *n.* the conception one has of oneself, of one's abilities and ambitions, etc.

se·mes·ter (sə mes′tər), *n.* a division, often one half, of a school year, usually lasting from 15 to 18 weeks.

sen·sa·tion·al (sen sā′shə nəl), *adj.* **1** very good, exciting, etc.; outstanding; spectacular: *the outfielder's sensational catch.* **2** arousing or trying to arouse strong or excited feeling. —**sen·sa′tion·al·ly,** *adv.*

sense (sens), *n.* **1** power of an organism to know what happens outside itself. Sight, hearing, touch, taste, and smell are the five principal senses. **2** feeling: *a sense of warmth.* (< Latin *sensus* < *sentire* perceive, know, feel)

sen·si·ble (sen′sə bəl), *adj.* having or showing good sense or judgment; wise. —**sen′si·ble·ness,** *n.* —**sen′si·bly,** *adv.*

sen·si·bil·i·ty (sen′sə bil′ə tē), *n., pl.* **-ties. 1** ability to feel or perceive. **2** sensitiveness.

sen·si·tiv·i·ty (sen′sə tiv′ə tē), *n., pl.* **-ties.** quality of being sensitive.

sen·si·tize (sen′sə tīz), *v.t.,* **-tized, -tiz·ing.** make sensitive. Camera films have been sensitized to light. —**sen′si·tiz′er,** *n.*

sen·ti·men·tal (sen′tə men′tl), *adj.* **1** having or showing much tender feeling: *sentimental poetry.* **2** likely to act from feelings rather than from logical thinking. —**sen′ti·men′tal·ly,** *adv.*

sep·a·rate (*v.* sep′ə rāt′; *adj.* sep′ər it), *v.,* **-rat·ed, -rat·ing,** *adj.* —*v.t.* **1** be between; keep apart; divide. **2** take apart; part; disjoin: *separate church and state.* —*v.i.* **1** draw, come, or go apart; become disconnected or disunited. **2** part company. —*adj.* **1** apart from others: *in a separate room.* **2** divided; not joined. **3** individual; single. (< Latin *separatum* put apart, divided < *se-* apart + *parare* prepare) —**sep′ar·ate·ly,** *adv.* —**sep′ar·ate·ness,** *n.*

se·quin (sē′kwən), *n.* a small spangle used to ornament dresses, scarfs.

ser·geant (sär′jent), *n.* a noncommissioned military officer ranking above a corporal.

ser·ies cir·cuits (sir′ēz sér′kits), the paths of electric current connecting several electrical devices one after the other so that the removal of one device breaks the electrical flow to the other devices.

ser·i·ous (sir′ē əs), *adj.* **1** showing deep thought or purpose; thoughtful; grave: *a serious manner.* **2** in earnest; not joking; sincere. —**ser′i·ous·ly,** *adv.* —**ser′i·ous·ness,** *n.*

scuba

a diver using **scuba** gear

a	hat	**ī**	ice	**u̇**	put	**ə** stands for	
ā	age	**o**	not	**ü**	rule	**a**	in about
ä	far, calm	**ō**	open	**ch**	child	**e**	in taken
âr	care	**ȯ**	saw	**ng**	long	**i**	in pencil
e	let	**ô**	order	**sh**	she	**o**	in lemon
ē	equal	**oi**	oil	**th**	thin	**u**	in circus
ėr	term	**ou**	out	**ŦH**	then		
i	it	**u**	cup	**zh**	measure		

set·ting (set′ing), *n.* **1** scenery of a play. **2** place, time, etc., of a play or story.

set·tle (set′l), *v.t.*, **-tled, -tling.** **1** cause to take up residence in a place. **2** establish colonies in; colonize. (Old English *setlan* < *setl* a sitting place, seat)

set·tle·ment (set′l mənt), *n.* **1** act of settling. **2** settling of persons in a new country or area; colonization.

sev·en·ty-two (sev′ən tē tü), seventy plus two.

shad·ow (shad′ō), *n.* an area that is not lit or is only partially lit because an object is blocking light from reaching it. **—shad′ow·er,** *n.* **—shad′ow·less,** *adj.* **—shad′ow·like′,** *adj.*

sheet (shēt), *n.* rope or chain that controls the angle at which a sail is set. (Old English *scēata* lower part of a sail)

shock (shok), *n.* condition of physical collapse or depression, accompanied by a sudden drop in blood pressure, often resulting in unconsciousness. Shock may set in after a severe injury, great loss of blood, or a sudden emotional disturbance. (probably < French *choc,* noun, *choquer,* verb) **—shock′a·ble,** *adj.*

shop·ping cen·ter (shop′ing sen′tər), group of stores built as a unit on or near a main road, especially in a suburban or new community.

sil·hou·ette (sil′ü et′), *n., v.,* **-et·ted, -et·ting.** **—n.** an outline portrait, especially in profile, cut out of a black paper or drawn and filled in with some single color. **—v.t.** show in outline. (< Étienne de *Silhouette,* 1709–1767, French finance minister)

sim·ple in·ter·est (sim′pəl in′tər ist), interest paid on the sum of money saved.

si·mul·cast (sī′məl kast′), *v.,* **-cast** or **-cast·ed, -cast·ing,** *n.* **—v.t., v.i.** transmit a program over radio and television simultaneously. **—n.** broadcast transmitted over radio and television simultaneously.

Sioux (sü), *n., pl.* **Sioux** (sü, süz) for 1. **1** member of an American Indian tribe living on the plains of northern United States and southern Canada; Dakota. **2** the Siouan language of this tribe.

sis·ter-in-law (sis′tər in lȯ′), *n., pl.* **sis·ters-in-law.** **1** sister of one's husband or wife. **2** wife of one's brother. **3** wife of the brother of one's husband or wife.

skyscraper
a modern **skyscraper** in Hong Kong

sit·com (sit′kom), *n.* INFORMAL. situation comedy.

sky·scrap·er (skī′skrā′pər), *n., pl.* **sky·scrap·ers.** a very tall building.

sla·lom (slä′ləm, slal′əm), *n.* (in skiing) a zigzag race downhill. (< Norwegian < *slad* bent, sloping + *lom* path, trail)

sleep·i·ness (slēp′ē nis), *n.* a feeling of drowsiness, almost sleeping.

sleuth (slüth), *n.* **1** bloodhound. **2** INFORMAL. detective. **—v.i.** INFORMAL. be or act like a detective.

slid·ing fric·tion (slīd′ing frik′shən), backwards force that exists between the surfaces of objects that are sliding over each other.

slosh (slosh), *v.i.* splash in or through slush, mud, or water. **—v.t.** pour or dash (liquid) upon. **—n. 1** slush. **2** INFORMAL. a watery or weak drink. (perhaps blend of *slop* and *slush*)

smoke de·tec·tor (smōk di tek′tər), *n., pl.* **smoke de·tec·tors.** a device that sounds an alarm when it detects the presence of smoke inside.

sna·fu (sna fü′), SLANG. **—n.** a snarled or confused state of things. **—adj.** snarled; confused. **—v.t. 1** put in disorder or in a chaotic state. **2** botch. (< the initial letters of "situation normal—all fouled up")

snor·kel (snôr′kəl), *n.* a curved tube which enables swimmers to breathe under water while swimming near the surface. **—v.i.** swim under water using a snorkel.

soft·ware (sȯft′wãr′), *n.* program for a computer system.

so·lar col·lec·tor (sō′lər kə lek′tər), *n., pl.* **so·lar col·lec·tors.** an object that traps the sun's energy and heats up a fluid.

so·lil·o·quy (sə lil′ə kwē), *n., pl.* **-quies. 1** a talking to oneself. **2** speech made by an actor to himself or herself when alone.

sol·ute (sol′yüt, sō′lüt), *n.* solid, gas, or liquid dissolved in a liquid to make a solution. (< Latin *solutum* dissolved)

so·lu·tion (sə lü′shən), *n.* **1** process of dissolving; the mixing of a solid, liquid, or gas with another solid, liquid, or gas so that the molecules of each are evenly distributed. **2** (in mathematics) a value of a variable that makes an equation true. (< Latin *solutionem* a loosing < *solvere* loosen)

solve (solv), *v.t.,* **solved, solv·ing.** find the answer to; clear up; explain. (< Latin *solvere* loosen)

sol·vent (sol′vənt), *adj.* able to dissolve: *Gasoline is a solvent liquid that removes grease spots.* —*n.* substance, usually a liquid, that can dissolve other substances. (< Latin *solventem* loosening, paying)

some·thing (sum′thing), *n.* some thing; a particular thing not named or known. —*adv.* somewhat; to some extent or degree.

soph·o·more (sof′ə môr), *n.* student in the second year of high school or college.

spa·cious (spā′shəs), *adj.* 1 having much space or room; large: *the spacious rooms of the old castle.* 2 of great extent or area. —**spa′cious·ly,** *adv.* —**spa′cious·ness,** *n.*

speak·eas·y (spēk′ē/zē), *n., pl.* **speak·eas·ies.** SLANG. place where alcoholic liquors are sold contrary to law.

spe·cies (spē′shēz), *n., pl.* **-cies.** group of related organisms that have certain permanent characteristics in common and are able to interbreed. A species ranks next below a genus and may be divided into several varieties, races, or breeds. Wheat is a species of grass.

speed (spēd), *n.* rate of motion; found by dividing the distance an object moves by the time the object takes to go that distance and usually expressed in meters/seconds.

speed·om·e·ter (spē dom′ə tər), *n.* instrument to indicate the speed of an automobile or other vehicle, and often the distance traveled.

sphere (sfir), *n.* a round solid figure whose surface is at all points equally distant from the center.

spir·i·tu·al (spir′ə chü əl), *adj.* 1 of or having to do with the spirit or soul. 2 of or having to do with the church; sacred; religious. —*n.* a sacred song or hymn as originally created or interpreted by the Negroes of the southern United States. —**spir′i·tu·al·ly,** *adv.* —**spir′i·tu·al·ness,** *n.*

splat·ter (splat′ər), *v.t., v.i.* splash or spatter. —*n.* a splash or spatter.

sports·cast (spôrts′kast′), *n.* broadcast of a sporting event.

sports·man·ship (spôrts′mən ship), *n.* qualities or conduct of a sportsman; fair play.

square root (skwãr rüt), number that produces a given number when multiplied by itself: *The square root of 16 is 4.*

squig·gle (skwig′əl), *n., v.,* **-gled, -gling.** —*n.* a wriggly twist or curve. —*v.t.* make twisting or curving lines. —*v.i.* twist and turn about. (blend of *squirm* and *wriggle*)

sta·bil·i·ty (stə bil′ə tē), *n., pl.* **-ties.** a being fixed in position.

sta·ble (stā′bəl), *adj.* 1 not likely to fall or be overturned: *a stable government.* 2 not likely to give way; steady; firm: *a stable support.* 3 not likely to change in nature or purpose; steadfast.

stage fright (stāj frīt), nervous fear of appearing before an audience.

stam·pede (stam pēd′), *n.* a sudden scattering or headlong flight of a frightened herd of cattle, horses.

stan·dard form (stan′dərd fôrm), the notation for writing numbers using the digits 0–9 and each place representing a power of ten.

star·board (stär′bərd), *n.* the right side of a ship, boat, or aircraft, when facing forward. (Old English *stēorbord* the side from which a vessel was steered < *stēor* steering paddle + *bord* side (of a ship))

states′ rights (stāts rīts), powers belonging to the individual states of the United States, under the Constitution. The doctrine of states′ rights holds that all powers which the Constitution does not specifically delegate to the federal government and does not specifically deny to the individual states belong to the states.

stat·ic fric·tion (stat′ik frik′shən), force in the direction that opposes any motion between the surfaces of objects that are touching but not moving past each other.

a	hat	**ī**	ice	**u̇**	put	**ə**	stands for
ā	age	**o**	not	**ü**	rule	**a**	in about
ä	far, calm	**ō**	open	**ch**	child	**e**	in taken
âr	care	**ȯ**	saw	**ng**	long	**i**	in pencil
e	let	**ô**	order	**sh**	she	**o**	in lemon
ē	equal	**oi**	oil	**th**	thin	**u**	in circus
ėr	term	**ou**	out	**ᴛʜ**	then		
i	it	**u**	cup	**zh**	measure		

stim·u·lus (stim′yə ləs), *n., pl.* **-li.** something that stirs to action or effort; incentive: *Ambition is a great stimulus.*

stor·age (stôr′ij), *n.* **1** act or tact of storing goods. **2** condition of being stored. Cold storage is used to keep eggs and meat from spoiling.

straight-faced (strāt′fāst′), *adj.* showing no emotion, humor, etc.

straight·for·ward (strāt′fôr′wərd), *adj.* **1** honest; frank. **2** going straight ahead; direct. —*adv.* directly. —**straight′for′ward·ness,** *n.*

strain (strān), *v.i.* be injured or damaged by too much effort. —*n.* **1** any severe, trying, or wearing pressure: *the strain of worry.* **2** effect of such pressure on the body or mind. —**strain′less,** *adj.*

stra·te·gic (strə tē′jik), *adj.* **1** of strategy; based on strategy; useful in strategy: *a strategic retreat.* **2** important in strategy: *a strategic link in national defense.* —**stra·te′gi·cal·ly,** *adv.*

stra·te·gi·cal (strə tē′jə kəl), *adj.* strategic.

strat·e·gy (strat′ə jē), *n., pl.* **-gies.** **1** science or art of war; the planning and directing of military movements and operations. **2** the skillful planning and management of anything. (< Greek *stratēgia* < *stratēgos* general < *stratos* army + *agein* to lead)

stren·u·ous (stren′yü əs), *adj.* **1** very active. **2** full of energy. **3** requiring much energy: *strenuous exercise.* —**stren′u·ous·ly,** *adv.* —**stren′u·ous·ness,** *n.*

struc·tur·al (struk′chər əl), *adj.* **1** used in building. **2** of or having to do with structure or structures: *The geologist showed the structural difference in rocks of different ages.* —**struc′tur·al·ly,** *adv.*

stub·born (stub′ərn), *adj.* **1** fixed in purpose or opinion; not giving in to argument or requests. **2** characterized by obstinacy: *a stubborn refusal.* **3** hard to deal with or manage: *a stubborn cough.* —**stub′born·ly,** *adv.* —**stub′born·ness,** *n.*

sub·com·mit·tee (sub′kə mit′ē), *n.* a small committee chosen from and acting under a larger general committee for some special duty.

sub·di·vi·sion (sub′də vizh′ən), *n.* **1** division into smaller parts. **2** part of a part. **3** tract of land divided into building lots.

sub·head (sub′hed′), *n.* a subordinate heading or title.

sub·head·ing (sub′hed′ing), *n.* subhead.

sub·ma·rine (*n., v.* sub′mə rēn′; *adj.* sub′mə rēn′), *n., v.,* **-rined, -rin·ing,** *adj.* —*n.* boat that can operate under water, used in warfare for attacking enemy ships with torpedoes and for launching missiles. —*v.t.* attack or sink by a submarine. —*adj.* under the surface of the sea; underwater.

sub·merge (səb mėrj′), *v.,* **-merged, -merg·ing.** —*v.t.* **1** put under water; cover with water. **2** cover; bury. —*v.i.* sink under water; go below the surface. (< Latin *submergere* < *sub-* under + *mergere* to plunge)

sub·or·di·nate (*adj., n.* sə bôrd′n it; *v.* sə bôrd′n āt), *adj., n., v.,* **-nat·ed, -nat·ing.** —*adj.* **1** lower in rank: *In the army, lieutenants are subordinate to captains.* **2** lower in importance; secondary. —*n.* a subordinate person or thing. —*v.t.* make subordinate: *He subordinated his wishes to those of his guests.* (< Medieval Latin *subordinatum* lowered in rank < Latin *sub-* under + *ordinem* order) —**sub·or′di·nate·ly,** *adv.* —**sub·or′di·nate·ness,** *n.*

sub·scribe (səb skrīb′), *v.i.,* **-scribed, -scrib·ing.** **1** promise to give or pay money: *subscribe to several charities.* **2** promise to accept and pay for a number of copies of a newspaper, magazine, etc.: *We subscribe to a few magazines.* (< Latin *subscribere* < *sub-* under + *scribere* write) —**sub·scrib′er,** *n.*

sub·script (sub′skript), *adj.* written underneath or low on the line. —*n.* number, letter, or other symbol written underneath and to one side of a symbol. In H_2SO_4 the 2 and 4 are subscripts.

sub·sec·tion (sub′sek′shən), *n.* part of a section.

sub·stance (sub′stəns), *n.* **1** what a thing consists of; matter; material. **2** the real, main, or important part of anything: *The substance of an education is its effect on your life.* **3** the real meaning: *Give the substance of the speech in your own words.* **4** solid quality; body. **5** wealth; property: *a person of substance.* (< Old French < Latin *substantia* < *substare* stand firm < *sub-* up to + *stare* to stand)

sub·stan·tial (səb stan′shəl), *adj.*
1 having substance; material; real; actual: *People and things are substantial; dreams and ghosts are not.* **2** strong; firm; solid: *The house is substantial enough to last a hundred years.* **3** large; important; ample: *make a substantial improvement in health.*
—**sub·stan′tial·ly,** *adv.*

sub·ter·ra·ne·an (sub′tə rā′nē ən), *adj.* underground: *A subterranean passage led from the castle to a cave.* (< Latin *subterraneus* < *sub-* under + *terra* earth)

sub·trac·tion (səb trak′shən), *n.* operation of subtracting one number or quantity from another.

sub·ur·ban (sə bėr′bən), *adj.* **1** of, having to do with, or in a suburb: *We have excellent suburban train service.* **2** characteristic of a suburb or its inhabitants. —*n.* **sub·ur·ban·i·za·tion.**

sub·ur·ban·ite (sə bėr′bə nīt), *n.* person who lives in a suburb.

suede (swād), *n.* a soft leather that has a velvety nap on one or both sides. —*adj.* made of suede: *a suede jacket.* (< French (*gants de*) *Suède* (gloves from) Sweden)

suf·fi·cient (sə fish′ənt), *adj.* as much as is needed; enough: *sufficient proof.* —**suf·fi′cient·ly,** *adv.*

suite (swēt; *also* süt *for* 2), *n.* **1** set of connected rooms to be used by one person or family. **2** set of furniture that matches; suit. **3** any set or series of like things. (< French < Old French *siute* < Popular Latin *sequita.*)

suit·or (sü′tər), *n., pl.* **suit·ors. 1** man who is courting a woman. **2** person bringing suit in a court of law.

su·ki·ya·ki (sü′kē yä′kē, skē yä′kē), *n.* a Japanese dish consisting mainly of cooked, thinly sliced meat, onions, bamboo shoots, and various other vegetables. (< Japanese)

sun·di·al (sun′dī′əl), *n.* instrument for telling the time of day by the position of a shadow cast by the sun; dial.

su·per·car·go (sü′per kär′gō), *n., pl.* **su·per·car·goes.** officer on a merchant ship who represents the owner and has charge of the cargo and the business affairs of the voyage.

su·per·fi·cial (sü′per fish′əl), *adj.* measurement. **1** on the surface; at the surface: *His burns were superficial and soon healed.* **2** concerned with or understanding only what is on the surface; not thorough; shallow: *superficial education, superficial knowledge.*
—**su′per·fi′cial·ly,** *adv.*

su·per·gi·ant (sü′per jī′ənt), *n., pl.* **su·per·gi·ants.** star more massive than the sun in a late stage in its life in which it becomes even larger and brighter than a red giant.

su·per·im·pose (sü′per im pōz′), *v.t.,* **-posed, -pos·ing.** put on top of something else.

su·per·mar·ket (sü′per mär′kit), *n.* a large grocery store in which customers select their purchases from open shelves.

su·per·nat·u·ral (sü′per nach′er əl), *adj.* above or beyond what is natural: *supernatural voices.*
—**su′per·nat′ur·al·ly,** *adv.*
—**su′per·nat′ur·al·ness,** *n.*

su·per no·va (sü′per nō′və), *n., pl.* **-vas.** explosive death of a massive, supergiant star.

su·per·script (sü′per skript), *adj.* written above. —*n.* number, letter, etc., written above and to one side of a symbol. In $a^3 × b^n$ the 3 and the *n* are superscripts.

su·per·sede (sü′per sēd′), *v.t.,* **-sed·ed, -sed·ing.** take the place of; cause to be set aside; displace: *Electric lights have superseded gaslights.* (< Latin *supersedere* be superior to, refrain from < *super-* above + *sedere* sit)
—**su′per·sed′er,** *n.*

su·per·son·ic (sü′per son′ik), *adj.* **1** greater than the speed of sound in air or in some other medium. **2** capable of moving faster than sound: *supersonic aircraft.*

supersonic (def. 2)
the **supersonic**
Concorde

a	hat	**ī**	ice	**u̇**	put	**ə** stands for	
ā	age	**o**	not	**ü**	rule	**a**	in about
ä	far, calm	**ō**	open	**ch**	child	**e**	in taken
âr	care	**ȯ**	saw	**ng**	long	**i**	in pencil
e	let	**ô**	order	**sh**	she	**o**	in lemon
ē	equal	**oi**	oil	**th**	thin	**u**	in circus
ėr	term	**ou**	out	**ᴛʜ**	then		
i	it	**u**	cup	**zh**	measure		

suspend (def. 1)
This bridge is
suspended on cables
between towers.

su·per·sti·tion (sü′pər stish′ən), *n.*
1 an unreasoning fear of what is
unknown or mysterious;
unreasoning expectation. **2** belief
or practice founded on ignorant
fear or mistaken reverence: *A
common superstition considers 13
an unlucky number.* (< Latin
superstitionem, originally, a
standing over, as in wonder or awe
< *super-* above + *stare* to stand)

sup·posed to (sə pōzd′ tü), permitted
to, expected to.

sur·face ar·e·a (sėr′fis er′ē ə), the
sum of the areas of all the surfaces
of a solid figure.

sur·geon (sėr′jən), *n.* doctor who
performs operations; medical
practitioner who specializes in
surgery.

sur·ren·der (sə ren′dər), *v.*
**sur·ren·ders, sur·ren·dered,
sur·ren·der·ing.** — *v.t.* give up
(something) to the possession or
power of another; yield (*to*): *The
general surrendered the fort to the
enemy.* — *n.* act of surrendering.
(< Old French *surrendre* < *sur-*
over + *rendre* render)

sur·veil·lance (sėr vā′ləns), *n.*
1 watch kept over a person.
2 supervision. (< French < *sur-* over
+ *veiller* to watch)

sur·vive (sər vīv′), *v.,* **sur·vived,
sur·viv·ing.** — *v.t.* live longer than;
remain alive after: *He survived his
wife by three years.* — *v.i.* continue
to live; remain alive; live on. (< Old
French *sourvivre* < *sur-* over +
vivre to live)

sus·cep·ti·ble (sə sep′tə bəl), *adj.*
1 easily influenced by feelings or
emotions; very sensitive: *Poetry
appealed to his susceptible nature.*
2 susceptible to, easily affected by;
liable to; open to: *Vain people are
susceptible to flattery.* (< Late Latin
susceptibilis, ultimately < Latin
sub- up + *capere* to take)
— **sus·cep′ti·bly,** *adv.*

sus·pend (sə spend′), *v.t.* **1** hang
down by attaching to something
above: *The lamp was suspended
from the ceiling.* **2** hold in place as
if by hanging. **3** stop for a while:
suspend work.

sus·pense (sə spens′), *n.* **1** condition
of being uncertain. **2** anxious
uncertainty; anxiety: *Parents may
feel suspense when their children
are very sick.* (< Old French (*en*)
suspens (in) abeyance, ultimately
< Latin *suspendere.*)

sus·pen·sion (sə spen′shən), *n.* **1** a
suspending: *the suspension of a
driver's license for speeding.*
2 support on which something is
suspended.

sus·pi·cious (sə spish′əs), *adj.*
1 causing one to suspect;
questionable; doubtful. **2** feeling
suspicion; suspecting; mistrustful.
— **sus·pi′cious·ly,** *adv.*
— **sus·pi′cious·ness,** *n.*

sus·tain (sə stān′), *v.t.* **1** keep up;
keep going: *Hope sustains him in
his misery.* **2** supply with food,
provisions, etc.: *sustain a family.*
3 hold up; support: *Arches sustain
the weight of the roof.* **4** bear;
endure: *The sea wall sustains the
shock of the waves.* **5** suffer;
experience: *sustain a great loss.*
6 allow; admit; favor: *The court
sustained his suit.* **7** agree with;
confirm: *The facts sustain her
theory.* (< Old French < Latin
sustinere < *sub-* up + *tenere* to
hold) — **sus·tain′a·ble,** *adj.*
— **sus·tain′er,** *n.*

sus·te·nance (sus′tə nəns), *n.* **1** food
or provisions; nourishment. **2** means
of living; support: *give money for
the sustenance of the poor.*

SWAT (swot), *n.* Special Weapons and
Tactics (a specially trained section
of police).

sweet (swēt), *adj.* **1** having a taste like
that of sugar or honey: *Pears are
sweeter than lemons.* **2** having a
pleasant taste or smell: *a sweet
flower.* **3** pleasing; agreeable: *a
sweet child, a sweet smile, sweet
music.* (Old English *swēte*)
— **sweet′ly,** *adv.* — **sweet′ness,** *n.*

swore (swôr), *v.* a pt. of **swear.**

sym·bol (sim′bəl), *n., v.,* **-boled,
-bol·ing** or **-bolled, -bol·ling.** — *n.*
something that stands for or
represents an idea, quality,
condition, or other abstraction: *The
lion is the symbol of courage; the
lamb, of meekness.* — *v.t.*
symbolize. (< Greek *symbolon*
token, mark < *syn-* together +
ballein to throw)

sym·me·try (sim′ə trē), *n., pl.* **-tries.** a
regular, balanced arrangement on
opposite sides of a line or plane, or
around a center or axis. (< Greek
symmetria < *syn-* together +
metron measure)

sym·pa·thet·ic (sim′pə thet′ik), *adj.*
having or showing kind feelings
toward others; sympathizing.
— **sym′pa·thet′i·cal·ly,** *adv.*

syn·chro·nize (sing′krə nīz), *v.*, **-nized, -niz·ing.** —*v.i.* **1** occur at the same time; agree in time. **2** move or take place at the same rate and exactly together. —*v.t.* **1** make agree in time: *synchronize all the clocks in a building.* **2** assign to the same time or period. —**syn′chro·ni·za′tion,** *n.* —**syn′chro·niz′er,** *n.*

T

tam·bou·rine (tam′bə rēn′), *n.* a small, shallow drum with one head, and jingling metal disks around the side, played by striking with the hand or by shaking it.

tan·ge·rine (tan′jə rēn′), *n.* a small, reddish-orange citrus fruit with a very loose peel and segments that separate easily. It is widely grown in the United States. (< French *Tanger* Tangier)

tar·iff (tar′if), *n., pl.* **tar·iffs.** list of duties or taxes that a government charges on imports or exports. (< Italian *tariffa* < Arabic *ta'rīf* information) —**tar′iff·less,** *adj.*

ta·ta·mi (tə tä′mē), *n., pl.* **-mi.** a woven straw floor mat traditionally used in Japanese homes. (< Japanese)

ted·dy bear or **Ted·dy bear** (ted′ē bãr), a child's furry toy bear.

tel·e·scop·ic (tel′ə skop′ik), *adj.* **1** of or having to do with a telescope. **2** obtained or seen by means of a telescope. **3** visible only through a telescope. **4** farseeing.

tel·e·thon (tel′ə thon), *n.* a television program lasting many hours, especially one soliciting contributions for a charity, etc.

tem·per (tem′pər), *n.* **1** state of mind; disposition; mood. **2** angry state of mind. —*v.t.* **1** moderate; soften: *Temper justice with mercy.* **2** check; restrain; curb. (Old English *temprian* to temper < Latin *temperare,* originally, observe due measure < *tempus* time, interval)

tem·per·a·men·tal (tem′pər ə men′tl), *adj.* subject to moods and whims; easily irritated; sensitive. —**tem′per·a·men′tal·ly,** *adv.*

tem·per·a·ture (tem′pər ə chər), *n.* the number that is a measure of the average kinetic energy of all the particles in an object or material, expressed in degrees.

tem·pest (tem′pist) *n.* a violent windstorm, usually accompanied by rain, hail, or snow.

tem·po (tem′pō), *n., pl.* **-pos. 1** (in music) the time or rate of movement. **2** characteristic pace or rhythm.

tem·po·rar·y (tem′pə rãr′ē), *adj., n., pl.* **-rar·ies.** —*adj.* lasting for a short time only; used for the time being; not permanent. —*n.* person hired for a limited period of time. —**tem′po·rar′i·ly,** *adv.*

ter·mi·nat·ing dec·i·mal (tèr′mə nāt ing des′ə məl), a decimal with an exact number of nonzero digits.

tes·ti·mo·ny (tes′tə mō′nē), *n., pl.* **-nies. 1** statement used for evidence or proof. **2** evidence: *The pupils presented their teacher with a watch in testimony of their respect and affection.* See **evidence** for synonym study. **3** an open declaration or profession of one's faith. (< Latin *testimonium* < *testis* witness)

ther·a·py (thãr′ə pē), *n., pl.* **-pies.** treatment of diseases or disorders. (< Greek *therapeia* < *therapeuein* to cure, treat < *theraps* attendant)

ther·mal (thèr′məl), *adj.* **1** of or having to do with heat; thermic. **2** warm; hot. —*n.* a rising current of warm air. —**ther′mal·ly,** *adv.*

ther·mo·dy·nam·ic (thèr′mō dī nam′ik), *adj.* using force due to heat or to the conversion of heat into other forms of energy.

ther·mom·e·ter (thər mom′ə tər), *n.* instrument for measuring the temperature of a body or of space, usually by means of the expansion and contraction of mercury or alcohol in a capillary tube and bulb with a graduated scale.

thermometer

The **thermometer** measures temperature in degrees.

a	hat	**ī**	ice	**ù**	put	**ə** stands for	
ā	age	**o**	not	**ü**	rule	**a**	in about
ä	far, calm	**ō**	open	**ch**	child	**e**	in taken
âr	care	**ȯ**	saw	**ng**	long	**i**	in pencil
e	let	**ô**	order	**sh**	she	**o**	in lemon
ē	equal	**oi**	oil	**th**	thin	**u**	in circus
èr	term	**ou**	out	**ᴛʜ**	then		
i	it	**u**	cup	**zh**	measure		

ther·mo·nu·cle·ar (thėr′mō nü′klē ėr, thėr′mō nyü′klē ėr), *adj.* of or having to do with the fusion of atoms through very high temperature, as in the hydrogen bomb: *a thermonuclear reaction.*

ther·mos (thėr′məs), *n.* container made with a vacuum between its inner and outer walls so that its contents remain hot or cold for a long time. (< *Thermos,* a trademark)

ther·mo·stat (thėr′mə stat), *n.* an automatic device for regulating temperature, especially one in which the expansion and contraction of a metal, liquid, or gas opens and closes an electric circuit connected to a furnace, air conditioner, etc.

the·ro·pod (thēr′ə pod′), *n.* a member of a group of meat-eating dinosaurs that had short forelimbs and walked or ran on their hind legs.

thor·ough (thėr′ō), *adj.* **1** being all that is needed; complete: *a thorough search.* **2** doing all that should be done and slighting nothing; painstaking: *The doctor was very thorough in examining the patient.* —**thor′ough·ly,** *adv.* —**thor′ough·ness,** *n.*

three-di·men·sion·al (thrē′də men′shə nəl), *adj.* **1** having three dimensions. **2** seeming to have depth as well as height and breadth; appearing to exist in three dimensions.

thrive (thrīv), *v.i.,* **throve** or **thrived, thrived** or **thriv·en** (thriv′ən), **thriv·ing. 1** grow or develop well; grow vigorously: *Flowers will not thrive without sunshine.* **2** be successful; grow rich; prosper. —**thriv′er,** *n.* —**thriv′ing·ly,** *adv.*

through (thrü), *prep.* **1** from end to end of; from side to side of; between the parts of; from beginning to end of: *march through a town.* **2** having reached the end of; finished with: *We are through school at noon.* **3** during and until the finish of: *help a person through hard times.* —*adv.* from end to end; from side to side; between the parts: *The ball hit the window and went through.* —*adj.* **1** going all the way without change: *a through flight from New York to Paris.* **2** having reached the end; finished: *I am almost through.*

through·out (thrü out′), *prep.* **1** in every part of: *The Fourth of July is celebrated throughout the United States.* **2** during the whole of (a period of time or course of action). —*adv.* in or to every part: *This house is well built throughout.*

thun·der·storm (thun′dər stôrm′), *n.* storm with thunder and lightning.

thyme (tīm), *n.* any of a genus of herbs of the mint family, with fragrant, aromatic leaves. The leaves of the common garden thyme are used for seasoning.

tim·id (tim′id), *adj.* **1** easily frightened; shy. **2** characterized by or indicating fear: *a timid reply.* (< Latin *timidus* < *timere* to fear) —**tim′id·ly,** *adv.* —**tim′id·ness,** *n.*

tim·pa·ni (tim′pə nē), *n.pl.* of **tim·pa·no** (tim′pə nō). kettledrums. (< Italian, plural of *timpano* < Latin *tympanum*) —**tim′pa·nist,** *n.*

to·bog·gan (tə bog′ən), *n.* a long, narrow, flat sled with its front end curved upward without runners. —*v.i.* slide downhill on a toboggan. (< Canadian French *tabagane;* of Algonquian origin) —**to·bog′gan·er,** *n.*

tow·el (tou′əl), *n., v.,* **-eled, -el·ing** or **-elled, -el·ling.** —*n.* **1** piece of cloth or paper for wiping and drying something wet. **2 throw in the towel,** INFORMAL. admit defeat; surrender. —*v.t.* wipe or dry with a towel.

tra·di·tion (trə dish′ən), *n., pl.* **tra·di·tions. 1** the handing down of beliefs, opinions, customs, stories, etc., from parents to children. **2** what is handed down in this way. (< Latin *traditionem* < *tradere* hand over < *trans-* over + *dare* to give.)

tra·di·tion·al (trə dish′ə nəl), *adj.* **1** of tradition. **2** handed down by tradition. **3** according to tradition: *traditional furniture.* **4** customary. —**tra·di′tion·al·ly,** *adv.*

trail drive (trāl drīv), during the cowboy era, a long trip in which cowboys drove their herds hundreds of miles to railroad stations for shipment to market.

Trail of Tears (trāl ov tirs), name given to the journey of the Cherokee nation from the Southeast to an area west of the Mississippi when they were forced to leave their ancestral homelands in 1830. Thousands perished from disease, starvation, and other hardships.

tradition (def. 1)
The Pipers of Scotland have been a **tradition** for more than 500 years.

tram·po·line (tram′pə lēn′), *n.* piece of canvas or other sturdy fabric stretched on a metal frame, used for tumbling, acrobatics, etc.

tran·quil (trang′kwəl), *adj.* free from agitation or disturbance; calm; peaceful; quiet. (< Latin *tranquillus*) —**tran′quil·ly,** *adv.*

tran·quil·li·ty (trang kwil′ə tē), *n.* tranquil condition; calmness.

trans·ac·tion (tran zak′shən), *n.* **1** act or process of transacting: *She attends to the transaction of important matters herself.* **2** piece of business. —**trans·ac′tion·al,** *adj.*

tran·script (tran′skript), *n.* **1** a written or typewritten copy. **2** copy or reproduction of anything: *The college wanted a transcript.*

trans·fer (*v.* tran sfér′, tran′sfér′; *n.* tran′sfér′), *v.,* **trans·ferred, trans·fer·ring,** *n.* —*v.t.* **1** convey or remove from one person or place to another; hand over. **2** convey (a drawing, design, pattern) from one surface to another. —*v.i.* change from one place, position, condition, etc., to another. —*n.* **1** a transferring. **2** a being transferred. —**trans·fer′rer,** *n.*

trans·fer·al (tran sfér′əl), *n.* transference; transfer.

trans·fu·sion (tran sfyü′zhən), *n.* **1** act or fact of transfusing. **2** transfer of blood from one person or animal to another.

tran·sis·tor (tran zis′tər), *n.* a small electronic device containing semiconductors such as germanium or silicon, used to amplify or control the flow of electrons in an electric circuit. (< *tran′*sfer) + (*re*)*sistor*)

trans·late (tran slāt′, tran′slāt), *v.,* **-lat·ed, -lat·ing.** —*v.t.* **1** change from one language into another. **2** change into other words. **3** explain the meaning of; interpret. —*v.i.* change something from one language or form of words into another. (< Latin *translatum* carried over < *trans-* + *latum* carried) —**trans·lat′a·ble,** *adj.*

trans·lu·cent (tran slü′snt), *adj.* letting light through without being transparent: *Frosted glass is translucent.* (< Latin *translucentem* < *trans-* through + *lucere* to shine) —**trans·lu′cent·ly,** *adv.*

trans·mit (tran smit′), *v.t.,* **-mit·ted, -mit·ting.** **1** send over; pass on; pass along; let through. **2** send out (signals) by means of electromagnetic waves or by wire. (< Latin *transmittere* < *trans-* across + *mittere* send) —**trans·mit′ta·ble,** *adj.*

trans·o·ce·an·ic (tran′sō shē an′ik, tranz′ō shē an′ik), *adj.* **1** crossing the ocean. **2** on the other side of the ocean.

trans·par·ent (tran spâr′ənt), *adj.* **1** transmitting light so that bodies beyond or behind can be distinctly seen: *Window glass is transparent.* **2** easily seen through or detected: *a transparent excuse.* (< Medieval Latin *transparentem* showing light through < Latin *trans-* through + *parere* appear) —**trans·par′ent·ly,** *adv.*

trans·por·ta·tion (tran′spər tā′shən), *n.* **1** a transporting: *The railroad gives free transportation to a certain amount of baggage.* **2** a being transported. **3** business of transporting people or goods.

trea·ty (trē′tē), *n., pl.* **-ties.** a formal agreement, especially one between nations, signed and approved by each nation.

tre·men·dous (tri men′dəs), *adj.* **1** very severe; dreadful; awful: *a tremendous defeat.* **2** INFORMAL. very great; enormous: *a tremendous house.* **3** INFORMAL. excellent; wonderful; extraordinary. (< Latin *tremendus,* literally, be trembled at < *tremere* to tremble) —**tre·men′dous·ly,** *adv.* —**tre·men′dous·ness,** *n.*

tres·pass (tres′pəs), *v.i.* **1** go on somebody's property without any right. **2** do wrong; sin. —*n.* a wrong; a sin. (< Old French *trespasser* < *tres-* across + *passer* to pass) —**tres′pass·er,** *n.*

transportation
(def. 3) a type of
transportation

a	hat	**ī**	ice	**u̇**	put	**ə** stands for	
ā	age	**o**	not	**ü**	rule	**a**	in about
ä	far, calm	**ō**	open	**ch**	child	**e**	in taken
âr	care	**ȯ**	saw	**ng**	long	**i**	in pencil
e	let	**ô**	order	**sh**	she	**o**	in lemon
ē	equal	**oi**	oil	**th**	thin	**u**	in circus
ėr	term	**ou**	out	**ᴛʜ**	then		
i	it	**u**	cup	**zh**	measure		

tri·an·gu·lar prism (trī ang′gyə lər priz′əm), a polyhedron whose congruent and parallel bases are triangles.

tset·se fly (tset′sē), any of a group of two-winged, bloodsucking African flies that transmit disease, including the one transmitting the trypanosome that causes sleeping sickness, and one that carries a disease of horses and other domestic animals. Also, **tzetze fly.** (*tsetse,* of Bantu origin)

tsu·na·mi (sü nä′mē, tsü nä′mē), n. an oceanic tidal wave caused by a submarine earthquake. (< Japanese)

tun·dra (tun′drə), n. a vast, level, treeless plain in the arctic regions. The ground beneath the surface of the tundras is frozen even in summer. Much of Alaska and northern Canada is tundra. (< Russian)

tu·pe·lo (tü′pə lō, tyü′pə lō), n., pl. **-los.** a large North American tree of the same family as the sour gum, whose flowers are often used by bees in making honey. (of Algonquian origin)

tur·quoise (tėr′koiz, tėr′kwoiz), n. 1 a sky-blue or greenish-blue precious mineral which is valued as a gem. 2 a sky blue or greenish blue. (< Old French *(pierre) turqueise* Turkish (stone))

tux·e·do (tuk sē′dō), n., pl. **-dos.** 1 a man's coat for semiformal evening wear, made without tails, usually black with satin lapels. 2 the suit to which such a coat belongs. (< *Tuxedo* Park, New York)

ty·coon (tī kün′), n. businessman having great wealth and power. (< Japanese *taikun* < Chinese *tai* great + *kiun* lord)

ty·rant (tī′rənt), n. 1 person who uses power cruelly or unjustly. 2 a cruel or unjust ruler.

U

u·ku·le·le (yü′kə lā′lē), n. a small guitar having four strings. (< Hawaiian, originally, leaping flea)

um·brel·la (um brel′ə), n. a light, portable, circular cover for protection against rain or sun, consisting of a fabric held on a folding frame of thin ribs, which slide on a rod or stick. **—um·brel′la·like′,** adj.

un·con·nect·ed (un′kə nek′tid), adj. 1 not joined together; not fastened. 2 not joined in orderly sequence.

un·daunt·ed (un dȯn′tid), adj. not afraid; not dismayed or discouraged; fearless. **—un·daunt′ed·ly,** adv.

un·der·ground (adv. un′dər ground′; adj., n. un′dər ground′), adv. beneath the surface of the ground. **—adj.** being, working, or used beneath the surface of the ground. **—n.** place or space beneath the surface of the ground.

Un·der·ground Rail·road (un′dər ground′ rāl′rōd), system by which the opponents of slavery secretly helped fugitive slaves to escape to the free states or Canada.

un·der·rate (un′dər rāt′), v.t., **-rat·ed, -rat·ing.** rate or estimate too low; put too low a value on.

un·der·stand·ing (un′dər stan′ding), n. 1 comprehension; knowledge. 2 a mutual arrangement or agreement. **—adj.** that understands or is able to understand: *an understanding reply.* **—un′der·stand′ing·ly,** adv.

un·doubt·ed·ly (un dou′tid lē), adv. beyond doubt; certainly.

U·NI·CEF (yü′nə sef), n. United Nations Children's Fund. (< U(nited) N(ations) I(nternational) C(hildren's) E(mergency) F(und), the original name of the fund)

u·nit pric·es (yü′nit prīs′es), prices that give both the total cost and the cost per unit of measure.

un·nat·ur·al (un nach′ər əl), adj. 1 not natural; not normal. 2 shocking; horrible. 3 synthetic; artificial. **—un·nat′ur·al·ly,** adv. **—un·nat′ur·al·ness,** n.

un·nec·es·sar·y (un nes′ə sâr′ē), adj. not necessary; needless. **—un·nec′es·sar′i·ly,** adv.

un·pro·nounce·a·ble (un prə nouns′ə bəl), adj. too complicated or too difficult to be pronounced.

un·re·al (un rē′əl), adj. not real or substantial; imaginary; fanciful.

un·u·su·al (un yü′zhü əl), adj. not usual; not in common use; uncommon; rare. **—un·u′su·al·ly,** adv. **—un·u′su·al·ness,** n.

u·su·al (yü′zhü əl), adj. 1 commonly seen, found, or happening; ordinary; customary. 2 **as usual,** in the usual manner; as is customary. **—u′su·al·ness,** n.

u·su·al·ly (yü′zhü ə lē), adv. according to what is usual; commonly; ordinarily; customarily.

UNICEF

UNICEF is an international organization that helps needy children.

u·til·i·ty (yü til′ə tē), *n., pl.* **-ties,** *adj.*
—*n.* **1** power to satisfy people's needs; usefulness. **2** a useful thing. **3** company that performs a public service; public utility. Railroads, bus lines, and gas and electric companies are utilities. —*adj.* used for various purposes: *a utility shed.*

V

van·dal·ism (van′dl iz′əm), *n.* willful or ignorant destruction or damaging of valuable things.

var·i·a·ble (vàr′ē ə bəl), *n.* a letter or symbol used to represent a number.

vaude·ville (vòd′vil, vò′də vil), *n.* theatrical entertainment featuring a variety of acts, such as songs, dances, acrobatic feats, skits, trained animals, etc. (< French, alteration of *vaudevire* < *(chanson de) Vau de Vire* (song of the) valley of Vire, region in Normandy)

ve·loc·i·ty (və los′ə tē), *n., pl.* **-ties.** quantity giving both the speed and the direction that an object is moving.

ven·det·ta (ven det′ə), *n.* **1** feud in which a murdered person's relatives try to kill the slayer or the slayer's relatives. **2** any bitter feud. (< Italian < Latin *vindicta* revenge, perhaps ultimately < *vis* force, strength + *dicere* say)

venge·ance (ven′jəns), *n.* punishment in return for a wrong; revenge. (< Old French < *vengier* avenge < Latin *vindicare* < *vindex* avenger)

ven·ti·late (ven′tl āt), *v.t.,* **-lat·ed, -lat·ing. 1** change the air in. **2** purify by fresh air. **3** furnish with a vent or opening for the escape of air, gas, etc. (< Latin *ventilatum* fanned < *ventus* wind)

ver·sa·tile (vèr′sə təl), *adj.* able to do many things well. (< Latin *versatilis* turning < *versare,* frequentative of *vertere* to turn) —**ver′sa·tile·ness,** *n.* —**ver′sa·til′i·ty** (vèr′sə til′ə tē), *n.*

vet·er·i·nar·i·an (vet′ər ə nàr′ē ən), *n.* doctor or surgeon who treats animals.

ve·to (vē′tō), *n., pl.* **ve·toes,** *adj., v.* —*n.* the right or power of a president, governor, etc., to reject bills passed by a lawmaking body. —*adj.* having to do with a veto: *veto power.* —*v.t.* **1** reject by a veto. **2** refuse to consent to. (< Latin, I forbid) —**ve′to·er,** *n.*

vice-pres·i·dent (vīs′prez′ə dənt), *n.* officer next in rank to the president, who takes the president's place.

vi·ce ver·sa (vī′sə vèr′sə), the other way round; conversely: *John blamed Mary, and vice versa (Mary blamed John).* (< Latin)

vic·to·ri·ous (vik tôr′ē əs), *adj.* **1** having won a victory; conquering: *a victorious team.* **2** ending in victory: *a victorious war.* —**vic·to′ri·ous·ly,** *adv.*

vic·tor·y (vik′tər ē), *n., pl.* **-tor·ies.** defeat of an enemy or opponent; success in a contest.

vin·dic·tive (vin dik′tiv), *adj.* **1** feeling a strong tendency toward revenge; bearing a grudge. **2** showing a strong tendency toward revenge: *a vindictive act.* (< Latin *vindicta* revenge < *vindex* avenger) —**vin·dic′tive·ly,** *adv.* —**vin·dic′tive·ness,** *n.*

vis·i·ble spec·trum (viz′ə bəl spek′trəm), part of the electromagnetic spectrum that people can see.

VIS·TA (vis′tə), *n.* Volunteers in Service to America (agency of the United States government established in 1964 to send volunteers to work and help in depressed areas of the country).

vo·cal·ize (vō′kə līz), *v.,* **-ized, -iz·ing.** —*v.i.* use the voice; speak, sing, shout, etc. —*v.t.* form into voice; utter or sing. —**vo′cal·i·za′tion,** *n.*

vo·ca·tion (vō kā′shən), *n.* occupation, business, profession, or trade. (< Latin *vocationem,* literally, a calling < *vocare* to call, related to *vocem* voice)

veterinarian

a **veterinarian** treating a bird

a	hat	**ī**	ice	**u̇**	put	**ə**	stands for
ā	age	**o**	not	**ü**	rule	**a**	in about
ä	far, calm	**ō**	open	**ch**	child	**e**	in taken
âr	care	**ò**	saw	**ng**	long	**i**	in pencil
e	let	**ô**	order	**sh**	she	**o**	in lemon
ē	equal	**oi**	oil	**th**	thin	**u**	in circus
ėr	term	**ou**	out	**ᵺ**	then		
i	it	**u**	cup	**zh**	measure		

woodwind instrument
A clarinet is a **woodwind instrument.**

vo·ca·tion·al (vō kā′she nel), *adj.* **1** of or having to do with some occupation, business, profession, or trade. **2** of or having to do with studies or training for some occupation, etc.: *vocational guidance.* —**vo·ca′tion·al·ly,** *adv.*

vol·ca·no (vol kā′nō), *n., pl.* **-noes.** an opening in the earth's crust through which steam, ashes, and lava are expelled in periods of activity. (< Italian < Latin *Vulcanus* Vulcan)

volt·age (vōl′tij), *n.* the push needed to move an electron from one place to another, in volts.

vol·ume (vol′yem), *n.* a number given in cubic units that indicates the size of the inside of a space figure. (< Old French < Latin *volumen* book, roll, scroll < *volvere* to roll)

W

warn (wôrn), *v.t.* give notice to in advance; put on guard (against danger, evil, harm, etc.). —**warn′er,** *n.*

wart (wôrt), *n.* a small, hard lump on the skin, caused by a virus infection. (Old English *wearte*)

weird (wird), *adj.* **1** unearthly or mysterious: *They were awakened by a weird shriek.* **2** odd; fantastic; queer: *The shadows made weird figures on the wall.* (Old English *wyrd* fate) —**weird′ly,** *adv.* —**weird′ness,** *n.*

well-known (wel′nōn′), *adj.* **1** clearly or fully known. **2** familiar. **3** generally or widely known.

wharf (hwôrf), *n., pl.* **wharves.** platform built on the shore or out from the shore, beside which ships can load and unload.

wheel·chair (hwēl′chãr′), *n.* chair mounted on wheels, used especially by invalids. It can be propelled by the person sitting in it.

white dwarf (hwīt dwôrf), *n., pl.* **white dwarfs.** rather faint, dead star about the size of the earth but containing about as much mass as the sun; the end state of stars containing as much mass as the sun or less.

white light (hwīt līt), light, such as sunlight, that is a blend of visible colors.

wife (wīf), *n., pl.* **wives.** woman who has a husband; married woman. (Old English *wīf*) —**wife′less,** *adj.*

wind·ward (wind′werd), *adv.* toward the wind. —*adj.* **1** on the side toward the wind. **2** in the direction from which the wind is blowing. —*n.* the side toward the wind.

wood·chuck (wùd′chuk′), *n.* a small North American marmot; groundhog. Woodchucks grow fat in summer and sleep in their holes in the ground all winter. (< Cree *otchek* or Ojibwa *otchig* fisher, marten; influenced by *wood, chuck*)

wood·wind in·stru·ment (wùd′wind′ in′stre ment), any of a group of wind instruments which were originally made of wood, but are now often made of metal or plastic. Clarinets are woodwinds.

wran·gler (rang′gler), *n.* (in the western United States and Canada) a herder in charge of horses, etc.

wreck·age (rek′ij), *n.* what is left by a wreck or wrecks.

Y

yacht (yot), *n.* boat equipped with sails or engines, or both, used for pleasure trips or racing. —*v.i.* sail or race on a yacht.

yam (yam), *n.* **1** vine of warm regions with a starchy, tuberous root much like the sweet potato. **2** its root, eaten as a vegetable. (< Portuguese *inhame* and Spanish *ñame*, ultimately < a west African word *nyami* eat)

yel·low jour·nal·ism (yel′ō jèr′nl iz′em), characterized by sensational or lurid writing or presentation of the news.

Z

Zep·pe·lin or **zep·pe·lin** (zep′e len), *n.* a large, rigid, cigar-shaped airship with separate compartments filled with gas. Zeppelins were mostly used between 1914 and 1937. (< Count Ferdinand von *Zeppelin*, 1838–1917, German general who invented it)

Zip Code (zip kōd), **1** system of numbers, each of which identifies one of the postal delivery areas into which the United States and its larger cities have been divided. **2** a number in this system. (< Z(one) I(mprovement) P(lan) Code)

zeppelin
The development of the airplane contributed to the decreased use of the **zeppelin.**